D1011102

A Special Gift

Presented to:

From:

Date:

Through him we have obtained access to this grace in which we stand, and we rejoice in our hope of sharing the glory of God.
—Romans 5:2, RSV

A Word From HOME

The Women's Devotional Series

Among Friends

The Listening Heart

A Gift of Love

A Moment of Peace

Close to Home

From the Heart

This Quiet Place

In God's Garden

Fabric of Faith

Alone With God

Bouquets of Hope

Colors of Grace

Beautiful in God's Eyes

A Word From Home

Ardis Stenbakken, Editor

A Word From HOME

REVIEW AND HERALD® PUBLISHING ASSOCIATION
HAGERSTOWN, MD 21740

The author assumes full responsibility for the accuracy of all facts and quotations as cited in this book.

This book was
Edited by Jeannette R. Johnson
Cover design by Tina Ivany
Cover photo by Getty Images
Electronic makeup by Shirley M. Bolivar
Typeset: Minion 11/13.5

PRINTED IN U.S.A.

09 08 07 06 05 5 4 3 2 1

R&H Cataloging Service
Stenbakken, Ardis Dick, ed., 1939- .
A word from home, edited by Ardis Dick Stenbakken.

1. Devotional calendars—SDA. 2. Devotional calendars—women.
3. Women—religious life. 4. Devotional literature—SDA. I. Title.

242.643

ISBN 0-8280-1905-3

The Future Is in God's Hands

"For I know the plans I have for you," declares the Lord, "plans to prosper you and not to harm you, plans to give you hope and a future." Jer. 29:11, NIV.

NEW YEAR'S DAY dawned bright and beautiful, but I was feeling sad—in fact, depressed. "Please help me, God!" I cried.

I hate to feel this way, I thought, *but I do.*

I knew I needed to do something, so I opened my cupboard to look for something to do. A printed page fell from the top of the cupboard as if it were a message from heaven. It was titled, "The Comfort of His Presence." I was amazed as I picked it up and read, "If at the moment you feel so deep 'in the valley' that life is a misery and holds little meaning, in simple faith place your hand into the hand of God, reaffirm your faith in Him who cares for you, and even in your depression you will realize the abiding presence of God. Before facing any problem, you will find it most helpful to concentrate your mind upon one of the Gospel stories where Jesus deals with a specific human problem. Capture the spirit of the story; then, in the spirit, turn to your own problem. You will find that God and you are looking at the problem together, and when this happens, the solution is not far away."—Anonymous.

Someone has said that "advice is like castor oil: easy to give to others but difficult to take yourself." Yes, it's easy to give others advice, but when our bag of problems seems too heavy, we still try to carry it ourselves.

I'm so glad God is always there. He never changes. He is the one and only constant in life, and the only one in whom we can place our reliance to see us through when days are dark.

As you live one day at a time throughout this new year, put your trust in God, who is the same yesterday, today, and forever.

I felt like a blind person groping in the dark, but with Jesus at my side I knew I could make it; He knows the way. Let Him be your constant companion. He knows what is best for us. He will comfort and protect us and give us hope.

"Days of darkness still may meet me, sorrow's path I oft may tread;
But His presence still is with me, by His guiding hand I'm led."

—Anonymous

May you enjoy a happy year, and may God's peace be with you, my sister and my friend.

PRISCILLA ADONIS

The Challenge for Today

So I commend the enjoyment of life, because nothing is better for a [woman] under the sun than to eat and drink and be glad. Then joy will accompany [her] in [her] work all the days of the life God has given [her] under the sun. Eccl. 8:15, NIV.

A PSYCHOLOGIST ONCE SURVEYED some 3,000 people picked at random from a telephone directory. The survey was brief. It asked, "What have you got to live for?" More than 90 percent of the respondents stated they were waiting—waiting for their marriage to improve, for their children to grow up, to become grandparents. They were waiting to retire and gain more leisure time. They were waiting for something exciting to happen. They were giving up today for the promise tomorrow held. These people failed to realize that today is the tomorrow they waited for yesterday!

It's a pity to endure the present while waiting for some future event that may, or may not, happen. Today you have been given a fresh beginning. Today you can open your eyes and find a new world. This world is yours. Enjoy every moment of it today because it will soon be gone. Thank God for the new beginning you can enjoy today!

Greet today with a smile. Breathe in the fresh, cool air and revel in the rays of sunshine. Beauty is God's therapy for the ugly side of life. Fear, anxiety, depression, and worry can be overcome with an appreciation of beauty.

Today is here. Don't think of what you would do if only things were different. Things are not different. They are what they are. Make the best of what you have.

Dream, if you will, but work to make your dream come true. Stop saying, "If only I had the time, I'd—" You'll never find time to do everything. Pick one thing you want to do, and do it.

Today act toward God and others as if it were your last day on earth. Life begins when you take charge of your attitude and begin enjoying what you have. Today determines your quality of life tomorrow. If you want freedom and happiness, you must fight for it now.

Today is the time to make the hard choices necessary to accomplish this. The greatest gift you can give the people you love is you. Now is the time to develop high-quality relationships. If you accomplish this you will be a happier person and touch lives around you in a positive way.

NANCY VAN PELT

A Lesson in the Face of a New Life

If ye . . . , being evil, know how to give good gifts unto your children, how much more shall your Father which is in heaven give good things to them that ask him? Matt. 7:11.

WAYNE AND I WERE blessed to see brand-new Ayiana Ayala last weekend. She is absolutely perfect! Ayiana resembles her mother, Natalie, and has her cute nose. She is a pink little thing, with coal-black hair that has a bit of wave in it.

I sat and watched Ayiana after the nurse came in the room to weigh her and check her temperature. Standard procedure. After she dressed her in a fresh gown and diaper, carefully swaddled and returned her to the tall bassinet, Ayiana finally opened her eyes. I stared as she seemed to be familiarizing herself with the world around her. They say that newborn infants can't visually focus right away, but it looked as if she was trying out those strangely blue/brown/black eyes in earnest. Her pretty pink mouth opened as wide as she could get it, obviously searching for her mommy's breast. It was too, too cute. I didn't want to take my eyes off that precious face.

Later I thought about the differences between a human baby and a newborn in almost any part of the animal kingdom. By the end of the day of its birth, a new giraffe has already learned to stand up. The baby bald eagle will eat its meaty meal with ease on that first day. But Ayiana will not stand up unassisted until she's somewhere between 6 and 9 months. She may enjoy her first unstrained or unmashed meal within that same period. Simply, Ayiana needs her mother, not just to survive but to get from place to place, to make decisions for her, and to provide security.

Watching our little goddaughter reminded me of how dependent I am on my heavenly Papa for survival—not just physically, but spiritually. I am as pitiful and as needy as a newborn babe when I set out to make it on my own. I am not equipped. I need a tender, loving, and doting Daddy.

How blessed we are to live in a world created by an awesome, eternal God who wants so much to be our Abba-Father as well. Such love, such condescension!

Thank You, Papa-God, for creating me, then adopting me, and providing everything I need to survive. I long to see You and to put my head on Your shoulder—forever.

Renee Verrett-Dooley

A Higher Standard

Do not be conformed to this world, but be transformed by the renewing of your mind, so that you may prove what the will of God is, that which is good and acceptable and perfect. Rom. 12:2, NASB.

MY HUSBAND DOESN'T CALL ME a gypsy for nothing; I love to travel, and I've gotten around to some places I never dreamed I would go. Recently I returned from a trip to Seoul, South Korea. It was truly a different world from the United States in more than one way, but there was one thing that stood out above all the rest—the people.

My flight stopped in Tokyo before going on to Shanghai, so there were mostly Asian passengers on board. I was really impressed with how quiet and calm everyone was for 13 long hours. They are truly to be commended for their respectful decorum.

On the streets of Seoul, or in subway stations, you have only to pause with a questioning look to draw someone to your side offering assistance. It seems to be their goal in life to be helpful. Riding on the subways and buses, even middle-aged women will give up their seats to someone older, with a disability, pregnant, or carrying a child. And I loved their habit of bowing to you as you go in and out of places of business. Their politeness is inspiring.

The most lasting impression, though, was the women—*meek* and *mild* are the words that come to mind. And they have beautiful smiles. Their modest clothing seemed to be in sharp contrast to that in other parts of the world where women are taken in by fashions that leave much to be desired. Sometimes we don't see ourselves as we are until compared with those who are different. In 1 Timothy 2:9 and 10 Paul admonishes those who claim godliness to dress properly.

Whether it's respect, humility, politeness, or modesty, if we try to be just a little better than the culture around us we'll go downhill with it, because it's getting worse with the passing of time. We should be a transforming example. My Korean trip was a wake-up call for me to live up to God's ideals—not the world's.

Lord, please help us renew our minds so we can be transformed to follow Your will instead of our own.

DONNA MEYER VOTH

Misconnected

Behold, I am coming soon! My reward is with me, and I will give to everyone according to what he has done. I am the Alpha and Omega, the First and the Last, the Beginning and the End. Rev. 22:12, 13, NIV.

CHECKING MY CORDLESS PHONE recently, I discovered what I thought was an expired battery, as I couldn't get a dial tone. So sure it needed a battery, I purchased one, and charged the new battery according to the instructions. When I rechecked the phone, I could see that there was some power as the messages and caller ID were intact, but I still couldn't get a dial tone.

I thought that maybe this phone had seen its best days, and relegated it to the trash and purchased a new one. The next day, while programming the new phone, I read this advice from the instructions sheet: "Once per month use a pencil eraser and clean the connections to maintain uninterrupted use." I retrieved my discarded phone from the trash and plugged it in again. I cleaned the connection points as outlined, and the phone quickly gave me a dial tone. Connection points accumulate corrosion that gets in the way of direct connections.

Sometimes our very lives get so corroded with the sins of anger, greed, guilt, envy, and jealousy that we can't get a direct connection with the Lord. The extra prayer is the eraser that removes the corrosion and allows connection with the Lord.

Sometimes as God's children we are seeking directions from the Lord as to what He wants us to do, but often we don't wait to get full instructions. The Lord has a plan for you to prosper and "be in good health, just as it is well with your soul" (3 John 1:2, NRSV).

We need a daily reconnection with the Lord so that when He speaks we will understand and be willing and ready to obey. The evil one has always tried to duplicate or outdo the Lord. If we aren't careful, even the very elect will be deceived, thinking we are connected with the Lord.

During the final days of this earth the evil one will try many things to deceive us. The devil knows his future and desires to keep us misconnected from Christ. God's Word tells us about all of these possibilities.

Dear Jesus, help me to keep connected with You so that I will know Your will in my life. Thank You for being my Lord and my Savior. Amen.

Betty G. Perry

The Desires of Our Hearts

Delight yourself in the Lord; and He will give you the desires of your heart. Ps. 37:4, NASB.

SINCE THE BIRTH OF OUR third child, a son, I had been begging, pleading, and yes, you might say even nagging, my poor husband to adopt a little girl. We had one daughter and two sons, and he just couldn't understand why I wanted another baby so badly.

I had been an only child for 11 years and had always wanted lots of children so that no child would have to be alone. When the doctor told me I could have no more children, I was devastated, but I knew there was another way to have children, and that was adoption.

I am a firm believer in prayer, so I prayed that God would change my husband's heart and help him to also want to adopt a little girl. I was sure that would be in God's plan, but year after year went by, and still my husband was opposed to the idea.

Then one morning, when our son youngest was 9, my husband walked into the bedroom where I was making the bed and calmly informed me that he had been thinking about it and had decided that it was probably a good idea for us to adopt a little girl. Almost without giving it another thought, I replied, "But honey, now it would be like raising her all alone; I think we should adopt twins." As he rolled his eyes, I knew that even though he was going to sputter, my prayers had been answered—times two. It was all in God's perfect timing.

Our physician, who was on the board of a well-known adoption agency, was a big help to us. At first there were no twins available, but when the time was right, the agency placed identical twin girls with us.

For nine years I had questioned why God was not answering my prayers for a baby girl, but I just thank Him every day that He saw fit to have me wait until the perfect time for the perfect little girls to become a part of our family. For 36 years they have been such a wonderful part of our lives, and we have no doubt that they were God's gift to us.

Nine years seemed like a long time to wait for an answer, but it was perfect timing, and God answered our prayers at just the right time. If He had listened to my demands and given me what I thought I wanted when I wanted it, we never would have known these beautiful daughters. He truly gave me the desires of my heart.

ANNA MAY RADKE WATERS

Who Shares Your Burdens?

Cast thy burden upon the Lord, and he shall sustain thee: he shall never suffer the righteous to be moved. Ps. 55:22.

I LOOKED AT MY LUNCH sack, my regular school bag, and the four bags of school supplies I had purchased the day before. How could I carry them all to school at the same time? Which one to leave? Which had priority? They all did, I assured myself. Why not leave some bags in the car and make a second trip? Too much trouble, I reasoned. I was determined to totter the two city blocks to the entrance of the school with my six packages.

Before I had gone 20 steps, I felt shooting pains in my abdominal region. That's when I realized that my hands were not alone in carrying my burden—internal organs were hurting as well. After one block I put everything down. I considered leaving the low-priority items—two hefty reams of paper—near a tree and returning for them later. Then I stubbornly decided against the idea.

Then I heard footsteps behind me, and, glancing over my shoulder, I saw a tall young man with a tall backpack. Although I didn't recognize him, I immediately asked, "Would you like to help your teacher?" Without hesitating, he grabbed the heaviest of my bags. What a relief!

"Thanks so much," I whispered.

As we walked toward the school I told him how happy I was that he had arrived at the right time to assist me. Silently, I wondered, *Why did he appear out of nowhere at the moment when I felt that I couldn't take another step?* As the young man placed my bags at the door of the school, I told him, "God sent you to help me today; do you know that?"

As I divided the bags, preparing for two trips to my third-floor classroom, the importance of the incident began to sink in. I thought of the heavy burdens I had been carrying all week. Stubbornly I had been struggling with them, praying about them, but not handing them entirely over to God. Now I thanked my heavenly Father for presenting an object lesson to me so vividly. Our God is just waiting for us to lay down our burdens so that He can carry them for us.

Today, place your burdens—large and small—at His feet. Then walk beside Him, knowing that your burden is now light.

ANNETTE WALWYN MICHAEL

The Birthday Party

That's how it is with the kingdom of heaven. Everyone is given a royal invitation to come to the wedding to celebrate with the King and His Son, but few will come wearing the robe the King has provided. Matt. 22:14, Clear Word.

SHE IS AN ELEGANT WOMAN, this friend of mine, with her svelte figure and shocking white hair. Her brothers acknowledge her as the mover and shaker in the family. It is because of her, they insist, that they and their children are where they are today—geographically and professionally.

Almost a year before her seventieth birthday, people started wondering how they could celebrate the milestone moment of the person they loved so well. Eventually the notion of a spectacular party took root. "She deserves something wonderful," someone said. All agreed.

And so it began. Work started on the invitations. She had not had a formal wedding when she got married more than 20 years before, but she always knew what she would have chosen. The embossed, rose-framed cards seemed perfect. Then there was the guest list. She came from a large, close-knit family scattered all over the globe—all had to be invited.

Next, arrangements were made for the banquet hall, the menu, and the program, and scores of minutiae in between. The last thing on her list was the gown. She had to find the perfect dress. She saw it, one day, in a bridal shop—a lovely, violet, sequined creation.

Opening my Bible one morning, I read again the poignant verses in Matthew 22: "The kingdom of heaven is like a king who prepared a wedding banquet" (verse 1, NIV). I smiled as I saw how closely the party checklist mirrored Matthew's—invitation, guests, food, clothes, and all. Spiritual similarities spilled over in my mind. Slipping the invitation in my beaded bag, just in case the maître d' had questions about my presence, I praised God for His guest list. He has invited me.

My friend was radiant as she greeted each perfectly attired guest. Nobody had dared to come unprepared. I prayed that we would all be as prepared for Him.

This party was only a foretaste of our heavenly party. Unlike what my friend's relatives affirmed, we will know that we do not deserve anything so wonderful. As we don those glory-bright robes, we will know that we are welcomed in that celestial banquet hall only because our Savior Redeemer chose to wear ragged, sin-splattered clothes in our stead. GLENDA-MAE GREENE

Good Works

But now God has shown us a different way to heaven—not by "being good enough" and trying to keep his laws, but by a new way (though not new, really, for the Scriptures told about it long ago). Now God says he will accept and acquit us—declare us "not guilty"—if we trust Jesus Christ to take away our sins. And we all can be saved in this same way, by coming to Christ, no matter who we are or what we have been like. Rom 3:21, 22, TLB.

THINGS WERE REALLY going great! For at least the previous two weeks I had been abiding by everything that I had taught as a health educator. Eight glasses of water? Done! Daily exercise? Done! Lots of fruits and vegetables? Done! Adequate rest? Done! Quiet time with God? Done! Good time management ? Done! The list went on—and so did my feeling of pride in a job well done.

Then it started: itchy throat, runny eyes and nose, chills, aches and pains. "Not now, Lord, when I should be experiencing perfect health after all that I have done!" I thought, *How could I possibly get the flu now?* After a brief period of denial, I finally accepted that I was sick despite all my efforts.

How many times have we patted ourselves on the back for how good we have been? Like the rich young ruler, we measure our works against the Ten Commandments, and wow! Don't we look good! Stealing? None! Murder? None! Bearing false witness? None! Neglect of the Sabbath? None! As the list goes on, so does our pride in our own self-righteousness. However, a closer look reveals that our "righteousness is like dirty rags," as described in Isaiah 64:6. Our honorable deeds are still tainted with sin. No matter how much good we do, we will never be deserving of the gift of salvation, for that is what it is—a gift.

God has indeed given me much more than I deserve. Every opportunity, every blessing—even every challenge—is a greater blessing than all my work could ever earn.

So yes, I have the flu—and I also have a life stained with sin. But today I can claim God's wonderful forgiveness and be happy as I accept the marvelous gift of His Salvation.

Dear Father, today may my eyes be opened to the wonder of Your grace as I accept the gift of Your righteousness. PATRICE E. WILLIAMS-GORDON

Filthy Rags

All of us have become like one who is unclean, and all our righteous acts are like filthy rags. Isa. 64:6, NIV.

MY DAUGHTER HAD JUST given me a new, dressy sweater blouse, and it was so pretty—white, with various shades of green and navy blue. Since my only navy pants were rather faded, I bought a new pair that I was sure would look nice with the sweater.

Then the day came when I was invited to a women's luncheon—just the occasion to wear my new outfit. I felt so good as I attended the luncheon with many other women, all wearing attractive clothes. I decided to make a day of it and did some errands while I was in town. No one complimented me on how I looked, but I didn't think much of it. I didn't really need any compliments, since I already knew I looked good.

Then I got home and went to change into other clothes so I could keep my new clothes nice. How horrified I was when I took off the navy pants and found that the back was covered with lint, fuzz from my seat covers, and cat hair from pets who like to sleep in my car when the windows are down! No wonder no one had complimented me on my pretty clothes! It would have been so nice if someone had said, "Excuse me; you have lint on the back of your pants." But no one mentioned that I needed to brush off the back of my pants, which would have been embarrassing but helpful.

There are times in my everyday life when I may think I look good because of what I do. I attend church regularly, help out with community service activities, share with neighbors and friends who have less than I do, and go on mission trips. These are all important, but in spite of the fact that they are "good" activities, according to Isaiah I can't depend on them, as they are like filthy rags. The only thing that will save me is the white robe of Christ's righteousness.

Dear heavenly Father, please help me today and every day to accept and depend on Christ's robe of righteousness instead of my own "filthy rags."

BETTY J. ADAMS

Keeping Things in Perspective

I will bless the Lord at all times. Ps. 34:1, NKJV.

RECENTLY I FELT I was experiencing a meltdown. Our daughter, Karimah, mother of two very young children, returned to school. We supported her decision even though it meant moving her family to England. Her husband, Michael, also supported her by aborting his career to make the move. We knew there were challenging times ahead. To help her, my husband and I tapped into our retirement savings. This was an investment we willingly made to help our daughter realize her dreams.

The challenges began when she started experiencing some unforeseeable difficulties. Her prearranged accommodation did not work, and when the children joined her the landlord gave her one week to find alternate accommodations. This was difficult on a limited budget in a very expensive city. Worst of all, shortly after her third move she discovered their passports were missing. Her passport contained the coveted five-year visa. Her husband's ability to work was incumbent on proof of the visa.

At first there was no panic, just concern. Three weeks of almost nonstop searching did not turn up the missing passports. Then sheer panic set in on both sides of the Atlantic. Thoughts of my daughter and granddaughters in a foreign country with no travel documents stirred in me a level of anxiety I had not experienced for a long time. I was praying also that Michael would receive a job offer before leaving Canada. That didn't happen. I prayed that Karimah would receive educational funding. That didn't happen. Most urgently I prayed for the return of the missing documents. That didn't happen.

What *did* happen was that while the adults were anxious, 3-year-old Naomi was thanking God for providing a "beautiful" home for them. Two-year-old Asha frequently invited us to "come see my 'blue' house." We subsequently found out that only the front door is blue, and structurally the building is less than beautiful. Obviously it's all about perspective. The documents are presently being replaced. Our son-in-law found temporary work in his field. Our daughter has not received funding, but our financial security is safe in God's hands.

Dear God, help each of us keep things in perspective and not be overwhelmed by life's daily trials.

Avis Mae Rodney

January 12

The Shower and the Pipe Wrench

You called in trouble and I rescued you. Ps. 81:7, NASB.

MANY YEARS AGO WHEN my husband and I moved into our first house we were so excited, even though the house needed some upgrades before it would be perfect. One afternoon while my husband was at work, I decided to change the showerhead myself to one that "massages." I found it in a box of supplies, then hunted until I found the pipe wrenches. The one I picked out seemed heavy, but I figured bigger was better for my plumbing job.

I climbed into the bathtub to take off the showerhead. It wouldn't budge with my fingers, so I fit the pipe wrench on it and pulled hard. Nothing. More strength was obviously needed. Again I fit the pipe wrench on the showerhead, climbed onto the edge of the bathtub, then leaped off, putting all my weight on the wrench. There was an ominous snap and a clang as something fell behind the wall of the shower.

Sick with terror, I pondered the situation. A sudden ring of the phone interrupted my thoughts. My mother cheerfully announced that she and Dad would be arriving the next day for a visit. I rushed down the street for some advice from my friend, whose father was a builder. When she called him, he said, "You'll have to get behind the wall somehow, because you've snapped a water line. Don't use the tub or shower until it's fixed."

Now I was really ill! My husband returned home late that night. His face was grim as we tried to think how we could possibly get the shower fixed before my parents arrived. It was time to bring in the heavy ammunition. Kneeling on the floor beside our bed, we gave the problem to the Lord, begging Him to help us. Then I crawled into bed and fell asleep. But He woke me early with this thought: *The wall behind the mirror in the master bathroom is shared with the other bathroom. Take the mirror off, cut a hole in the wall, and you can fix the pipe.* What relief! I got up quietly and wrote it all down.

When my husband woke up, I excitedly told him what our Lord had told me, and He was exactly right! We took the mirror off and cut a big hole through which we could see the copper pipe. We bought copper pipe and soldering supplies, and by the time my parents arrived the pipe was fixed, the "shower massage" head was on, and the lovely big mirror covered the hole.

Thank You, Lord, for still speaking to us today and hearing and answering our prayers.

CHERYL HURT

Cataracts

For now we see through a glass, darkly; but then face to face. 1 Cor. 13:12.

WE LIVE IN A retirement apartment complex and are fortunate to have our "villa" bus take us where we wish to go. One Sabbath my husband and I had boarded the bus for church, and I remarked to him how nice he looked in his brown suit. "It isn't brown," he replied. "It's blue."

I felt sorry that he was so off on the color of that beautiful suit, and ever after, when he wore it, I reminded him it was not blue, but brown. He failed to be convinced, and our different opinions became a private little joke.

By nature, I'm an early riser. I cherish the early-morning hours when my concentration is best. I love talking with my Best Friend and listening to His words to me from His Book. It sets the tone for my day. For several months, though, I had been having problems with focusing. I was definitely troubled with eyestrain. I looked forward to my routine visit with my ophthalmologist. New lenses, I knew, would correct my problem.

When my doctor suggested that I had cataracts, I was not a little surprised. Before I left his office I had been scheduled with the surgeon for cataract removal. The procedure went well, and I was amazed at the clear lines and brilliant colors I was now seeing—I was observing things as they are in the real world. What a difference! Reading was a pleasure. I reveled in the bright colors of the out of doors.

One Sabbath my husband pulled out his favorite suit to wear to church—the brown one, of course—and at that moment I realized how wrong I had been. His suit *was* blue! He had been right all along and had been so gracious about it.

This experience taught me a lesson I never want to forget. When I see flaws in those around me, I must remind myself that it could well be my spiritual cataracts. I know my Great Physician wants more than anything else to correct my vision by cutting away the defects in my character. My prayer is that when I am tempted to see flaws in others, I will ask Him to stand between us where I can catch a glimpse of His loving face. Then, by keeping my focus on Him, I will reflect His beauty to everyone I see.

LORRAINE HUDGINS-HIRSCH

Tomatoes and Parking Spaces

Trust in the Lord with all thine heart; and lean not unto thine own understanding. In all thy ways acknowledge him, and he shall direct thy paths. Prov. 3:5, 6.

THERE ARE MANY THINGS I remember about Madeline Schmida. She lived in Huntington Beach, California. She had a strong personality and a big smile. I also remember her energy to serve Christ and study His Word. But what I remember most about Madeline were her comments regarding tomatoes and parking spaces. At a Bible study I attended at the time, several of us were having a discussion on faith. Some of the attendees gave examples of how they exercised their faith. I found Madeline's method very interesting.

She stated that she had learned to pray over everything, even things that would seem insignificant to most people. She described being at a grocery store and trying to select the best food for her family. For example, before she picked out the tomatoes to purchase, she would pray over them. She did this with all her grocery shopping, asking for God's guidance to make the best choice. At the time it was hard to fathom doing this over produce, but I realized the issue at hand was bigger than the tomatoes themselves.

Madeline went on to say that she also prayed to find parking spaces. As she entered a parking lot, she would pray to find the spot the Lord wanted her to have. Upon hearing this, I could feel my left eyebrow arching, and I was beginning to look like Sherlock Holmes. Nevertheless, I found what she said interesting and insightful. I yearned for that kind of faith and trust.

Since then, when I am in the produce section of a grocery store, I seem to always think of Madeline and the lesson that God showed me through her. How can I trust God in the big things if I cannot trust Him with little things such as tomatoes and parking spaces?

Lord, I pray that my faith will continue to grow as I learn to depend on You with the big and little things in my life. Whether it is tomatoes, parking spaces, or anything else that comes up in my life, guide me to seek You out in prayer instead of making a decision based on my weak human understanding.

MARY M. J. WAGONER ANGELIN

A Time to Be Born

To every thing there is a season, and a time to every purpose under the heaven. Eccl. 3:1.

MY HUSBAND AND I started our family early in our marriage. Like many new families, we faced many of life's difficult challenges and decisions. Money wasn't always abundant, living space was limited, and time was lacking. When our son was about 3 years old and our daughter was only 1, we faced more questions: How many children were we intended to have? What did God have in store for our family? Were two children all God had planned for us? We carefully pondered the pros and cons of having more children. We discussed advice given to us by our peers and mentors. We discussed the financial burdens that sometimes come along with an additional family member. We even discussed how it would affect our car and house arrangements. In the end, however, we could come up with no definite answer.

One fall day I decided to take it as a petition to my heavenly Father in my daily devotions. I prayed, "Lord, You know what the future holds. You know what tomorrow brings. You know from the beginning to the end, so please impress upon my husband and me what Your will is for us. We want to be happy, and we know that the best way to accomplish this is to abide in Your plan for us. Please, help us to know Your will and to follow Your leading." We agreed that if we felt impressed to do so, we would start trying to have another baby in the spring.

Two weeks later our answer came. It was neither what nor how we had imagined it, but it was an answer: I was pregnant with our third child. We were thrilled! God had definitely answered our prayers. Many times we have an idea of how our life should go. We think that we know the right road and the right time to take it. We expect God to follow along behind us to catch us if we fall, but we seldom let Him take the lead. I am thankful that we serve a God who cares so much for us. He is always willing to show us His plan if we only allow Him to do so. He too wants us to be happy.

Thank You, Father, for allowing us the freedom of choice. Please help us each day to choose You and Your guidance for our lives. May we remember to do this every moment of each day. Amen.

MANDY LAFAVE-VOGLER

Our Turn to Be the Good Samaritan

Which now of these three, thinkest thou, was neighbour unto him that fell among thieves? Luke 10:36.

THIS IS BILL'S STORY, as told to me by his friend, Elsie.

Bill fell slowly to the ground as he was crossing the busy street. He picked himself up and felt that tingling in his hands and experienced the blurred vision that reminded him once again of the recent stroke he had suffered. As he leaned heavily on the lamppost, he thought of his plight. It was a beautiful, sunny day, and he had walked a long way from his house—more than a mile. He knew there was a hospital just a few blocks in the opposite direction. He slowly walked to it, thinking they would take care of him. He stopped at the admitting desk, and the nurse asked many questions. The doctor asked even more. Bill tried to tell them he thought he was having a stroke. Either they didn't hear him or didn't believe him. No, they said, they could not (or would not) take care of him. He could go home or to the veterans' hospital.

Bill turned away, not quite understanding what was going on. He managed the walk as far as the bus stop and took the bus to Harvard Square. Again he almost fell as he was getting off. A young woman student grabbed onto his arm and held him upright, asking what she could do for him. Bill explained his problem. "I guess I need to go to the veterans' hospital across town." The student flagged a taxi and helped Bill into the back seat, making sure he was comfortable. Handing the taxi driver a $20 bill, she said, "Please take him to the veterans' hospital. If there is any change, give it to him." And with a smile and a little wave, she called, "Goodbye; take care of yourself!" He blew a kiss to her as the taxi pulled away.

She was a young student, but quickly became a good Samaritan. She didn't see his ethnicity, only his need. She put him, not on a donkey, but into a modern taxi, and, like the Samaritan of old, provided funds to take care of his problem—enough for the taxi and a little extra. The stories are so similar. May we not fail the test when our turn comes in this our modern age.

Dessa Weisz Hardin

Answered Prayer

And I will do whatever you ask in my name. John 14:13, NIV.

I WORKED IN A telecommunication business, where there were 90 women in the same sector. Distributing vacation periods in a manner that pleased everyone was impossible.

I was one of those who could take their vacation in the "good" period, between January and February. (In Brazil it is summer in January and February.) In 1994, to benefit a friend, I changed my vacation period from February to May, which is a colder season of the year. When my vacation arrived, my children and husband left for their regular activities, and I had more peaceful time with God.

Soon after this I did some research and went out in a nearby neighborhood. I found 18 people wanting to study the Bible. So every morning I left home at 8:00 and returned at noon, ate lunch with my family, and went out again from 2:30 to 6:00 p.m. It was gratifying to see people willing to learn of the love of God!

I prayed in gratitude: "Thank You, Lord, for using me. I want to see the fruits of this work." When vacation ended, I prayed, "Lord, give me the opportunity to work for You."

When I returned to work on June 5, my colleagues asked how my vacation had been. I answered that it had been the best vacation time ever because I had studied the Bible with several people and had made new friends. Ending the conversation, I stated, "I would like Jesus to give me a special leave of absence from work so that I can finish these Bible studies." Some colleagues thought I was strange and even laughed at me.

I have a health problem that in the past has caused me to be away from work as much as eight to 10 days at a time. This problem involved terrible crises. On June 7 the Lord answered my request, made two days earlier. The company doctor called to say, "As of tomorrow, you will have a 15-day leave of absence, and then go to the National Institute of Social Security Office."

I was able to finish those Bible studies, and eight people accepted Jesus. Praise the Lord! I never returned to secular work. I was considered disabled for four years, and today I am retired and work for Jesus. I believe that if we ask in His name He will answer according to Psalm 37:4: "Delight yourself in the Lord and he will give you the desires of your heart" (NIV).

Edileuza Nascimento Ramos

My Supper With Jesus

Here I am! I stand at the door and knock. If anyone hears my voice and opens the door, I will come in and eat with him, and he with me. Rev. 3:20, NIV.

I LOVE TO OPEN MY home to people, to have them come in and share my sofa, my music, my kitchen, my cooking. There's something about sharing a meal with someone that draws us closer together. That's why my most precious mental picture of Jesus is that of having Him come into my home and and eat the meal I cook for Him. I imagine baking for Him my own homemade bread and letting its aroma fill the air. When Jesus knocks at the door, I open it, and He says, "Oh, something smells good!"

"Thank You, Lord!" I reply. "I'm so glad You came. I've looked forward to our time together."

I usher Him into the living room and seat Him on my comfortable sofa. (I have carefully fluffed and arranged the throw pillows ahead of time.) I get out an album of the most recent family pictures for Him to look at while I finish preparing our meal. In the background beautiful music is playing for Him to enjoy.

"Lunch is ready. Please, come join me," I invite. I lead Jesus into the kitchen to my table that is loaded with good things for us to share. After giving thanks, Jesus Himself breaks the bread, and we eat together. Of course, He loves my cooking. He can taste the love I have stirred into every morsel. But what I love most is His presence in my home—being able to look into His face, to feel His love, to talk to Him about everything.

Of course, it's only a fantasy, but not entirely. I may never get to bake bread for Jesus and have Him come and sit on my sofa. But His presence is with me—in my home and wherever I go. I can feel His love, and I can talk to Him about everything. Someday I will even be able to look into His face. But until then, I will enjoy our quiet times together—sweet fellowship with Jesus.

O my Jesus, let me never get so busy that I forget how important it is to have sweet fellowship with You every day! LYNDA MAE VANDEN TOORN

Young at Heart

Let love and faithfulness never leave you; bind them around your neck, write them on the tablet of your heart. Then you will win favor and a good name in the sight of God and man. Prov. 3:3, 4, NIV.

I'M NOT 16 ANYMORE. I accept that fact, and most of the time I'm heartily glad that I'm not. But sometimes I look in the mirror and wonder: Who is that middle-aged woman staring back at me?

God has made us wonderfully well, and I'd rather be getting older as opposed to the alternative. But when parts of me don't move as well as they used to, or work as easily as I'd like, I begin to complain.

My problem is that behind this face I still feel 16. My mind still thinks I'm a teenager. (I think my mom does, too.) Granted, I've packed quite a few years of experiences into this body, and, as a result, I'm probably smarter than I was at 16. I know I make better decisions than I did then.

My epiphany came today. I was driving along in the 90-degree, humid August weather, thinking about how great a jump into a nice cool swimming pool would feel, and I realized that even though I'm thinking like a kid, that doesn't make me a bad person—I must be what they call "young at heart!"

But the important thing I have to remember is that the past is over. It's finished and done with. I can't go back and live over the past—I can only learn from it and go on. Some people I know like to live in "the good ol' days" and complain about how terrible everything is today. But God doesn't want us looking back. He wants us to look forward, using the knowledge we've gained from the past. That's why He gave us the past, the present, and a future.

Today is a new day. There are more possibilities today than during any other day you've ever lived in the past. Today is your opportunity to do something worthwhile—for yourself and for others. If you think you're too old or too young or too tired or too busy, you're absolutely wrong. You are in the best possible place to make a real, positive difference in your life and in the world surrounding you.

Today is the best opportunity anyone could ever imagine, because what you do with your today is completely up to you. Make it the best day ever with God's help.

FAUNA RANKIN DEAN

Passions of the Mind

But thou, O Lord, art a God full of compassion, and gracious, long-suffering, and plenteous in mercy and truth. Ps. 86:15.

HAVE YOU EVER BEEN judged unfairly by someone you know and love? It isn't a pleasant experience, is it? Do you ever forget it? I never have!

About 30 years ago my husband and I were spending a quiet evening at home. He was watching sports on television, and I was lying comfortably on our sofa reading *The Passions of the Mind,* a story about the famous psychiatrist Sigmund Freud. The title of this paperback book was superimposed onto a cover of bright-orange flames. I'm sure it was deliberately designed to be noticed on any store's bookshelf.

Suddenly there was a knock on our front door. Looking through the foyer, I saw that our unexpected visitor was our pastor. I placed my book on the coffee table in front of me and went to the door to greet him. After his visit, I returned to my comfortable sofa to continue reading. However, my book was missing. Puzzled, I asked my husband if he had seen it.

"Oh," he replied, "when I saw who was at the door, I threw your trashy novel into the stairwell. You wouldn't want the pastor to know what you were reading, would you?"

It's probably best *not* to share my reply to my husband! The point is, he saw the title and the bright flames on the cover of a paperback book and decided it was a trashy novel. He didn't ask. He didn't read the synopsis on the back cover. He just made a judgment—and then acted on erroneous information.

This seems to be the way we humans behave. However, it should not be the way Christians behave. Everyone should receive the benefit of the doubt before we speak or act. In our homes, schools, communities, and churches we often base our opinions of other people on a thread of gossip, a partially overheard conversation, or something we *think* we saw. Sadly, our hasty judgment divides, wounds, and hurts those whom God is tenderly seeking.

Today let's determine that we will find out *all* the facts before jumping to any conclusion. And even if we find we are correct in our judgment, let's *still* give that person love, kindness, and understanding in the name of Jesus—just as He has so mercifully given to us.

Ellie Green

Count My Blessings

But if we walk in the light as he himself is in the light, we have fellowship with one another, and the blood of Jesus his Son cleanses us from all sin.
1 John 1:7, NRSV.

I WAS HAVING LUNCH with a friend. We laughed and chatted as we enjoyed Indian food. She began to share with me little stories of God's guidance and love from when she was very young in northern Japan. God helped her to go to Christian school, sending her to Yokahama Seventh-day Adventist Academy and Cheba Seventh-day Adventist College. From there she got a job for the mission. And that's where our friendship began.

In 1976 I was a student missionary and she was working at the office in Yokahama. We had a lot of fun hiking, and she also took me out to eat great Japanese food. I even remember playing the piano one Sabbath while she sang in church. I have to say we did a great job with God helping us. I didn't speak any Japanese and she knew very little English, but we managed to get though the song, being inspired by the music and the words. Music was the way we shared God's love that day.

Time went by—almost 30 years. Then one Sabbath in a church in the United States I noticed a Japanese woman sitting in front of me. More then once I glanced at her, thinking, *I know this woman. . . . Is she Kasuko?*

Saying a short prayer, I approached her after church. "Excuse me," I began, "but are you Kasuko?"

"Yes," she replied. She looked at me a moment, then asked, "Are you Susen?" We hugged and rejoiced at finding each other after so long, realizing anew how much God looks out for us. Both of us know God's love through all the ways He leads us in our lives.

Finding a friend who knows Jesus is very important. I am glad that I have great friends who love Him, and with whom I can share times such as this.

It was wonderful finding friends again after many years. The fellowship You give us is just a glimpse of what You have for all who choose to walk in the light. We count our blessings and give You thanks. SUSEN MATTISON MOLÉ

The Attic Room

I will lie down and sleep in peace, for you alone, O Lord, make me dwell in safety. Ps. 4:8, NIV.

WHEN I WAS A CHILD we lived on the upper floor of an old villa. My bedroom was a little room with a slanting roof and a door leading to the attic. During the day I had no problem with this—I would even go into the attic to play. But in the evening, when it got dark, I was scared of this attic. In my imagination there were all kinds of creeping animals living there—snakes and other crawling things I was so afraid of. I imagined that they would creep under the door from the attic and come and wait for me under my bed. I didn't want to go to this bed.

"Please, please carry me to bed," I begged my parents. I reasoned that the animals under my bed would not know that I was lying there if they saw only adult feet coming and going. They would think it wasn't a bed after all, but only a chest of drawers, and that no small child had lain down there. I would then lie very quietly so that no movement would betray me.

Often I woke up again in the night, and my fear would overcome me once again. What should I do? The animals were under my bed—I was sure of that. I couldn't sleep because I was so scared. So I put my pillow under my arm and took a big leap, as far as possible from my bed, and raced to my parents' bed as fast as my little legs could carry me.

Jumping into their bed, I crawled under their blankets and pulled the sheet over my head so that the pursuing snakes would not find me. Now nothing could happen to me. I was safe. Sheltered by the presence of my parents, I instantly fell asleep again.

You may laugh at my childish fears, but for me they were no trifle. The safety I felt in the presence of my parents reminds me that God is my Father who wants to give us this security in our adult lives, as well.

The psalmist found this safety in God's presence. Only God was able to protect him. So he was able to write, "I will lie down and sleep in peace, for you alone, O Lord, make me dwell in safety."

Do you, too, want to flee to God when life's fears and worries get too heavy to bear? He is waiting for you and will cover you with His sheet of love and give you shelter. HANNELE OTTSCHOFSKI

The Begats in My Life

But as many as received him, to them gave he power to become the [sons and daughters] of God, even to them that believe on his name. John 1:12.

WHENEVER I READ my Bible I am always tempted to just skip the "begats." I'm sure most of you know what I mean. "And Abraham begat Isaac . . ." and on down the line. I've always had a difficult time getting through those parts of the Bible. But that was before I got into genealogy.

For some time now one of the genealogy commercial Web sites has sent me enticing offers to try out their site for free for 14 full days. I managed to ignore their generous offer for about six months, but then I succumbed and began searching to see what I could find. Since most of my family has been gone for many years, I thought, *They won't have anything on my family; they weren't famous, or anything.* However, much to my amazement, I found family trees for both of my grandmothers. One dates back to Scotland, and the other back to England. At that moment I was hooked. I even began to appreciate all the begats in the Bible for the first time. Just as it was important to the Jewish people to be able to trace their ancestry, I was fascinated with what I was finding about my own family. I am still finding precious gems about where I came from as I search. Since my mother passed away when I was only 4, it is like finding her again.

We know that pedigrees are important when it comes to purebred dogs, cats, and livestock; and some think it very important to know the backgrounds of people. While I'm enjoying finding my own roots, I believe that the most important kind of roots is to know that I am a daughter of the living God and a sister to His Son, who came and died for me. Ultimately, we are all sons and daughters of Adam and Eve, and heirs of the kingdom.

My prayer for you today, dear reader, is that you will accept that precious gift that God the Father, and His Son, and the Holy Spirit offer to you: to be His child, and live with Him in His kingdom when He comes to take us home.

LORAINE F. SWEETLAND

Company's Coming

And the Spirit and the bride say, Come. And let him that heareth say, Come. And let him that is athirst come. And whosoever will, let him take the water of life freely. Rev. 22:17.

COMPANY'S COMING FOR DINNER. I have prepared for six guests, but I don't know who they will be. I set the table with my mother's heirloom china and with napkins that matched the burgundy border on the plates. I planned a tasty menu and garnished the lemon dessert with mandarin orange wedges and a sliver of maraschino cherries to resemble butterflies.

Once or twice a year our church social committee plans a surprise guest-and-host Sabbath dinner. We have a choice of being guests or hosts. I always sign up as a host. I feel that hosts get the biggest surprise—all we know is how many to prepare for. The guests are given an address and, with a bit of ingenuity, they can figure out who their hosts will be.

The social committee mixes and matches the hosts and guests so that we get to fellowship with folks with whom we may not be well acquainted. It is a week of pleasant anticipation, wondering who's coming to dinner.

A banquet table is being set in heaven. We're all invited. The choice is ours to accept the free invitation. Unlike our church's "Company's Coming for Dinner" event, though, the Host in heaven knows who's coming, but we, the guests, don't know who will be there. When the festive day arrives, I can imagine there will be a lot of talking and laughing around the table as we renew acquaintances and meet new friends.

For some unknown reason, one couple notified the social committee that they had to cancel as my Sabbath dinner guests. However, they would be able to come for supper that evening or for dinner the next day. However, this was not an open invitation for guests to come at their convenience. Neither is the feast in heaven being served when it fits into our schedule.

Like the king in the parable of a wedding feast for his son recorded in Matthew 22, I was able to invite another couple who didn't have other plans for the day.

Let's accept the invitation today—and every day—to meet around God's throne and feast on the tree of life and drink from the river of life. Nothing this world has to offer should tempt us to neglect or postpone our commitment to receiving eternal life.

EDITH FITCH

Bone-Marrow Crisis

For the word of God is living and powerful, and sharper than any two-edged sword, piercing even to the division of soul and spirit, and of joints and marrow, and is a discerner of the thoughts and intents of the heart. Heb. 4:12, NKJV.

I'D NEVER THOUGHT MUCH about bone marrow. Not until the day my white count, following a chemotherapy treatment, dropped from 1.9 to .7. (Normal starts around 4.4.) My doctor quickly ordered daily injections that would stimulate the bone marrow to produce more white blood cells. The nurse administering the daily injections tried to prepare me. "When this med takes effect in about four days," she said, "be prepared for some potentially major pain."

Now, I've never desired pain. Yet in this particular instance the worry of my compromised immune system not being able to fight off a serious infection deeply troubled me. Three days after the first injection I began to feel a bit achy. *If this means my immune system is getting stronger,* I thought, *bring on the pain!* Little did I know.

The next morning I awoke to pain such as I haven't experienced since childbirth. Every joint in my body screamed. I felt trapped inside a throbbing rib cage with sledgehammers pounding front and back, at the base of my skull, and on both hips. The pain was so intense I couldn't even cry.

A quick checkup call from my doctor's office gave me permission to take some light pain medication. I prayed that I could bear this trial bravely. What helped the most during the next few days of suffering was remembering that this pain was an indicator of something very positive. My immune system was being strengthened precisely because of this painful activity.

In Hebrews Paul describes the Word of God as being powerful, sharp, and able to penetrate between the joints and marrow. It even discerns my thoughts and hidden motives. Now that can hurt! Yet the resulting spiritual, and even emotional, pain caused by spiritual conviction is a very clear indicator of something most positive occurring. The spiritual immune system is growing stronger precisely because the "sword" of God's Word is at work.

How infinitely good God is to "activate" our spiritual bone marrow now (despite some painful aching in our "joints") so that we can throw off the infectious temptations of sin.

Carolyn Rathbun Sutton

Super Bowl Sunday

The Lord will make a list of those who are His and will take into consideration where they were born. Ps. 87:6, Clear Word.

IT WAS THE BIG DAY—Super Bowl Sunday, January 26, 2003. The Tampa Bay Buccaneers and the Oakland Raiders were playing in San Diego, California. My husband was excited and wanted me to share in his enthusiasm for the game.

You will need to understand the difference in our backgrounds. Bill's mother died when he was 3, and his father when he was 5. Since his dad had been an engineer on the railroad, he and his two older brothers were sent to Junior Order Home in Tiffin, Ohio, in 1920. There, he and 1,000 other children were well nourished, clothed, and schooled. They were also thoroughly immersed in sports, including baseball and football. He proudly showed me the stadium where they played when we visited there after we married.

The only other person we know who was in the home at the same time Bill lived there, and later joined our church, was Robert Francois. He learned linotype while in the home and later used that training to work his way through the theology course, becoming a professor of religion. Before his death he and Bill enjoyed reminiscing about the sports program at Tiffin.

As for my background, my family was very poor. The eldest of seven children, I learned early in life to enjoy work more than play—and still do! So I can't get enthusiastic about Bill's game, though he has begged me to watch at least the first quarter with him as he patiently explains the different plays and interprets the signals of the referee.

So I decided that instead of thinking it a waste of time, I could pray for each player. Bill pointed out one of the team members who was religious and could be seen making the sign of the cross while on the field. He assured me that their team would win the game.

It was estimated that 8 million people around the world, including the soldiers preparing for war with Iraq, watched that game. I'm not sure what the Lord thinks about football, but I do know He loves all those players out there on the field, and I trust Him to answer my prayers on their behalf.

By the way, the Bucs won, 48-21! RUBYE SUE

Procrastination

Thou wilt keep him in perfect peace, whose mind is stayed on thee: because he trusteth in thee. Isa. 26:3.

THROUGHOUT MY DEVELOPING years and into my adult life, my mother often said to me, "Never put off for tomorrow what you can do today; tomorrow you may never see the rising of the sun." I don't know where she got that saying, but it has proven to be true. Perhaps she observed that I was always putting off doing things. I'm one of those people who have to think things through before coming to a decision; meanwhile, time and opportunities pass by.

The building of the church where I worship was recently completed, and it was decided to have a grand-opening celebration. This necessitated having a souvenir journal, and a drive was on to solicit donations. I mailed letters to friends far away, but because of time constraints I decided to deliver letters to my neighbors personally. One neighbor in particular I was impressed to visit. As I passed her house on my travels, I'd look over and think, *I have to stop by.* But I never did. It was always *I will do it tomorrow.* But tomorrow never came.

One morning as I left home to run errands I decided, *Today, on my way back, I will stop.* I even took a copy of *Steps to Christ* with me in case I hadn't given her one before. My intentions that morning were all good. There was even a strong prompting by the Holy Spirit to visit her. But I still did not stop.

That night guilt overwhelmed me. I decided not to let another day go by without calling, regardless of the lateness of the hour. I'm glad I did. When her husband answered the phone, I asked, "May I speak with Phyllis?"

"She is no longer here," he replied. "She left yesterday." I didn't grasp what he meant. Recognizing the hesitation in my voice, he added, "She died yesterday."

Never put off for tomorrow what you can do today. It could be someone's last day—or it could be yours or mine.

Lord, please help me to be obedient to the Holy Spirit and not pass up the opportunity to be of service to others while there is still time. DOLORES SMITH

January 28

All Things Work Together for Good

And we know that all things work together for good to them that love God, to them who are the called according to his purpose. Rom. 8:28.

I LEARNED EARLY ON THAT one of the most important things a Christian must do is attend prayer meeting on a regular basis. Herein lies power and a constant source of encouragement and strength. I have also learned that it is safe to depend on this weekly spiritual nourishment and sheer joy to drink in the rich fellowship shared with other spiritual believers.

Rushing to church one prayer meeting night to be sure not to be late, I hurried across the street to the bus stop. *Oh, here it comes!* I thought. Confident that the driver saw me, I ran across the street, waving to attract his attention, fully expecting him to pull to a stop and let me on. He did not. He didn't even slow down.

I couldn't believe it! Why would the Lord let this happen to me? He knew my purpose in going to prayer meeting. He knew missing that particular bus would also mean missing the connecting bus, which would get me to the church late. Oh, how I hurt, feeling that the Lord had forsaken me. Didn't He want me to go to prayer meeting? Sulking, I waited impatiently for the next bus, my thoughts running wildly into the net of doubt. I felt as if God were far away.

Then a strange thing happened. A car approached and pulled to the curb directly in front of me. A friend poked his head out of the window and asked if I wanted a ride. I gladly got into the car, and he took me directly to the church door.

How chagrined I felt for having chided the Lord. Has He not promised, "And we know that all things work together for good to them that love God, to them who are the called according to His purpose"? He can make even a missed bus work together for our good.

God cares about every little thing that concerns us, and He meets our needs in many unexpected ways. I felt so grateful, for He had saved me both time and money, and I had arrived at church not only on time but early.

Trust Him. He never fails.

AUDRE B. TAYLOR

Colors of Cheer

Children are a gift from God; they are his reward." Ps. 127:3, TLB.

COME ON AUNTIE! Let's paint!" my 3-year-old nephew, Brendan, exclaimed. Smiling, I scurried to the table and sank into the chair beside him. Then, gazing out the window, lost in the white wonderland of snow, I sighed at the gray sky producing freezing flakes.

"Auntie, look at this!" Brendan cried as his brush swiped broadly across the paper.

But the only colors I saw were as gray as the sky above us. The dreary New York weather was in sharp contrast to the mild California winter I'd left behind to assist my sister, Lisa, with Brendan, and his little brother Cameron during her husband's military deployment.

Despite the blessings, I was lost in a fog and couldn't see my way out. It felt as though nothing mattered anymore as I struggled each morning to climb out of bed. Two years before an illness had taken over my life with depression, a vicious cycle of the illness. Brendan and Cameron were the bright spots in this ongoing battle.

"Auntie, come on! Paint with me!" Brendan implored. Obediently I picked up a brush. "OK, Auntie, here's what you do," he commanded.

I paused. What color should I choose? None looked very cheery to me. Looking over, I observed Brendan painting only with black. "Bren, I don't see any color."

Startled, he replied, "Auntie, there's a little blue right there!"—plopping his finger into a puddle of paint. Looking closely, I saw a blur of blue paint mixed with his black clouds.

"You're right! There is some color there!" I exclaimed, sweeping my paintbrush across the soggy paper.

"That's it, Auntie! You're painting just like me!" Brendan encouraged.

When circumstances fall beyond our control, God is there encouraging us. Can't you hear His cries of exuberance? "My child, come on, paint with Me!" I couldn't see any color on that gray day, yet Brendan could see what I couldn't.

Not long after this experience the world opened up with color, if only for a day. God used my small nephew to brighten "just a little bit" of my world when all I could see was darkness. I can hear Jesus echoing Brendan's words: "Can't you see it? There's a little bit of color here." LORI L. MANTZ

January 30

My Silent Partner

And after the earthquake a fire, but the Lord was not in the fire; and after the fire [a sound of gentle stillness and] a still, small voice. 1 Kings 19:12, Amplified.

WHEN I WAS A little girl I remember hearing my businessman father come home and tell my mother about his day. Many times he mentioned that "so-and-so can go on with that deal now; he's found a silent partner."

I wondered what a silent partner was. One day I asked him.

"When two people start a business project," my father explained, "many times one person has the know-how, and he's up front doing what needs to be done. The other person doesn't do any of the work or have much to say about how it should be done, but he provides the money to get the project started. He's the silent partner. One can't function without the other."

That simple explanation was enough for me then, and even now I use it to illustrate a point. All my life I have been a doer. If I saw anything that needed to be done, I couldn't rest until it was done by me or someone else. I often acted too soon, spoke too fast, gave help where it wasn't needed, or barged into someone else's domain. My good deeds were often misunderstood, and I spent a great deal of time explaining or apologizing, feeling unhappy and full of remorse when neither of those options was possible.

Now that I'm older and learning more about living a Christian life, I have a Silent Partner to work along with me. My Silent Partner provides not only money but everything else I need. Unlike other silent partners, He also gives direction and knowledge. He doesn't interfere with what I plan to do unless I ask His advice; then He provides me with printed instructions.

He has even given me a special "hotline" I can use at any time or in any place. I talk over my problems with Him, and He immediately understands. If I wait quietly, I hear His reply in a still small voice that seems to come from inside me. He doesn't speak aloud, but His directions are so clear that He doesn't need to do so. If I begin to do something wrong, He is quick to point out my error. If I persist and end up in disaster, He doesn't gloat or berate. He helps me pick up the pieces and start again.

My Silent Partner's name is Jesus Christ, and He wants to help you, too.

GOLDIE DOWN

Borrowing the Priceless

I am the door: by me if any man enter in, he shall be saved, and shall go in and out, and find pasture. The thief cometh not, but for to steal, and to kill, and to destroy: I am come that they might have life and that they might have it more abundantly. I am the good shepherd: the good shepherd giveth his life for the sheep. John 10:9-11.

HAVE YOU EVER BEEN responsible for something priceless? No? Are you sure? What about a friend's baby? Some say that children are expensive—and they're right—but that cost is just maintenance. The children themselves are priceless, from birth to death. (Yes, that includes you.) They are priceless because they cost the life of God's own Son.

There is something else that is priceless: time. Some think it's priceless because it's free. Time isn't free; it's borrowed.

When I worked in a nursing home, I once heard one of the men say one morning that he was living on borrowed time. I just smiled and said I was glad that he was still around. Recently, though, I have really started to think about that expression, "borrowed time."

I see so many people—in and out of the church—who are passive about the truths of God. Truths such as judgment and the Second Coming. Some might say, "My great-grandmother thought God was coming in her day, and He still isn't here. So He probably won't come until my great-grandchildren's day. I have plenty of time."

I find a fatal flaw in this logic. Jesus may not have come physically yet to declare the end of the age, but for all those who have died, the next thing they will see is Jesus coming in the clouds of glory. Each day is a gift that we borrow from God. He is the giver of life and the sustainer of life. God can exist without us, but we can't exist without Him.

We borrow every moment from God. He gives us these moments so that we can form a relationship with Him. He gives us innumerable chances to have and develop this relationship. But just because the chances are innumerable doesn't mean they are infinite.

The time you have is priceless. It is a gift from God. May He bless you today as you use it to strengthen your relationship with Him. JULI BLOOD

Who Shall Stand?

For the great day of his wrath is come; and who shall be able to stand? Rev. 6:17.

ONE OF THE JOYS I have in traveling is seeing the awesome might and majesty of God's creative power everywhere I go. Such was my feeling while visiting Korea to do women's ministries leadership training with the women of that country.

Our three-hour journey from Seoul to Muju seemed quite uneventful. Korea is 70 percent mountainous, and mountains lined the roadway on our journey. The meeting place was nestled in a beautiful valley, and the mountains there reminded me of stately vanguards around the building where we stayed. They were very close and very overwhelming, but they also gave a feeling of safety and security. We were in our own little world.

The words of today's verse talk about the end of this world when Jesus comes. If you read Revelation 6:14-17, you will see that when Jesus comes the heavens will depart, the mountains and the islands will be moved out of their place, and people will seek to hide themselves in these very mountains. Their cry will be "Fall on us, and hide us from the face of him that sitteth on the throne. . . . For the great day of his wrath is come; and who shall be able to stand?" (Rev. 6:16, 17).

As I think of these mountains now, my perspective has changed. The mountains that seem to be safe, strong, and secure will one day be a place of disaster for many. The question that came to mind was "Where do I feel safe and secure?" The psalmist reminds me that if I dwell in God's secret place I will find refuge (Ps. 91). The psalmist also tells me that my strength does not come from the hills but from God (Ps. 121).

So what about you? When you think of that "great and dreadful day of the Lord" (Mal. 4:5), when the skies will burst open and the earth will be moved, where will you be safe? Will you be able to stand? The wonderful thing is that those of us who know God and are known by Him will stand, safe and secure.

Lord, help us to make You our "dwelling place" each day so that on that day when You return we will rise above the terror of this earth into Your loving arms.

HEATHER-DAWN SMALL

Eventually Is Now

I tell you, now is the time of God's favor, now is the day of salvation. 2 Cor. 6:2, NIV.

YES, I'D LIKE TO learn to play the piano. Eventually I'll take lessons. Maybe by then I'll find time to join a church, too, and I can help with the music." Her curls shone golden in the sunlight, her green eyes danced. "Too busy right now. Gotta run." And we parted. Fast-forward 30 years.

We met again in the waiting room of a prominent dermatopathologist. It wasn't planned—I was having another invasive basal cell carcinoma removed from my face. Sun damage, the doctor said. Hers was significantly more serious. We both exclaimed in surprise and picked up where we had left off. Taking turns, we caught each other up-to-date with highlights from the past three decades.

"Thirty years!" she exclaimed at one point. "Where did they go?" Her curls were much shorter. Still golden. But her eyes, though still green, no longer danced.

"I don't know," I replied reflectively. "Just poof . . ."

"Do you still play the piano?" she asked.

"Some. Not as much as I used to," I admitted. "Travel and seminars seem to have taken up a bigger chunk of time than they used to." There was a pause, each lost in our own thoughts.

"What about you?" I asked. "Weren't you planning to take piano lessons?"

"I was always going to do that, eventually." Her smile was rueful. Her face sad. I wasn't sure it would be a good idea to mention her plans for church, but she did it for me.

"I was always going to join a church, too," she admitted. "Eventually. Somehow eventually never came. Now it's too late."

"Never!" I smiled in return. "Eventually is now!" And before she could interrupt with the proverbial "but" I added quickly, "I know a retired piano teacher who would love to coach another student, and I just happen to be playing the organ for church this weekend, if you'd like to come along." She would.

And I thought about some of the eventuallys in my life. Eventually *is* now!

ARLENE TAYLOR

Ask, Seek, Knock

Ask and it will be given to you; seek and you will find; knock and the door will be opened to you. Matt 7:7, NIV.

WHY IS IT THAT we continue to deny the Holy Spirit the authority to supply our needs according to God's riches in glory? When will we take God at His word? Why do we continue to worry? Have you ever asked yourself these questions? Or have you kicked yourself when you came back to the realization that you have, for some reason and some time, withdrawn yourself from relying on God to relying on yourself?

As a Bundjalung (indigenous Australian from the northern part of the state of New South Wales, Australia) "warrior" woman of God, I kept others busy and organized, managing this and that in a big way. Then one day I realized that I had been relying on my own devices and wearing myself out. When I was at my lowest point of exhaustion and tears were streaming down my face, my mind was saying, *No matter what, keep going, keep doing.* Then a voice from deep within said, *No, my God is sufficient for me; just ask, seek, and knock.* And I thought, *I can do all things through God who strengthens me.* It was then that I realized I was doing lots for lots of people for God, but I wasn't doing it for me with God. In other words, my motivation was sincere, but it was bound by my own resources instead of tapping in daily and moment by moment to the eternal life and energy source. So it was at that moment that I surrendered my plans, my present, and my future, to my God.

If your life is overwhelmingly full and crowded (and maybe confused)—if you are feeling empty and lonely, even though you may be very busy and have many people around you—I encourage you to turn back to the Life Force, drink at the spring of living water daily, talk continually to Him who is the universal manager, universal organizer, universal planner. He can be your continual life source each day.

Heavenly Father, thank You for reminding me of Your unwavering willingness to supply my needs according to Your riches and Your glory. Please continue to remind me that all I have to do is to ask, seek, knock, and believe that You will fulfill Your word.

JULIE NAGLE

No More Tears

And God shall wipe away all tears from their eyes; and there shall be no more death, neither sorrow, not crying, neither shall there be any more pain. Rev. 21:4.

THE PHONE RINGS at 6:30 a.m. Argelia's mother has had a stroke. I pray for God's will to be done and for her to be comforted and strengthened.

Beulah's father is found dead, sitting in his living room. I call to offer a helping hand. Her baby is only 1 month old.

A young couple walks into church. I had run into them at the supermarket a couple months before, and she had told me happily about her 12-week pregnancy. She should be about 20 weeks along by now, but there is no protruding belly. She tearfully tells me her baby had been born alive, but because he was so premature he lived only 12 days. I whisper a petition for the right words of healing.

Tricia's 3-month-old boy is diagnosed with cancer. I ask for God's will to be done. Another friend's husband is having an affair. I pray again and again and again.

Lately it seems as though everybody I know is having some type of difficulty. My prayer list grows longer every day. I wonder how life can seem so unfair. So many things happen that we can't understand or explain. Women all around are going through difficult situations and enduring unbelievable physical and emotional pain.

Yet God is still standing by. He's still in control, and He's more than able to take our pain and suffering and transform them into victory. Not a tear is shed that God doesn't see. He hears every single prayer, and every wounded and broken heart will be healed.

Like so many others, I long for the day when God Himself will wipe away all our tears and put an end to pain and sorrow. That will be the glorious day when we are reunited with our loved ones who have rested in Jesus. Then we shall not even remember all that we went through.

But until then, encourage one another. Minister to other women who might be going through what you've already conquered. Your testimony will help them to see that God never leaves us to fight our battles alone.

Remember, "tears may flow in the night, but joy comes in the morning" (Ps. 30:5, TEV).

DINORAH BLACKMAN

Marah or Elim?

My help cometh from the Lord, which made heaven and earth. Ps. 121:2.

WHERE ARE YOU? Are you at Elim, or are you at Marah?

Jesus didn't promise that in this life we would live on a bed of roses. Beautiful as the roses are, each rosebush has its thorns. Life is a mixture of the bitter and the sweet; sadness and happiness; sorrow and joy. Bitter as it is, there is a lot we can learn at Marah.

Someone once said, "I walked a mile with pleasure; she chattered all the way, but left me none the wiser for all she had to say. I walked a mile with sorrow, and ne'er a word said she; but oh, the things I learned from her when sorrow walked with me."

Exodus 15 tells of some of the bittersweet experiences of the children of Israel. They had just left the Red Sea where the Lord had worked a mighty miracle and delivered them from the evils of Egypt. They lifted up their voices and sang, danced, and praised God for His leading.

After only three days had passed, they seemed to have forgotten the way the Lord had led. Water ran out, and they were thirsty. Instead of looking to God, their deliverer—who just days before had plagued Egypt with severe plagues and set His people free, and who later led them through the Red Sea and destroyed their enemies—they forgot, only three days later, what God could do.

Many of us have camped at Marah far too long. What is keeping us so long at Marah? Isn't it time for us to cry to God for help? We have power available to us, only for the asking. Some Marahs can become sweet only through prayer and fasting and constantly calling on God. Like Jacob of old we should say to the Lord, "I will not let you go until you bless me." Or perhaps we are looking to the wrong source for help. The psalmist David says, "My help cometh from the Lord, which made heaven and earth."

When the Israelites journeyed from Marah, God led them to Elim, an oasis with 12 wells of water and 70 palm trees. What a refreshing change! The joyful voices of the people made the barren desert come to life when they saw the cool palms and the wells of water.

Life's journey has its Marah. But we also encounter the Elims of refreshing. As long as we follow the Lord's leading, the bitter experiences as well as the times of refreshing can develop in us strength for our homeward journey.

JACQUELINE HOPE HOSHING-CLARKE

Witness of Hope

In hope we wait on the Lord; He is our help and our shield. Ps. 33:20, Clear Word.

MY MOTHER AND I sat in the reception room at the Adelaide Hospital awaiting results of her scan. Nothing could have prepared us for the unexpected news that lay beyond the closed door. "Mrs. Aunger, you have a malignant tumor the size of football on your right kidney and attached to your liver. I'm sorry; we can do nothing. You may have only three months, and you would be better to spend it at home."

I prayed for comfort as grief overwhelmed our family. The words "Thy will be done" rang in my ears. My mother, a sincere and faithful Christian woman, claimed the promises Christ gives, and together we encouraged each other with reassurances of "the blessed hope."

Throughout her life Mom had served her Savior tirelessly by helping others, and her example of faith and acceptance in what she now faced continued as a true witness to all.

She was anointed, and soon after this church friends offered her a product known for helping tumors. Praying sincerely about this, we believed God was guiding, and it was accepted, along with their continued friendship and support.

In the months that followed, my mother inspired everyone with her enthusiasm to be involved in whatever she could do. Her right arm had been rendered useless because of lymphodema, resulting in the sacrifice of many of her interests. However, it didn't stop her from learning to write left-handed, or digging in the garden she loved so much.

Her smiles and messages of cheer embraced us all, especially Dad, her devoted companion of 56 years, and, in turn, strengthened our faith.

Mom was granted an extension of life for three and a half years. In her final days we talked together about the resurrection and heaven, as well as the gift of care from those who had brought the product to her in their thoughtfulness. No one knows if it contributed to her longer life, and it matters not, for when we live in accordance to God's will, He can use others to fulfill His purpose in sharing hope through loving friendships.

The hope of the coming of the Lord burns within our hearts!

LYN WELK

God Does Not Show Favoritism

For there is no respect of persons with God. Rom. 2:11.

I USED TO WORK IN an institute of the European Commission where nuclear research for peaceful purposes is undertaken. For the first few months on my duty there, I had to work in the so-called control area, where the actual research is done. Although I was an administrative assistant and not part of the scientific staff, I always had to wear a long white coat in my office as a precaution against radiation exposure. When I first met my boss, the head of the unit I worked in, the first thing he said was "I'm also wearing such an item," and pointed to his white coat. I think he wanted me to feel more comfortable.

I found his remark quite funny because it made it very clear to me that there were no outward differences among the people working in that control area. It didn't matter if one wore a shirt with some famous brand, a miniskirt, designer shoes (they had to be exchanged for white shoes before entering the radioactive zone), or anything else that could be somehow flashy or distinctive. Everyone looked the same in a white coat.

I learned in primary school that all people on earth are equal before God. He doesn't show favoritism. For Him, it doesn't matter how we present ourselves outwardly—He sees us the way we look inwardly. "And if ye call on the Father, who without respect of persons judgeth according to every man's work" (1 Peter 1:17).

So what is going on with me inwardly today? Are my works in accordance with what I profess? Do I have a clean, white heart? Do I have the fruit of the spirit—love, joy, peace, longsuffering, gentleness, goodness, faith, meekness, and temperance?

"Create in me a clean heart, O God, and renew a right spirit within me" (Ps. 51:10). This was the earnest prayer of David after he indulged in sin. Shouldn't we ask our heavenly Father every day to clean us inwardly? Isn't He the one who can show us all our negative traits of character, the one who is able to keep us from falling?

Dear Lord, I'm so glad that You know me to the core, and that I don't have to put on something special before You. Please help me today to become a woman after Your own heart. DANIELA WEICHHOLD

Let God Fight Your Battles

Don't fret or worry. Instead of worrying, pray. Let petitions and praises shape your worries into prayers, letting God know your concerns. Phil. 4:6, Message.

IT NEVER CEASES TO amaze me what God can do when we give our difficulties to Him and watch the way that He is able to work.

When we lived in Cheltenham, a certain girl at school bullied Rima, our eldest daughter, who is very small for her age. This girl was big and intimidating, and had a terrible reputation for being a tough person. Everyone was frightened of Kathy, and no one wanted to mess with her.

It was an awful time for Rima. Every day she left home crying and returned from school, sobbing. Even though my husband and I wanted to do something about Kathy, Rima was so frightened of the consequences that she begged us to do nothing.

We asked God to do something about the situation that we felt powerless to deal with. We thanked Him for what was going on, praised Him for His ability to deal with the problem, and gave Him permission to provide a solution to the situation. It was probably the hardest prayer we ever prayed.

Each day as Rima left for school, Jonathan and I would talk to God. Several times throughout the day we would continue to praise and thank Him and to ask for His will to be done.

A few days later Rima came home full of smiles. The situation had been resolved.

Kathy had been showing a photograph to members of their class. It was a picture of her cousin, Jodie, and her aunt Sarah. As Rima looked at the picture, she blurted out, "But that is my cousin and *my* aunt, too!" Rima and Kathy are actually cousins. Jonathan's sister and Kathy's uncle are Jodie's parents. After that Rima never had a problem with Kathy. Apparently Kathy didn't "beat up" on family, and if anyone tried to give Rima a hard time, they had to deal with Kathy first!

God says, "I am the Lord God; I can do anything!" (see Jer. 32:27). It is true: nothing is too hard for God. Give Him your problems and ask Him to give you a solution for which you can praise Him.

Mary Barrett

The Lord Made Us All

The rich and the poor meet together: the Lord is the maker of them all. Prov. 22:2.

THE YEAR WAS 1935. On a very cold winter evening I walked across town to try to borrow $2 from Aunt Mary so we could buy some groceries, only to be turned away, empty-handed, because they too were feeling the crunch of the Great Depression.

In those days $2 went a long way toward feeding even a family as large as ours. Day-old bread was 10 cents a loaf, a large box of oatmeal was 11 cents, and five pennies would buy a gallon of kerosene for our stove and lamp.

As a child of the 1930s I was aware of the responsibilities my father carried as he tried to provide for his family. I saw my parents struggle every day as we witnessed poverty firsthand.

The gap between the haves and the have nots was brought home to us each time I walked to our landlord's big house to tell him that once again we didn't have the $6 rent that month.

By the time I married in 1940, I was already primed for the hard times that were to come because of World War II. Harold had a job as a welder, one he held until he retired in 1981, so we got by. We always had a house to live in, even if it was an old house. We always had a car to drive, even if it was an old car. And we always had food to eat, although it might be mush and milk for supper more often than we liked. Vacations usually consisted of packing up the old tent and a box of groceries and heading for the nearest state park for a week. There were times we returned home with only a few dollars to our name. Since we lived from payday to payday we didn't have the luxury of a bank account, but we paid our tithe, and our two children always went to parochial school until they finished high school. Looking back, I have to say it was a good life. We didn't always have everything we wanted, but we usually had everything we needed.

We learned early on that to be poor is not necessarily the absence of money; neither is having a vast amount of money in the bank a sign of wealth. We discovered we were rich in other ways—love for God and love for family and friends.

"There is that maketh himself rich, yet hath nothing: there is that maketh himself poor, yet hath great riches" (Prov. 13:7).

CLAREEN COLCLESSER

Roll Call

Then the Lord said to Cain, "Where is your brother Abel?" "I don't know," he replied. "Am I my brother's keeper?" Gen. 4:9, NIV.

WHERE'S MARGARET?" I asked my husband. "She's not in church." I'd been away myself for 12 weeks, and since my husband doesn't go to just one church all the time he couldn't tell why Maggie was absent. He told me that when he met her one day she had told him she was working for Gracie, the baker. I was a bit worried about Margaret's not being in church, because she's usually the first person to be there to welcome everyone with hugs and smiles. Maggie is a deaconess with a heart of gold—always cheerful and ready to serve.

I decided to look for her myself, and, as expected, I found her in Gracie's house. She was so ill she couldn't walk. Even though I was disturbed to find her that way, I was glad that I had found her. She was expecting someone to come and look for her. She called Gracie and said, "I told you that as soon as my pastor's wife comes back from England she would look for me." I tried to console Maggie, prayed with her, and left her with words of encouragement.

We prayed for Maggie at prayer meeting, and the whole church visited and prayed with her, and that lifted her spirits. Maggie was comforted because she realized that she belonged to a group that was ready to help her. By God's grace, after a month she got well and rejoined us.

Often we go about our business without knowing what is happening to our friends, and we ignore their absence from church. Are we going to ask God someday, "Am I my brother's or sister's keeper?" No! Let's be our sisters' keepers, please! We should remember that Christ said the Good Shepherd will leave the 99 on the hill and go after the one that has wandered away (Matt. 18:12, 13). If we forget about absentees and members who are irregular in attendance, they may never come back to us.

Master Shepherd, please teach us to encourage each other. We are almost home, and as You lead us on, make each of us a shepherd's helper to those who wander from the fold. It is my humble wish that when You call the roll up yonder we will all be there.

MABEL KWEI

Comfort Ye

Who comforts us in all our troubles, so that we can comfort those in any trouble with the comfort we ourselves have received from God. 2 Cor. 1:4, NIV.

I WAS SCHEDULED TO have outpatient surgery in the same hospital where I work. I needed to have two skin cancers removed from my nose; the diagnosis was confirmed by biopsies. During my nursing career the Lord has given me frequent opportunities to help and comfort many frightened and suffering patients. I never believed that I would be in need of such comfort.

The morning of my surgery I felt calm and confident that my surgical procedure and recovery period would be uneventful. My husband, sister, and daughter were there as my support system. The chaplain came for a short visit and had prayer with us. The anesthetist spoke briefly with me about the type of general anesthetic to be used. I was unafraid as I was rolled into the operating room holding area—I was among friends and staff that I had worked with for years.

When I awoke several hours later, my first thought was *What is wrong with me?* I was perspiring profusely; I had pressure in my chest; I felt short of breath, and the nausea was unbearable. I was given medication for nausea and was placed on oxygen. I was then taken to the outpatient area, where I was supposed to stay for a few hours before returning home. The more awake I became, the worse I felt. My nurse, Tonya, did everything in her power to accommodate my every need, and my family was in constant attention. Even so, I felt so bad, and my symptoms persisted.

Finally, after several hours, the nurse manager checked on me. Jane asked me what was wrong as she began to gently rub my head and back. At that moment I felt so reassured and comforted. I began to feel that everything was going to be all right. The doctor did, however, give some orders to rule out any serious complications, and I was admitted to the telemetry unit overnight. In the morning I received a clean bill of health and was discharged.

Before that time I didn't fully realize the true value of human touch given in love. You can be assured that since then I've been much more generous with my talent of touch, for I have realized that others can feel the touch of Jesus through my hands. So, parents, spouses, friends, and nurses, do not selfishly rob others of this precious gift!

Rose Neff Sikora

Beyond Belief

Inasmuch as ye have done it unto one of the least of these my brethren, ye have done it unto me. Matt. 25:40.

JUDGMENT WOULD BEGIN at the door of the church." I'd heard the statement before, but I'd failed to understand it until the Friday night I sat in on my daughter's youth Bible study. The leader asked each person, "What are you grateful for this week?"

Then a girl, who had a history of problems but had tried so hard to fit in with the others, came in late with her cell phone in her hand. The leader turned her attention toward her with a reprimand about the phone and asked her the question she'd asked everyone else. Embarrassed and uncomfortable, the girl stuttered shyly, "I don't know; my family—and an A I got on my test."

Suddenly insults and a burst of laughter sprang from two other young people, and a third laughed so hard she almost fell to the floor. Two adults looked at the girl in disgust and spoke words of distaste. No one came to the girl's rescue. Her face flushed with hurt. The undiscerning leader went on with the class, untouched by the girl's obvious look of pain. The girl got up and walked out.

When she didn't return after a few minutes, I went to look for her and couldn't find her on the church premises. Appalled by this kind of behavior, I spoke to the class leaders. They still failed to see the depth of the pain they had caused, or that this girl was also a person for whom God cared so dearly. I told the leader that the girl who had been humiliated probably had a better understanding of her need of Christ than those left praising God when their behavior indicated they did not know Him.

How often we forget that the church is supposed to be a sanctuary where we should find peace from a world that's full of cruelty. Instead, sometimes we find more cruelty among those who profess to know God.

As Christians we often fail to realize that evangelism really *does* begin with one another, and it's impossible to witness to others if we ourselves fail to live what we say we believe.

"Above all, love each other deeply" (1 Peter 4:8, NIV).

TERI DEANGELIA ROULHAC

Just Friends

And we know that in all things God works for the good of those who love him, who have been called according to his purpose. Rom. 8:28, NIV.

I THINK YOU HAVE A lot in common," she insisted.

Oh, great. My friend Barbara had someone she wanted me to meet—her brother! At first I wanted nothing to do with him. I didn't want him to write, call, e-mail, or show up on my doorstep. Period.

But Barbara gently suggested it again. She explained that she understood my hesitance but thought that we had a lot to offer each other, since our situations were so similar. Grudgingly I e-mailed her back that if he wrote me a letter I might write back—but only if it was completely and totally clear that it was on a friendship/mutual support basis. No funny business.

To make a long story short, he did, and—you guessed it—we fell in love.

I found out later that he wrote many drafts of his original letter, placing it in the mailbox with both hands. He also dropped it in a big blue public mailbox so that he couldn't change his mind and take it out again!

When I received his well-written, carefully scripted letter, there was a phone number at the end. He had written that I needn't feel any pressure to call, but should I ever need to talk, to feel free. He didn't have e-mail, so I figured we could get to know each other a lot quicker over the phone than waiting for letters. So I called. And we talked for the next three and a half hours. The rest, as they say, is history; and two years later we publicly thanked Barbara at our wedding.

This story amuses me now because of my cynicism. Today my husband is my best friend. He is my buddy—we laugh, pray, and talk together. We're not perfect, but we are totally committed to God and to each other. Although I don't believe that some of the things we went through were good, I do believe that God used them for good because we allowed Him to. Today's verse doesn't say all things are good—we all know what our world is like. It says that all things work together *for* good if we let Him handle them. Even the darkest, most dismal, difficult, painful things can be used for good by God. Hang on—He will bring you through the difficult times and will, in His time, create something beautiful from them.

VICKI MACOMBER REDDEN

Valentine Balloons

The Lord hath appeared of old unto me, saying, Yea, I have loved thee with an everlasting love: therefore with lovingkindness have I drawn thee. Jer. 31:3.

IT WAS A LARGE, heart-shaped Mylar balloon. I'd given it to my husband, attached to a flower-filled, hearts-and-kisses mug on Valentine's Day. Written across both sides of the balloon, in big, pink letters, were the words "I love you." We both enjoyed the beautiful, fragrant gift as it sat on our kitchen table. Then, when the red, white, and pink flowers faded, I snipped the ribbon that held the helium-filled balloon to the cup and allowed it to float lazily to the ceiling.

As the days progressed and the helium began to slowly escape from its prison, my husband and I began to notice the balloon making its way around our house. It floated from room to room on the air currents, and we laughed as we found it in the strangest places. For several weeks it seemed as though it followed us around, constantly reminding us of the love for each other we have shared for more than 45 years. We found it bobbing in the basement, or riding high in our upstairs bedroom. One morning, as my husband was fixing his breakfast in our kitchen, he was startled when it gently landed on his shoulder. And, strange as it may seem, when my husband left on business for a few days, I found it resting on his favorite chair, as if to remind me that even in his absence we are blessed to share this wonderful love.

As I watched that balloon invade the various rooms of our home, I realized that everywhere we go, wherever we look, we find constant reminders of God's love for us. I laugh with delight when I watch the antics of the little frogs in my yard or see the animals in the zoo. He shows us His love through the beauty of nature, the singing of the birds, the sweet scents of the flowers, an unspeakably beautiful sunset, the blessings of life itself. All are God's way of telling us, "I love you, and you are precious to Me." Just as that valentine balloon continued to remind my husband and me of our devotion to each other, so also we continue to find evidences of God's love for us all around. My heart is filled with thankfulness that my God continues to draw me to Him with an everlasting love and that He shows that love to me in so many ways.

Lord, please help us to see the "balloons" all around us that remind us of Your love for each one of us. BARBARA HORST REINHOLTZ

A Gracious Gift

For it is by grace you have been saved, through faith—and this not from yourselves, it is the gift of God. Eph. 2:8, NIV.

IT WAS A FOREIGN country, and I didn't speak the language. However, after the meetings I was attending were over, there was some time before my plane was due to leave. I was keen to explore the city and asked that my hosts leave me near the places of interest, assuring them that I would be able to find my way to the airport alone.

Arriving with a few minutes to spare before the airport bus was due to leave, I noticed that people were purchasing their tickets before boarding the bus. I had assumed, wrongly, that the ticket could be bought from the driver. When I tried to purchase mine, I discovered that the machine didn't take notes—and I didn't have the correct coins! My heart sank, and I wondered what I was going to do. The shops were closed by this time, and I could think of nowhere to find change. Noticing my predicament, a kind young woman purchased a ticket and handed it to me. When I tried to pay her, she refused my proffered note with a gracious smile and a wave of her hand. All I could do was to try to convey how immensely grateful I was.

As I boarded the bus I felt overwhelmed by her kindness and generosity, saving me—a stranger, a foreigner—from an embarrassing and potentially dangerous situation. I gave thanks to God for her graciousness. I was on the bus to the airport, and the journey was costing me nothing.

It reminded of the verse in Ephesians that tells how Christ, through His grace, has saved us. Our currency in His country is worthless, so He paid the ultimate price—His life—so that the journey to our heavenly home is completely free. It struck me then that the gratitude I felt for my earthly "savior" is nothing in comparison to the debt I owe, every day, to Jesus.

I have kept that bus ticket that was given as a gift. It reminds me that I am a stranger here on earth, but soon I will be going home. In the meantime, I have resolved to pray for opportunities to repay my earthly benefactor by helping others and to repay my Savior by sharing the good news that He has purchased our salvation.

AUDREY BALDERSTONE

Awesome Answers to Parents' Prayers

Be anxious for nothing, but in everything by prayer and supplication, with thanksgiving, let your requests be made known to God. Phil. 4:6, NKJV.

MOM, I HAVE A new sister!" These words greeted my husband and me as we telephoned our youngest daughter from our holiday destination in Ireland.

The background to my story started in the early years of my eldest daughter's time in high school. Kylie loved food and found many opportunities to visit the local take-away shop. The more we encouraged her to exercise, the less she listened. The years of overeating and lack of exercise caused Kylie's weight to balloon. Even her forthcoming marriage failed to create a desire to live a healthier lifestyle.

We decided on a new strategy: no more nagging, only fervent prayers on Kylie's behalf. I was not prepared for the awesome answers that our family received.

Shortly after we started to earnestly pray for our daughter's situation, she visited her doctor and was told that she was suffering from high blood pressure. The doctor explained to her that she needed to lose weight and also start exercising on a regular basis.

That, then, brings us back to the introductory statement made by her sister. We have all watched in amazement as God has created a metamorphosis in Kylie's habits. She has now lost approximately 71 pounds (32 kilograms). She joined a gym, walks the dog every morning for an hour, and spends a great deal of her spare time studying about healthful living.

But God hadn't finished answering our fervent prayers yet. Apart from our petition for her health situation, we were praying for a greater interest in the things of God. We were concerned about her reading fictitious novels and her desire to watch the soap operas on television.

Last week Kylie visited us and requested some of our spiritual reading. Now, instead of the usual time spent watching television, she is enjoying discovering the truths of the Bible! It is little wonder that I can only say, "When the Lord answers our prayers, He does it in an awesome way!"

Parents, sisters, friends, "be anxious for nothing," but "let your requests be made known to God."

LYNN HOWELL

We Shall Obey the Voice of the Lord!

Whether it is favorable or unfavorable, we will obey the Lord our God, to whom we are sending you, so that it will go well with us, for we will obey the Lord our God. Jer. 42:6, NIV.

I WOKE UP VERY CONCERNED, my mind confused. My husband and I worked in the suburbs of the city with the highest altitude in Bolivia, "El Alto." In two years of activities, our work had been well developed through the help of God. We were happy. However, there was something wrong, and this hung over me like a dark cloud announcing a storm on a sunny day.

My husband's health—his heart—seemed to grow worse each day. The doctor suggested that he seek treatment abroad. For a long time, my husband thought that the climate aggravated his illness. He told me that he had decided to request a transfer.

For me this would mean leaving behind unfinished activities. This brought great sadness to me because everyone was motivated and there was still much to do. My heart had thrilled when I had the opportunity to share the message of the return of Christ, my precious Savior.

On the other hand, I had a new challenge to my faith. I asked myself, *Can my husband's heart condition improve if he is far from his cardiologist?* I was afraid, thinking of the long roads in distant places. What would I do in one of these locations if his heart suddenly began to beat at 380 beats per minute?

But I was not alone—I had a wonderful God at my side. This morning when I said "Good morning, God," I asked, "What should I do? Should I urge my husband to give up on the transfer, or should I accept his decision?" When I opened my Bible, I found an answer from Him: "Whether it is favorable or unfavorable, we will obey the Lord our God, to whom we are sending you."

This year has meant a greater degree of faith in our life. The Lord has guided us and increased our trust in Him. Through His marvelous care in tenuous moments, we have returned to our work with more energy.

Dear sister, have you ever been at a crossroad in your life? Do you want to know what God's will is? Each morning seek the living source of His Word. This is where you will find an answer. Obey, and you will be blessed.

CLAUDINA MENA DE PACO

Three Margarets

I thank my God always when I remember you. Philemon 4, RSV.

I HAVE THREE FRIENDS, all named Margaret. Interestingly, I got acquainted with all three of them in Harare, Zimbabwe.

I met Margaret Clark in a Bible study group. Her infectious smile and loving spirit drew me to her. In our many lovely visits together—a meal in her garden, a drive to her son's farm, an afternoon tea or stroll—I came to admire her strength and faith. She's had her share of grief; she was widowed at a young age and lost a teenage son to illness. I treasured the walk to her place on Sabbath mornings to share the blessings of the week while she had tea in bed. Her cat Ginger joined us, and she poured cream for him. We exchanged letters after I left Harare. Now in her 90s and almost blind, I visit with her on the phone, and we talk and laugh.

Margaret and Ron Parker came to Harare in 1990 from California, where Ron was to serve as a relief orthodontist for one month. I love the spontaneity of Margaret's friendship. Margaret loves to share God's love in her own shy way. She has a tender heart and is drawn to the needs of those around her. Now we keep in touch conveniently by Internet. She keeps me abreast of their travels to welcome the birth or celebrate the birthday of each grandchild. I was privileged to have had a visit from them when they came to the East Coast for the birth of their twin grandsons. Their joy is boundless.

Margaret and Winston Fletcher visited Harare in 1991 to see the countryside. Together we marveled at the majesty of Victoria Falls and gawked at the big-mouthed fat hippos as our boat glided on the Zambesi River. The evening and early-morning game viewing at Hwange Game Park was an experience I will long remember. I visited the Fletchers in their home in Australia. They never cease to talk of God's goodness. Lovers of nature, their garden blooms profusely with flowers. Colorful Australian birds frequent the feeders, butterflies flit, and bees buzz. Sadly, Margaret lost Winston to cancer and has now moved to a retirement village in Tasmania. I phoned her last week. She was recovering from a serious car accident; her voice was faint but her trust in God still strong.

Thank You, Lord, for bringing these three Margarets into my life. I am profoundly blessed by their love and friendship. LINDA ALINSOD

My Father's Daughter

I will be a Father to you, and you will be my sons and daughters, says the Lord Almighty. 2 Cor. 6:18, NIV.

IT WAS MY EIGHTH birthday. My dad had given me a nice bicycle as my birthday gift. I was so happy with my new bike. The only problem was that I didn't know how to ride it.

Every evening after he came from work my dad would give me lessons on how to ride my new bicycle. I always looked forward to his coming. We went to the empty parking lot of the office building opposite our house. It was fun learning to ride a bicycle, though I was a little scared at first.

On the third day of practice I felt a little easier. My scared feeling started to disappear. I felt more relaxed as I enjoyed riding on my new bicycle. My dad also realized that I felt more comfortable. The first two days he had held onto the back of my bike and run alongside as I pedaled, but this time he started to let me ride my bicycle without his holding on to it. But I didn't know he had let go.

When I glanced back and didn't see my dad holding my bicycle, I panicked. As a result, I lost my balance and ended up hitting the wall of the office building. My dad quickly ran toward me and helped me.

Many years later I still hold this memory dear. Although I lost my dad a couple years ago, this memory, and other memorable experiences I had with him, will always be in my heart. I'm so thankful that God gave him to me. His love and kindness toward me and the whole family were the biggest treasure I ever received in this life, and I couldn't have asked for more than that.

Although I lost my father here on earth, I'm grateful to know that I will always have my Father in heaven to guide and look after me. "I will be a Father to you, and you will be my sons and daughters," says the Lord in 2 Corinthians 6:18.

Heavenly Father, I'm so grateful and proud to be Your daughter. Thank You for being my Father and for Your promise to stay with me.

LANNY LYDIA PONGILATAN

Angels in the Early Morning

The angel of the Lord encamps around those who fear him, and he delivers them. Ps. 34:7, NIV.

WE WERE ALL SOUNDLY asleep on that winter night. My husband had snuggled near to me and was sleeping calmly. Back pain had caused him to have a terrible night, and he had used the electric heating pad, which was somewhat old but still worked well, giving heat and relief.

Still half asleep, I moved carefully not to wake him. I took a deep breath, and became aware that the air smelled terrible, a bitter odor that made me wake up completely, although I still didn't understand what was happening. Then I heard excessive coughing from my husband and from the children's room.

We sat up in the bed and turned on the light. A cloud of thick, dark smoke brought tears to our eyes. We were suffocating! But what was happening? Jumping up, we saw that where the heating pad had been, there now was a smoking hole that completely penetrated the mattress and the slats of the bed, reaching the rug, which was starting to flame.

We rushed to open the window so we could breath pure air. My husband lifted the mattress and the smoking blankets and carried them downstairs and outside, while I explained to the children what had happened and calmed them.

Evidently the control on the well-used heating pad had malfunctioned, and all this burning had taken place while we were sleeping.

What a scare! Who had awakened us from certain death by asphyxiation? It was in the wee hours of the morning and not yet time for our "biological clock" to wake us, and with the tiredness caused by pain, my husband's sleep was very deep. Certainly, it was a miracle. I do not have any doubt there are angels who stand vigil while God's children sleep. They carefully pay attention to their task, and what great work they have at times! During that night we once again had proof of what angels do for us.

"Praise the Lord, O my soul, and forget not all his benefits" (Ps. 103:2, NIV).

Thank You, my God!

LENI UŔIA DE ZAMORANO

February 21

The Steel Trunk

Cast thy burden upon the Lord, and he shall sustain thee: he shall never suffer the righteous to be moved. Ps. 55:22.

FOR MANY YEARS, though I had lots of happiness, I would dwell on the hurtful and unpleasant experiences that came my way. Fortunately, they were not too many. During the day I was too busy to think about them, but at night, usually after a fresh hurt, when everyone was asleep I would think about the hurts and wonder why I should be treated so. I would feel very sorry for myself. Each fresh hurt would bring to the surface all the past hurts. Of course, every time I was hurt I would kneel and pray and feel better after that; but after laying all my troubles at the feet of Jesus, I would unconsciously pick them up again and store them safely. This continued for years.

One night, after recounting all my hurts yet again, I found it difficult to sleep. I prayed as usual and was asleep in a few minutes, but I woke up suddenly after a terrible dream. I dreamed I was standing alone on a narrow path in the middle of a forest. Beside me was a large, heavy, steel storage trunk. It was getting dark, and I was afraid and anxious to get out of the forest. I tried to pick up the trunk many times but was not even able to lift it off the ground. I didn't want to leave it behind. I was so depressed and afraid. Suddenly I woke up, relieved that it was only a dream.

The dream taught me a good lesson. I was very foolish for storing my hurts and taking them with me everywhere as if they were precious cargo. I would take my troubles to Jesus, then foolishly pick them up again. It was a heavy burden indeed! Only after that dream was I able to learn to take all my troubles and hurts to the feet of Jesus and leave them there.

For many years now I have enjoyed freedom from this unpleasant habit. Sometimes when I feel tempted to indulge in nursing my hurts, I remember the dream of the steel trunk. I have thanked God many times for that dream. I believe it was God who gave me the dream in order to help me out of my problem. Satan takes delight in our suffering; he is happy when we wallow in self-pity. God loves us so much He wants to deliver us from this bondage. None of us is free from trouble, but if we learn to take all our troubles to God, He will take care of them.

BIROL CHARLOTTE CHRISTO

The Accident

And all things, whatsoever ye shall ask in prayer, believing, ye shall receive. Matt. 21:22.

ON A SNOWY WINTER Saturday afternoon, Ruth and her son were driving to a family gathering when suddenly she lost control of her car and hit the car in front of her. Ruth was in shock and thought she was dreaming, but it was real. The distraught woman in the other car called the police, and Ruth was served with a moving violation. There were some damages to both cars, but Ruth was grateful for God's protection and that her car still worked.

Eventually, Ruth made it to the family gathering and thanked God for His loving care and protection. However, the story doesn't end there. Three years after the accident, the woman sued Ruth for $1 million for physical and emotional injuries and car damages. The insurance companies tried their best to settle this matter out of court, but the woman was adamant about taking the matter to court and insisted on the $1 million.

Finally, the court date was set for a Thursday. Ruth was very nervous and anxious over this terrible situation. She prayed earnestly and talked to her lawyer, asking that he talk to the woman once more. She called her extended family and friends and requested that they also pray.

On the day before the court hearing, Ruth went home after work, cooked dinner for her family, and rushed to prayer meeting. She told her church family about the court hearing, and they had a special season of prayer that evening.

As soon as Ruth arrived at work the following morning, the phone rang. When she heard the lawyer's voice, she froze, wondering what he would say. "Ruth, enjoy your summer vacation; the woman has agreed to settle the matter out of court for only $15,000." Ruth was speechless. Now she didn't have to go to court, and the insurance company was going to take care of all expenses.

Ruth was so happy. She immediately called her family and friends and shared the great news of how God answered everyone's prayers and touched the woman's heart.

Our God is a personal God. He knows our every heartache, problem, sorrow, and sickness. There is nothing He cannot do. He rules the world; let us make Him ruler of our hearts today!

STELLA THOMAS

The Taillight

Thy word is a lamp unto my feet, and a light unto my path. Ps. 119:105.

MY HUSBAND AND I, along with our daughter's family, were going to Bangalore, nearly 30 miles (45 kilometers) from Hosur, where we lived. My husband drove us through the busy morning traffic, heavy with people going to work, shopping, or other business. We began discussing cars, specifically a car directly ahead of us and its attractive taillights. The discussion was so interesting that when that car turned right, we turned right, too, instead of going straight. After we had gone quite a distance my husband exclaimed, "Oh! We are on the wrong road. Why did I take this turn? I should have gone straight." We could still reach our destination, but it would take more time. He had been so attracted by the beauty of the taillights that he followed them unconsciously instead of concentrating on the road.

We are on a heavenward journey. Satan, the adversary, doesn't want us to reach heaven, our destination. He entices us with numerous attractions and pleasures of this world that are so seductive we deviate from the right path. Sometimes we are carried too far away. But the Holy Spirit, who convicts us of the right, gives us a warning signal through the Word of God, messages from the pulpit, printed material, and people who care for our well-being. Quite often we don't give heed to the warning. Sometimes we're so enchanted by the pleasures that seem pleasant to the eyes that we choose to go our own way. The farther we go astray, the harder it is to come back. If we are alert, though, we will give heed to the warning, realize we are on the wrong path, and come back.

Our heavenly Father is so loving, gracious, and forgiving that He warns us repeatedly. He doesn't want anyone to be lost!

I thank You, Father, for the gift of Your Word and the Holy Spirit who warns me when I go the wrong direction. Please help me to give heed to the warning and stay on the right road that will take me to the eternal home Your Son Jesus is preparing for me. Help us today to keep our eyes on You, following in Your path.

HEPZIBAH KORE

Why Not Me?

Faith is the substance of things hoped for, the evidence of things not seen. Heb. 11:1.

HAVE YOU EVER heard of someone writing their own Bible verse? I have, and I decided to pick up the challenge and do it. First, I carefully read Hebrews 11, the faith chapter.

Abel had faith to trust God with the kind of offering he was asked to bring. Noah believed God would keep His promise and send a flood. Abraham knew that when God was asking him to offer up his only son it was for a God-given reason. Moses chose to suffer rather than to enjoy the pleasures of sin for a season. By faith, the walls of Jericho fell down. And there were others.

Out of their weakness they were made strong. I am in awe of the terrible things some of these faithful ones had to go through in the times of the Bible: they subdued kingdoms, stopped the mouths of lions, quenched fire, escaped the sword. Others were tortured, cruelly mocked, scourged, and imprisoned. They were stoned, sawed up, tormented; they wandered in the desert; they hid in mountains, dens, and caves. Yet they received no promise. So much they had to endure! We are fortunate not to suffer most of those things today.

Faith is the substance of things hoped for—and not yet seen. Only faith can explain a song of praise and thanksgiving when times are bad. So here is my faith verse, paling when compared to those above: "By faith, Vidella, after having a heart transformation and coming to a knowledge of God's will for her, not fully understanding the when, how, and whys of God, believed His words and stayed steadfast in her beliefs. By faith, she believed she is a child of the King and an heir according to His promise. She stands for the right when faced by opposition from family and friends. By faith, she believes Jesus is coming soon, even though she's heard that same thing for 50 years. By faith, Vidella believes."

Mentally scan over your life—past and present—and see how you can write about your life, what God has done for you; and then write your own faith verse. It can be Hebrews 11:41. It can be a positive reinforcement when you think of the times in the past when you have exercised the faith that you have. Try it!

VIDELLA MCCLELLAN

The Mallard's Song

Blessed be the Lord, who daily loads us with benefits, the God of our salvation! Ps. 68:19, NKJV.

IT'S ON THE GLOOMY, cloudy, and sunless days that I get the most discouraged. My problems seem to be 10 times bigger than on sunny days. On one of those low days, after many days of gloomy weather, I was walking to school, feeling sorry for myself. Along my path is a river. When I was halfway over the bridge, I saw on the surface of the water ripples going out in a circular pattern. Curious, I looked over the rail and saw three mallard ducks perched on a log in the middle of the shallow river. At the end of the log sat Mrs. Mallard, serenely preening herself. Each time she lifted her foot and put it down again a ripple went out across the water, expanding and enlarging. Fascinated, I watch for a few minutes. If ripples could have words and a melody, this would have been the most peaceful and glorious song ever heard. Happiness and peace flooded my soul.

I didn't feel discouraged anymore. A smile spread over my face. I could picture God laughing and saying, *See? I got your attention! I'm still here. My presence is all around you, like the ripples on the water. I stand at the center of your life and bath you in My love. Do not fear the gloomy days; I am with you through it all. Look up, not down!*

Oh, how I needed that message! Mrs. Mallard's song stayed with me all day. Now when the gloomy days come, I remember Mrs. Mallard's song and smile. I may feel like God is far away, but He isn't. He is always somewhere in my life, ready to give me what I need to make it through each day. Yes, life can be hard; but it is the little everyday gifts from God that make the journey through all the difficulties possible. Oh, I am so thankful that I have Someone who walks this life with me and stands at its center and makes sure I am protected and loved, even when I don't feel that way.

Thank You, Lord, for always, always being there when I am low; and for sending me messages of encouragement by such ordinary means. Draw near me this day and open my eyes to see You at work in everything.

RISA STORLIE

You Are Chosen for a Purpose

Because he hath set his love upon me, therefore will I deliver him: I will set him on high, because he hath known my name. Ps. 91:14.

CAN YOU IMAGINE what would have happened if Moses had been killed along with all the male children of Egypt? You might say, *Well, God would have raised up someone else.* But when we look at it optimistically, Moses was that someone through whom God chose to do His will; and as long as Moses was willing to do God's will, he fit perfectly into His plan. We understand that once we submit ourselves to His will, He takes charge of us and protects us from all the snares of the devil.

When I was 15 years old, I fell seriously ill. Doctors could not diagnose the disease precisely, though it was similar to cholera. I was admitted to the public hospital, along with a few others suffering from the same disease.

My mother sat by my bed and wept and prayed: "Lord, we are Your children, and You have chosen us to do Your will. I have none but You."

My father couldn't help me much, since he was ill himself. Every day I had to take 18 injections at three different times, and salines dripped 24 hours a day. I lost my appetite. Only medicine and tonics went into my stomach. My back became numb, and my skin started peeling off like scales. Our hope dwindled as patients with the same sickness as I had began to die. Finally the doctors gave up too. They asked my parents to take me home, as it would be of no use to keep me in the hospital any longer.

Then the person in the next bed died too. All was lost. Or so we thought. Then it happened. My mother began to beg the Lord to give my life as alms. She wept for a week. I began to recover miraculously. It took a year for me to recover completely, but I was made whole by my Lord who chose me.

Today I am the mother of two children and serve as office secretary in the headquarters of our church in India. Every Friday evening, along with my husband, I go to a nearby village to share God's love. I stand as a living witness to God's miraculous power. I know that He is fulfilling His will in my life. And He will fulfill His purpose in your life as He did for me and for Moses.

ARUL MARY DANIEL

Above the Clouds

But those who wait on the Lord shall renew their strength; they shall mount up with wings like eagles, they shall run and not be weary, they shall walk and not faint. Isa. 40:31, NKJV.

HAVE YOU EVER FELT as if life has slipped you a situation and you can't quite get your footing? It's that exasperating feeling that flips you upside down, and you don't know what to do. As a mother, I've had my share of these experiences as my children have metamorphosed through life.

When my son graduated from high school, I presented him with a new leather Bible carrier that had Isaiah 40:31 inscribed on the outside. The scripture was suitable because he was leaving for a Christian university to study aeronautical engineering. Since the time he was an adolescent, he wanted to become a pilot—and by no means just any ordinary pilot. He wanted to be a top gun pilot, and to fly in the armed forces. Therefore, I knew that after his college education, he would be heading there. However, I wasn't prepared for the news that he was leaving to pursue his dream sooner than expected. The news was shocking because it was February 2003, and the United States was contemplating a war. Part of me wanted to cry in agony, and part of me wanted to support his dream. I had ambiguous feelings about his decision because he is my only son, and I felt his life was in peril. There was only one thing for me to do: I went above the clouds to inquire of the Lord.

God, in His infinite mercy, understood my anguish. He lifted my spirits by reminding me that I had raised my son in the fear of Him. He reminded me of His covenant promise that His protection extends to my children, and that Jon was not my child, but His. He reminded me of my frequent prayer of protection that I continuously pray for both my children. Then, as only God can do, He bestowed on me His peace.

It was time to turn my prayer into an act of faith and watch God work in my son's life. It was time for me to let go and let God. And once again God renewed my strength. He lifted my spirit up on eagle wings, and under the shadow of His love I soared above the clouds.

Thank You, Lord, for reminding me of Your faithful promises, and for being a loving, protective Father. And Lord, no matter what happens, I will trust in You!

EVELYN GREENWADE BOLTWOOD

Life Is Good?

Thou will keep him in perfect peace, whose mind is stayed on thee. Isa. 26:3.

IT WAS AN ABSOLUTELY glorious morning! The sun was shining; the sky was a vibrant blue, dotted with cotton-candy clouds to add a bit of variety. During the winter months in Florida we do get some rather cool weather; this is always a surprise to visitors who pack only shorts and tank tops, and a delight to vendors who are ever willing to remedy the situation. Having lived in New York through many a winter, I found the crisp air quite refreshing.

The traffic was moving at a nice pace, in time with the cheery, upbeat song playing on the radio. I was even ahead of schedule for a change. I felt good; I felt I looked good; the kids were behaving. *Life is good,* I thought. I truly had a song in my heart and a prayer of thanksgiving on my lips.

Then, out of nowhere, another motorist cut right in front of me. I had to do everything possible not to meet him—and the other cars around me—by accident!

"You nut! What are you, crazy?" I shouted. I was boiling. I wished I had a big car with a big rubber bumper so I could—

"What happened, Mom?" Two excited voices from the back seat reminded me that I wasn't alone. "Is this an accident?" the oldest asked.

"No, sweeties." I smiled at them in the rearview mirror. "No accident."

"Jesus took care of us?" Brandon, my oldest, asked.

"Jesus took care of us?" Jonathan, the younger, parroted.

"That He did, hon," I had to agree. "That He did."

Yep, I had to admit as we continued on our way. *Life is good.*

Lord, how quickly I forget to count my blessings. When I do the math, I always find that the blessings far outnumber the annoyances. Today, help me to keep things in an eternal perspective, because with You, Life is good.

Maxine Williams Allen

Icy Weather

My health may fail, and my spirit may grow weak, but God remains the strength of my heart; he is mine forever. Ps. 73:26, NLT.

THE ONLY PLACE THAT was free from icy winds and gaping holes in our bungalow was in our cozy little study. The place was its usual clutter of papers, pens, and assorted whatnots. I had tried on many occasions to clean, dust, and sort out; if the whatnots didn't get me, my husband, David, and his gadgets did.

Was this really what my life was about? Always sorting and in the end giving up on the whole idea of ever getting the study to look welcoming? Every time David or I wanted to work in this place either all my papers went onto his desk or his papers went onto mine. In my weekly cleaning I would pop my head around the study door, flick the duster over the computer screen and the bits I could see of the desktops, then shut the door behind me.

But now an extension was being built, and old windows were coming out and new ones replacing them. Ben, the builder, plodded back and forth with barrow loads of cement and bricks, smiling and trying to keep warm. Dave, the window changer, worked quietly, opening doors, closing doors, and leaving huge holes in the walls, also trying to keep warm. David and I hid away after making a hot drink for the workers and tried to get some of our own work done in the study. Everything was shifted and our desks were clear; however, a heap of papers had now appeared on top of the photocopying machine.

I've been sitting here wondering if God has had to do the same sort of thing with me over the years. Has He had to bring me in from the cold and settle me somewhere warm and quiet? Has He tried to help me unclutter my mind so I could see Him more clearly? Has He had to remove all my old and decayed thoughts and actions? Oh, yes, yes!

The Lord has taken and thrown away all my old sins and forgiven me, and He has given me a new future. My Creator has come to earth for me and for David and for you. He has sped through the universe and said, "Here I am, and I love you. Take my hand, and I will give you a new world, one filled with love for each other."

WENDY BRADLEY

But You Brought the Lord!

Now then, we are ambassadors for Christ, as though God were pleading through us: we implore you on Christ's behalf, be reconciled to God. 2 Cor. 5:20, NKJV.

WE HAD JUST ARRIVED on the Big Island of Hawaii for a year's assignment to pastor the church in Kohala. Looking at the church directory, we were told that several church members had taken their long sabbatical leave. My husband and I decided to visit those particular members who, for one reason or another, had really taken a long vacation from church. We began calling each one to make an appointment to visit them. Some were very gracious to accept our offer to visit them right away; others were hesitant and gave several excuses why it wasn't time yet for us to see them. One couple hadn't come to fellowship with fellow believers for quite some time. The lady of the house sounded very accommodating, saying we could come anytime we wanted.

When we arrived at their home, the couple eagerly welcomed us. Toward the end of our friendly visit, the man requested that he be excused, as he and his adult son had an appointment. However, he asked his wife if she could show us their fishing boat since he had invited us to go fishing with him whenever we could. In the process of the wife's showing us how big the boat was, she also showed her fruit trees in the backyard. Later, she gave us some local lemons, avocados, tomatoes, and butternut squash. I didn't want to accept the produce, because I felt I was taking her food; however, she said she had plenty. I thanked her profusely, and then we said goodbye.

Because she hadn't been feeling well on the day of our visit, I phoned her the following day to ask how she was. After exchanging pleasantries, I mentioned how grateful my husband and I were for the visit we'd had with them and thanked her again for the produce she'd shared with us. "We came without anything to give you, but you loaded us with goodies. Thank you for your kindness and generosity," I told her.

I had hardly finished my sentence when she replied, "But you brought us the Lord!"

It truly behooves us to remember that we are Christ's ambassadors (2 Cor. 5:20).

OFELIA A. PANGAN

Spring Is Coming

Let us try to know the Lord. He will come to us as surely as the day dawns, as surely as the spring rains fall upon the earth. Hosea 6:3, TEV.

IT IS WINTER. Where I live, winter is only about three months long, and this has been a mild one for us. On the news I hear of blizzards in the Northeast—record-breaking blizzards. I live in the mid-South and, so far, there haven't been any blizzards that I remember. I hear the kids wish for snow every year and tell them they live in the wrong place for that. (I, for one, am glad!)

I'm waiting for spring. I'm ready for spring. I really like spring! New life, new growth. Beauty just springs out all over. Maybe that's where the season's name comes from. Colorful and refreshing. We can feel alive again after the cold and drudgery of Old Man Winter.

Can one get for ready for spring? Flower bulbs can be planted in the fall so that they will bloom in the spring for our enjoyment. Rose bushes can be trimmed so they will yield fragrant, lovely, vibrant flowers for bouquets and corsages or for giving to someone who is sick and needs a lift. Some trees are pruned so they will yield crops of nuts or fruit. But whether we do any of these things or not, spring is coming.

Jesus is coming.

We have lived in the drudgery of this old, cold world with its record-breaking crime and the blizzards of sin for a long time now. Are we waiting for Jesus to come? Are we ready for Jesus to come? Do we *really* want Jesus to come? With Jesus' coming there will be a refreshing in our lives such as we have never experienced before. We will feel more alive than ever.

Can one get ready for Jesus to come? Love can be planted so that it will bloom not only in our hearts but also in the hearts of those with whom we share it. We can be trimmed and pruned, cutting off all withered, ugly things in our lives that might hinder our growth in Jesus Christ. But whether we do any of those things or not, Jesus is coming. What a wonderful time to be alive! Let's be ready.

DONNA SHERRILL

God Is Always With Us

I can do all things through Christ who strengthens me. Phil 4:13, NKJV.

IT WAS FEBRUARY. My son, Terry, and his wife, Nancy, had planned a dinner for couples and singles in the church. They had thought of everything, right down to providing a babysitting service at the church with their three older children and a friend serving as the babysitters.

They had invited me to the dinner, and afterward I stopped by the church to pick up Tiffany, my 14-year-old granddaughter. About 7:00 p.m. we began our three-hour drive home. As we turned onto the expressway out of Gaylord, the car began making a noise. Soon it was making a louder noise—then a loud bang! I knew I had thrown a rod. I managed to get the car off the road.

I tried calling on my cell phone, but it wouldn't work. Since we didn't know what was up ahead, we had no choice but to walk back to the last exit. It was very cold, and after walking more than a mile we were getting *really* cold. Tiffany suggested we should hitchhike. I said "No!" and told her God would provide a ride. At that instant a Jeep Cherokee pulled up. A man put the window down and introduced himself, saying he was a paramedic from Gaylord. He offered us a ride to a McDonald's restaurant.

We found the phone number for the church but had trouble getting through on the pay phone. McDonald's was closing in 20 minutes, and we had to catch Terry and Nancy at the church before they left to spend the rest of the evening at a friend's home. We were praying!

Because of the trouble with the pay phone, I went inside the restaurant and asked to use the inside phone. The manager said that wasn't permitted. When I explained the situation he finally agreed to dial the phone number of the church. I was so relieved when Nancy answered. I was praising God!

I'll never forget that night. When it was so bitter cold God provided a ride for us and took care of the phone situation. We are told if we just have faith, God will provide our every need.

Today may I have faith and know my God is in control and will take care of my every need. Praise God!

ANNE ELAINE NELSON

March 5

What Are You?

Behold what manner of love the Father has bestowed on us, that we should be called children of God. 1 John 3:1, NKJV.

IT WAS ONE OF the strangest questions I had ever been asked. I was in the grocery store, looking for the lavender pen that had fallen out of my mother's checkbook, when a small, freckle-faced, straw-haired child looked up at me with the biggest smile ever and asked, "What are you?"

Now I have been asked many times *who* I am, but never has anyone asked what I am. Having worked with young people for many years, I always pay special attention to children and try to answer their questions, but this one had me thinking for a moment. But as soon as she repeated the question, her mother whisked her out the door.

I thought about that question all through the evening. How could I have answered that dear little girl? I could have told her I am a daughter, a sister, a wife, a mother, a grandmother, a niece, an auntie, even a great-auntie. But really, *what* am I? I could have told her I am a lover of people—especially children—and that I am a great cook and I love to read and play games and give Bible studies. But those are all answers about *what* I do, not what I am.

The more I think about it the more I realize that the most important thing I can say about what I am is that I am a child of God. When I was growing up I didn't get to spend a lot of time with my father, and some of the times we did spend together weren't always pleasant.

However, I remember the very first time I heard the hymn "I'm a Child of the King"—how it touched my heart, and how I clung to those words. No matter what may happen, what I may like or dislike, or what my station in life may be, I am a child of the King. I am a child of God. How I wish there had been some way I could have shared that with that child. At least it made me stop and think about what I am.

So if anyone ever asks, "What are you?" you can assure them that what you are is a child of God and that they are too. ANNA MAY RADKE WATERS

A Present Help in Trouble

But my God shall supply all your need according to His riches in glory by Christ Jesus. Phil. 4:19.

IT HAD BEEN A hectic day getting my husband to the hospital through the ice and snow for his shoulder surgery. A dear friend took us in his four-wheel-drive vehicle and returned for us later in the day when I could bring my husband home. Now it was time to deliver the evening paper down two long streets. It was going to be a real challenge. After seeing that my husband was comfortable in his chair, I bundled up in heavy winter clothes and boots. Then I loaded the paper-carrier bag; with its big pouch in front and another in the back, putting half the papers in front and the other half in back.

I had no staff to balance myself as I waded through the deep snow, and I fell twice but managed to reach a fence to get up, and once a schoolboy helped me up. Finally I was on the last street and started delivering the papers to the homes when I fell again after tripping on something under the snow near a tree. I crawled to the tree and tried to pull myself up, but the tree was too big around on which to get a grip. A woman in a car came along and helped me up. I thanked her profusely and told her I needed a stick very badly to steady myself.

At once a car stopped and a nice gentleman, elegantly attired in a suit, hat, and dress shoes, stepped from his car and asked, "May I help you?"

"Oh, yes! I need a stick to steady myself."

He reached into his pocket and pulled out a pocketknife. He looked for a tree limb within reach, and with one slash of his knife he had the branch cut. He trimmed off the excess little branches and handed them to me. "I think this will help you," he said.

I thanked him for his kindness, then turned to watch him go—but he had disappeared. And so had his car. There were no footprints in the snow where he had walked. Then I knew the Lord had sent His angel to help me.

I still have the stick, and I marvel how that small stick helped me up. I know the Lord made it strong enough. It reminds me that I need never fear, for God will always provide what I need. RUTH GANTZ WEIS

Foiled

I will praise you, Lord, for you have rescued me. You refused to let my enemies triumph over me. Ps. 30:1, NLT.

HAS ANYONE EXPERIENCED a miracle in her life recently?" someone in our prayer circle asked. Good question. Several women shared very moving experiences. I could think of nothing more than the amazing miracle of life itself, but I wished I could share a spectacular story.

As a friend and I passed a service station a few days later I saw an ancient white Fiat. Suddenly memories, four decades old, flooded my consciousness. I remembered waking up to the midnight commotion of my father's urgent distress call that long-ago night in rural Jamaica. "Stop, friend. Stop! That's my car." My father's pleas seemed incessant.

I slid out of my little bed and hurried to the front room. I could see my father on the porch, his cupped hands encircling his mouth as he beseeched the thieves. I could hear my mom begging him to be quiet. I could feel my heart beating rapidly. "My friend, please leave the car."

The car tires crunched on the gravel of our long driveway as the men pushed our little Fiat down the gentle incline. Then there was silence, followed by the sound of the emergency brake being pulled, car doors slamming, and the rush of fleeing feet.

The policeman who came by shook his head. "You are so lucky." He told us that the would-be burglars were part of a drug heist and that three other cars had been stolen along this coastline.

Later, friends argued that our car had not been stolen because my father had called the criminals friends. My mother knew differently. "What happened was a miracle," she told us in no uncertain terms. "It was God who foiled their plans."

I still remember going back to bed that night, comforted by that knowledge and by the fact that I need not trudge those four long miles to school the next day. Years later I came across a powerful phrase Ellen G. White once penned: "We cannot know how much we owe to Christ for the peace and protection which we enjoy" (*The Great Controversy,* p. 36).

Thank You, majestic Maker of miracles, for foiling the enemy's plans every day of our lives. Thank You for the privilege of calling You Friend.

GLENDA-MAE GREENE

Freed During a Time of Tests

Be merciful to me, Lord, for I am faint; O Lord, heal me, for my bones are in agony. Ps. 6:2, NIV.

WHEN I WAS EXPECTING my first daughter, near the sixth month I began to have unwarranted fears that continued to grow until the end of the pregnancy. When my daughter was born I suffered from phobias and panic. My town is not very big, and there are few doctors. The doctors available were unable to diagnose my problem, which frightened me more and more.

One day a Christian neighbor to whom I had turned during moments of crisis told me that she was going to visit her mother. I immediately panicked. What would I do while my husband was at work and without my neighbor nearby? I thought I was going to go crazy with the entire responsibility of caring for the baby. The lack of this support terrified me.

My neighbor prepared a folder with Bible promises that I clung to in the times of crisis. On the night before her departure my crisis was greater. My husband didn't know how to help me. I sat on the floor in despair while I read the promises and prayed, asking Jesus for help. Then a miracle happened. How had I not seen it before, that very, very precious promise? It said that God cares for me. Even before I had read the promise carefully, the panic disappeared, replaced by an incredible peace. I liked the promise so much that I immediately memorized it. The Bible promise and peace embraced me.

After one week my neighbor returned. Joyful and feeling victorious, I wanted to show her the promise that had done so much good for me. To my surprise the promise was not in the folder. It simply was not there!

I have saved the folder as a reminder that God is no further from me than a prayer. He has compassion and immense love for each one of His children. Every day the Lord performs miracles in our lives, perhaps not like this one, but He renews His mercy over me and makes me feel thankful and safe that I have such a loving Father.

If you are not feeling good today, pray, because God is willing to pour out His blessings on His children. Wait patiently and with faith for the answer, because "now I know that the Lord saves" (Ps. 20:6, NIV).

MARIA ALEJANDRA LOSTRA DE PERUCCI

Christians With Attitudes

Your attitude should be the same as that of Christ Jesus. Phil. 2:5, NIV.

NOT LONG AGO I overheard a mother counseling her teenage daughter against displaying a certain attitude when being corrected. That incident prompted me to reflect back on my attitude in my teenage years. I recall being disciplined for wearing a certain look, responding in a certain tone of voice, walking away with a certain stride—all interpreted as lack of respect.

Often the accusation of "having an attitude" is a result of a negative observation which, warranted or not, encourages self-examination. Would it not be a pleasant twist to be labeled "Christians with attitude," based on positive brushstrokes we paint on the canvas of people's lives? If we were thus labeled we would be in preferred royal company since Jesus was known for His "attitudes": an attitude of pardon for sinners (Matt. 11:19); an attitude of compassion for crowds that followed Him in search of healing and/or food (Matt. 9:36; Mark 8:2); an attitude of welcome for children (Matt. 19:14); an attitude of acceptance for women at a time when they were considered by the majority to be inferior in many ways (John 4:4-29).

Perhaps Christ's greatest attitude was that of humility, accompanied by unparalleled love for His human creation. Who else but Jesus would do the unthinkable (in human terms) and volunteer to die, guaranteeing salvation for saints, as well as every repentant serial killer, terrorist, or crook who ever breathed? Who else but the Son of man would choose to retain His human form, forever to identify with those who would accept His righteousness?

Undoubtedly, it would be a powerful testimony if Christ's disciples today were known for their positive attitudes: attitudes of compassion in the face of pain, pardon in the face of betrayal, involvement in the place of indifference, acceptance in the face of bigotry, control in the face of provocation, contentment in the face of want, peace in the face of adversity, joy in the face of loss, calm in the presence of frustrations, courage in the presence of criticism, hope in the presence of panic, love in the presence of repugnance, forgiveness in the face of bitterness. Our world can surely benefit from more Christians possessed of these attitudes.

Father, I pray that You will bless others through me as I prepare to face the challenges today will present. May Your Spirit be at work in me to reflect that Christ's attitude lives in me.

MARIA G. MCCLEAN

The Leaking Cylinder

For he shall give his angels charge over thee, to keep thee in all thy ways. Ps. 91:11.

THE SKY WAS CLEAR that Sunday. I woke up with the pressing burden of numerous tasks that had to be accomplished. I had to wash clothes, scrub floors, cook, and any number of other things that would make me dog-tired by the end of the day. Would I be able to do it all? I was anxious about it.

After asking for the fulfillment of the promises from the Bible, I went into the kitchen to fix breakfast. Just as the last dosai (lentils and rice) finished cooking, the cooking gas cylinder emptied.

After eating the breakfast, my son David (13), daughter Hannah (11), and my aged mother, and I cleaned the house. The clothes were washed and hung on the line to dry.

Soon it was time to cook dinner. As I pulled out the cap of the new cylinder to attach it to the stove, the gas suddenly started leaking with a loud hissing sound. Then it blew clear to the ceiling with full force, like water gushing from a fountain. I was stunned. The smell of the gas soon filled the whole house. Afraid that the house would explode, I shouted for my children and mother to get out. My mind reeled. My husband was doing some extra work as the principal of the school, so he was no help. I couldn't think what to do because the appliance was new to me. The gas continued to spew for 15 minutes.

I ran to our neighbor's house to ask Mr. Jayasingh for help. He covered his face with a wet cloth then simply placed the cap over the leaking cylinder without any incident. The gas stopped leaking.

I didn't have enough words to thank him for his help. He could have found many excuses not to help us, including possible danger, but he came at the critical moment and extended his helping hand. As I thought through the events of the day, I knew God had fulfilled His promises, sending angels seen and unseen to give us protection.

Lord, I know You will be with us today as well. Regardless of what may happen, may we know that You love and care for each of us.

Soosanna Mathew

Safe Journey

The Lord shall preserve you from all evil; He shall preserve your soul. The Lord shall preserve your going out and your coming in from this time forth, and even forevermore. Ps. 121:7, 8, NKJV.

ONE FRIDAY MORNING I got a call from my mother saying that my dad had met with an accident. My heart was clouded with sadness, and I wanted to see him right away; however, I live in Hosur, 280 miles (450 kilometers) away from my parents' place. As the only daughter, I am very close to my dad. My husband and I got permission to leave our work early to travel home. We told our 2-year-old daughter that "Grandpa Simon is sick."

She felt bad and said, "Let's go to Grandpa's house." We had a short prayer and went to catch the bus. "Do you think this bus will be on time?" I asked my husband.

"I don't think so!" he answered, but during our conversation the bus pulled out. I wanted the bus to fly fast so I could get home early, but there was a mechanical problem. The bus moved slower, stopping and starting. Some of the passengers became very angry, and a few of them asked the conductor to give back the tickets so that they could take another bus, but he refused.

Finally the bus stopped completely, and the conductor decided to return our tickets. All the passengers got off with the luggage and stood in the middle of the main road. I noticed my husband standing right in front of the bus, and the bus driver was starting to board the bus. I called my husband to come up to the pavement where all us where standing. While he was walking toward the pavement, there was a huge bang at the back of the bus and the bus lurched forward. The driver jumped onto the bus to stop it. When we went to the back of the bus, we saw that a van had rammed our bus. I thanked God for saving all the passengers. *Praise the Lord!*

We got onto another bus and reached home four or five hours late. I was happy to learn that my dad had only slight injuries. While trying to cross the road, he had felt dizzy and fallen down in the middle of the road, where a bike hit him. He was unconscious for about a half hour; the doctor gave him medicine, cleaned his wounds, and sent him back home the same night.

Lord, thank You for preserving us from evil. SOPHIA JASMINE SAMSON

Time Will Tell

To everything there is a season, a time for every purpose under heaven. Eccl. 3:1, NKJV.

I OPENED THE WHITE envelope carefully, holding my breath, hoping that it would bring good news. The return address read *Guideposts.* I tore it open and my eyes dropped down to the words neatly printed on the form letter: "Your document does not meet our standards. Please try again sometime." For the first time in my short life as an aspiring author, I held in my hands a rejection letter that strangely seemed to energize me. With great fanfare I tacked the letter above my desk—the first of many yet to come, certainly. I was on my way, I told myself. Where should I try next?

Silently, a glimmer of hope entered my mind—there was still one more story out there in *Guidepost* land, for I had sent off two articles, the second a story about "my friends in blue." With seesaw determination, I reviewed my prospects. The following day I stalked the mailbox again. "No *Guidepost* mail." (Sigh.) "Good!" I was elated and proclaimed throughout the house, "Hurray, no rejection letter today!" Perhaps the second story had a chance. Like a puppet on my shoulder, the old phrase slipped into my ear: "Time will tell!" Time plays the part of the messenger when we take on new ventures. That evening, I opened my Bible to a familiar text in Ecclesiastes: "To everything there is a season." *Perhaps,* I said to myself, *there is a time to write and be accepted!*

Dear, Lord, I prayed, *thank You for this rejection letter. May there be many more as they indicate I am trying.*

Then God spoke to me. "If you share your story with Me, I won't reject it."

Wow! I hadn't thought about that; when I share my life, my insignificant and earth-shattering life moments, with Christ, He takes them all. He isn't bored; no big yawn from Him. He loves to hear our stories. Occasionally I've heard people say that God shouldn't be bothered with the little problems in our lives. He has bigger things to deal with. What about the woman who barely touched His clothes as He was surrounded by a crowd walking down the road? He could have let that go! But He didn't because Jesus is into the acceptance business, and He's sent us a letter, too.

NANCY NEUHARTH TROYER

Ridiculous Blessings

With men this is impossible; but with God all things are possible. Matt. 19:26.

WEBSTER DESCRIBES *RIDICULOUS* as "contrary to reason or sense." I'm reminded of God's "ridiculous" blessings as I review my prayer journal. It is amazing to me how concerned He is with the details of our lives and the lives of those for whom we intercede.

I smile as I think of Stephanie, a colleague who wanted a Christian companion. Prayers were offered on her behalf, and almost out of nowhere an ex-boyfriend crossed her path again. They began dating, and it's been a year since their wonderful wedding. Ridiculous blessing!

Recently I felt impressed to share a monetary gift with a friend, not knowing that she had been praying for a monetary blessing. When I presented the gift to her, tears of joy began to flow down her cheeks. God's timing is perfect, and His provision is sure. Ridiculous blessing!

Another friend asked God for specific clothing items, while at the same time God was impressing me to clear the clutter in my closet. The items I placed in the care package were the specific items she asked God for. Ridiculous blessing!

I have to pinch myself as I think of God's favor and the way He engineers the circumstances in our lives and gives us what we need when we need it, or who we need when we need them.

Errol is one such blessing in my life. What is unique about our encounter is that we have only seen each other twice in 12 years—once at our meeting, and another time while I was in the Caribbean. Yet there was a brother-sister bond developed that is simply God-given. I have been planning a fall trip to the Caribbean and needed a serious blessing regarding my hotel stay. I was impressed to call Errol since he is the vice president for one the hotel/resorts in the Caribbean. We reconnected, and he informed me that he manages one of the hotels on the specific island I was visiting. When I gave him my itinerary, he said he would work something out that wouldn't "burn a hole in your pocket." Last week I received an e-mail from Errol: the arrangements have been made; my seven nights in the Caribbean are "completely complimentary." Ridiculous blessing!

Whatever we need, God's got it (Matt. 21:22). He's got showers of blessings, ridiculous blessings!

TERRIE RUFF

Step Into the Water

Commit your way to the Lord, trust also in Him, and He shall bring it to pass. Ps. 37:5, NKJV.

YOU WOULD TAKE A chance like that?" my friend asked.

"It's my only choice," I answered, knowing the chances and also God's promise. I chose to walk out in faith, to step into the water, the water of faith, as God told Joshua to do. He sent the priests, carrying the sacred Ark, to put their feet into the water of the Jordan River and promised the water would part. And it did.

I believed that if God called me to do a job, He would provide the way to do it. I remembered that Ellen White wrote: "All His biddings are enablings" (*Christ's Object Lessons,* p. 333). I asked God to fulfill that promise as I packed my bags.

Tickets and passport in hand, I boarded a plane to a country I had never seen. There I was to find the necessary visa to complete my journey farther away into the strange country where my assignment awaited me.

God's blessed assurance filled my heart as I clung to His promises. Over the ocean I memorized the words I needed to say as I prayed for guidance. Those words are still clear in my mind, though it happened long, long ago. I know God gave me those words. It was He speaking through me; I felt the Holy Spirit in those moments.

And God's timing was perfect at every step of the way. I obtained the needed visa just before the embassy closed for a long weekend that Friday afternoon. With God's help I was ready and on my way to my faraway missionary job. I prayed for safety all the rest of the way as I rested that Sabbath.

I continued on plane after plane, stop after stop, experiencing miracles all the way, even the jammed wheel carriage on the last plane. It loosened after we circled the airport three times. When we landed, fire trucks and ambulances lined the airstrip. When I had deplaned safely, I knew it was God's power that had kept me safe.

Dear Lord, we give You all the praise and honor today as we submit our way to You and Your guidance for this day. Help us to step into the water today and share Your good news with others. BESSIE SIEMENS LOBSIEN

Cats at Play

I will rejoice in the Lord, I will be joyful in God my Savior. Hab. 3:18, NIV.

LOOKING OUT MY kitchen window I watched Mother Cat escort her two children from the barn through the yard on their way to the woods behind our house. The kittens decided to stop and play for a while. Little Calico dashed here and there through the flower garden, enjoying the cool morning air. Black-'n-White followed the same path. Changing their plan, they chased each other through the garden as two children would if they were allowed to run free. They dashed into the shrubs for a time to play in the shadows of the leaves. Little Calico would run and hide under a plant, waiting for Black-'n-White to come by. Without warning, Calico would jump upon Black-'n-White, resulting in a time of playful tussling.

Feeling free and happy, the kittens enjoyed their romp in the garden. Mother Cat decided she'd had enough of their kittenish foolishness and strolled off into the woods with the dignity that only a mother possesses. Neither of the kittens paid any attention to what their mother was doing. They were having fun.

My heart was lifted as I laughed at the antics of these two kittens. I was reminded of the blessings that come because we were created with the ability to laugh. When the burdens of life seem too heavy and we do not know what we should do, finding something to laugh about is often the one thing that lifts the burdens. God must wonder at our concerns and why we choose to dwell upon the negatives when He has provided so many reasons for us to be cheerful.

Just as the kittens made me laugh, the antics of children provide us with many situations where laughter is the only proper response. Seize the opportunities to look at the happy side of life. Just for today keep an account of the occasions when laughter is a good response. When speaking to various groups I often have suggested they keep a happiness journal. Recording happy moments in a book will give us a resource to look back upon when days are not so bright.

I want to always look for the happy things in life because it makes me a better person. My physical health benefits when I am happy, and I am able to do my work more efficiently. I am also a more pleasant person to my family, friends, and coworkers. My prayer is for God to keep reminding me of the joys in my life that give me a reason to laugh. EVELYN GLASS

Tank Burst

Our God shall come, and shall not keep silence. Ps. 50:3.

I WAS BUSY IN THE nurse's station that night, writing out the duties for the following week. Absorbed in what I was doing, I was not disturbed by any noise, even the opening of the duty-room door. Suddenly I heard a voice saying softly and gently, "Are you still here?" I looked up in amazement. It was the night supervisor.

"Are you aware that you are the only nurse on the floor?" she asked. I was astonished. She then said, "The town is on fire, and your colleagues have left to see to their families; anything could happen. Come and see." I walked down the hall in the direction of the railway station when a huge, red flame shot up into the sky. A noise like great thunder followed. A petrol tank had burst.

The windows were red from the heat, but my curiosity drew me closer. In the middle of that night I saw traffic rushing at high speed in all directions—family cars, trucks with household furniture, all accompanied by a great buzzing. The seriousness of it all hit me. I thought of my mother and grandchildren at home. *How am I going to get there?* I wondered. I had no transportation and no idea how far the flames reached. I began praying for the safety of my family. I was torn between two options: home and the helpless patients.

I went into the ward, which was really packed with patients—we even had beds on the floor. Standing in the middle, I heard a faint voice say, "Are you also going to leave us?"

I was overwhelmed; the decision now became harder than ever as I stood in that dark ward with the seriously ill patients. I again prayed for God to keep control of the situation until dawn so doctors could discharge these patients or have them transferred to some other hospital. The Lord answered my prayer when a few of my colleagues returned after they had made sure that their families were safe.

There is a another day of decision coming. People will be crying to the mountains to hide them from the face of the coming One. Others will be crying over their fate as the long-awaited-for Savior appears. Graves will open, and the dead in Christ will rise to meet their Savior. I want to be ready to meet my Jesus, don't you? ETHEL DORIS MSUSENI

Strong or Weak?

Lord, thou hast been our dwelling place in all generations. Ps. 90:1.

HAVE YOU EVER experienced especially difficult moments in your life during which you felt sad, alone, tired of everyone and the world around you; moments in which you had feelings of such despair that you even reached the point of questioning the reason for your existence? I have been through moments like these. There have been times in my life when I thought I would not be able to face an entire day, much less make it halfway through the week. During these discouraging moments, those I contacted thought I was strong, full of life, capable of supporting all the storms and torments of life. However, I greatly needed someone with whom I could share my situation, and I did not find anyone to help me carry the weight of my burdens or the bitterness of my soul. When I reached the very bottom, the encouraging words found in Psalm 90:1 told me of my unchangeable God. This spoke to my frailty and helped me tremendously.

I was reminded that a refuge exists, that there is Someone who is interested in me—not just in the strong, dedicated, capable woman who I am most of the time, but Someone who is concerned with the person who exists deep within me—the lonely, sad, and tired woman who sometimes feels that she does not have the strength to continue.

There is Someone who has His arms opened wide and is always ready to hear all that I have to say, Someone who is always willing to offer counsel. He embraced me; He listened to me, and still hears me. He was there all the time. I was the one who didn't realize His presence.

When I put myself in His arms, He allows me to overcome everything. When I speak with Him, I feel relief. He cures my wounds and prepares me for the daily battle. Even more than this, He is right by my side in the battle. He never leaves me alone.

If you feel lonely and discouraged today, go to a place far away from everyone and rest in the arms of the heavenly Father. Talk to Him about your anguish; let Him know how you feel, and with complete trust you may go out to the battles of life and become victorious.

Dear Lord, thank You for listening and understanding how I feel today. Thank You for being by my side at all times, even when the battles of life seem to be more than I can bear. AURÍSIA SILVA BRITO RODRIGUES

Lost for a Moment

Then the man and his wife heard the sound of the Lord God as he was walking in the garden in the cool of the day, and they hid from the Lord God among the trees of the garden. Gen. 3:8, NIV.

MY 4-YEAR-OLD DAUGHTER and her friend had gone to our neighbor's house to play with her little boy. The silence was absolute in my house, but for a moment I was not concerned. Panic began to take hold of me when my neighbor came to look for the children at my home, confirming that they were no longer at her house. In an instant I grabbed my bicycle and began looking for them up and down the streets of the neighborhood. All of our friends and neighbors joined our search for the children.

We notified the police so they could help to find the three children who had disappeared. All schools and nearby parks were searched. After 20 minutes of despair, I sat on the sidewalk in front of my home, crying out to the Lord. Far off, I heard the noise of some children. I entered my neighbor's home, searching for the source of the noise. To my relief I found the three children in a cluttered room, hidden under the bed. They had hidden because they were afraid. They knew they would be punished for cluttering up the room, and that's why they didn't answer when someone had called them. I still shudder when I remember that day and consider that I could have lost my rare jewel.

There was a long-ago day when Adam and Eve hid from God with fear because they had sinned. And like them, we sin and hide from the presence of the Lord. Ashamed of our sins, we no longer feel the desire to pray because we do not think that we are worthy. We forget that God is searching for us because we are precious jewels. And even if punishment comes as a consequence of our sins, when we respond to the call and return to the loving arms of the Lord it will always be worthwhile and give Him great joy.

Thank You, Lord, for always protecting my daughter with Your angels. Teach us to return to Your arms after each fall. May we realize that You are always ready to receive us, and that with You we have nothing to fear.

PATRICIA FERNANDES DOS SANTOS DA SILVA

Fire!

Aha, I am warm, I have seen the fire. Isa. 44:16.

IT WAS A DREARY winter afternoon. The day was foggy, damp, gloomy, and very cold, just the kind of day for a good book in front of a roaring fire. I was prepared to spend my day off all warm, cozy, and comfortable, waiting for my husband to come home from work.

We had a large supply of wood by the side of the house and a lovely fireplace just waiting for it. Building a fire was not difficult, I knew, because I'd watched my clever husband build many of them. "Build it properly and it will burn," he used to tell me, so I piled several large logs on the iron grate in the fireplace. After many attempts to start a fire, I figured I'd take a shortcut because what I had been doing just wasn't working.

In the garage I looked for some liquid fire starter. Spying a gallon can of lacquer thinner on the shelf, I lugged it through the kitchen into the family room. I unscrewed the shiny silver cap and poured some of the clear liquid over the logs. Putting the lid back on, I knelt down, struck another match, and watched in horror as flames leapt up the fireplace and engulfed the can sitting on the hearth! The can was on fire, so I pushed it into the fireplace. Then, realizing the can could explode and burn down the whole house, I grabbed the flaming can again and raced through the kitchen into the empty garage.

I placed the flaming can in the middle of the empty garage floor. Staggering back into the house, I collapsed in the kitchen and crawled to our bedroom. My heart crashed with fear. Adrenalin coursed through my body and I shook, a mass of hysteria, all alone. My heart begged the Lord for help, but my lips couldn't even open, frozen with terror. Minute after minute passed without any sound of explosions while I continued to pray. He had heard me!

When my husband came home that night, he asked me why there was a blackened can of lacquer thinner in the middle of the garage. I had to explain my idea of using a shortcut to start a fire and all that happened because of it. He was very pale when I'd finished talking. He didn't need to tell me how foolish I'd been and what could have happened. The Lord heard the unspoken cries of a desperate heart, and once again He saved me.

"The way of a fool is right in his own eyes" (Prov. 12:15).

CHERYL HURT

O Give Me That Book!

Your decrees are my heritage forever; they are the joy of my heart. Ps. 119:111, NRSV.

I WANT TO KNOW one thing—the way to heaven; how to land safe on that happy shore. God himself came to teach the way; for this very end He came from heaven. He has written it down in a book. O give me that book! At any price, give me the book of God! I have it; here is knowledge enough for me. Let me be *homo unius libri* [a man of one book]"—John Wesley, 1746.

One day while shuffling through a pile of old books, I came across a really old-looking, fabric-bound book. It looked very worn and used, and gave off an old, musky smell. I had a sense that within its pages were some possible answers to life's secrets. A treasure! And now I had it! But I didn't reckon on what I would find in that book.

I was 35, extremely busy professionally and personally, and I had decided that it was time to get away. I went to my Nan's house, which sits between a peaceful river bordered by tall green trees and the Pacific Ocean. The ocean gave me a sense of peace, freedom, release. This place to me was a little bit of heaven on earth—just what I needed. The sea breeze swept past me, violently, taking with it all of my anxiety. As its intensity decreased, I was left with its gentleness brushing past my skin and sweeping my hair from my face.

John Wesley wrote two centuries before my time, and it hit me like a lightning bolt during a summer thunderstorm. I asked myself the hard questions about God's Word that John Wesley desired: Did I really know the power spoken of within the pages of the Holy Book? Did I feel passionately about this Book? Did I acknowledge that this "book of God" has within it the map to land "safe on that happy shore"? Would I pay any price to access the information in its pages?

I asked myself, *Why is my life so chaotic?* My response: *Because I don't desire the book of God enough to give it time. I don't desire the book at any price, and therefore I don't desire the blessings in its pages.* But I do now.

I believe that the only source of life's fulfillment is God the Creator, and we access Him through the map, the love letters, the journal about Him for us and to us as written in the Bible.

Father God, thank You for guiding and leading us through the writings of others.

JULIE NAGLE

Seatmates

When the Counselor comes, . . . he will testify about me. And you also must testify, for you have been with me from the beginning. John 15:26, 27, NIV.

IF YOU HAVE FLOWN with Southwest Airlines, you know they don't give you a seat assignment. Rather, you receive a boarding card with an *A*, *B*, or *C* designation. *A's* board first, *B's* next, and *C's* last. My husband and I had a *B*. Dick said, "When we get on, all the window and aisle seats will be taken, so we may be seated separately." As we began walking down the aisle, I was surprised to see the center and aisle seat in row three empty. And then I saw why. Next to the window sat a young mother with a baby. The mother looked at me with frightened eyes as if she were saying, "You don't want to sit by me, do you? I'm so afraid my baby will misbehave." Ordinarily I don't like sitting near babies, but this was not going to be a long flight; so I asked Dick, "This OK?" and we sat down.

Little Isaac turned out to be a charming little 7-month-old who immediately gave me a big smile when I spoke to him, and his mother seemed to relax. As we took off I saw her make the sign of the cross on baby Isaac and herself, so I knew she was a Christian. We began to visit, and I learned that she was a young Army wife who had just been to Maryland to visit her parents. Her husband, assigned to the 101st Airborne, had been sent to Kuwait. American troops had just invaded Iraq the day before. As far as she knew, his unit had not yet moved into battle.

We talked a little about her fears and the challenges she faced. I was able to share with her that I had been left with an infant almost the same age as hers, as well as a toddler, when Dick had gone to Vietnam many years before. It created a common bond. The mother relaxed, and soon she and Isaac were asleep. As we landed, I shared a couple small pamphlets with her, including one on prayer, saying I was sure that at this time in her life she would be appreciating prayer.

There have been times I have prayed for a good seat for myself. Sometimes I get it; sometimes I don't. I have prayed that God would seat me by someone to whom I could witness for Him. Sometimes I have found that person; sometimes I have not. It did seem, however, that the Holy Spirit had led on this particular day. Did I say what He wanted me to say? I hope so. He opens opportunities. It is up to us to be open and available to His leading.

ARDIS DICK STENBAKKEN

Best of All Seasons

For everything there is a season, and a time for every matter under heaven. Ecclesiastes 3:1, NRSV.

SPRING! THE WONDROUS season—theme of innumerable songs, paintings, and poems. Time of young love, budding blossoms, flowering fruit trees, strengthening sunshine, nesting birds—wondrous lifegiving season. My heart throbs with joy when winter takes her leave and I turn off the heaters, pack my woollies into plastic bags with suitable moth repellent, and fluff the feather quilt for the last time. Frosts and cold and drab gray mornings are gone for another year.

Slowly the days lengthen, the morning light strengthens, until by 6:00 I can see the first blush of dawn through my bedroom window and hear the birds twittering in the camellia bush. Glorious spring! I greet each shiny new day with the wonder of a child.

Then *wham!* By government edict we are slammed back into dark again. Instead of blushing dawn, 6:00 brings dreary gray half light, and we resentfully stagger off to work when the sun is scarcely above the horizon.

At the other end of the day we drag ourselves home, hot, tired, and irritable—ready for a shower and an evening's relaxation. But no! The sun is high in the sky; its accusing glare highlighting the lawn that needs mowing, the weeds that need pulling, the garage that needs painting. There is no plausible excuse. We grit our teeth and work a 12-hour day.

Six months later our biological time clocks are thrown into confusion again when daylight saving time ends, and we return to standard time.

And what is all this for? Energy consumption saved? What nonsense! What difference is there between electricity used at the beginning of the day and energy used at the day's end?

In the wintertime I bid the sun goodbye about 5:00, draw the curtains, and settle down to a long evening of reading, writing, or watching TV before I turn off the heater, turn on the electric blanket, and snuggle into bed.

In the summer I turn up the cold setting on the refrigerator and freezer. I keep the air-conditioner on full blast and have two showers a day instead of one; and I don't use cold water.

What about you, my friend? What does God want of you in this season? How does He want you to spend the hours and use the light He has given you?

GOLDIE DOWN

Only One Thing

You are worried and upset about many things, but only one thing is needed. Mary has chosen what is better, and it will not be taken away from her. Luke 10:41, NIV.

ONLY ONE THING. The words kept sounding in my mind as I tried to get our new multimedia projector to work properly. They were the words of Jesus I had read that morning. *Only one thing is needed.* The projector, purchased from our Christian Women's Retreat offering, was being sent to the Southern Mindanao Mission for our JITA (Jesus Is the Answer) Philippine mission project. I tried everything I could think of to correctly hook up the projector, and then tried it again and again. I even read the manual! Still, there was no signal. One after another, I sought the help of three electricity-knowledgeable men in our office who frequently use multimedia projectors. They accepted this as their challenge for the day. Hours later there was still no signal. "It must be defective," they decided.

"Lord," I pleaded, "before I send this projector to the Philippines I need to know it is working properly. What is the 'only one thing' that is needed?" No answer. Finally I took the projector all the way across town to the company from which it came. They checked it out, and it was as I suspected. Only one thing was needed—the provided adapter! I needed to use the provided adapter. The adapter made the proper connection. I just had to use it.

"Corleen, Corleen," I heard Jesus say through His words to Martha, "you are worried and upset about many things, but only one thing is needed. Mary has chosen what is better. And it will not be taken away from her."

Lord, You have given me yet another invitation to come to You, sit at Your feet, and enjoy Your presence as Mary did. I come on a quest to find the "only one thing" that is needed: a vital and constant connection with You. I have learned from experience that this connection comes only through spending time with You, meditating on Your Word, and remaining in constant prayer contact with You. This is Your provided adapter. It makes the connection that allows You to shine through my life to others. Yes, it is the only one thing that is needed.

Corleen Johnson

A Forever Guide

I will lead the blind by ways they have not known, along unfamiliar paths I will guide them; I will turn the darkness into light before them and make the rough places smooth. These are the things I will do; I will not forsake them. Isa. 42:16, NIV.

DAYLIGHT HAD NOT yet arrived. I couldn't sleep—my mind was whirling with excitement, questions, and apprehensions. A childhood dream was about to become a reality, but I wasn't sure I was ready for it. My family was traveling from New Jersey to California to bid our families and friends goodbye before flying to a mission field in eastern Asia.

I cautiously crawled out of bed, dressed, and crept past my husband and four children sleeping in our tent trailer. Outside the tent flap a glorious scene opened up before me. Dawn began to light up the sky. Pine trees and mountains were reflected in the mirror lake beside me. The rickrack strata of Maroon Belles in the Colorado Rocky Mountains framed the backdrop. An alpine glow was growing brighter in the West. A beaver crisscrossed the lake, gathering boughs for his den not far from where I was standing. Just beyond was a big flat rock beckoning me to sit for a while and reflect on my past and future.

Suddenly I looked up from my rocky perch to see one of my boys come tripping down the trail. The beaver slapped his tail with a resounding whack on the water and disappeared. Even though my tryst with my heavenly Guide ended, my soul was refreshed.

Through the beauty, the silence, and the peace surrounding me I felt God's presence. I knew He could answer all my questions "in His time." I knew He would lead and guide me in the unfamiliar paths ahead. Best of all, I knew He would never forsake me no matter how difficult the road might be.

When life faced me with seemingly insurmountable obstacles, I could return to this hallowed spot. In my mind I could walk that woodland trail, sit on that rock amid the wonders of nature and splendor of that sunrise, and know that ultimately my heavenly Friend would turn the darkness into a glorious dawn.

DONNA LEE SHARP

Angels?

For he will command his angels concerning you to guard you in all your ways. Ps. 91:11, NIV.

I *HAD IT ALL,* I thought. A great job. Friends I'd known since I was a kid. A family who loved and supported me. But it wasn't enough. I had decided to live my life for God, and living in a town without a church of my persuasion just wouldn't do anymore. So I packed my little car to the roof and moved to Lacombe, Alberta, about 1,000 miles away from home. I was only 20 years old, and I was spreading my wings!

I didn't realize how hard it was going to be to make new friends, find a job that would satisfy and sustain me, and make myself at home in this unfamiliar place.

I was a shell of the girl I had known not long before. I had loved to laugh, and now it seemed all I did was cry. I hated being alone. I made myself go to church in the hope of meeting some new friends. I sat alone in a church that held 1,000 people and was the loneliest I've ever been. I was scared to let anyone know that I needed them, but I was determined to stay; my pride was stronger than I was.

Six months later I hit rock bottom. I was weeping and praying, "God, Father, please help me. I want to know that someone cares. I need a hug—I don't remember the last one anymore. Please, God, give me the strength to face another lonely day."

The next morning, pushing my desperate prayer of the night before to the back of my mind, I left for church. I was teaching kindergarten Sabbath school, one of the joys I was holding on to. I had just finished the lesson story when I looked up and saw the cutest little boy running in my direction. Before I could see what his name badge said, he wrapped his little arms around my neck and squeezed. I was stunned, but I hugged him back—my mind a blur. Then he let go and ran back to his teacher. Or so I thought. I wanted to thank this child that I had never seen before, but I couldn't find him anywhere. He was gone. My heart filled, and so did my eyes, as I said, "Thank You, God, for loving me."

Now I know there are angels. My little angel is about three feet tall with blond hair, and he gives the best hugs!

LORI C. WIENS

Be Not Dismayed

Why are ye fearful, O ye of little faith? Matt. 8:26.

PRIOR TO MY RETIRING, I made frequent visits to the dentist. As she examined my mouth, she informed me of a crack in the center of a jaw tooth; she then proceeded to hand me a mirror that clearly confirmed her findings. I asked her if she would remove the filling and replace it with a new one. She explained that she could run into unforeseen problems, including a possible root canal. "You will have to make a decision sooner or later," she reminded me.

Several years passed. I had no savings and no dental insurance. It was the first of the month. The bank that I usually dealt with merged with another bank, and the rules of banking had recently changed. I had very little money on hand.

As I approached the teller with my check for the month I was told I would have to wait for three or four days for the money to clear. As it was, some of my bills were already due on the first with a few days of grace period. I went to the manager, explaining that I was having a major problem with their new banking rules. I always paid my bills on time, in spite of my situation.

My financial matters were totally out of my control, although the bank manager promised that I would not have to wait in the future for my funds to clear because of my good standing. Nevertheless, I was not a happy camper. This meant I had to juggle to pay the most important bills first with the little I had on hand. I was faithfully returning my tithes and offerings.

I'd had a busy day and decided to buy an order of rice and broccoli in garlic sauce on the way home. As I chewed a hard grain of rice off the top of the container, I heard a crackling sound. I ran my finger lightly over the tooth to see if any part of it would dislodge, but to no avail. I immediately made a dental appointment for the next day.

The dentist X-rayed the tooth without a charge. He could not pull it, so he sent me to an orthodontist on day two. The third day of the month my check cleared and somehow—I don't know how—I had $200 more than I had expected after paying my monthly bills. All my creditors received their money on time. Had my check cleared on the first of the month, I could not have covered my dental expenses in full.

Thank You, Father, for taking care of me. CORA A. WALKER

Stuck at Traffic Lights

The Lord shall preserve thy going out and thy coming in from this time forth, and even for evermore. Ps. 121:8.

IT WAS WINTERTIME, and the roads in Germany were snowy and icy. During the week it kept snowing, and the temperature dropped to 15° F (–9.5° C). We woke up earlier that day so we could be on time for church only as we are the ones to hand out the church bulletins.

Normally it takes us almost an hour to get to church, but on that day our car behaved very unusually. It stalled every time we stopped at a traffic light, and it took four or five minutes before we were able to get it running again. Sometimes other drivers passed us on all sides; sometimes they got upset and honked at us. I was getting impatient and worried because we would arrive late for church. We were already 20 minutes past our schedule when we reached the highway. That's when we discovered the reason our car kept failing us at every traffic light: The Lord had kept us from being involved in a mass accident that had happened less than 20 minutes before—just the time we lost getting stuck at the three traffic lights. The police had blocked the highway in order to let the helicopter rescue the victims. We saw cars facing in every direction, most of them totally wrecked.

We couldn't say a word. Our attitude of feeling impatient and upset for the delay turned to joy and thankfulness. After we passed the accident scene our car ran smoothly, and we had no further problems at any of the traffic lights we passed on our way to the chapel.

At church we heard different kinds of testimonies. Other members had encountered similar experiences while on their way to church. How the Lord protected and kept us safe that day! Our hearts filled with gladness, gratitude, and praise. We were thankful for what He had done for us.

Never again has our car stalled as it did that day. Only once, on that special Saturday, did this happen to us. We can witness that God is faithful to His promises all the time. We can count on Him—He will always be there in the time of need. We thank the Lord and give glory to His name for the thousand ways He protects us. LOIDA GULAJA LEHMANN

Time-out Praises

Because thy lovingkindness is better than life, my lips shall praise thee. Ps. 63:3.

IT WAS OBVIOUS from the distress cry coming from the diningroom that my 18-month-old son was stuck on a piece of furniture or on the converter unit in the apartment. He loves to climb up "mountains," and anything that is high is a mountain—bookcase, table, desk, entertainment center, you name it. As he climbs he sings one of his favorite songs: "Climb, Climb Up Sonshine Mountain."

I ran to the room to see what was going on and, sure enough, he was on the converter unit. He had run out of room to put his little legs, and his hands were pressed flat against the wall. His legs were too short to reach the floor, so fear had taken over. At the sight of Mommy coming to the rescue again, he started smiling. I took him off the converter unit, sat down, placed him in my lap, and said, "OK; since you don't want to listen, you'll have to have a time-out. You need to know that climbing on the furniture is dangerous, and you aren't too little to learn." I pulled out a chair and placed him on it, knelt down beside him, and said, "From now on you are in time-out. Please sit here for two minutes and do not move; do you understand?" He looked at me and nodded, then smiled.

Returning to my household duties, I heard him singing, "This is the day that the Lord has made, I will rejoice and be glad in it."

Can't win, I thought. Time-out usually makes children sad, but not this child. Should he be joyful in everything? Oh, yes! Philippians 4:4 tells us to rejoice in the Lord always. My desire was to teach my son a lesson, but this sad time became praise time. It didn't matter what the circumstances were.

This is the truth: in all things, rejoice. This is what God want us to do as His chosen generation. He has given us seven days, and each is a new beginning to rejoice in Him. When we acknowledge His lovingkindness, our lips should praise Him no matter what a minute, an hour, or a day may bring. When life's problems cloud up our day, praises will send rays of sunshine through.

Lord, through Your strength please help my lips to always praise You, no matter what.

VELNA WRIGHT

Our Awesome Heavenly Father

Bring ye all the tithes into the storehouse, that there may be meat in mine house, and prove me now herewith, saith the Lord of hosts, if I will not open you the windows of heaven, and pour you out a blessing, that there shall not be room enough to receive it. And I will rebuke the devourer for your sakes, and he shall not destroy the fruits of your ground. Mal. 3:10, 11.

THE MANY DEMANDS of spring housecleaning and planting a garden left me totally exhausted. Hence, an afternoon nap strongly appealed to me, and I succumbed to a horizontal position for a much-needed rest. After a short snooze, I was abruptly awakened by a deafening pelting on our roof, as though someone were pouring a truckload of rocks onto our abode. I jumped up and looked out the window. I couldn't believe what I saw. White, marble-sized—and even golf ball-sized—hail bounced all over our lawn.

Breathless, my eyes immediately focused on our vegetable garden. *Will the tender young plants survive this trouncing of ice pellets?* I wondered.

To my surprise, I couldn't see hail bouncing in our garden. I blinked and looked again. I watched hail dance on our lawn, but our garden seemed free from hail. To obtain a better view, I ventured out to the patio. I found no hail falling on our garden. Immediately I realized who was responsible for this awesome display of protection. Aloud I whispered, "Thank You, Father in heaven, for protecting our garden from this unusual hail storm! You are an awesome God!"

Our tomato plants stood tall—not a leaf missing or harmed in any way. I discovered our zucchini, beets, carrots, and lettuce were all unscathed. I didn't find one particle of ice anywhere in the garden. All the new plants stood tall and safe. In the midst of our garden I stood fixed and in awe for a few moments—exceedingly thankful that our heavenly Father had spared our garden from destruction.

Again I said, "Thank You, Father in heaven, for sparing our garden! You have truly and faithfully fulfilled your promise found in Malachi 3:10 and 11."

I called my husband and pointed out the difference between the white ice pellets on the lawn and none in our garden. He, too, stood in a moment of silent awe, then said, "God truly protected our garden as He promised us in Malachi, didn't He?"

NATHALIE LADNER-BISCHOFF

Prayer and an Old Shoe Rack

God is our refuge and strength, a very present help in trouble. Ps. 46:1.

M*Y GRANDPARENTS could die."* The thought slammed into my brain through the darkness of sleep. I jumped up, disoriented. *It's only 11:00 p.m.,* I thought, looking at the clock. *I just went to sleep!* I tried to fight the anxiety that started my stomach churning. But the thought of my grandparents dying refused to go away, and my panic built by the second. I tried to rationalize my fear. Perhaps I was feeling this way because I was all the way in California and was homesick. But what a strange time to be homesick! *It's 2:00 in the morning over there,* I told myself. *They're fast asleep.* I didn't want to call Trinidad at that hour of the morning just to see if they were OK. So I did the only thing I could do from 6,000 miles away. I dropped to my knees and pleaded with my heavenly Father for my grandparents' safety. I calmed down by about midnight and slept peacefully for the rest of the night.

Two weeks later my mother called. "I didn't want to worry you," she said, "but thieves broke into Granny and Popsy's house two weeks ago." She told me that the thieves woke my grandmother during their search. When she called out, the burglars went into their bedroom and put a gun to my grandmother's head. They said that they would kill her if they didn't get money. My grandmother, always courageous and known for her unusual sense of humor, informed them that they should have come at the end of the month when people got their pensions! My grandfather, with the spiritual strength that characterized his life, said that they had no money and were prepared to die. Then he prayed, "Father, forgive them, for they know not what they do."

The burglars, startled at the unusual responses, moved away from my grandparents' bed just long enough for my grandfather to grab an old iron shoe rack filled with shoes and throw it at them. In the darkness the thieves didn't know what hit them, and they bolted for the window as shoes scattered everywhere. I asked my mother what time the incident took place. She told me that it was about 2:00 in the morning.

When you face your next impossible situation, remember that God saved my grandparents' lives using only their faith in Him, an old shoe rack, and the prayers of a granddaughter 6,000 miles away. There is no limit to God's resources. So do not be afraid!

Karen Abdool

Hidden Sin

Search me, O God, and know my heart; test me and know my anxious thoughts. See if there is any offensive way in me, and lead me in the way everlasting. Ps. 139:23, 24, NIV.

I WAS SHOCKED! The conviction came to my heart as a blow. I had sinned! I was partaking of the Lord's Supper, and I had asked God to search my heart. I was not prepared for what He would reveal. Since renewing my walk with the Lord several years ago, I felt that all wrongdoings on my part had been dealt with in a timely manner.

I had stolen from someone. Six years before when my husband and I were getting married, we had paid half of the floral bill before the ceremony; and the balance was to be paid after. We received the bills but set them aside until our finances were on a sounder footing. Over time we began to almost ignore the bills as they came in the mail.

We would discuss the issue from time to time, and my husband advised me to pay the bill. By this time I felt quite embarrassed that we had let it go for so long, so I continued to put it off. I knew that we should clear the balance, but I didn't think that we were doing anything harmful to anyone by not paying.

Until the Communion service. With stark clarity I saw my sin. I asked God for courage to make it right. Before my resolve could fade, I drove to the florist early in the following week. I had to pray for courage with every step. Inside, I approached the counter. I told the clerk that I had a balance that I would like to pay. She took my details and looked up my account on the computer system. She informed me that there was a zero balance on the account.

I had to pray for even more courage to not thank her and walk out right then. God gave me the courage, and I asked for the manager. When she appeared, she looked up my account and explained that the balance had been written off a few months earlier. Close to tears at this point, I told her that I had to pay the bill and asked for the total figure. She quoted me the figure as the original balance without the added finance charges. I paid the bill and left, thanking God for His blessings. He searched me and showed me the offensive way in me and gave me the courage to make it right, with the added bonus of removing the penalty. What a great God!

Abigail Blake Parchment

Choosing to Camp Under the Stars!

May the Lord direct your hearts into God's love and Christ's perseverance. 2 Thess. 3:5, NIV.

CHRISTIANS THINK AND act within the framework of eternity. When things don't turn out as they planned, they don't get bitter. They know that the sufferings of this world are not worthy to be compared to what we can look forward to in the new earth, and so they choose to focus on the joy in their lives—no matter how small that portion may be.

One day a mother got a phone call from her daughter who was just bubbling over with excitement. The daughter would be able to travel to places she'd only dreamed about; she'd be able to learn a new language and make new friends. Life was going to be sweet!

A few months later the mother received a letter laced with complaints. Her daughter complained of being homesick, of having no friends, of not being able to understand the language. The wise mother decided that she would respond with a simple two-sentence fax: "Two women looked through prison bars. One saw mud, and the other saw stars!"

One day I sat in the living room of a dear friend whose family had suffered unspeakable atrocities while being held as prisoners in Auschwitz, a World War II extermination camp. "How do you deal with the dark memories of your youth?" I asked her.

"Oh, Rose," she replied, "it's true; I pass through those dark valleys. But long ago I made a conscious decision. I determined that I would not camp there, and this decision has made all the difference in the world in my life."

Satan is the destroyer; God is the restorer. Jesus calls Satan the ruler of this world but then hastens to add in John 16:33, "I have told you these things, so that in me you may have peace. In this world you will have trouble. But take heart! I have overcome the world" (NIV).

Are you finding it difficult to focus on the positive? Perhaps you need God's emergency number. Let me share it with you. I promise you will find it a source of comfort and hope. The number is Psalm 91:1: "He who dwells in the shelter of the Most High will rest in the shadow of the Almighty. I say of the Lord, 'He is my refuge and fortress, my God, in whom I trust' " (NIV). I encourage you to call on God's 911 number whenever you need a spiritual lift. He will never fail to answer! And He will empower you to view your life in the framework of eternity!

Rose Otis

Lesson From a Toothbrush Holder

And the blood of Jesus Christ his Son cleanseth us from all sin. 1 John 1:7.

THE BLUE TOOTHBRUSH holder sat at its usual place on the washstand. For days now I had noticed that it could do with a good scrubbing, but I kept putting it off until a more convenient time. Then the thought hit me as to how embarrassed I'd be if friends had to use my bathroom and noticed the advanced stages of lack of cleaning that small item was experiencing. Motivated by the thought, I armed myself with soap and scrubber and took on the long-overdue job. When I took off the cover I realized that there was much more grime on the inside than I could have imagined.

As I scrubbed, the thought struck me that we humans are somewhat like that toothbrush holder. First, we try to conceal from our friends those spots in our lives that we have not yet yielded to the cleansing blood of Jesus. But evidence of lack of cleansing can be seen on our outside—the harsh words, the unkind actions, gossip, and lack of trust in God are all evident. Yet these are all really manifestations of the deeper spiritual "spring cleaning" that needs to take place on the inside.

Like the toothbrush holder, we are incapable of cleaning ourselves spiritually. Often we can't even see the grime of sin in our own lives, but it is so easy to see stains of sin in the lives of others. How often we criticize and point fingers at others when God is still working with them. However, the good news is that the only One who can cleanse us is He who alone can see all the dirt that's on the inside. The toothbrush holder had to wait to be scrubbed, but we don't have to wait. Our cleansing job was completed before we were created. God in His wisdom knew that we were going to mess up, so He provided the fountain before the foundation of the world.

The toothbrush holder will get grimy again, and I will have to scrub it again, but the lesson will always be clear: as long as we yield ourselves to Christ, He will wash away our sins. And should we get grimy again, "he is faithful and just to forgive us our sins, and to cleanse us from all unrighteousness" (1 John 1:9).

Awesome God, I thank You today for Your shed blood. Help me daily to accept the cleansing that only You can give. LILITH ROSE SCARLETT

The Little Paper Happiness Boxes

We give thanks to You, O God, we give thanks. Ps. 75:1, NASB.

I USED TO BUY LITTLE boxes and put Bible verses in them with certain subjects such as "Assurance of God's Love" or "Thoughts for a New Mother" or "Thoughts From Famous People" such as "A thing of beauty is a joy forever." Then one day a friend said, "I can teach you to make boxes, and it will hardly cost you anything." It was such a joy, as each box was a surprise and a joy to make. Each item took only two to three minutes to produce. It was fun to have learned something new and exciting to share with others.

One day I was getting ready to go to the dentist's office to have my daughter clean my teeth. (She insists on doing it four times a year because of some medicine I take. I think once a year is enough; but she will just not agree, so I try to be appreciative.) I was hoping she would look in my mouth and say, "Oh, they are clean, so we won't need to clean them today." But no such luck.

It's really not too bad an experience. She thinks it's relaxing; but I can't quite agree with that idea, especially when she probes at the bottom of each tooth.

As I was getting ready to leave the thought came to me: *How about taking nine little paper boxes I had made and fill them with candy kisses?* There would be one for each of the staff and the dentist.

Then I thought, *No; they will think it is silly. Anyway, Christmas is over. . . .* Well, I'll pray about it. But God didn't answer. I think now maybe God was telling me, "Remember, without Me you can do nothing. Didn't I give you the idea in the first place?"

I didn't have time to put pretty ribbons on the boxes, but I took them in to see what the reaction would be.

You wouldn't believe how thrilled they all were! At least five thanked me again and again, and one gave me a hug. She walked off saying how delighted she was with the idea. Even the woman dentist thanked me several times.

The lesson I learned: Little things make people happy and reflect God's love.

Frieda Tanner

April 4

Singing in the Dark

Sing praises to God, sing praises; sing praises to our King, sing praises. . . . Sing to him a psalm of praise. Ps. 47:6, 7, NIV.

EVERY MORNING AS consciousness creeps into my dreamy thoughts, I'm fully alerted to the realities of a new day by the song of a little bird. Before sunrise, while it's still dark, this little bird begins to sing.

Twa-twa-twi-twi-twa; twi-twi-twa. My little bird friend begins to sing before any other birds and continues pouring forth its song of praise in the dark to the Creator.

What an inspiration! Singing praises in the dark. Of course, it is easy to sing praises when all is bright and skies are clear. David admonishes us to sing praises to God. He knew what it was like to sing praises in the dark. When troubles assailed him, he sang in the dark—and even while running for his life.

We too must sing in the dark. When problems are too difficult for us to solve, when trials beset us from all directions, when pain wracks our body and the night is long, sing praises in the dark to our Lord.

Singing dispels the gloom, lifts the spirit, and gladdens the heart. Singing assures us that there will be a brighter tomorrow. Just as laughter does a body good, so singing praises brings healing balm to troubled and weary minds.

I always have been inspired by this quotation taken from one of my favorite authors, Ellen White: "The melody of praise is the atmosphere of heaven; and when heaven comes in touch with the earth, there is music and song—thanksgiving, and voice of melody'" (*Education,* p. 161).

The melodies we learn to sing here will go with us to our home in the earth made new. However, there will be one great difference. There we will never need to sing in the dark, because there is no night there.

The same author says, "We may catch the themes of praise and thanksgiving from the heavenly choir round about the throne; and as the echo of the angels' song is awakened in our earthly homes, hearts will be drawn closer to the heavenly singers" (*ibid.,* p. 168).

Dear Lord, please help me today to sing praises to You—even in the dark.

Olga I. Corbin de Lindo

Spring of Living Water

Jesus answered, "Everyone who drinks this water will be thirsty again, but whoever drinks the water I give him will never thirst. Indeed, the water I give him will become in him a spring of water welling up to eternal life." John 4:13, 14, NIV.

WHEN I WAS YOUNGER our family lived in a little town in Michigan. Actually, it was more of a wide spot in the road, and if you blinked you could easily miss it. There were several nice things about it, however. Strangers were easy to identify and avoid, and children could be left outside to play and explore all day without fear of being kidnapped or run over by cars.

It was on one of these carefree days that some friends and I found a clear and cold spring. It was in the woods near an intersection of two dirt roads. The water from this spring tasted great. This was before the bottled water revolution hit America, and now I'm sure that if a bottling company could find this water they would love to use it. Personally, I hope they don't find it. There was just something special about drinking fresh water as it bubbles up from the ground, and then gurgles a few feet over the pebbles before it is absorbed into the rich soil again.

Many people can't tell the difference between different kinds of water. Other people can taste the difference but, like everything else, they like different tastes, thereby explaining all the different brands of bottled water.

Part of the enjoyment of drinking from the spring was that it was different and surprisingly cold—no matter how hot the day. After we had tasted the water from that spring, no other water around was nearly as good. I think it's like that with the living water that Jesus offered the woman at the well. Once you have tasted the best, nothing else even comes close.

Have you tasted and seen that the Lord is good? Have you filled up on His living water today? Most important, have you shared this living water with others around you?

You see, one of the greatest blessings in life is that the living water of God is available to everyone at no charge, and it never runs out. As a matter of fact, many believe that you only truly taste its richness when you share it with others.

May God bless you today and quench your thirst with His living water.

JULI BLOOD

Consider and Be Wise

Consider her ways, and be wise. Prov. 6:6.

ANTS AREN'T POPULAR items in anyone's kitchen. They are swept out, washed down the drain, and sprayed away. Determined little creatures, they keep coming back. My cat especially hates ants. If he spies even a single ant in his dry cat food, he tilts his ears forward, looks at it, and refuses to eat from his dish until the offending creature is removed.

Bible writers took note of ants and favorably mention them. King Solomon suggests that the unindustrious person should consider the ant and be wise. In Proverbs 30:24 Agur says, "Four things on earth are small yet they are extremely wise" (NIV). Ants are one of the four. What might look like a mess of ants in a hill is actually a highly organized, committed ecosystem.

They are dedicated to the welfare of the community, protecting the queen ant, and regulating the nest chambers for the eggs, larvae, and pupae. Worker ants transport these little creatures-to-be to the top chambers near the sun-warmed earth in winter, and to the bottom chambers for the dark coolness in summer. Ventilation shafts are opened and closed according to the weather. Workers gather food and bring it to the nest where other ants store the food; then they run to gather more. Others are hygienists, whose job is to keep the nest clean.

Plucky and energetic, they faithfully do their work in the face of horrendous odds, especially one little ant I noticed one morning as I filled the sink with water. She had fallen in. Normally, I would have washed her down the sink; but that ant began swimming with all her might, legs flailing out to her side, pedaling fast. And she was keeping afloat, although she wasn't getting anywhere. I watched in fascination. She didn't give up, just kept churning and churning.

I admired the plucky way she kept at it. She wasn't going to give up! Yet there was no way she was going to swim across the sinkful of water without a rescuer. I gave in and put my hand down to save her.

Then I thought of how hard we work, how hard we try, to make it in our little world. Yet even using all our common sense, brainpower, work power—everything—we will never make it unless we have a rescuer. Christ is that rescuer for each of us. How foolish to think we can do it all on our own, because we don't see the big picture of the "water" all around us.

Edna Maye Gallington

God of Praises

But You are holy, O You Who dwell in [the holy place where] the praises of Israel [are offered]. Ps. 22:3, Amplified.

SOON AFTER I ACCEPTED Jesus as my Lord and Savior, my family and I moved to Africa. There, I started to seek God by studying the Bible. But something troubled my mind. I heard some ordinary Christians saying that God spoke to them. This is not the Bible times, so how did God speak to these people? How did they hear His voice? Was it through their intuition, or was it something else? Then I met Julie.

Julie was a new Christian who was trying desperately to have a baby. She told me that her only hope was Jesus. So she set aside five days to fast and pray. She spent the first four days weeping before God and asking why she could not conceive. On the fifth day, she was exhausted. Sitting quietly in her living room, she said in her heart, "Lord, I told You everything that I could think of. What else should I say now?" Right at that time she heard a voice saying, "Your God is a God of praises and not of lamentations." She looked around and saw nobody. "How did you hear that voice?" I asked her.

"It was audible," she replied.

Audible? That was beyond my understanding! Even though Julie's story sounded weird, it did not leave me indifferent. I began to praise God more than before.

About a year later, again I was facing challenges. I was looking for a job in a country where the unemployment rate was very high. It was rare even to see a job announcement in the local papers. I was desperate, and I knew that Jesus was my only hope. Inspired by Julie's story, I set a day aside to ask for God's grace. I locked myself in a room, and for two hours I praised God through the Scriptures and songs. Then I said in my heart, "Where in this city can I be hired?" At that very moment I heard a soft voice whisper the name of an international organization in my left ear. A month later I was working in that organization.

Our Lord is a loving and merciful God who reveals Himself to ordinary people. He is alive and still speaks to us through ourselves, other people, or even little children. Isn't that a sufficient reason to put our trust in Him and praise Him?

NICOLE SALIFOU

Itsy-bitsy Spider

All a man's ways seem innocent to him, but motives are weighed by the Lord. Prov. 16:2, NIV.

RECENTLY I HAD AN unusual pet in my home for a short time. I came into my kitchen one morning and noticed, as the sunlight filtered through the window, that a little spider had made a web between a potted plant I had on the windowsill and the window frame. The spider had taken considerable trouble to weave the web on two levels, one near the bottom of the plant and another near the top. I wondered to myself whether this was a male or female spider.

As my husband was away from home at the time, I decided to ease up on the housework and let the spider stay. After a few days the spider had collected lots of small insects in the web. I wondered how much a spider really needed to eat! As I continued to observe, I noticed that the little spider was changing. A white line had appeared down its back, and the spider was putting on weight. I came to the conclusion that this was a lady spider about to give birth. She was collecting as much food as she could so that she would have plenty of nutrition for her babies.

However, much as I liked the little spider, I was getting a bit frustrated about not being able to clean that area of my kitchen. My husband came home from his trip, and I wondered what he would say about the cobweb on the kitchen window! He must have seen it, but he said nothing. After a few days I broached the subject and suggested that perhaps if we did it very gently we could remove the spider and her web to the garden so that I could clean properly. Unfortunately, in the removal process the web was destroyed, but I really had to clean my kitchen!

Sometimes my relationship with Jesus is a bit like my relationship with the spider. Rather than allowing Him to spring clean my life, I hang on to cobwebs. My motives may seem good to me, and I find all sorts of reasons not to remove the cobwebs, but in reality the cobweb is impeding my need for cleansing. If that is your problem, too, why not join me in asking God to remove both the spider and the cobwebs, and make our hearts clean?

BASMA SALEEM

Refusing the Easy Way

He who is in you is greater than he who is in the world. 1 John 4:4, NKJV.

WATER CAN BE AN unpredictable thing at times. If I were to spill some on my kitchen counter it would run wherever it wanted to. If I use too much when watering my houseplants it can run out the bottom of the pot and maybe all over some important papers, the furniture, or onto the floor.

A river or stream of water will go wherever there is a path of least resistance. The river does not decide one day to run uphill. If there is the least bit of downhill slant, the water will go in that direction. It simply goes with the flow. Where the banks are weak and not reinforced, water will break them down. When it does, it carves out its own branch of that river and makes another way, taking the easiest way to do so.

The same can be said for me. Sometimes I give in to wrong things that I still love to do. I can deviate from the path that God—for my own good—would have me follow. I can be led easily down the path of least resistance, going with the flow, doing things the easy way without standing for the right. Letting little habits carve away at my bank of life. Sometimes I give in to eating foods that are not good for my health. Or I may not keep the Sabbath day holy. I am not carving out my own river of right, but letting the compromises of the world carve away at me.

There are people in the Bible who stood for the right no matter what. Daniel was one of them. He would not defile himself with what the king wanted him to do.

I am so glad that the Holy Spirit is still striving with me, and through Him I can recognize what I'm doing. I can be victorious in my struggle against evil because, as the *Good News Bible* puts it, "the Spirit who is in you is more powerful than the spirit in those who belong to the world." This tells me that I can, through Christ, overcome anything the world throws at me. Through His power I don't have to just "go with the flow"; I don't have to follow the path of least resistance. With His Word, the Bible, and my special prayer time and a daily relationship with Jesus, I can reinforce my spiritual banks. I can stay strong and flow ahead on my way to the kingdom.

Vidella McClellan

Picture This!

From heaven you heard them, and in your great compassion you gave them deliverers, who rescued them from the hand of their enemies. Neh. 9:27, NIV.

PROBLEMS ARE JUST opportunities dressed in work clothes," the sign on the church lawn read. I thought, *This is truth, neatly presented in a catchy little phrase. Amen!*

My children, Andrea and Sonny, and I, along with some friends, planned to spend the day sightseeing on Salt Spring Island in beautiful British Columbia, Canada. We had moved our things from Andrea's car, which was parked on the street, into Leslie's vehicle. Andrea went back to her car one last time for her camera. Then the unthinkable happened. Andrea dropped her ring of keys. We helplessly watched as they disappeared through the grate under her car into the storm sewer system. Instantly and silently I began praying, *Jesus, would You please help us not to panic, and please help us retrieve the keys?*

Andrea and I were able to lift up the rusty, heavy iron grate and push it under the car. Massive cobwebs lined the sides of the cavity, but thankfully we didn't see any spiders. Andrea stretched out on the grass beside the curb and thrust her arm into the opening. Her fingertips couldn't quite touch the thick, black, nasty water below. Disappointment was written all over both our faces.

"Andea, find me a broom; I want to measure how deep this hole is," I said.

We were both encouraged when the broom handle hit bottom about six inches beneath the water's surface. I tried sweeping the sludge up the side of the hole, but had no success. Kneeling beside the curb, shielded by Andrea's car in front and bushes behind me, I changed my clothes, replacing my new white blouse with a T-shirt. I then stretched out on the grass and gracefully slid over the curb and under Andrea's car. In the first handful of filth the keys were retrieved. Andrea and I rejoiced as we washed ourselves and the keys with hot soapy water and lots of bleach. I smiled and reminded Andrea of the 15 pounds I had shed over the summer holidays, enabling me to fit under her Mazada Protege.

When God reached down into the filth of this world to save us, He never hesitated. He only thought of how He loves us. *Thank You once again, Father.*

DEBORAH SANDERS

What a Little Bird Told Me

But ask the animals, and they will teach you, or the birds of the air, and they will tell you. Job 12:7, NIV.

WHEN WE MOVED into our new home, we fell in love with gorgeous little eastern rosellas that belong to the parrot family. They were well groomed in their scarlet, gold, blue, and green feathers as they plucked at seed heads in the garden.

This led to my husband installing a bird feeder for them. He bought the food best suited to their needs—and we watched. Delightedly we would call to each other, "The redheads have come!" I would then tease my spouse that he was in love with redheads.

Other birds raided the feeder—especially the wood ducks, who carelessly swished most of the seed onto the ground and greedily gobbled it up. One day as I looked through the large windows in the family room I saw 10 wood ducks waddling along nonchalantly in a group. Then a magpie, neat in his black and white feathers but smaller than any of the other ducks, flew down and assessed the situation. In bird talk he told those wood ducks to move off his territory, and supervised them until they were out of sight. The poor wood ducks seemed to be out of luck.

After many experiments and great determination we had a feeder modified solely for the redheads. Soon there were at least eight of them coming to the feeder right through the day. They also sipped at the birdbath and made the area their home. We were delighted.

When galahs or green king parrots put their beaks in the feeder, the little eastern rosellas let them have some time, then fearlessly swooped down to send them away.

Those jewel-feathered little birds have taught me an important truth: when you find the best food, keep going there for your nourishment. For my spiritual needs, that means the Bible. Then share this discovery with your friends. If others—even those who are dauntingly large—block your path, do not let them obstruct your access to the best.

You can be sure that on God's feeder you will find the exact mixture to keep you strong, happy (as a bird), comforted, and well cared for, no matter what the circumstances of your life—rain, hail, or shine. God never forgets us, and we can depend on His provisions. URSULA M. HEDGES

The New Flute

He who was seated on the throne said, "I am making everything new!" Then he said, "Write this down, for these words are trustworthy and true." Rev. 21:5, NIV.

IN 1997, THE CITY where my family lived was devastated by a flood. About 50,000 people were evacuated; and then they returned to the job of cleaning up homes, property, and possessions that had been severely flood-damaged. Several weeks into the cleanup, a friend stopped by to speak to my husband (who cleans and repairs musical instruments). Then he displayed the flute he had brought along. It was a terrible sight! It had soaked in river water, flood mud, and sewage backup in a flooded home for several weeks. It was caked with filth and grime, not looking even worth the time it would take to clean it. The friend assured us that the flute was solid silver, a prized possession of his wife's. Upon finding her flute in such a condition, she had tearfully placed it on the pile of garbage at the curb, sure it was beyond repair. Her husband, seeing her tears, took the flute from the garbage pile and placed it under the seat of his car without telling his wife.

My husband spent many hours working on that flute. It required oil and tiny screwdrivers to remove the rusted screws and other small parts. When the flute was finally taken apart, he began the long process of cleaning. After that there were a number of repairs to be made to keys and springs. New keypads were added. Then he polished until the flute was shiny and beautiful.

Our friend brought his wife over one evening and told her he had a gift for her. When my husband brought out the flute, she began weeping and thanking her husband for buying her a new flute. When it was explained to her that this was her flute—cleaned, repaired, and made like new again—she was even more overwhelmed with emotion. She could barely believe that this beautiful instrument was the same one that had been so devastated in the flood.

What a wonderful thing it is that Jesus does for us when we bring Him our ruined, filthy lives, corroded by the sewage of sin. Not with cleaning fluid or silver polish, but with His own precious blood He cleans away every trace of the grime of our devastated condition and makes us completely new in Him. He has promised us this, and His words are trustworthy and true.

What a beautiful promise to claim this day and every day!

SANDRA SIMANTON

God's Promises

Your promises have been thoroughly tested, and your servant loves them. Ps. 119:140, NIV.

MY GRANDDAUGHTER, MISTY, comes bounding through our back door and spies the trophy on the counter. "Grandma!" she exclaims. "Where did you get that?"

The trophy had been sitting on the kitchen counter for more than a week. I hadn't yet decided on a permanent location for it.

I explained that I had played in an alumni golf tournament with another couple. Since we were the only mixed doubles, we were given the trophy for first place. It wasn't as if we had really won it. "That doesn't matter," she retorted. "I am so proud of you! Good job! It's beautiful!"

Her enthusiasm for our so-called achievement gave me a glowing feeling inside. I smiled as I remembered the very cool, breezy day we spent hitting and chasing that little white ball. In my estimation, however, Misty was my real trophy! This is another occasion when she made me feel very loved and special.

Isn't God good? He blesses us with people like Misty, who encourage and affirm us even in the smallest things. The sensitivity and joy over even our insignificant achievements brings to our hearts a feeling of specialness.

However, those who are in tune to our joys and sorrows are not always there to give us the boost we desire. Yet there is Someone who is always there through the promises in His Word. Any of these abundant promises may be claimed at any hour of any day or night. He promises never to leave us or forsake us (Heb. 13:5). He also says, "I am with you always" (Matt. 28:20, NKJV). My favorite promise is "My God will meet all your needs according to his glorious riches" (Phil. 4:19, NIV). His rich promises apply not only to our spiritual needs; but also to our physical, emotional, financial, social, and psychological needs as well. He knows us so intimately that He's numbered the hairs on our heads (Matt. 10:30).

What is more encouraging than knowing that Someone loves us unconditionally, no matter who or where we are? When the Mistys of our lives are nowhere around, we need only recall a promise from God's Word. When we bask in it and internalize it we know—not just feel—that there is One who has the most intense desire for our best good. It can't get any better than that!

Marian M. Hart

Good Friday, Horrible Friday

At the place where Jesus was crucified, there was a garden, and in the garden a new tomb, in which no one had ever been laid. Because it was the Jewish day of Preparation and since the tomb was nearby, they laid Jesus there. John 19:41, 42, NIV.

WHY DO WE CALL it *Good* Friday? True, for some it is a holiday—school is out, the stock market and banks are closed, so you can't fail a test or lose money. That's good. And we can call it good because we have read the last chapter of the Book—we know the outcome of the story. Death is not final. But for those living that preparation day—that Friday so long ago—it was *horrible* Friday, not *Good* Friday.

There were women there that day, and for them it was truly Horrible Friday. There was His mother who had cared for all His needs for years, and when He was old enough to care for Himself she still worried constantly. It was a horrendous day for her. And it was dreadful, too, for the women who had followed Him and had cared for His needs. Some of them were mothers of young men of the same age as Jesus, and this day was agonizing.

The women knew the trials had gone all wrong, even though they were not allowed in. They had followed the mob to the cross, mourning and wailing. They were about the only ones to whom Jesus really did speak that day. He had turned to them and said, "Daughters of Jerusalem, do not weep for me; weep for yourselves and for your children. For the time will come when you will say, 'Blessed are the barren women, the wombs that never bore and the breasts that never nursed!'" (Luke 23:28, 29, NIV). For them it was a horrible, awful, frightening, nightmarish, cruel, sadistic day of ultimate hurt and death.

Nevertheless, the women stayed nearby, even following the dead body to the tomb. To them it did not seem like a good Friday.

Many women are living a horrible Friday because they don't know the end of the story, either. They, too, are buried under hurt, abuse, rejection, worry, grief, and care. They don't know Jesus. If they ever knew about Good Friday, they have forgotten. They have not only a horrible Friday, but Sunday, Monday, Tuesday, Wednesday, and Thursday, as well. Oh, how they need to know Jesus won the victory for them—a victory that turned a *horrible* Friday into *Good* Friday!

ARDIS DICK STENBAKKEN

The Cry of My Heart

That's how much you mean to me! That's how much I love you! I'd sell off the whole world to get you back, trade the creation just for you. Isa. 43:4, Message.

ONLY A SHORT WHILE ago the Lord's friends gathered around to hear Him speak of great and wonderful things. The things of God. Eternal things. We hung on every word. Savoring it. Digesting it. Now, they are gone and I alone remain, sitting at His feet. The sound of His voice lingers in the air. I breathe in the essence of His presence and sigh. It is good that I should be here. I want to stay forever. All at once the child in me comes alive as Yeshua lifts me to His lap and cradles me in His arms. Tears of joy fill my eyes and overflow, cascading down my cheeks.

Who am I that my Lord should hold me so tenderly? Did He hear my anguished cry for more of Him? Had He peered into the depths of my heart and dug through the sin and deeply-rooted pride and greed and actually found some good buried there? Is there any good in me? I am still so slow to learn. So quick to fall. As Yeshua draws me closer to Himself, He holds me, not because of my goodness, but His. Not because of my love for Him, but rather because of His extravagant love for me. My thoughts become a blur, struggling to grasp what is unimaginable for my human mind. He is "able to do exceeding abundantly above all that we ask or think" (Eph. 3:20). My Lord and my God loves me.

As I listened to the Savior's heartbeat, He must have been listening to mine. What I couldn't put into words He heard from the cry of my heart. My love for Him. My longing to be with Him. And the heartbreaking sorrow I felt for ever having done anything that puts distance between my beloved Lord and me.

I am reluctant to look up because I know that my eyes will meet His. What I have longed for all my days now suddenly fills me with dread. I fear what He will see in me.

He cups my cheek and wipes away my tears with His thumb. God's thumb wiping away my tears! Amazing! His eyes seem to plead with me as He speaks. "This is why I did it. So I could hold you and love you for all eternity." The passion in His voice reaches to the depth of my heart and I am undone. Nothing else matters. I fall in love again with Love Himself.

Deborah Frans

Share the Hope

Jesus said, "Don't cling to me, for I have not yet ascended to the Father. Go to my brothers and tell them, 'I ascend to my Father and your Father, my God and your God.'" John 20:17, Message.

WHEN I FIRST LEFT school I spent four months training to be a nurse. During that time there was one particular experience I will never forget. It happened when we visited the hospital morgue.

While we were being taken around the morgue, a woman was brought in on a trolley. Our guide explained that the 30- to 40-year-old woman had just died of a heart attack at home. One of her friends had called an ambulance, but it was too late. The guide informed us that the police were rushing to the workplace of her husband and then on to the local school to break the devastating news to her family.

As I stood looking at the cold, inanimate body of the woman on the trolley, I felt for her. I thought of the pain that her death would bring. And I felt for her husband and children whose lives would never be the same.

When Jesus Christ died, life was never going to be the same for each of us. His death was the beginning of our eternal life, if we so choose.

Just pause for a moment and imagine what it must have been like when Jesus conquered death. Imagine his heart starting to beat again, the gentle movements of His chest as He started to breathe once more, the wriggling of His toes, the stretching of His fingertips as life flowed back into His body. Imagine the scene in heaven as Jesus started to slowly open His eyelids, raised His eyes heavenward and opened His mouth to utter the name "Father." The angels, peering down from the blue expanse, must have danced and hugged one another with exuberant joy, and the Father must have wept to know that nothing could ever separate Him from His Son again.

We have the most amazing hope to share with those who are dying every day. Death no longer is the end, but the beginning of life—with no end to those who love God. Jesus said to Mary, "Don't cling to me. . . . Go to my brothers and tell them, 'I ascend to my Father.'" He says the same to each one of us: "Don't keep the good news to yourself; do all that you can to share Me."

MARY BARRETT

Easter Reflections

O Death, where is your sting? O Hades, where is your victory? 1 Cor. 15:55, NKJV.

IT WAS EASTER. The Easter blossoms were out in their full splendor, hanging in golden cascades from the trees that lined many roads in Singapore. As many Christians celebrated the death and resurrection of Christ, I was about to receive two pieces of news 12 hours apart that would point me to the meaning of Christ's resurrection.

My phone rang just before 7:00 a.m., before I could get out of bed that Sunday. My daughter sounded serious on the other end as she spoke a few words and then burst into tears. Five-year-old Sandra had suffered a final fatal heart attack and passed away.

This miracle child who had been snatched from the jaws of death at birth had finally succumbed to the heart condition with which she was born. She had been healthy, with intermittent coughs and colds so typical of childhood, but otherwise an active child. Her time on earth was over. All day I was in an attitude of prayer for the grief-stricken parents of this only child.

Less than 12 hours later my phone rang again. A friend who had been the focus of my personal prayer had also succumbed to death. In the wake of severe acute respiratory syndrome (SARS), Henry had contracted the disease and had been fighting for his life. The doctors were puzzled why this apparently healthy young man in his 30s was not turning around as he should. Just the week before I had received news that the doctors were giving up on him. A few days later they discovered the cause. Henry had not only SARS, the atypical pneumonia, but also the typical pneumonia as well. They had concentrated so much on treating the SARS that they had overlooked the typical pneumonia that was zapping away his life.

As I struggled with the loss of these two lives that had crossed mine, my thoughts turned to the resurrection morning. God whispered His assurance to me as I grieved. Their earthly struggles were over; they were at rest. "O death, where is thy sting? O grave, where is thy victory?" (1 Cor. 15:55). Their lives are hid in Christ until the resurrection morning, when death will be conquered once and for all.

SALLY LAM-PHOON

O Lord, Be Merciful

Yea, mine own familiar friend, in whom I trusted, which did eat of my bread, hath lifted up his heel against me. But thou, O Lord, be merciful unto me. Ps. 41:9, 10.

DAVID WROTE THIS text from his own experience. His friends may have turned against him many times, but the worst was when his own son sought to kill him and snatch away the kingdom from him. Yet when David's men finally killed Absalom, David cried with a loud voice, "O my son Absalom, O Absalom, my son, my son!" (2 Sam. 19:4). Oh, what father's love for a son—who was a traitor! Even as a young boy, David had been ridiculed by his brothers. As a faithful soldier for the king, who was his father-in-law, he was in danger of his very life being hunted by the king. When David danced before the Lord, his own wife mocked him.

Joseph too experienced cruel treatments from his own brothers. In obedience to his father he walked a long way to search for his brothers. He was glad to find them and to give them the food their father had sent. He was tired and perhaps hungry; yet the brothers threw him into the pit, intending to kill him. Then they sold him off and deprived their own father of a beloved son. Their father lived a life of sorrow for many years as a result.

Moses worked hard for the deliverance of his people from Egypt in leading them through the wilderness for 40 years. Yet his people disappointed him. There was no payment or even a word of thanks—only complaints, murmuring, and threats. Worst of all, his own brother and sister were against him and his wife. Though appointed by God, they questioned his authority.

Whenever you feel betrayed, remember these men of God. David loved his son who was a traitor. Joseph forgave his brothers and helped them to prosper. Moses was willing to forgo his place in heaven if his people could be saved.

Above all, look at the life of Jesus. His own disciple sold him. Peter denied him three times when Jesus was suffering the most. His own family members gave Him a hard time. His own home church people were ready to stone Him. Jesus said, "A prophet is not without honor, save in his own country, and in his own house" (Matt. 13:57). His own people rejected and crucified Him. So let's not be too surprised if we suffer the same way. Let's pray as did David, for mercy alone brings healing and reconciliation.

BIRDIE PODDAR

Sit and Stay

Be still, and know that I am God. Ps. 46:10, NIV.

NEW NEIGHBORS HAVE arrived. They are newly married and pastoring a nearby church. Their two dogs, Charlie and Chester, are old. But the wife is young and not familiar with how to handle them. So Jana is taking the dogs to obedience school. It's just as much a training school for her as for the dogs.

Jana will be taught how to communicate with her dogs so that they understand her commands. Most likely she will first learn primary commands such as "Sit!" and "Stay."

One morning while I was having my quiet time, I realized the Lord was trying to teach me those first commands that dogs learn: "Sit" and "Stay."

I'd had the privilege of receiving a small stipend for working with my husband, John, as an assistant pastor for almost three years. It had been our delight to work together for our two churches. Showing my own misplaced identity, the loss of that job brought me face to face with a character deficiency: my identity had been wrapped up in that job. And now, having lost it, I felt lost and alone—somehow adrift.

Taking time to "regroup, refocus, and step back" had brought me face to face with my own insufficiency. I needed to figure out where my identity truly came from; to do that, I needed to learn to sit and stay.

My friend Debbie has two dogs. Gypsy is the old one. Hearing "stay," he actually retreats backward, ears drooping, eyes falling. With all of himself he wants to "go," but he stays, though very unhappily.

Trooper, the younger dog, is the picture of exuberance. When he is told to sit and stay his tail wags, his tongue hangs out, he looks left and right. It's all he can do to sit still.

How like these two dogs I have been. To sit and to stay seems to me to be disciplined. I want to be working, producing, making money. But to sit and stay? How unlike me this would be. And yet how necessary to learn. "Be still and know that I am God," the Bible says. Have I yet learned the spiritual art of being still, of "sitting" and "staying"? BECKI KNOBLOCH

The Aroma

We are to God the aroma of Christ among those who are being saved and those who are perishing. To the one we are the smell of death; to the other, the fragrance of life. 2 Cor. 2:15, 16, NIV.

WHILE OUT ON A sightseeing excursion on the beautiful island of Lanzarote, I was so taken with the breathtaking view of the valley below that I missed a small step and fell onto the tarmac pavement, landing awkwardly on my left shoulder.

When we arrived back at the hotel at the end of the day, I decided to massage my bruised shoulder with some Olbas Oil I had brought from home. After applying a warming compress, I rubbed in some massage oil followed by a few drops of Olbas Oil. The warmth and the oil were soothing, as was the smell that soon filled the room—a comforting smell of eucalyptus, menthol, and other oils (or so I thought).

I have always kept a bottle of Olbas Oil in the family medicine cabinet and used it on many occasions as a massage or inhalant for common ailments. My children never liked the smell and always complained about it, but they put up with it when they were younger. Now young adults, they generally refuse it. My husband doesn't like the smell, either; and his reaction was immediate. "I've just settled down to look forward to a good sleep," he said. "If I'd known you were going to use that I'd have stayed in the other room." But he turned over and was soon fast asleep, all the same. I couldn't help smiling to myself as I continued to rub the oils in. It's amazing how a smell so pleasant and soothing to one person can be totally repugnant to another.

I thought of the text in 2 Corinthians 2:15 and 16. Christians presenting the gospel of Christ, the Good News of Salvation, can be to one group of people the sweet aroma of life, and to another the repugnant odor of death.

Lord, help me to be sensitive to the sweet aroma of Christ; and wherever I go, may I become a pleasing aroma to God and to "those who are being saved, and those who are perishing." ANTONIA (ANN) CASTELLINO

Innocent Things

I said, "I will confess my sins to the Lord," and you forgave my guilt. Ps. 32:5, NCV.

GARDENING BRINGS SUCH joy! After the last frost, out come the seeds, then the plants. The soil is prepared, and the rows look so neat and tidy. All is done—and now the waiting period begins. One day little green leaves begin poking out of the ground, saying "There is life!" I begin to think of how good everything will taste.

As the plants grow I notice some volunteer plants growing where I didn't plant them. Now my rows don't look so neat anymore. What looked like plenty of room between the plants and rows shrinks dramatically as plants mature. It's a challenge to get between the rows without stepping on tomatoes, cucumbers, or squash.

However, the biggest challenge each year is the weeds. I've tried several things to keep them out: rolls of black plastic, and piles of leaves or grass as mulch down each row and around the plants. Letting it be without any protection really invites the weeds. When there is a lot of rain, it's almost impossible to keep up with them.

Then the summer gardener's guilt sets in: *I should really be out in the garden weeding. But it's too hot. I'm too tired. There's no time to cover myself with bug spray before venturing out. I'll work on it the next cool day.*

And so the weeds really get a foothold before I get back to the garden. *How could they get so big in such a short time?* I ask myself. So I pull weeds or hoe them while the sweat drips off my nose. It's a constant battle. As everyone knows, weeds grow three times better than any other plant.

Ever notice how something small gets out of hand in just a short time? "It's only a dish of ice cream . . ." Then five new pounds show on the scales before you know it. "He's only being friendly by inviting me to eat lunch with him at work . . ." But now lunch has become a special time to be with him. "I'll keep my notes where I can see them during the test—just this time . . ." All situations that get out of hand started out innocently. That's so like sin in our lives. It leaves an imprint. Just as not weeding ruins a garden, our sins have a permanent effect.

LOUISE DRIVER

Warrior Tree

He is like a tree planted by streams of water, which yields its fruit in season and whose leaf does not wither. Whatever he does prospers. Ps. 1:3, NIV.

I ALWAYS WANTED TO have an ornamental tree planted near my home. One day I obtained one and planted it right in front of the kitchen window so that I could see it while I cooked or washed the dishes. It was beautiful! When it was in flower, large pink clusters of blooms formed.

One morning I received an alarming surprise—ants! Thousands of them were attacking my defenseless little tree, stripping it completely of its leaves. After the damage was done the ants left; and my poor, rickety, ugly tree seemed to ask for help to survive. Finally—and apparently all of a sudden—after a rain the process of restoration began. A small sprout appeared, and then another. Suddenly my tree was once again covered with strong, beautiful, green leaves.

This was not the only time that my tree was attacked by ants. This incident was repeated several times. At times I had the impression that my tree would not resist another attack of the enemy ants, or even the ant repellent that I put at its roots in an effort to protect it. However, my tree continued to grow through struggle and pain. That's why I call my tree a "warrior." Now the ants aren't able to climb up the entire trunk. They stay in the lower parts, while from the top of the tree the green leaves and lovely pink-hued flowers decorate my yard.

What gave this suffering and mistreated tree strength to be able to grow? It had a strong root system that sustained the tree even when it seemed to be dead and there was no one to appreciate or value it. The tree always had life within, a strength coming from its roots that was much stronger than ants and bad weather.

What gives us strength and power that does not allow us to become discouraged or die spiritually? Prayer and daily Bible study in a complete relationship with Jesus. Only in this manner can we make our roots go deeper so that we do not keel over when struggles come. God did not promise to free us from suffering, but He promised to be by our side if we trust in Him.

Lord, I want to have deep roots that sink into You, to be nourished and to grow according to Your plan. This is my prayer for today. EDIT FONSECA

Written Records

But there are also many other things which Jesus did; were every one of them to be written, I suppose that the world itself could not contain the books that would be written. John 21:25, RSV.

THIS VERSE USED TO bother me. Was John exaggerating when he said that the world could not contain the books that would be written about the things that Jesus did? Just what were those things, for example? What a big disadvantage that the computer came too late for John! Writing by hand limited what he could write after having been with Jesus.

Some years ago a small group of us were praying in an anteroom for evangelistic meetings being held in our church. Before prayer, opportunity was given to testify of what God had done. Elena, one of the group, told how the Lord had led her to Him. She had much to tell, and the church meeting had long been over when we ended our session of prayer. Elena concluded, "That's not all! The Lord is still doing many things for me today." It seemed that she had told only a chapter of her life story; many more could be written. And more experiences were forthcoming!

John would have had a lot to write about, given the time and a keyboard. So would have each of the disciples, Judas Iscariot included. The demoniacs of Gadara, formerly blind Bartimaeus, and every sick person Jesus had healed—each could write a book about all Jesus had done for them. The 5,000 and the other group of 4,000 who had eaten of the miraculous bread and fish and had followed Jesus the whole day; the women who ministered to Jesus; those who had met Jesus—each could have written a book telling how Jesus had blessed their lives. The 144,000, and the multitudes besides them, will have at least a book each to write, and each experience will be unique. I too have much to share about things that Jesus has done and is doing for me.

John was right. If we would all write about what Jesus has done for us the world would be full of books to read. Eternity will surely come in handy to allow us time to read them all and to share our testimonies!

I too have a testimony. Lord, today I need the courage and direction for knowing how You want me to share our story with a waiting world.

Bienvisa Ladion-Nebres

April 24

Joy in the Night

I know you are with me, Lord. By day I see evidence of your presence, and at night your love fills the air like a song. Ps. 42:8, Clear Word.

MY NIGHT-BLOOMING CACTUS had bloomed again, in profusion, after the recent showers of rain. The perfect arrangement of the sepals and creamy white petals of the blooms, with scores of filaments seeming to beckon from the center, create such rare beauty that it seems a shame that this flower only lasts for a night. Every time it blooms it evokes within me such sheer joy that I feel like waking up everyone in my neighborhood to join me in enjoying its delicate perfume and unmatched beauty.

Why should I want to call perfect strangers to show them what God has wrought?

This beautiful flower reveals itself only at night, when so few can see it in the darkness. But isn't that like God? He sends us songs in the night, "the oil of joy for mourning" (Isa. 61:3). Wherever there is darkness, He seeks to dispel it with light. In a world darkened by sin, He sets His children to reveal the beauty of His love and re-creative power. Like a magnet it draws perfect strangers to praise Him and find sweet fellowship together.

This cactus plant is covered with prickles that are painful to the touch. But out of this plant that has the potential to give an intruder a painful stab, grows a magnificent flower that calls forth the admiration of all who see it. It provides sweet nectar for the bees and other creatures that seek food in the night or early morning hours. In life there are often many difficult situations that grieve the heart and cause it to be sorrowful. It is often that we come closer to God at those times and witness the unfolding of a deepening relationship with the Master. It is in the tunnels of a dark experience that the beauty of God's loving care is revealed to His children. It is when the ugliness of sin presses against the soul that the Lily of the Valley perfumes the atmosphere, reminding us that He is near, and that we are enveloped in His loving-kindness. Then our hearts can be lifted up in a song of praise, with a sense of inner joy as we reach out to Him in perfect trust, allowing Him to illuminate our darkness. CANDACE SPRAUVE

Powdered Face

But God commendeth his love toward us, in that, while we were yet sinners, Christ died for us. Rom. 5:8.

I WAS VISITING WITH MY favorite aunt when our quiet moment was interrupted by silence in the house. Where is Kadia? I realized then that I hadn't seen her for several minutes, and that meant trouble. I decided immediately to investigate. When I opened my aunt's bedroom door, there sat Kadia in the middle of my aunt's precious silk bedspread. It was so covered with powder that it was difficult to see the patterns on the spread.

"Look at me, Mommy; I am all pretty."

Kadia sat in a pool of white talcum powder, lotion, and face cream. Pinkish-white glue caked her face and hair, leaving beautiful brown eyes and pink lips smiling at me. What does one do at a time like this: scold or laugh?

I should have known that the silence spelled trouble. This 2-year-old didn't know how not to get into trouble. I lifted her off the bed, dusted her off, washed her face, and cleaned up the mess.

Christ is willing to do the same with us. He cleans us up, dusts us off, and makes us new again. What a wonderful Savior! What matchless love! Today we again have the opportunity to be cleansed by a loving Father. He comes searching for us. He is willing to clean us up and make us ready.

Yes, Kadia's face was covered with powder, but the powder did not hide her beautiful smile. Jesus covers us with His righteousness so that our Father's smile is not hid from us. What a beautiful experience!

Dear God, You have done it again. You have come in search of me, found me, and washed me completely in Your kindness. Even when I didn't know I was lost, You have brought me home. You have covered me with Your love. You didn't hide Your face from me. Thank You for Your cleansing grace.

GLORIA GREGORY

April 26

Pesky Ants!

Go to the ant, you sluggard; consider its ways and be wise! Prov. 6:6, NIV.

LOVING THE BEAUTY OF the peony flower, Diane planted several and faithfully attended them. Whenever the ants began to crawl all over them, she carefully sprayed and destroyed the pests. However, her peonies never bloomed. An accomplished gardener, she was frustrated. When she told her mother about the problem, the first question her mother asked was: "Did you spray them for ants?" Diane assured her she had. After all, she didn't want those pesky ants around. Then her mother told her how she had made the same mistake, and when she allowed the ants to attend to the peonies they bloomed prolifically. Following her mother's advice, Diane allowed the ants to remain; and her peonies also bloomed.

I've often read the above verse and associated it with laziness. The ant is a very industrious creature and always seems to be on the move, doing whatever it was designed to do. I've drawn the lesson that I should also be industrious in order to succeed. After hearing about my friend's experience I wonder if there isn't a deeper meaning. Did God create the lowly ant with a purpose, to be a factor in creating a beautiful flower?

You and I also have many irritants that seem to be detracting from the perfection we are seeking. Instead of going to great lengths to destroy the irritants, we may need to tolerate them. By tolerating these pesky little things we can choose to grow in spite of the detractions that we face each day. Nothing is ever as perfect as we wish it would be. There will always be people, things—and even ants—that do not please us. It may surprise us to know that we also may be the irritant in someone else's life.

Tolerance is necessary in order to keep things on an even keel. Churches, families, work environments, schools, and personal lives are all affected by the amount of tolerance we have for each other. By forgetting our selfish desires and allowing each person to be an individual, we can capitalize on their unique talents and grow as a family or organization.

Go to the ant and consider its ability to bring the peony into its full glory. The beauty we behold is well worth tolerating the pesky ants. Learn a new lesson from the life of the ant and agree that tolerance of little irritants is necessary to live a happy life today.

EVELYN GLASS

Something About Loneliness

The man and woman heard the Lord God walking in the garden. They were frightened and hid behind some trees. The Lord called out to the man and asked, "Where are you?" Gen. 3:8, 9, CEV.

LONELINESS IS PROBABLY the greatest curse of life. Being alone and being lonely are not the same things at all. At our home this spring we have three little calves. In less than two days they were bonded by the herd spirit. They stay together. In the winter when it is cold and dark, Amber and Fluffy (our dog and cat) sleep together in the doghouse. Migrating birds fly in flocks. One fall I watched a cloud of blackbirds fly over our orchard for 15 minutes without a break. Many kinds of blackbirds flew in that flock—redwings, cowbirds, grackles. Nature's company.

I postulate that God also loves company. Perhaps the creation of people was the act of a lonely God. Perhaps He longed for a creature made in His image. How else can one explain creating a race that has brought unhappiness to millions and death to the Son! Perhaps love and loneliness came together to take the risk.

Sin is the great separator, the source of our loneliness. All of us have felt its sting. We may not realize that when sin separates us from God both of us become lonely. For His part, God constantly seeks to restore the relationship. For our part, we often fill the void with other things. And even when we get right with God, we long for someone with skin on them.

Do you see any lonely faces? Maybe they're hoping for someone with your skin (or mine) to help them back to God. Maybe I'm saying, "Not my skin, Lord. I burn too easily. Someone else's skin, Lord."

Lonely people without God need to know that they are never abandoned by Him, that they are cared for as if they were the only person on earth. Discouraged, many have already discovered that they cannot perfect their hearts through fear of punishment or hope of reward. They, with us, are hopeless unless . . .

We see—really see—God slip down into human skin and experience humanity firsthand. See Him separated from the Father, between heaven and earth—alone, and fatally lonely. Only this vision will prepare us to show others what Jesus is really like. But first I must see Him!

Have you seen any lonely people lately?

BETH CARLSON

Faith of a Little Child

Verily I say unto you, Except ye be converted, and become as little children, ye shall not enter into the kingdom of heaven. Matt. 18:3.

I LIVE IN AN AREA that has four seasons, and they are displayed very well. In the spring, summer, and fall no one can resist its beauty. In the winter it is messy, cold, and sometimes very icy. When spring comes, we all enjoy it, but with spring sometimes comes severe thunderstorms or heavy rainstorms. Believe me, we get our share of storms!

I picked up my son, Joseph, from his day care on my way home from work one lovely spring day. Joseph, 3 years old, was always a happy child, except when it stormed. When it stormed he had such fear!

We still had about five miles to drive before we would reach home. For the first mile it was a beautiful day—sun shining, birds singing, flowers blooming. But before we knew it, a terrible storm came up—hard rain, thunder, lightning, and heavy winds.

Joseph was so afraid he was shaking. This day I told him, as I always do, "Put your head on the headrest and close your eyes. Before you know it we will be home." I didn't let him know I was almost as afraid as he was; we parents sometimes hide the way we really feel.

Joseph said, "Mommy, I'm going to pray to Jesus because I know He will help me." He bowed his head, closed his eyes, and prayed out loud. "Dear Jesus, please help me and Mommy to get home safely. I'm afraid of the storm; please make the storm stop." He held his head up and said, "Jesus is going to stop the storm."

I had seen this type of storm before, so I knew it was not about to stop. The sky was so dark. But when we were about a mile from home the storm did stop, and the sun shone again beautifully.

Joseph looked at me and said, "I told you Jesus would stop the storm." Then and there I saw what Jesus meant when he said that unless we become as a little child we will not enter the kingdom of heaven.

Lord, help me to have the faith and trust in You as does a little child.

Odessa S. Gentles

Rainbows

I have set my rainbow in the clouds, and it will be the sign of the covenant between me and the earth. Gen. 9:13, NIV.

I SAW ANOTHER ONE last night. It was a rare one. Both ends met the horizon from east to west. It was huge! It wasn't raining where I was, but it was toward the mountains. As we drove along I said to my husband, "Just look at it! You can see the whole arc; you can see every color. It's so beautiful."

Red, orange, yellow, green, blue, indigo, violet. One color blended into the other so perfectly. My thoughts flashed back to a time four years before. I'd returned home after my father's funeral. There was a heaviness hanging over me that was unusual and uncomfortable. Since the iris needed to be watered, I went outside and began to water the bloomless plants. The sun was behind me and getting low in the sky. As I made a sweep with the water hose, the sun caught the arc of the water and made a rainbow. Wow! I made another one. Higher and higher I swung the hose, making rainbow after rainbow.

As I walked back into the house the heavy and uncomfortable feeling that I'd been experiencing had left. I recognized that my depression had been lifted. *Thank You, Lord, for allowing me to make rainbows.* Things were going to be different, but all right.

When a friend lost her husband in an accident, she was at a loss concerning the future. The light of her life was gone. One day as she was driving, there before her was the most beautiful rainbow she'd ever seen. *Thank You, Lord, for sending the rainbow,* she thought. *I know You are in control and things will work out.*

I discovered a beautiful verse written by Emily Matthews entitled, "Look for the Rainbow." A line in it says, "For rainbows are simply reminders we see/ Of God's endless love for you and for me."

Thank You, Lord, for causing us to look up when we are down. For sending such beauty to lift our spirits to remind us to remember that Your promises are true. Thank You that we can choose to make rainbows.

May you have a rainbow day.

RITA KAY STEVENS

April 30

Discipline

Discipline your son while there is hope: do not set your heart on his destruction. Prov. 19:18, RSV.

I WAS ABOUT 5 YEARS OLD when my mother tied me to the laundry basket on the back porch of our house. I had strayed too far from our yard, and that was Mom's way of punishing me rather than giving me a spanking. (Come to think of it, I can't recall ever having a spanking—maybe a light swat on the backside sometime, but I don't remember it if I did.)

Our mom was one of the sweetest, most gentle women I ever knew. She raised 16 children, and each one loved her dearly. The fact that she was always patient and fair contributed to that.

Children have to be disciplined at times, and our family was no exception. Because Mom was our primary disciplinarian, she had to devise her own method of punishment. Her method was simple. First, she'd give us that disappointed look. There wasn't a lot of lecturing—that wasn't Mom's style. Then she might set us in a chair for a designated time. For the most part, it worked.

The only temper tantrum I can remember was performed by me when I was about 8 years old. I wanted to go somewhere and Mom said no. When she said no, she usually meant just that—not "Maybe," or "I'll think about it." I guess she figured if I didn't have an audience my fire would burn out, so she ignored me. I knew she was going to hold her ground, so I finally decided: "What's the point?"

It was one of the best lessons I ever learned, because it helped me as I was raising my own two children and the four small children we cared for through the years.

I learned early on that discipline must be carried out on occasion, but it must be done in love. I truly believe my mom disciplined her children because she wanted to teach us obedience, not to unleash some pent-up frustration she may have had. And with eight boys and eight girls to contend with every day, I'm certain there was plenty of frustration.

Ephesians 6:1 says, "Children, obey your parents in the Lord, for this is right" (RSV). In looking back on those years I believe we did that.

CLAREEN COLCLESSER

The Hurried-Life Syndrome

"Martha, Martha," the Lord answered, "you are worried and upset about many things, but only one thing is needed. Mary has chosen what is better, and it will not be taken away from her." Luke 10:41, 42, NIV.

IT WAS ANOTHER OF those days—so much to do, so little time. I was trying to write letters, edit material, and create agendas while sitting in still another committee meeting. And that was just at work. At home there were all the regular chores—tax time looming, a personal promise to a friend to read a manuscript, and a project my husband and I had agreed in a weak moment to write. When was there time for me? Especially, how was I going to have time for exercise, or even to read a book—to say nothing at all of spending personal time with Jesus?

The previous week I'd been at a woman's retreat—no, not retreating, but as a speaker. The leader had mentioned that there is a new sickness, a new syndrome now showing up in doctors' offices: the hurried-life syndrome.

This makes me think of Martha. Poor Martha. So like all of us: overwhelmed. Thirteen—or more—men coming to dinner. So much to do, and no one helping. But she had one very good strategy when she was overwhelmed—she went to Jesus.

His answer? It makes no sense at all, as far as time management is concerned. He suggested that Martha had her priorities out of kilter. She was busy and concerned about many things, but she had neglected the most important part: spending time with Him. She had been spending time with Jesus as her guest, Someone who was visiting for only a short time and must be pleased. But Mary, her sister, was spending time with Jesus as a friend, developing a relationship, getting to really know Him. And which did Jesus appreciate more? I'm sure He enjoyed the good food, but He loved His time with Mary.

Is Jesus a guest in my life, someone invited occasionally for a visit, or is He a friend? Someone who is frequently invited to lunch, to spend time in deep soul sharing; someone with whom I can share plans and dreams, as well as the one to whom I go when my heart is aching?

The hurried-life syndrome. *Thank You, Jesus; there* is *a remedy.*

ARDIS DICK STENBAKKEN

The Hole in the Garage Wall

Be strong and of a good courage; be not afraid, neither be thou dismayed: for the Lord thy God is with thee whithersoever thou goest. Joshua 1:9.

HAVE YOU EVER HAD a problem that seemed unsolvable? No matter how hard you try, the situation doesn't improve. I have such a problem.

Every time I drive into our garage I hit the wall in front of my car. A sizable hole has developed. I've grown weary of confessing that I've hit the wall again. My husband doesn't understand why it is so difficult to stop my car before I hit the wall. He always asks, "Don't you know what your brakes are for?" Of course I know what my brakes are for!

My brother-in-law, Jim, offered a solution. He bought us a rather expensive traffic-light gadget. It was very clever, and I was excited the day my husband installed it. When I drove into the garage, the green light came on. As I drove closer to the wall, the light turned yellow. When I was within inches of the wall, the light turned red, signaling me to stop. We were ecstatic to think the problem was solved! Then, a few days later, I failed to watch the little lights closely enough and plowed into the sensor. I smashed it right into the wall. We haven't had the nerve to tell Jim what happened to his clever, expensive gift.

Next, we tried a tennis ball hanging from the ceiling of the garage. I was instructed to stop when the ball touched my windshield. That worked well until one night I pulled into the garage during a terrific rainstorm and failed to see the tennis ball through the wet windshield and movement of the windshield wipers. I really whacked the wall that time! My husband now plans to install several pieces of lumber at bumper level across the hole I've made in the garage wall.

We all have problems and trials that seem unsolvable. God, who reads our hearts, knows that without His help we are going to keep "hitting the wall." For this reason He makes provision for us, through the power of His blood, to overcome all obstacles in our lives. He says, "Fear thou not; for I am with thee: be not dismayed; for I am thy God: I will strengthen thee; yea, I will help thee; yea, I will uphold thee with the right hand of my righteousness" (Isa. 41:10).

Today, let's give all our problems and concerns to the Lord and let Him solve them—even those that seem unsolvable. He has promised His help for every need. Let's trust Him.

ELLIE GREEN

Lesson From the Playground

As for me, I will call upon God; and the Lord shall save me. Ps. 55:16.

RECENTLY, DURING A WALK on the track at a local city park, I decided it would be a good time to talk to the Lord. I told Him that I wanted to know my purpose; and because I have a burden on my heart for young people, I prayed that He would help me hear the cries of children when it seems that no one else around can hear them.

About 60 seconds later, my thoughts were interrupted by what seemed to me to be the faint yelp of a child. My eyes searched the playground in the middle of the track as I heard a second yelp which was now distinctly louder. A little Hispanic girl, about 3 or 4 years old and obviously distressed, was hanging midway between the two ends of the monkey bars and seemed to be struggling to maintain her grip. I could only imagine her fear as she looked up at her hands that must have been tired and hurting from the weight of her small frame, then down at the ground beneath her, which most assuredly seemed to her to be too far to jump.

After hesitating only a second to see whether a caretaker or older sibling would come to her aid, I rushed over and reached up to her with both hands. In a calm voice I began to ask whether she wanted to get down, not sure if she could understand English. Almost immediately she let go of the bars and dropped into my hands. She seemed relieved as I placed her on the ground.

Without looking around, I went back to the track to resume my walk. As I walked that last lap, I reflected on the lesson that the brief encounter had taught me; and I thanked God for the awesome ways He manifests Himself to us.

Just like this dear little one, might you be experiencing paralysis (emotional or spiritual) because of fear, pain, or even anger? You've looked at the totality of your situation, and it seems a painful struggle to maintain your grip under the weight of your burdens and trials. The alternatives don't seem to offer a viable solution to your dilemma. Don't despair. Call on God while you still have the strength. Let go, and trust Him to keep you from falling.

BRENDA THORNTON

The Airport

Yes, I am coming soon! Rev. 22:20, NEB.

THE ARCHAEOLOGICAL DIG was almost over, and at the dig house people were smiling as they planned their return to North America. I was excited too, although I wasn't leaving the country. I was anticipating walking into Petra with its elaborately carved sandstone cliffs, strolling along the Roman road in Palmyra, and exploring Jerusalem—all in the company of my husband, Larry, and his parents.

His parents' plane was to arrive at 7:00 p.m. At 5:45, unable to wait any longer, Larry and I began the 30-minute drive to the airport. The airport was so small that only passengers were allowed in the terminal, so we waited outside, scrutinizing each plane as it descended. Even though it was 6:45 we said, "That looks like TWA—maybe it's them! Maybe they got a tailwind."

Although we knew they faced lines at immigration and customs, we stood on tiptoe, trying to find two familiar faces. By 7:45 we were worried, and Larry talked to the attendants. "The flight from London won't arrive until 9:00 p.m," they said.

Crestfallen, we sat in our rental car. At 8:45 we started craning our necks again. At 9:30 a surge of people exited the terminal. Soon the surge became a trickle—and then no one.

Larry again asked. "Another delay, sir. Your passengers should be here by midnight."

Disappointed, we drove back to our quarters. We read, but our adrenaline was still too high to doze. At 11:30 we returned to the airport. This time there were no crowds, and the attendant volunteered, "Another delay. Flight 968 will arrive at 2:00 a.m."

At 2:30 Mom and Dad emerged from the airport. "Did you get tired of waiting for us?" Dad asked as we walked to the car.

"Each time there was a delay we were disappointed, but that just made us more eager to see you," Larry replied, "I'm glad you're here now. Let's go home together."

More than 20 years later that night seems larger than life: I remember the ever-growing anticipation, despite setbacks. It is a good parallel to our life on earth as we wait for our heavenly Father. Someday our waiting in the darkness will end, and we'll all go home together.

Denise Dick Herr

My Father's Love Letter

Every good and perfect gift is from above, coming down from the Father of the heavenly lights, who does not change like shifting shadows. James 1:17, NIV.

MY LIFE IS VERY FULL, as I am the only dietitian at a delinquent juvenile facility for 254 youth. In addition, I run a soup kitchen, do the PowerPoint presentations for my church's praise service, and conduct Bible studies at the soup kitchen.

I have a wonderful relationship with my Lord and Savior; however, there are times when even though I remember from where my God has led me, I am so busy that I don't feel connected to my heavenly Father. These times are generally whenever I come back from vacation and have piles and piles of paperwork to wade through, the soup kitchen is not running smoothly, and I just plainly am out of time. Something that reminds me that God loves and cherishes me is the special gift He sends at times like these. One such occasion happened to me in May a few years ago.

I was driving to work at 4:30 on a Tuesday morning. God and I have had this special love relationship with deer. At one time He sent them to me in the woods in California. As I had been praying and asking Him to show me His Glory, out walked two deer. So whenever I'm having a difficult time, He sends deer to remind me of His love.

On this particular Tuesday, as I rounded the corner at my work place, I was sobbing and crying out to the Lord about all my problems and mountains in my life. I looked up; and there were six deer, standing on their hind legs, prancing with each other. I have worked at this facility for 15 years and have never seen deer there before—and certainly not six of them. There are no woods around there; no one else has ever seen them. It amazes me that I go for months without seeing them; but when I am crying out to the Lord and overwhelmed after my vacation, around the next corner were six deer to remind me that God loves and cherishes me, that He is in control and will work everything out.

Lord, help me to remember that even though I don't feel Your presence, You have promised never to leave me nor forsake me. DONNA M. DUNBAR

The Blue Bowl

And when he saw a fig tree in the way, he came to it, and found nothing thereon, but leaves only, and said unto it, Let no fruit grow on thee henceforward for ever. And presently the fig tree withered away. Matt. 21:19.

HAVE YOU EVER COME across something that wasn't as it appeared to be? I once bought a bowl that seemed to be deep blue, transparent, cut glass.

One day I put a vegetable salad in it as part of my contribution to a special family meal at my mom-in-law's. When we were almost through eating, we heard a knock at the back door. It was an antique dealer who was passing through. Seeing my dish, he said, "I want that! I'll give you $5 for it." I shook my head.

"But it's quite valuable. Please, I'll give you $7.50."

I refused. When he offered $10 and I still refused, he asked, "Why won't you sell it? Twelve-fifty, and that's my final offer."

"Sir," I explained, "it really isn't worth that much. I bought it at the dime store for 50 cents. Plus, I'm sentimentally attached to it."

"Very well," he sighed. "If that's how it has to be." My mom-in-law sold him some things, and he left. While clearing the table, I left my salad container soaking in the dishwater.

"Bonnie! Come here!" Mom called. "The color's coming off your dish!"

She was right. The dishwater was full of pieces of blue film. How glad I was that I hadn't sold it, for the dealer, or perhaps whoever bought it from him, would have been cheated.

"What will you do with it now?" Mom asked.

"Let the rest of this stuff soak off. I can still use it as a clear crystal bowl."

We shared a good laugh about the "valuable" dish.

As a Christian I may appear truly fine and be well thought of by many. But am I as good as I look? Is my Christianity just a thin veneer? How do I fare when I'm soaked by the waters of affliction?

The fig tree was useless. The bowl could still be used. Hopefully, God can use me as He continues His transforming work in my life. And I won't have to worry, because what I seem to be is what I will be—an accurate reflection of Christ's character.

BONNIE MOYERS

Day-Planner

Oh, the depth of the riches both of the wisdom and knowledge of God! How unsearchable are His judgments and unfathomable His ways! Rom. 11:33, NASB.

IT WAS 2:00 ON a hot, humid, Florida afternoon. The road was congested, and the other drivers were impatient. I had gotten up at 5:30 that morning and was giving insulin to my first patient by 7:00. As a home-care nurse I had spent the rest of the day instructing one patient on ways to lower his blood pressure, removing staples from a lady's reconstructed knee incision, changing the dressing on an elderly patient's bedsore, and drawing blood from an overly medicated man.

Now, finally on my way to my last patient's home, I was about to drive by a small day-care center that I routinely passed each day. I knew that Linda, a good friend, worked there, and I suddenly felt an urge to stop in and say hi. It made no sense—I had never been in the day-care center and didn't even know if you were allowed to talk to the employees. I still had another patient to see, paperwork to complete, and supper to prepare before my family trooped home for the evening. While I was thinking it would be better to call Linda later that night, my car pulled into the parking lot, and I turned off the ignition.

Still very unsure of why I was doing this, I got out of the car and headed into the center. After explaining who I was and whom I wanted to see, I was escorted to the 2- and 3-year-old room. When Linda saw me her eyes grew wide, her mouth dropped open, and she said, "God sent you to me!" She then told me how she had unexpectedly had to take Isaac, her 2-year-old grandson, to the doctor that morning, and because of complications he had had to have a tube inserted into his bladder. Before they had gotten to the doctor, Linda had promised Isaac that she wouldn't let anybody do anything to hurt him, and the whole experience had been very traumatic—for both of them. Linda had been crying and said she just wanted a hug from somebody who cared. We talked and hugged, and after finding out that Isaac would be fine, I left. But I wasn't the same as when I had arrived. I felt so humbled and awed that the mighty, all-powerful God of innumerable worlds would allow someone as insignificant as me to be used in His incredibly wonderful plans!

I pray that my "day-planner" will always be open for His appointments!

Susan Wooley

May 8

Spina Bifida Blessing

But God gives it a body as he has determined, and to each kind of seed he gives its own body. 1 Cor. 15:38, NIV.

I LIVE WITH SPINA BIFIDA. This is a congenital disability, causing paralysis from the point of the spinal damage down. My spinal lesion is at the bottom of my back; therefore I have no feeling in my legs and have no bladder control. I've had to use a wheelchair from the age of 13, after having used crutches and leg braces until then. At 13 I had an operation in which my tibia was broken in order to reset the angle of my foot. I hadn't been eating properly, trying to lose weight in order to look good; and therefore my bone didn't heal. For 10 months it didn't heal; finally the doctor realized what the problem was and gave me calcium, zinc, and vitamin D supplements. But by then it was too late; my paralyzed muscles, which had miraculously worked until that point, withered and would not regain their usefulness.

Spina bifida is, in part, caused by a pregnant mother's poor diet. If a pregnant mother has enough fruit and vegetables in her diet, the chances are that her baby will be fine. My mother lived on a low income while she was pregnant with me and, as many mothers do, sacrificed her own quality of food for the sake of the family's financial needs. Consequently (not that I blame her), I live with spina bifida, and probably will until I die.

If God gave me this body, and should you one day pick up this book and read this piece and realize how important it is to look after your body, then it will all have been worth it. Eat plenty of fruits and vegetables and praise God for His advice given through the Bible. If you then read further you will realize how much God has given me, despite my disability: loving parents, a university place that enabled me to train as a teacher, two teaching jobs over seven years through which I climbed the career ladder and held a Head of Year job down for four years, a husband and son, a postgraduate diploma in counseling, and a private counseling practice that I run from home. Aren't you glad God gave me the body He did, so that I, through what has happened to me, could sow the seed of hope in you? This hope says, "If she in her wheelchair can do all these things with God by her side, couldn't I do even more?"

Then it really will have all been worth it.

TRACY DIXON

The Time God Hovered Over Us

I have given them the glory that you gave me, that they may be one as we are one. John 17:22, NIV.

THE WOMEN'S RETREAT leadership team was new, and I could sense God rearranging things for me as well. Our last retreat had been a Spirit-filled success; and as we began the task of preparing for the next retreat, we settled on the theme "The Power of His Presence." I longed for the unity that I felt was God's will for us. Our women's ministry retreat looked like a beautiful rainbow of women representing the 42 people groups in our area. As we developed the plan the weekend fit together, but none of our guests wanted to speak Sunday morning—and the budget was zero. I now see that it was in God's divine plan.

As women's ministry director, I felt fully responsible that the ending should bring unity of heart, mind, and Spirit. I took responsibility for Sunday's closing and began an intense study to get a clearer picture of the body of Christ.

His message was specific to "time." Two of us spoke on God's timing for all seasons of life and the time for His coming. We all stood together to close, and then walked together, singing, to an outside grassy area. We formed a large, tight circle. A rendition of "The Midnight Cry" played as brides from each culture came into the center-stage area. Each bride was radiant; each had accepted without reservation the call to wear the bride's dress and walk beautifully adorned to meet her Bridegroom. No bride was informed of the meaning of this grand event; there was no rehearsal.

As we sang "and at the midnight cry, the bride of Christ will rise," the brides released hundreds of balloons into the air. We felt as though we were being swept up to meet with Jesus at that very moment. A few feet above us, God formed a small wisp of a cloud. First, it hovered over us, then broke into three pieces before becoming one cloud again as the song concluded.

The balloons circled above us for nearly an hour. Women stood still, waited, sat on the lawn, were stunned and wept as they each experienced God's presence. Many women recall this event as life changing. I know I experienced His presence in a new and profound way. I was humbled as I had answered His call to bring people into His presence. NANCY WALLACK

Be Alert

Stay alert and be careful because the devil is roaming around like a hungry lion seeking to destroy anyone he can. 1 Peter 5:8, Clear Word.

THE GROUNDS OF THE retirement village where my husband and I reside are quite spacious, and numerous birds frequent the many trees and shrubs surrounding our unit. We receive much pleasure from our feathered visitors.

The brightly colored rainbow lorikeet parrots are regular visitors to the flowering trees. They chatter nonstop while feeding, and I like to think that they are thanking their heavenly Creator for supplying them with such abundant food and are calling their friends to come and to join in the feasting.

A shy dove built her flimsy nest in a shrub by our back door. One morning at the nearby clothesline, I surprised a kookaburra with a near-naked baby dove in its powerful beak. The dove's mate was lying on the ground nearby.

Another dove built a nest in the bougainvillea shrub by the front door. She laid her eggs and sat on them for a couple of days, and then she and the eggs disappeared. Some days later we found that a snake had shed its skin by the nest. I guess it ate the eggs.

Later the dove took courage and built another flimsy nest nearby, and two baby doves hatched out. She cared for them until they were almost ready to leave the nest. One day we found one lying dead on the ground under the nest. A butcher bird which thrills its listener with its varied repertoire of songs had apparently killed it. The butcher bird—though not a large bird—will kill smaller birds for the sheer joy of it, and so is aptly named.

The aggressive minor bird, though not as large as most of our visiting feathered friends, will attempt to frighten all other birds away. All is not peaceful in the bird life around our home.

As I observed the life of these birds and how they constantly have to be on the alert for danger, it reminded me of our lives. We enjoy many pleasures, but we have to be watchful and on the alert all the time. Satan and his helpers use many different ways to attack and to destroy us when we least expect him.

JOY DUSTOW

Crawl Before You Walk

I understood as a child. 1 Cor. 13:11.

SYDNEY AND I WERE playing with the ball on the floor. When the baby in the swing started to cry, Sydney jumped up and ran to try to comfort her. She said to me, "Ms. Elaine, when I grow up I'm going to work in the baby room, just like you!"

It's amazing how infants, toddlers, and young children can imitate adults. I've often heard them referred to as "miniature adults."

During the past 22 years, working with children at home as well as in day-care facilities, I have discovered that no matter what your physical or mental condition, most children have a warm smile, a forgiving spirit, a need to be loved, a willingness to learn, and the ability to soak up knowledge like a sponge! When I am with these children, they become the teacher and I become the pupil. It's awesome how God has so magnificently and wonderfully made each one of us in His image!

I learned that by my facial expressions I can communicate very well with these children, and they're able to pick up on my emotions and act accordingly. If I'm stressed, they become stressed. If I am sad, they feel it.

The developmental stages children go through have their counterpart in our Christian development. When we accept Christ into our lives, we go through a maturation process from infancy to adult Christian. Out of our parent's womb, we're crying. In Christ we're being fed through the Word in order to live in this world. As a newborn we learn "I can do everything through him who gives me strength" (Phil. 4:13, NIV). In infancy we begin to crawl. In Christ we learn that some things are at our fingertips, and sometimes we have to ask for help. In infancy we start pulling up on things, only to fall down. Through Christ we learn that God is our anchor, and we must take hold and hold on! Then we take those first few steps. In Christ we learn to step out in faith. Finally, we're able to move about on our own. We become independent, and with further training we can then help fulfill the gospel.

Thank You, God, for Your gift of children, who help us learn that we must crawl before we walk! ELAINE J. JOHNSON

The Left Turn

Fear thou not; for I am with thee: Be not dismayed; for I am thy God: I will strengthen thee; yea, I will help thee; yea, I will uphold thee with the right hand of my righteousness. Isa. 41:10.

I WAS APPREHENSIVE AS I waited for my appointment with the doctor. I reached for the Bible lying on the coffee table. It opened to today's text. I breathed a sigh of relief. Everything was going to be all right, the verse seemed to say. And it was, the physician confirmed.

But as we were driving home, my daughter asked me to make a detour to a nearby store. It was almost noon, and the lunch-hour traffic was beginning to swell. Indicating that I needed to make a left turn, I waited for the oncoming traffic to pass. The cars kept moving in an incessant stream until a woman finally stopped and motioned for me to cross over. As there were no other cars in the lane beside her, I began to make the turn. My daughter's horrified scream signaled impending disaster!

Apparently, another driver two cars behind the helpful driver had needed to be on her way in a hurry. Changing lanes quickly, she crashed into us. The burly police officer who came to the scene almost immediately gently informed us that it was my fault as he wrote out a ticket and called a tow truck to pull my car away.

I was shaken, devastated by the disaster I had caused. I took the blame for everything. That evening I read the text in a different version. "So do not fear, for I am with you; do not be dismayed, for I am your God. I will strengthen you and help you" (Isa. 41:10, NIV). I felt the strong assurance in the promise I had mistaken for a simple assessment of my medical report. Even though the car was badly damaged, we were unhurt. He was with me. I had firsthand experience of the strength in His hand.

I learned an unforgettable lesson that day. I am accountable for every decision I make—regardless of how thoughtful and considerate others may be. When we finally got our car back, I praised Him once more for reminding me of a dramatic irony. There are some left turns in life only God with His righteous right hand can make with me; but I need not be afraid, because He is right beside me.

CAROL JOY GREENE

The Mother's Day Amaryllis

Love is patient. 1 Cor. 13:4, NIV.

OUR SON, NATHAN, CAME home from school with three plastic cups filled with potting compost and what looked like a few blades of grass. I didn't know what the plants were, but Nathan's teacher had told him that she had saved the seeds from an amaryllis and planted enough to grow seedlings for the whole class. "It'll be a few years before they'll flower," she told me. "Until then, just give them plant food and water."

So for four years we watered and fed as the skinny little shoots turned into long, wayward leaves. I tried to arrange other plants around them on the windowsill to make the plain leaves look more attractive. Occasionally a leaf would die back, and new ones would come. Several times they needed special care when they were attacked by plant flies. Sometimes I wondered why we bothered to keep nurturing the leaves. I could easily buy a cheap amaryllis bulb that was ready to bloom without watching over these flowerless plants month after month.

One day, as I rearranged the plants on my windowsill, I decided to move the amaryllis plants into the office where they would be less visible. But a few weeks later, as I was watering them, I noticed a thick shoot rising between the leaves. It looked very different from the shoots that heralded a new leaf, and it grew amazingly fast. Soon there were two large buds, and we all tried to guess what color the flowers would be.

Finally, on the morning of Mother's Day, the buds burst open into glorious deep pink flowers, exquisitely formed. Our patience had been rewarded; our faith in those tiny green shoots had helped them to develop into something incredibly beautiful.

I often thought of Nathan's teacher and what she was hoping to teach the children when she gave them the tiny plants. I wondered if the other plants had survived to produce a flower.

As it was Mother's Day when our flower finally blossomed, I reflected on what it means to be a mother; and how it can take many years of patient love before we see the beautiful results of our care. I also thought about what it means to be the heavenly Father, lavishing us with patient love, never giving up on us, feeding us, watering us, and removing the dead leaves, until we also blossom into something beautiful for Him.

KAREN HOLFORD

Shared Joy

Who is like the Lord our God, the One who sits enthroned on high, who stoops down to look on the heavens and the earth? Ps. 113:5, 6, NIV.

ONE MOTHER'S DAY the church we attend honored mothers with flowers and a delicious snack. Later that same day the school my sons, Daniel and Yuri, and my nephew, Kevyn, attended prepared a special program with student participation. After the church program Daniel helped his father clean up the social room rather than participate in the school program.

My sisters-in-law and I arrived at the school early and sat on the first row so we would have a good view of the stage. While we waited for the program to begin, the teacher responsible for the students' practice came to me and wanted to know about Daniel. She told me that she needed him so that the choreography that had been practiced would turn out according to plan. I assured her that I would go get him and left quickly, ready to bring him back as soon as possible.

When we arrived back at the auditorium, I recognized the music playing—it was the choreography for Kevyn's class. I ran down the steps, and when I reached the door of the auditorium I found it filled with people who struggled to have a chance to see their dear ones. What would I do if I could see nothing?

Forgetting my shyness, I began to squeeze through the crowd saying, "Excuse me! I need to see my nephew!" Finally, I was able to reach my seat and see my nephew's performance. How he smiled with joy as the audience applauded!

After this, I began to remember my attitude of being a proud aunt and realized that God reacts in the same manner toward us, His children. He isn't concerned about opinions or worried that His attitude may seem ridiculous. He simply leaves His throne of grace and comes to us to be overjoyed with our successes. He opens His arms of love and says, "This is My child! I created you; I gave you My life, and I will never leave you, because heaven would never be the same without you by My side!"

Vera Lúcia Rosembaum Silva

Saved From the Shark

Choose you this day whom ye will serve. Joshua 24:15.

OUR DAUGHTER WAS breathless with excitement as she told us her aunt and uncle had invited her to accompany them on a trip to Hawaii. She eagerly counted the days until it was time to go. One of the events Duane and Carolyn enjoy is whale watches, often going several times each Hawaiian trip. The year our daughter was to go with them whale watches were definitely part of the planning.

The day dawned bright and clear; a perfect day for a whale watch. They boarded the boat with Captain Dave at the helm, the same boat they'd taken many times before with Captain Dave. It was a great watch. Whales jumped everywhere, in and out of the sparkling-blue waters. The watchers used sonar equipment to hear the whales communicate beneath the surface of the water. It was truly a memorable experience for everyone on board!

Now, it happened that Captain Dave was quite taken with our daughter and offered to take her boating and snorkeling the next day at Molokini, a favorite place of divers and snorkelers. That invitation had appeal as a great adventure, of course; but the next day she would be going to church with her aunt and uncle, so she turned him down.

The next morning they attended a lovely Hawaiian church service—complete with Hawaiian music and flowers. Church members wore flowers on clothing and in their hair. A potluck that included all sorts of delicious tropical fruits followed. It was a very special day!

On Sunday morning they heard that out on Molokini, the very place and time that Captain Dave had planned to take Tami snorkeling, a 12-foot-long, 1,000-pound tiger shark had been seen swimming all around. Goose bumps sped up and down Tami's spine when she realized that she could well have been in serious danger. She was so thankful she had made the right choice that day.

Our choices are important. More times than we would like to admit, they can be a matter of life and death.

Dear Father, help us to hear Your voice when You speak that we might choose the right way. DARLENE YTREDAL BURGESON

Friendship Gardens

Honor the Lord. . . . with the firstfruits of all your crops. Prov. 3:9, NIV.

GARDENS ARE FOR SHARING." That idea probably came from my grandmother, from whom I inherited the gardening gene. Mama, as we call her, would labor in her garden; then take the baskets of fresh veggies to her pastor when she might have taken a siesta instead to escape the hot, non-air-conditioned Southern afternoon.

When Mother was a child, the garden was in their front yard, and she was embarrassed when their corn would wave to flowers across the street. It helped when Mama would take her, a knife, and a salt shaker, and go to the garden and eat tomatoes and cucumbers right then and there.

Before we had a place for a garden, we were blessed by others sharing with us. As a young married couple struggling to finish college, we helped one semester with evangelistic tent meetings. My husband and the friend working with us visited attendees in the country—and would come home with the car loaded with farm-fresh vegetables. What rejoicing there would be!

Now, we have a garden spot in our backyard. Even though the gardening catalogs come while it's still winter, I begin poring over them eagerly, planning what to order. Tomatoes are a favorite, and we always have several varieties, including my "Gracie" tomato. Grace is our young neighbor who likes the little "tommytoes" for school lunches, and that variety is especially for her. This year we bought 24 tomato plants; then more than 20 volunteer plants came up! My husband calls them my orphans because I transplant each one. We harvest enough to share with many others and still preserve plenty for winter.

Now it's fall, and the garden is looking very ragged. The cornstalks and many other plants have been uprooted. There are still a few treasures to be found, and some plants are full of blossoms, although there isn't time for them to produce. I suppose I should breathe a sigh of relief, but the final harvest always seems to come before I'm ready for it. "The harvest is past, the summer is ended" (Jer. 8:20, NIV). But that's not all. The verse goes on to say some of the saddest words I can imagine: "And we are not saved." I pray that instead of those mournful cries my loved ones and I can say, "This is our God; we have waited for him, and he will save us" (Isa. 25:9). Won't you make that your prayer too?

MARY JANE GRAVES

The Daughter Game

Whoever wants to be first must be slave of all. Mark 10:44, NIV.

AS A CHILD I competed with everyone and everything for my mom's attention. Nobody told me that being an adult daughter would prove to be just as much of a struggle.

When competing with my sister, I always come out the loser. She has a great job, a big house, and—the crowning achievement—her original husband. She has raised homemaking to an art. When she took up knitting, for example, she bought two sheep and a spinning wheel and—you guessed it—she sheared her own sheep, spun her own wool, and then knit her own socks. She also cans her own peaches. (Don't they come that way?) My domestic skills consist of being a great shopper, assisted by my calculated use of double coupons and the ability to slap together a decent meal in my trusty microwave.

Then there's my mom's best friend, Ellie. Ellie has five kids, all doing well financially. Whenever Ellie needs something replaced, say, a water heater, her kids chip in and buy it for her. They see to it that her car is serviced and her home in good repair. They also invite their mom and mine to numerous family gatherings. I don't have the money or the family to compete with Ellie's kids, so I had to give up on that, too.

My final defeat came when Mom took a vacation with my aunt and cousins.

"They just cherish my sister," Mom said. "They wait on her hand and foot."

"I cherish you, Mom," I told her. "I can't wait on you or buy you things the way my cousins do their mom, because I live too far away—and I'm broke."

Mom looked surprised. "You don't have to compete with anyone. You're my daughter."

Now she tells me!

In His earthly ministry Jesus had trouble with his disciples jockeying for position. At one point James and John asked Jesus if they could sit on either side of Him in heaven. The other disciples became angry. Jesus settled the dispute by telling them they were all there to serve.

I'm glad that my cousins cherish their mother. I'm thankful that Ellie's kids are generous enough to treat my mom like a member of their family. And I'm certainly grateful that my sister has a home and a husband to love. Now, if only I could afford to send Mom on a cruise. GINA LEE

My First Piano

Ask and it will be given to you; seek and you will find; knock and the door will be opened to you. Matt. 7:7, NIV.

I WAS IN A STRANGE country, experiencing what you would call homesickness. I was a young, pregnant wife going through months of morning sickness with no mother or sisters to whom I could talk. My husband worked during the day. I was all alone at home.

One morning, while reading my Bible study guide, I talked to my Father in heaven. "Father, You know how sick I am with this pregnancy, how trapped I feel with no one to talk to." I looked around the front room where I was sitting. "Lord," I prayed, "I can't play it, but please send me a piano." And with those words I got up, stretched my arms from the window to the corner where I had been sitting, "Yes, Father; my piano will fit right here."

Early one morning when I was about three months pregnant and still very nauseous, I lay in bed. The doorbell rang. Fortunately, Charles was already up and dressed. Going to the door, my husband greeted an old friend who had stopped by to visit. The two men stood talking by the entrance when a large truck stopped at our house.

Suddenly Charles rushed to my bedside. "Lizzie, your piano's here!" He was as excited as I was. I had forgotten that I had asked God for a piano. But He hadn't.

In the minutes that followed, I saw how God had taken care of even the minutest details of the whole transaction. He had sent my husband's friend to visit at the right time. Then the three men could lift the piano up the flight of stairs and into its proper place without a problem. The spot I had prayed about was perfect for the piano. I had no doubt. God was in control. Faith unlocks doors, breaks down barriers, and makes the crooked paths straight.

As my family grew, so did our musical talents. Eventually my husband and I sang with our middle daughter; the other children each learned an instrument. Friday night family worship around the piano brought gladness to my heart, a tight-knit bond to the family, and peace to our souls.

"Ask, and it shall be given you; seek, and ye shall find; knock, and it shall be opened unto you" (Matt. 7:7). My God said it. I experienced it.

Elizabeth McIntosh

A Wider Version of Motherhood

He settles the barren woman in her home as a happy mother of children. Ps. 113:9, NIV.
I will bless her so that she will be the mother of nations; kings of people will come from her. Gen. 17:16, NIV.

MISS ELIZABETH LOTHIAN was salt in our oatmeal, hot cocoa in our cup, rubbing alcohol on an outbreak of teenage acne. Our mothers were too young to have been her natural daughters, but our grandmothers could have been.

My freshman year at Maplewood Academy I had red measles. Too sick to be taken home until my fever went down, I was moved to the "infirmary" across the hall from the dean's apartment. More than once when my fever soared I awoke during the night to see Miss Lothian sleeping in a chair at my bedside. My junior year there was an outbreak of flu, during which more than half of the West Hall residents were down. If Miss Lothian experienced any of the symptoms that laid us low, she gave no indication. Students well enough to climb stairs carried the soups and juices; but she was the one to enter the sickroom, insisting that the well students must not go in or handle returning trays. She washed us up when were too weak to make ourselves decent after vomiting.

Miss Lothian had never married, had not been a mother. But as she often reminded us, she had begun her deaning career in 1901, and there wasn't much girls our age thought or suffered or were tempted into that she hadn't seen up close hundreds of times. "It's the same problem that made your grandmothers weep," she would say. "Not much changes."

Of course, everything changes, and Miss Lothian knew that, too. In fact, that year of the flu was her "last year." Even she had to face the facts: she had grown too old to keep up with the demands of a dormitory full of teens, though she was still a beautiful and charming woman. We imagined her at 21. I suppose generations of girls before us had also speculated about the great love of her life—a young man handsome and gallant enough to be worthy of her.

Actually, at 21 she was probably managing a dormitory. The work God gave her was her "husband and children." We were daughters and granddaughters and great-granddaughters. She taught us to be daughters of God.

Father, expand my capacity to love Your sons and daughters as You do.

HELEN GODFREY PYKE

Answered Prayer

For your Father knoweth what things ye have need of, before ye ask him. Matt. 6:8.

A COUPLE I KNEW celebrated their tenth anniversary with a renewal ceremony. As beautiful as it was, I didn't enjoy myself. The bride was about my age, and not only had she already been married for 10 years, she had children old enough to be in the service! It made me sad. I had recently ended another dead-end relationship, and although I did not miss this particular relationship, I did want to find a relationship that could lead to a lifelong commitment.

On the way home I felt better. I spoke with God as I drove, telling Him I realized that I might never marry, and that was fine. I focused on different things in my life and found peace. About nine months later I met the man I would marry. We talked for a while and exchanged numbers. Eventually we started talking on the phone, and I found myself drawn to him. I fell in love with him over the telephone! Our courtship progressed rapidly. Before I knew it, Mom and I were asking God if this was the man I should marry. He was sweet, attentive, kind, and giving; but he was not of our faith, was divorced, and was the father of a 9-year-old girl. The wedding date was set for one year to the day after we first spoke on the phone.

One night about three weeks before our wedding, my fiancé was agitated. We were discussing the wedding and which bills were still outstanding, when he concluded we were $500 short. I said, "Don't worry. I'll pray about it."

"*Pray* about it?" he asked incredulously. "What are we going to do?"

I told him to relax, that God knew we needed the money, and He would provide. The next day I received a note, along with a check, from my uncle who knew nothing of our financial needs. The note said, "Sweetheart, I was thinking about you and felt impressed to send you a check. I hope you can use this toward something for your wedding." I took the note and the check to my fiancé and let him read them. He looked up at me, amazed. "I told you God would provide," I said.

God says He will answer if we but ask. Had my uncle not allowed the Holy Spirit to impress him, or had I not said I was going to pray—and prayed—we would have missed an opportunity to witness God's care and power. Three years ago my husband gave his life to God, and I would like to think that prayer for $500 started everything. TAMARA MARQUEZ DE SMITH

God Is So Good to Me

Fear thou not; for I am with thee: be not dismayed; for I am thy God: I will strengthen thee; yea, I will help thee; yea, I will uphold thee with the right hand of my righteousness. Isa. 41:10.

SOMETIMES, WHEN WE ARE well and feeling great, we don't think about the wonderful bodies God has given us. We become complacent until we are overcome by sudden illness. This was my experience several months ago. I'd developed a severe allergic reaction to the smell of cologne and other scents that manifests itself in elevated blood pressure and rapid heartbeat. I was admitted to the hospital for 24-hour tests to ascertain the cause. The tests were completed, and everything seemed fine. While I was awaiting discharge orders, someone entered my room, and the smell of her cologne triggered a reaction. More tests were done. A little later a nurse hurried in to inform me that one of the tests revealed a pulmonary embolism. She told me not to move or get out of bed. Immediately I was transported to the cardiac-care unit. Instead of 24 hours, I spent 15 days in the hospital.

One night as I sat on a chair with my right leg propped up and questioning Why me? I was touched by God's Holy Word and inspiring songs playing on a Christian radio station. The cardiologist had inserted a Greenfield filter to filter out future clots, and IVs were in my arm. Feelings of loneliness, despondency, and homesickness enveloped me. I was in the dungeon of despair. The nights were long, dark, and dreary. I couldn't sleep. It seemed that every time I blinked, the lab technicians were poking me here and there, trying to extract more blood. Warm tears rolled down my cheeks. Like the psalmist David, "in my distress I . . . cried unto my God: He heard my voice" (Ps. 18:6).

Instantly, God spoke to me through a familiar song on the radio: "Tell Jesus when the way is dark before you and the path is hid from view; when you grope with steps uncertain and you know not what to do, . . . tell Jesus, blessed Jesus. He has grace to meet your need."

My focus on myself and my illness had blinded my view of the presence of the Holy Spirit and prevented me from praising God for saving my life. Some people never recover from pulmonary embolisms. He had performed a miracle, and instead of rejoicing I was downcast.

God, You're so good to me; thank You for reminding me how much You love and care for me.

Shirley C. Iheanacho

Promises Made, Promises Broken

Blessed be the Lord, that hath given rest unto his people Israel, according to all that he promised: there hath not failed one word of all his good promise, which he promised by the hand of Moses his servant. 1 Kings 8:56.

THERE ARE MANY seven-letter words in the dictionary, but there's only one that frequently comes to my mind—*promise.*

I've encountered promises made—some kept and some broken. For example, taking my car to the shop for repair and being promised it would be ready the next day. Instead, I receive it three days later. Or taking clothes to the cleaners, and it takes five days instead of the promised three.

A promise made to me years ago comes to mind. Sometimes my mother gave me small tasks to do and always promised to reward me for doing a good job, which she did. However, one day she promised that if I did a good job cleaning up my room we would go buy candy.

How happy I was as I began thinking about candy as I cleaned my room! After I finished my task, Mother inspected and said, "What a good job you have done! But honey, we can't walk to the store today."

Sadly, I asked, "Why, Mother? You promised."

Giving me a hug, she said, "Your mother is too tired to walk to the store today." Mom's answer didn't mend the broken promise.

As years go by, the word *promise* is still used as a basis for expectation. I recall a promise I made to my first-grade class: if they were good children for the day, I would have cookies for them the next day. But on the way home I forgot to stop to buy the cookies. And on my way to school the next morning there was a traffic jam, and I couldn't stop. I hoped that the children wouldn't remember my promise and that I wouldn't have to give an excuse. However, one little girl was brave enough to ask about the promised cookies.

After explaining why my promise had been broken and letting the class know I was very sorry, I made sure the second promise was kept, and cookies were in the class the next day.

I thank God for His precious promise, given to me and all who follow and believe, that He will give eternal life. I look forward to that blessed promise, knowing that He has not—and will not—fail one word of all His promises.

ANNIE B. BEST

Taxi Bargain

For what shall it profit a man, if he shall gain the whole world, and lose his own soul? Mark 8:36.

MY FRIEND BRENDA and I had a long layover at Manila airport. We decided to go to a recommended hotel where we could rest in comfort. We hailed a metered taxi and paid 50 pesos for the short ride. When we finished lunch we asked the hotel doorman to call a metered taxi for us. "Airport," we told him. We put our luggage inside, and he took off. However, a half block away he stopped and asked, "How much you pay?"

"The meter," I said.

"No meter!" he shook his head. "How much you pay?"

"Fifty pesos," I said. "Coming we paid 50 pesos."

"Now too much traffic," he insisted. "Three hundred pesos."

We could see traffic was moving very slowly, but we said, "Too much! One hundred only."

"One hundred fifty. Last price," He said. When I refused, the driver got out of the taxi and put our luggage on the sidewalk. We got out.

Taxi after taxi went by. At last we got another one to stop. He asked 500 pesos and drove off when we refused his last price of 300.

It was late afternoon. The tropical sun beat upon us. Exhaust fumes choked us. Taxi after taxi refused to stop. Brenda decided to try bargaining when the next one stopped.

"How much to airport?" she asked.

When he said "Two hundred," Brenda wisely agreed, and we got in. It took nearly an hour to get to the airport in rush-hour traffic, a distance we had traveled in minutes coming the other way. We paid four times what we had paid in the morning, but we felt we got a real bargain. At that point we were willing to pay whatever it took to get us to the airport. After all, what was the gain of a few hundred pesos if we missed our flight?

I wonder sometimes if I'm not like that when it comes to my journey to heaven. I try to bargain with God, thinking I can have my way, "hold on to my pesos," so to speak. However, He insists that I give up *all* if I want to reach my heavenly home. As long as I insist on having it my way, I'm not going to get there. There is no bargaining with God.

DOROTHY EATON WATTS

Good Gifts

If you, then, though you are evil, know how to give good gifts to your children, how much more will your Father in heaven give good gifts to those who ask him! Matt. 7:11, NIV.

LORD, I NEED a car." I had just moved back in, temporarily, with my parents and was without transportation. Or money. I didn't know what else to do, so I prayed. (Why is it that so often prayer is a last resort?) During the next few weeks my dad and I did online researches and pounded the pavement at every dealership in town. I really wanted a Honda Civic.

Finally, we found a 3-year-old blue Civic that I only "kind of" liked and could "more or less" afford. Nonetheless, I was excited, as everything seemed to be working out. It was late Friday afternoon by this time, so we told the salesman we'd be back on Monday to fill out the paperwork.

Saturday night my friend Dean called. "You haven't bought a car yet, have you?" he asked. I filled him in on the pending deal, and he said, "Don't do it. I think I might have something better for you." Then he proceeded to tell me of a Honda Civic EX (top-of-the-line model) that was less than a year old. It had power everything, a CD player—even a moon roof. And only 15,000 miles on it. My obvious question came next: "How much?" My jaw dropped when he told me it would be nearly $5,000 less than the car I had on hold. It was even my favorite color. Before letting my hopes rise too much, I asked the next obvious question: "What's the catch?"

It had been in a wreck, but Dean fixes and resells cars for a living. He promised me there was no frame damage. All he'd have to do was fix a headlight, replace two doors, and repaint the whole thing, and I'd have a brand-new car. Not only that, but he'd give me a lifetime warranty on his work for as long as I owned it.

I could almost see God smiling as He said, "Vick, not only am I going to give you a car; I'm going to give you a *car!*" Not only did He answer my prayer for transportation; He dropped a reliable, beautiful little car right in my lap—and even gave me all the extras I could never have afforded!

Read today's verse again. Trust Him. He means it.

VICKI MACOMBER REDDEN

When I Was on My Knees

Be joyful in hope, patient in affliction, faithful in prayer. Rom. 12:12, NIV.

THIRTY-FOUR OF US from our church in Maryland joined more than 500 young people from all over the world to do community projects in Thailand. There were several projects to choose from, but our group chose the Elephant Reforestation Project, whose goal was to help preserve the habitat of the elephants. The project site was located about four hour's drive from Bangkok.

We started early that Monday morning in Bangkok to get to the work site, because that was the same day more than 500 volunteers were to meet not only the governor of Thailand but other dignitaries from the government of Thailand and from the world headquarters of our church. The program began with the volunteers marching in as a special band played music. We were seated at our beautifully decorated tables and listened as the world youth director welcomed us; followed by the governor, who expressed his appreciation to the volunteers.

Then came the best part: it was time for my daughter, Susan, to give her response to the governor's speech. I'd been wondering how I would squeeze in through the many photographers to get a good picture of Susan. There was simply no way I'd be able to get to the front. Then an idea came to me: Use my knees! This was great! I'd surely be able to get through if I crawled on my knees. So I got down on my knees and without any difficulty was right there in front—very close to the stage—and was able to get a good picture of Susan.

Even during the convention that followed there in Bangkok, I knew the technique to use for getting through the crowds of photographers: get down on my knees. When I was on my knees, I was able to get a good view of whatever picture I wanted to take.

When we are on our knees we can easily see the picture that our Lord Jesus wants us to see. Our only way to understand what is happening in our lives and to be able to move on through is to be down on our knees.

Today let's "be joyful in hope, patient in affliction, faithful in prayer."

JEMIMA D. ORILLOSA

Waiting on God

Your word is a lamp to my feet and a light for my path. Ps. 119:105, NIV.

HAVE YOU EVER BEEN in the dark and not known which direction to go? The light that is supposed to light the path beneath your feet isn't leading forward; it has stopped. The only light you see ahead is the flickering light of fireflies. You're stopped, but you're ready to go. You put a small step forward this way, and then a small step forward that way. You long for that path of light beneath your feet. *I'm ready, Lord. Where are You?*

When King Saul needed direction, and God was silent, he sinned by trying to consult with dead Samuel. When the path was seemingly blocked by old age, Abraham and Sarah also decided to take the dark path of human reasoning. We may give excuses, but we really still have direction—from the Word of God. We still know to choose right from wrong. We still know we are to love our neighbor. We still know not to consult spirits. And sometimes, even when we walk the lit path, it may seem to lead to trouble, as in the case of Joseph and Potiphar's wife.

Sometimes, when we're stopped, I believe God is allowing us to see our character. We really are still walking in the pathway, but in the realm of patience and trust in Him. Patience and trust—two attributes God values much higher than we do. In the case of Abraham and Sarah, they needed patience and trust to believe God would deliver on His promise. Job stated, "Though he [God] slay me, yet will I trust in him." Joseph knew his path could not include sinning against God.

Being stopped may also allow time for repentance and renewal in the Lord. Had King Saul repented of his actions and sought the Lord in fasting and in prayer, his story could have been much different. If we look at being stopped as a blessing from the Lord, as a time for repentance, for recommitment, for developing patience and trust, for refreshment in the Lord, we may actually enjoy waiting. Our desire, after all, is to be in God's will. If we are stopped, that's just where God wants us to be. We can enjoy the extra time spent exclusively with Him.

In direction, in opportunities, in open doors, it is best to be aware that God is growing our insides to be able to handle the outside. When that is done, it will be time to be moving on again, walking in the path of light unto our feet.

JOYCE VICKARYOUS

A Tiny Miracle

Behold, I am the Lord, the God of all flesh; is there any thing too hard for me? Jer. 32:27.

A CHURCH CAMPOUT WAS the last place I wanted to go. It had been only a few months since my husband had passed away, and I had a lot to sort out in my mind. I didn't need anything else to add to my list. However, my 9-year-old twin daughters delighted in the idea. So with my enthusiasm low and my stress level high, we began packing. In addition to sleeping bags, clothing, and food, we added hearing-aid batteries because the girls are hearing-impaired.

Singing around the campfire that evening began to lighten my heavy heart. The following morning, after an outdoor church service and potluck luncheon, someone organized a treasure hunt for the youngsters. I walked down to the nearby river to be alone with my thoughts.

I'd been there only a short time when Tracy rushed up to me. "Mother, Dawn lost her hearing aid! Running made it jiggle, so she put it in the pocket of her jeans to keep from losing it, but it's gone!" We looked at each other, then without a word ran back to the camp.

When I saw the large area that the treasure hunt encompassed, my hopes, like my faith, began to dim. It had been a dry summer. How would we ever find a tiny, tan hearing aid tucked between weeds and grasses of the same color? There was only one way possible. We joined hands in a circle and asked the Lord for a miracle.

Then people formed a line, walking close to one another, carefully looking between dried-up wildflowers, foxtails, and other thirsty plant life. Ten minutes into the search, Dawn and a friend broke from the line of volunteers and went back to a spot where they had previously searched.

They've already covered that area, I thought, a bit dismayed. *Why don't they find a new place?"*

Then I saw my daughter bend down and pick up something from the ground. Her face beamed as she ran over to me, waving her hearing aid in the air. Everyone cheered!

A new prayer circle began to form. As we gave thanks to the Lord, He gently reminded me that when people join hands and pray, He loves to work miracles; whether it's finding a tiny hearing aid for a little girl, or renewing the faith of a discouraged mother.

MARCIA MOLLENKOPF

May 28

Living for the Lord

For none of us lives to himself alone and none of us dies to himself alone. . . . So, whether we live or die, we belong to the Lord. Rom. 14:7, 8, NIV.

A STUDENT WHO HAD BEEN dismissed from his school in Erfurt, Germany, saw no other solution to his problems than to kill as many of his teachers as possible. Fourteen teachers and two students were shot dead within 10 minutes. This action plunged the whole German nation into shock. Most people can't comprehend such things.

Our feelings are blunted by all the terrible news provided through the media. We can deal only with a limited amount of pain and suffering. I was aware of the tragedy, but it left me more or less cold. Only when I saw the piles of flowers on the steps of the school did my tears start flowing. On a card with a picture of one of the teachers were the words "Mummy, why did you have to die?" This card made the people real for me—tangible and personal.

Johannes Rau, president of the German republic, spoke moving and earnest words at the memorial service. I watched the service on the TV, choking back my tears. "We live next to each other and often don't know each other. We go to school or work together and don't care one for another. If our society, our families, small entities, schools, and companies are to hold together, we have to care one for the other. . . . We need two things: we must respect each other, and we must care one for the other. We must respect each other: nobody should be pushed to a point where he thinks that his life is worthless. . . . Nobody can live without kindness, security, and love. Everybody has worth because of who he is, and not because of what he does. . . . To care for others means to help them on, to be there for them."

Even we Christians don't always care for others as we should. We often think that we don't have the time to care for others. Our personal struggles seem to be all that we can handle. So we live our lives for ourselves. But God wants us to be there for others. To take care of God's children for Him. To live for the Lord, and to open our eyes to the needs of the people around us. To care for them in love. We do not live for ourselves. We live for the Lord.

HANNELE OTTSCHOFSKI

Blessed Hope

For I know the thoughts that I think toward you, saith the Lord, thoughts of peace, and not of evil, to give you an expected end. Jer. 29:11.

DEAR LORD," I PRAYED one morning, "please find me an afternoon shift. It would be so much easier to manage." I had just recuperated from surgery and was ready to start work. Even though I didn't see how I could get the shift I wanted, I had decided to pray about it.

The phone rang within the hour. It was the nursing registry. "Can you work the afternoon shift?" the woman on the phone asked. "We have a patient whose family wants to have an RN rather than an LPN. You would be perfect." Before I called, God had answered!

I went to the hospital the next day and met my new patient. Mr. J. was conscious and responsive, but I could see that the end was near. So could his family and the hospital staff. Driving home the second night, a Voice said to me, "This is the most important part of this man's life. What are you doing about it?"

I replied instantly. "Lord, You know I'm not permitted to talk about religion in the hospital. But if You want me to talk to him, keep him alive until tomorrow."

Mr. J appeared unconscious when I arrived that afternoon. His vitals had just been taken, so I sat down. The voice spoke again: "If you want to talk to him, do it now."

I got up and walked to the side of his bed. Mr. J's eyes were closed. His breathing was labored. He was sweating profusely. Taking a towel to dry his face, I whispered. "Mr. J, I don't know if you are Christian." Then, as if prompted by the Spirit, I began again. "Mr. J, I want to tell you that Jesus loves you. If you ask Him to forgive you of your sins, He will forgive you."

Mr. J opened his eyes immediately and looked upward. A gentle peace came over his face. His labored breathing slowed. His eyes closed. His elegant, 80-year-old mother seemed comforted when I told her that God had been with us as her son breathed his last.

God always has a bigger plan, but He let me see His handiwork all through that experience. He answered my prayer for the afternoon shift. He let me hear Him speak. He gave me time to witness to the patient before he died. Our God is able to use us in ways we will never understand until He comes.

MADGE S. MAY

May 30

My Bed of Affliction

The Lord is not slow in keeping his promise, as some understand slowness. He is patient with you, not wanting anyone to perish, but everyone to come to repentance. 2 Peter 3:9, NIV.

I CAN NEVER READ today's text without thinking of a defining moment in my spiritual life. It happened a long time ago when I was seriously ill, my condition worsening daily. The fevers and diarrhea persisted. Nothing I ate or drank could be digested. I was becoming weaker and more emaciated by the moment. Nothing seemed to help. *What is happening to me?* I wondered.

Eventually, I had to be taken to the hospital. Diagnosis: malaria and pneumonia. I did not improve. In fact, I became even more ill. Temporarily deaf because of incorrect medication, I lay in bed with my eyes closed, not even conscious of the summer sunshine I had once enjoyed so much. I was too weak to speak, too fearful to try. Only the breath in my body remained.

For an entire month I lay at death's door, unresponsive to my surroundings. All hope for my recovery had vanished. Tearfully my family made plans for my burial.

But one day I awoke to the sound of music, sweet singing. Opening my eyes, I saw a dais descending from heaven toward my hospital bed. On the dais were beings whose flowing white robes seemed ruffled by a gentle breeze. As the dais drew nearer, they sang, "Daughter of Zion, awake from thy sadness; awake, let thy sins oppress thee no more." Even in my semiconscious state, I knew that I had changed the word—from 'foes' to 'sins.' I began to pray, pleading and bargaining with God, begging for His healing, and confessing my sins. Almost immediately I began to improve, but the process was very slow—four and a half months slow. The most difficult part was learning to walk again and to overcome fear. After a while I learned to tell others of His glorious, saving power.

Thank You, dear Father, for rescuing me from my bed of affliction. Thank You for reminding me that the time is Yours. No longer will I fear. Thank You for Your patience, love, and grace. May I continue to be a witness of Your almighty power.

God is not slow in keeping His promise—it is just that His timing and purposes may be different from ours. May we each have His patience today.

EILEEN FURLONGE

Heavenly Home

Eye hath not seen, nor ear heard, neither have entered into the heart of man, the things which God hath prepared for them that love him. 1 Cor. 2:9.

FINALLY, A TRIP TO the mountains! This long-awaited jaunt seemed overdue. Together with friends, Ziata and Helen, I began to eagerly explore towns, shops, and anything that appeared interesting. A visit to the Biltmore House, while in the Asheville, North Carolina, area, was on our "must" list. How we oohed and aahed at the furnishings and architectural splendor. Each space and room seemed grander than the one before.

The rich brocades, velvets, satins, and leathers are far more luxurious than any in our homes; the woodcarvings were something to behold. Such opulence! After hours of admiring the house, we proceeded to the nursery and gardens. We enjoyed many plants that were new to us and reveled in their exquisiteness. The variety and beauty were almost overwhelming.

What must our heavenly home be like? We know the plantings and things of this earth are such a faint reflection of what is being prepared for us. Nothing can compare to the preparations that are being made. When we contemplate this, we know we cannot even begin to imagine the glorious home Christ is arranging for us. Temporal things become insignificant—no longer desirable. "And he shewed me a pure river of water of life, clear as crystal, proceeding out of the throne of God and of the Lamb. In the midst of the street of it, and on either side of the river, was there the tree of life, which bare twelve manner of fruits, and yielded her fruit every month: and the leaves of the tree were for the healing of the nations" (Rev. 22:1, 2).

Even the magnificent flowers and wonderful vegetation that we so delight in now will pale to nothingness then. The delightful scenery that so enthralls us here will not compare to what is being prepared for us. What excitement to remember the words: Eye hath not seen, nor ear heard, nor entered into the heart of man, the things God has prepared for those who love Him.

Whom does God love? You and me! Today is the day to establish our plans to be there with Him, through His grace.

DOROTHY WAINWRIGHT CAREY

Two Are Better Than One

Two are better than one, because they have a good return for their work: If one falls down, his friend can help him up. But pity the man who falls and has no one to help him up! Also, if two lie down together, they will keep warm. But how can one keep warm alone? Though one may be overpowered, two can defend themselves. A cord of three strands is not quickly broken. Eccl. 4:9-12, NIV.

I FACED THE MOUNTAINSIDE with trepidation. It was a steep slope, unmarked by a path, and well strewn with rocks and roots. My daughter, two granddaughters, and I had just arrived at a well-marked path, but now my daughter decided that we had come too far to go back the way we had come. However, she was sure that if we zigzagged across this slope to a lower elevation and hiked around the mountain we could find a shorter path back to our campsite.

I agreed to her proposal, but I wondered at my ability to carry it out. My daughter, Julie, and 6-year-old Tami started down the hillside, carefully avoiding the pitfalls. Four-year-old Kimi and I followed. Kimi had no doubts: she and Grandma could do anything. My problem was that I wasn't sure that I could have covered that assignment alone with ease. How could I protect and help a chubby 4-year-old when it was difficult for me by myself? It was then that I learned the lesson of "two are better than one." Kimi's two sturdy legs—connected to me by her hand in mine—balanced my unsure legs, and we made a great team as we slowly traversed the hillside. Four legs are surely better than two! Besides, she sang her happy little song, "God made the mountains, He made the trees, He made the rocks—and He made me," as we followed in the footsteps of Julie and Tami, laughing at the hard places.

Soon we were at the bottom and, sure enough, we found the trail home.

What a lesson I learned that day! When we are too fearful to go ahead in life, too wounded even to smile, we must look beyond our pain for another wounded soul and start out on the trail of life together. If we never withdraw into ourselves, choosing rather to share someone else's grief and pain, our own pain will be lessened. That is God's plan for us women: to share each other's burdens. The hillside won't seem so treacherous, so fearful, when two of us, hand in hand with each other and God, set out to cross the uneven ground.

CARROL JOHNSON SHEWMAKE

Thoughts on Prayer

Pray continually. 1 Thess. 5:17, NIV.

YOUNG JIMMY AND BOBBY once were asked if they prayed every day. Jimmy said, "Not in the morning, because I'm not scared in the daytime." And Bobby truthfully answered, "Well, no, not every day. Some days I don't need anything."

Although many of our prayers are self-centered, we should pray for others just as we would like them to pray for us. Does God want us to pray only when we are scared or in need of something? No; indeed not!

While it is true we don't have to talk to God because He knows what we need and want before we ask Him (see Matt. 6:8), He longs for us to talk to Him, just as we sometimes long to talk to an earthly friend.

Ellen White, who wrote a great deal on the topic of prayer, said: "Keep your wants, your joys, your sorrows, your cares, and your fears before God. You cannot burden Him; you cannot weary Him. . . . 'The Lord is very pitiful, and of tender mercy!' (James 5:11). . . . Nothing that in any way concerns our peace is too small for Him to notice" (*Steps to Christ,* p. 100).

In today's verse Paul tells us to "pray continually." If we did that we wouldn't get anything else done! I feel Paul means we should be in an attitude of prayer continually.

I've had people tell me, "I will say a prayer for you tonight," and I hope they don't forget! If I promise to pray for someone, I try to do so as soon and as often as possible. And when I hear sirens or see a car alongside the road with the hood up, I promptly say, "Please be with whomever and whatever."

I believe we all wonder what to ask God for sometimes. Romans 8:26 helps: "We do not know what we ought to pray for, but the Spirit himself intercedes for us with groans that words cannot express" (NIV). And, praise God, He understands!

Heavenly Father, I am so grateful that prayer is spiritual communion with You and awareness of Your presence. It can be in the form of thanksgiving, praise, confession, or even talking to You as a friend!

PATSY MURDOCH MEEKER

Preparation, Preparation

You also be patient. Establish your hearts, for the coming of the Lord is at hand. James 5:8, NKJV.

EVERYONE AT HOME was very busy collecting the addresses of friends and family members in preparation for the wedding. All the relatives, colleagues, neighbors (known and unknown), and friends (near and far) were invited to the wedding. This was the first wedding in our family—the day I was to be married. The wedding went well, and everyone at home felt relieved that the preparations were over.

A few months later, when our parents found out that I was pregnant, everyone was very happy and suggested lots of rules and regulations for the mother-to-be to follow. Other mothers became instant doctors with lots of advice: don't eat this, don't sleep straight, don't do this, or that. It would be very hard for any mother-to-be to heed all their rules and suggestions. I obeyed some of the advice, and dismissed others.

I longed for a daughter, and my wish came true when we got the scan report. I wanted to buy clothing and essential things for her, but I was told it was best to wait until after the birth of the baby to buy most things. Even so, I insisted on buying a few things. The day came for me to be admitted to the hospital to await for the anticipated arrival. I was the first one in the family to have a Cesarean, and my parents were unhappy about that. But when they saw the baby they were very happy, as they had become grandparents.

In both instances—my marriage and the baby's arrival—much preparation was involved. In fact, at times we thought that no one had ever prepared better. But how happy we were to prepare! There were lots of dreams involved in the preparation for various reasons—sometimes successful, and sometimes unsuccessful.

My attention is drawn to Jesus' second coming. Am I prepared for His coming? Am I even thinking about it? Am I careful about my actions and talk? What will I answer to all these questions? I need to remind myself that His coming is soon, and that I must be prepared before it is too late.

Lord, speak to my heart and help me to prepare, for the coming of the Lord is at hand.

SOPHIA JASMINE SAMSON

A Dress for Every Occasion

And He said to me, "My grace is sufficient for you, for My strength is made perfect in weakness." 2 Cor. 12:9, NKJV.

WHAT IS IT ABOUT a woman's wardrobe that makes her life so difficult? Could it be that just this morning you noticed a bulge or two in a new spot? Or you've even caught yourself breathing in just to button your skirt?

We've all been there. My fear may be that a slight weight gain could spiral out of control. You, on the other hand, may fear that you will be forever too thin; and yet another friend will ask you if you are sick or anorexic. Today, don't look in the mirror. Accept yourself just as you are. Begin to deal with the things that bring you grief. Then go to your closet, and pick out the prettiest dress you have.

Let me tell you about my favorite. It's called "grace." You could say it's the only thing I wear these days. I'm sure you have the same dress hanging in your closet, but perhaps you haven't realized it. As I describe it, you'll see why I choose no other.

God's grace is the ultimate garment. You never tire of wearing it, especially since it shows itself in different colors on different days. It feels very comfortable. In fact, often you forget you have it on. It is easy to clean—even the worst spots can be washed away. Others see it and want an exact copy of what you are wearing. Although they put on the same garment and others can tell it is from the same designer, your grace is especially tailored for you—and you alone! Grace is made from priceless material—there is nothing else like it. The give-and-take of the fabric causes it to resize every day to your exact dimensions. Grace looks best when worn naturally. The wearer has no need to be self-conscious. You are assured of a perfect fit and that the garment given you is the exact one you would choose if you had all knowledge and saw things clearly rather than darkly.

The price, too, is wonderful: it's free! Yet you cannot buy it for yourself for all the money in the world. You come to appreciate the grace you have been given most when you know the Designer intimately. GINGER CHURCH

Staying Close

But let all those that put their trust in thee rejoice: let them ever shout for joy, because thou defendest them: let them also that love thy name be joyful in thee. Ps. 5:11.

HAVE YOU FELT CLOSE to anyone? When you hold your children, hug a friend, or kiss your husband? God is like that, but I think in a much bigger and more fantastic way.

I went to boarding school in India in the first grade, up in the Himalayan Mountains. My mother was not very happy about it, but there weren't very many choices. I thought it was great fun, but I would also get very lonely. Night was the worst. They would put us little girls to bed, then turn off the lights. (I still don't like to sleep in the dark.) I knew that when I slept God was with me because I could feel His presence every night. When I was lonely in that dark room, I would say a prayer and truly could feel His angels around me!

A few years ago I visited my parents in Bangalore, India. I felt sure I wouldn't get sick since I believed that I had a strong immune system. Because I had lived in India all my childhood, I was in good health—for about two days. Then I got sick. My mother helped me by feeding me soup and the things that I needed to get well. I started to feel better but seemed to want to sleep a lot. About the third day I woke up to my little sister (an adopted Indian girl, then 3 years old) singing "Jesus Loves Me" while sitting on the side of my bed. I felt so much better hearing her sweet voice. That feeling of love has held me close many times, again and again.

We all have many memories, and I think that if we ask God to help us remember some of the good ones it will help us get through the bad situations that we encounter in our lives.

Lord, it is when we forget how You have led us in the past that we become fearful. Help us each to remember Your goodness that is revealed in so many ways. May that memory give us joy as we walk through both the light and the dark hours of this day.

When we are feeling alone or sick or just wanting assurance of love, Scripture can meet our deepest need. You may want to memorize today's text; then you too will want to shout for joy! SUSEN MATTISON MOLÉ

No Disaster Will Come Near Your Dwelling

If you make the Most High your dwelling—even the Lord, who is my refuge—then no harm will befall you, no disaster will come near your tent. Ps. 91:9, 10, NIV.

AS I OPENED THE drapes in my dining room one morning, I looked up at the opening in the roof over the front garden area. Much to my surprise, two of the beams in the opening were hanging down several inches and didn't appear to be attached on one side.

In southwest Florida your first thought is termites. A close inspection from the termite company determined that it was not termites—much to my relief! A water problem had rotted one end of the beams. Since I would be leaving Florida to spend the summer in Michigan with my family, I was thankful to have discovered this problem before I left so the repairs could be done.

The carpenter came and removed part of the obviously rotted wood, but found some more in the facing around the opening. When he took off part of the facing, he called me to take a look at what he had discovered. Behind the facing, at least two feet of the wood was scorched and black from a fire that had smoldered, hidden by the facing. His discovery was quite a shock to me. He asked me if we had ever had a light fixture or Christmas decorations mounted in that area that might have shorted out and caused a contained fire. At first I couldn't think of any electrical problems. After a few minutes, though, I remembered that seven or eight years earlier we had had a very severe lightning storm with lots of rain. At one point during the storm one of our tall palm trees, close to the front of the house, had been struck. The power of that bolt of lightning shorted out our security system and our Malibu lights and sent tiny stones from our landscaping into our car with such force that they dented it in several places. It was evidently then that a small fire had ignited behind the facing. The Lord was good and sent an angel to put out the fire so that the rest of our house didn't also catch on fire. This was all unbeknown to us.

Someday our guardian angels will reveal to us how many times we were protected from harm while we were unaware. What surprises we are going to enjoy hearing about from these angels!

I'm looking forward to that wonderful day. What a day that will be!

PATRICIA MULRANEY KOVALSKI

The Accidental Thump

Thou wilt keep him in perfect peace, whose mind is stayed on thee. Isa. 26:3.

I WAS STOPPED AT A traffic light some distance from our church one Sabbath evening, when I suddenly felt a huge thump to the rear of my car. Glancing behind me, I noticed a police cruiser. *What happened?* I asked myself. *I know I did nothing wrong.*

Still sitting in my car, I waited for the officer's next move; I could see him on his phone. Finally he came to my window. "I'm so sorry, ma'am," he began. "I was looking at a rather unusual occurrence across the road and didn't notice that the light had turned red. I'm so sorry," he apologized again. "I had to call my boss to report this accident. That's why it took so long for me to get to you. May I see your license and insurance, please?"

When I handed the documents over, he asked me to pull over to the right side of the road. I knew I was going to be late for the vesper program. But in what seemed no time, three police cruisers surrounded my car—the chief and two other patrol officers!

The patrol cruiser had sustained extensive front-end damage. My Toyota, however, was dusty but not even scratched. "Look," I suggested, pointing to my undamaged vehicle, "this is the type of car you should be driving." Smiling, the chief gave me his card and asked me to call should I need his help in the future. I'm sure he thought that I might have some delayed reaction to the accident. Fortunately, I've never experienced any ill effects from the crash that occurred years ago.

My daughter-in-law, who is a lieutenant state trooper, was amused when I told her about the incident. "Now you know from personal experience how good it is to have all your documents on hand should you suddenly need to present them."

Relating the experience to my husband that night, I thought of how wonderfully dependable my heavenly Father is. He is all-seeing. There will be no bumps, accidental or otherwise, that He caused. Nor do I need a phone to contact Him. He is always with me. And I have His insurance. He knows who I am and immediately sends scores of angel guards whenever I need them. All I have to do is trust Him.

Thank You for keeping me safe, heavenly Father. My peaceful mind is stayed on You.

MARJORIE HALL

Thanks Be to God

I have been young, and now am old; yet I have not seen the righteous forsaken or his children begging bread. Ps. 37:25, RSV.

EVERY DAY I THANK God for life and all the surprises—happy surprises—disappointments, pain, and discipline the day has brought. These are what have sustained me. My teenage life was not full of happy surprises. Those were the Depression years. Parents had to be very inventive to provide their children with surprises that brought laughter and joy.

Marriage and families brought both happiness and disappointment and occasional sorrow, depending on the choices we made through the years. Those we faced and made the best of were the most successful.

Now the final chapter approaches, blending all the years' activities, failures, and achievements into a composite memory. If we are still blessed with physical and mental capabilities, we see how people, events, and all other things we have encountered have influenced us. In the mirror I see my mother; I see my father in the way I drum my fingers when I'm nervous. I even understand my siblings better.

I appreciate my many dear friends so much more, especially so since a number of others have passed away and I can no longer enjoy their friendship. Some were so close that I credit them with keeping me close to my Savior.

My children are mature now and oh, the joy when I see them overcoming problems in situations similar to my own—and sometimes doing it better than I did. When they succeed where I feel I failed, I am thankful for their success and happiness. Their success is my success. However, I attribute all our successes to God for the promises He has kept. I think of the man who thought himself walking alone on the beach until God reminded him that where footprints were missing he was being carried in God's arms. I know that feeling in my own life.

The joy of seeing a child returning to the Lord after meandering and losing focus on life for a time is something which must be experienced to be appreciated. Truly I can say, "I have not seen the righteous forsaken or his children begging bread."

Thank You once again, kind heavenly Father. GRACE STREIFLING

June 9

Beyond Results

In all things God works for the good of those who love him. Rom. 8:28, NIV.

ONE SABBATH MORNING a big, beautiful, fresh flower arrangement of roses decorated the center table in front of the pulpit. I love flowers, but I can't afford to buy them. After the worship service I took them home and displayed them in our living room.

Thursday evening my husband arrived home from his job upset and sad because his bag of electrical tools had been stolen. It would be very hard for us to find the money to replace them, as we have Shelah in college, and a son, Seth, in high school. We both also volunteer in God's work by holding evangelistic meetings, following up on Bible studies, and nurturing newly baptized members.

That Friday evening at the vesper service I heard my brother-in-law, our church deacon, lose his temper because the previous week the flowers he had provided for church were stolen. I was shocked and guilty—I had thought they were of no value to him. I had followed the example of some other women who had picked up flowers and taken them home after the service.

Days passed, and my husband lost his job. I borrowed some small capital so I could buy and sell fruit. Always in a hurry because of responsibilities at home, in the church, and in the community, I bought 36 kilograms of watermelon at P6.00 per kilogram. I gave P125 in good faith that it was enough. When I arrived home, I realized it should have been P216. I failed to return because I had no money. Two days later I discovered that the fruit was full of worms and had to be destroyed. No capital, no gain.

Sometimes we are depressed because of our failures, problems, and our own ignorance. But I praise God in my mistakes, because I learned that God still loves me. He reminds me, however, not to keep on sinning. Yes, He has promised that we can walk in the right way, living in truth because God has decided on an even better plan for us. Hebrews 11:40 says that it is His purpose that we will be made perfect: "God had planned something better for us so that only together with us would they be made perfect" (NIV).

Lord, I ask for Your forgiveness, and I look forward to what You plan to do through and for me. ANNIE RUIZ

My Father Loves Me

The Lord thy God . . . will joy over thee with singing. Zeph. 3:17.

SUNDAY MORNING'S WARM sun streamed in my windows, warming my covers. It was especially welcome because of our long, dreary winter. Warming me even more were thoughts aching to be processed. Our weekend speaker had said that we each have God's approval, that God even says about us, "This is my beloved daughter in whom I am well pleased." I can personalize that text: "This is my beloved daughter Becki, in whom I am well pleased."

As a little girl I'd wanted my father's approval, somehow feeling as if I never quite had it. One day, as my dad was finishing lunch, I wiped the table. *He must be so proud of me,* I thought, *doing my best.* But as I finished with a flourish, he pointed out some crumbs I had left behind. I was crushed! Nothing I could do ever seemed enough to please him. Much later, as I was finishing my master's degree, I asked him if he was pleased with me. He put his arm around me and reassured me that he was proud of me and that I did please him. Yet 25 years later I was still hearing more of his criticism and disapproval than of his love.

Still leading me, God brought my thoughts back to the beginning of my life. One of my favorite childhood photos is one of Heidi, my older sister, sitting on the grass, with me on my dad's shoulders. That picture confirms to me that he did want me and loved me. But because of his own upbringing he had a difficult time showing it; and, naturally, I couldn't perceive it.

Tears flowed as I let the realization of my earthly father's love wash over me. Only then was I able to realize and feel my heavenly Father's love, as well. God's love is without condition and doesn't depend on my performance. He approves of me and is pleased with me.

God brought to my mind a text and scripture song already personalized. "The Lord, my God, in the midst of me is mighty, mighty. He will save, He will rejoice over me with joy, with joy. I will rest in his love, He will joy over me with singing. The Lord, my God, in the midst of me is mighty, mighty, mighty" (see Zeph. 3:17). God delights over me, sings over me. Amazing!

I have always been driven, always trying to prove my worth and value to those around me. Now, I can relax, slow down a bit, smell the roses. As a reminder, I have that photo beside my bed. Daily it reminds me of that early-spring morning as the sun streamed warm onto my bed.

Becki Knobloch

The Hope We Have

May the God of hope fill you with all joy and peace as you trust in him, so that you may overflow with hope by the power of the Holy Spirit. Rom. 15:13, NIV.

IT HAD BEEN ALMOST a year since my father passed away. Not one day had gone by when I didn't think about him. Standing near the baggage compartment in a busy airport, waiting for my daughter to arrive, I was barely conscious of the usual airport noise around me—people talking, laughing, rushing here and there. Then a voice rang out above the general hubbub, and I heard, "Daddy! Daddy! I've never been so happy to see you! I'm so very glad you're here!"

I looked up and saw a woman, probably in her late 40s or early 50s, moving quickly through the crowd. I turned in the direction she was heading, and then I saw him—an old man, thin, quite frail looking, shuffling down the hallway toward his daughter. This was the way my father had looked the last few years of his life. How I envied that woman! I wanted to run over and tell her how blessed she was and how much she needed to treasure every moment she had with her dad. But I didn't do that. Looking at her face, I didn't think I needed to do so. She already knew.

My dad and I had always been close. He was a quiet man who enjoyed nothing more than puttering around his small yard or lying on a lawn chair reading a book and soaking up the sunshine. I would sit in a chair beside him, reading my own book, and we would talk occasionally about family situations, world events, or religion. Religion was never a comfortable topic for us, though. My mom, my older brother, and I had been Christians for many years, but my dad had never made that decision. Events during his early years had "soured" him on God, and he never quite seemed to come to the place where he could accept Jesus as his Savior. However, many changes had occurred in my dad's attitude and behavior over the years. They were gradual, but when they came, they stayed. And they gave us hope.

Now my dad is no longer with us. The backyard at my mom's house is empty without him. I miss him very much. But in my mind's eye I visualize meeting him again. I see him walking toward me, no longer frail and weak, but strong and happy and smiling. I rush to him, and I say, "Daddy! Daddy! I've never been so happy to see you! I'm so very glad you're here!"

This is the hope we have in Jesus. This is what life is all about.

SANDRA BLACKMER

We Are Light

While I am in the world, I am the light of the world. John 9:5, NIV.

I WAS TOTALLY EUPHORIC! That afternoon I had gone to the hairdressers, my new outfit was ready, my shoes were intact, and I was ready! After all, it had been four years that I had closely watched the struggle that my husband had experienced to finish a theology degree. This would be the great day, the day of victory. Finishing college was a dream that was now coming true. Our parents had come from Minas Gerais just to attend the graduation.

We arrived at the church as the day was ending. The photographers were waiting for us at the door; there was illumination everywhere as people recorded this historic moment.

At the exact moment when the ceremony was ready to begin, the lights suddenly went out. The electrical technicians quickly worked to restore the electricity. We waited a short while, and the solemnities continued. The much awaited graduation ceremony had begun. What a surprise and disappointment when the lights went out once again—this time for good.

I wasn't able to see my husband receive his diploma; no one was able to see anything. It was at that time I realized the great importance of light. We can see only the beautiful events and scenes of this world if we have at least a small amount of light.

We are the light of the world. We have the responsibility of illuminating the lives of other people; through our acts and deeds we are transmitting light to other people. Jesus is our generator. He offers us energy so that our lights continue to shine. And this Generator is never defective; He is continually giving us more and more energy. Oh, dear ones! How wonderful it is to know that Jesus does not let our light go out! All we need to do is seek Him every day so that we may have a complete supply of energy.

We need to shine in the darkness of the world. Because of our life many people will come to know Jesus. Jesus tells us, "In the same way, let your light shine before men, that they may see your good deeds and praise your Father in heaven" (Matt. 5:16, NIV). Each time that our light shines, God is being glorified. May our loving God never allow our light to go out, and may we spread light throughout the world so that everyone may come to know Jesus.

LEILA M. GOMES FERREIRA

June 13

A Meaningful Act

Though you have not seen him, you love him; and even though you do not see him now, you believe in him and are filled with an inexpressible and glorious joy. 1 Peter 1:8, NIV.

HOW SURPRISED I WAS last Sabbath! Church announcements had just finished, and the worship service was about to begin. I walked into the sanctuary to find a spot to sit down when Marty, the primary class leader, tapped me on the shoulder and handed me an attractive looking, personalized thank-you card. I read my name on it, and checked the sender's name. I asked Marty who the sender was, because I didn't recognize her name. She told me she was one of the students who attended class that morning.

Apparently the whole class was assigned to write thank-you cards to all church leaders, and this girl named Kristen wrote and decorated a beautiful card for me. I was impressed at her willingness to acknowledge her assignment and to choose to actually make a personalized thank-you card, addressing me as a wonderful person! It is not the compliment I am hoarding, but the blessing; Kristen hadn't seen or met me before. In my mind I thought how easy it would have been for her to refuse doing such an assignment—writing to someone she didn't know—and I found out that she was only 9 years old.

I concluded that her action illustrated the message in 1 Peter 1:8: "Though you have not seen him, you love him; and even though you do not see him now, you believe in him and are filled with an inexpressible and glorious joy."

I asked Marty which girl was Kristen; then without hesitation I went and hugged her, thanked her, and told her that I loved her!

I learned a meaningful lesson from what Kristen did: to believe and to love God, even though I have not seen Him and I do not see Him. I need to build my faith one block at a time to grow into a stronghold of great faith by practicing what I learned.

Lord, thank You for speaking to me through Kristen. Help me learn and continue to be able to hear Your small voice and learn of You, whoever Your messenger may be.

EUNICE URBANY

She Washed Her Hands With Kool-Aid!

Who shall ascend into the hill of the Lord? or who shall stand in his holy place? He that hath clean hands, and a pure heart; who hath not lifted up his soul unto vanity, nor sworn deceitfully. Ps. 24:3, 4.

RECENTLY, MY HUSBAND, Carl, and I went out-of state to attend his family's reunion. We have a nice time at this annual event, enjoying nature, the food, and the conversation, and catching up on everyone's lives.

One of the most unusual happenings this year involved a small girl cousin who was about 5 or 6 years old. "Tiffany!" her father called. "Come! It's time for us to pose for our family pictures before we go home."

"Just a minute, Daddy. I'm washing my hands!"

I looked at her and my jaw dropped. She was washing her hands by running Kool-Aid over them, and they were becoming very red-splotched.

"Tiffany!" Her father's voice rose somewhat. "Come. *Now!*"

When Tiffany protested that she wasn't ready yet, her father strode purposefully over to her, grabbed her by the hand, and took her to their group. Of one thing I am certain: early into their return trip, after realizing how red and sticky her hands were, her family had to stop at the nearest public restroom and give her hands a good scrubbing with soap and water!

Earlier I had spilled some baked bean sauce on my hands while packing things into our cooler for our ride home. I had rinsed my hands, using water from a spouted thermos jug. Had Tiffany seen me and followed my example, but ended up using from the wrong jug?

Like Tiffany, we adults get ourselves into messes, doing things we shouldn't that get not only our hands dirty but our hearts as well. Tiffany's mistake was probably an innocent one. But often we walk into our situations with our eyes wide open, knowing that what we're doing is wrong. Like Tiffany, we try to "fix things," only to realize that we can't undo the damage.

Tiffany needed help. And so do we. God the Father, Christ, and the Holy Spirit are more than willing to cleanse us from all unrighteousness. The choice is ours to make. If we haven't already become "new creatures in Christ," what better time than now to make that full surrender?

Bonnie Moyers

The Good Life

If your only concern is to hold on to life, you'll lose it, but if you're willing to lose your life for my sake, you'll find it. Matt. 10:39, Clear Word.

LOUNGING BY THE POOL of an exclusive country club, I hugged myself and thought, *Mmmm, this sun feels so good.* Thus began my summer routine of swimming and sunning every day while the children either swam or played golf or tennis. Sounds like the good life? Wrong! The thought that I should be doing something more constructive often plagued me. I wasn't praying for something more constructive to do, but in His wisdom God gave it to me anyway.

Circumstances drew me away from what seemed to be the "good life" to what I described as "thrown to the sharks." Now I was totally dependent on the Lord to provide for me and to show me His will for my life. Servanthood was not a spiritual gift I sought. However, it turned out that serving others was what I was most comfortable doing. I loved "serving" my children, even as a single parent—even if a mother is expected to do that. As a teacher I experienced tremendous satisfaction in "serving" my students—but I was paid for that. Amazingly, it was not until my retirement that I discovered unselfish servanthood that really "improved my serve."

Mentoring nursing graduates from the various schools in my area, who have not been successful in passing the national exam for nursing, and sharing their jubilation when they do pass, is a ministry that has been divinely appointed. God also nudged me in my retirement to use my nursing skills to serve those who are distraught and don't know where to turn when a crisis arises. It seems the darkness of night brings with it scary situations, and that's when I get calls for help. As I get in my car to see what I can do, I always pray for wisdom. Sometimes the situation seems like a 911 call to me, but after I assess the problem it usually turns out to be noncompliance with medication.

Unclogging a urinary catheter on a friend with a cancerous kidney so they can have a good night's sleep, or sharing a friend's sorrow in a dysfunctional marriage, or suggesting what to do for a dehydrated child brings a peace that "passeth all understanding." Now, *this* is the good life!

BONNIE HUNT

The Day He Called My Name

Jesus saith unto her, Mary. She turned herself. John 20:16.

IT WAS A BRIGHT spring morning in the Bronx, New York. The air was filled with loud music emanating from speakers everywhere. The stores were getting ready for another busy day as the early customers filled the streets with laughter and chatter.

Early walks to the supermarket are lovely in this kind of weather, Laly thought to herself. *Nevertheless, I'm grateful I have to walk only a mile to and from there.*

The morning breeze softly caressed her face as she walked slowly, gazing joyously at the stores' colorful windows. Soon the supermarket came into view, and duty brought her back to reality. "I guess I have to do what I have to do," she sighed as she entered the store and left behind all the beauty of the morning.

It was a quick stop: a few bananas, potatoes for her mom's soup, some egg noodles, tomatoes, and, of course, fresh bread. Having everything packed and paid for, Laly began her trip back home. She looked forward to the colorful windows and window shopping along the way.

Lost in thoughts of ever being able to buy lots of things, everything known suddenly turned unknown—a walk between reality and imagination. Reaching a side street and still lost in thought, Laly proceeded to cross. As she was about to walk into the street, a still small voice called behind her back: "Laly, Laly." Immediately she turned around just in time to miss a speeding car that appeared out of nowhere and crossed within inches of her.

She stood speechless. She looked around for a friendly face but found none. *Who called my name?* she pondered. *I know I heard the voice. Who just saved my life?* Tears now clouded her view, and a thankful prayer lifted her heart toward heaven. Seconds seemed like years as she walked back home. Her heart raced; yet every second that passed, every pump of her heart was a tearful and joyous *Thank You, Lord, for sending my angel.*

Father, today I may find loads of problems, worldly windows full of temptations, loud gossip, and hurtful comments trying to get my attention. Yet help me to hear Your still small voice calling me to fellowship with You, to ponder Your love and mercy. Teach me today to sit still and hear when in love You call my name. Amen!

GLADYS S. (GUERRERO) KELLEY

June 17

Her Tell Me No!

Your ears shall hear a word behind you, saying, "This is the way, walk in it," whenever you turn to the right hand or whenever you turn to the left. Isa. 30:21, NKJV.

WE WERE ENJOYING ONE of our occasional get-togethers. After a delicious potluck meal and cleanup time, we all ended up in the living room, where we spent time talking, laughing, and generally relaxing away from the stresses caused by the challenges of the day-by-day world.

Most of us were adults; but two little boys, Christian (2½) and his baby brother, Gabriel (6 months), and one little girl, Megan (7 years), were there with their respective parents. Because of the wide age differences, there was little interaction among the children. So as the evening wore on, young Christian began looking for his own entertainment—under the watchful eye of the grown-ups, of course.

When Christian found some crayons, he pictured what he could do if he tried them out on the big white wall that seemed to be inviting his attention. But his plans were interrupted by offers of white paper instead. He ran to his grandpa sobbing, "Her tell me no!" the bright colors still in his little hand. Grandpa soothed his feelings, while the rest of us tried to hide our chuckles.

Soon Christian was off on another adventure, but found that climbing up on a big chair only brought more adult interference. Once again, baby boy headed to Grandpa, loudly proclaiming, "He tell me no!" as he pointed to his daddy.

What a frustrating evening it must have been for a little tot trying to have fun in a grown-up world. And yet how great it was that he could find comfort in his grandpa's love.

Some of our adult experiences bear similarities to what little Christian went through that evening. We make plans or have ideas that somehow don't work out. So we may burst into tears, or even throw an adult temper tantrum, because we fail to understand God's leading and wisdom when He closes doors or in some other way tells us no.

What a blessing it is when we realize it is our heavenly Father who is denying our unwise wishes, and the same loving Father who comforts us and desires to give us what is best.

MILDRED C. WILLIAMS

True Greatness

For God so loved the world, that he gave his only begotten Son, that whosoever believeth in him should not perish, but have everlasting life. John 3:16.

I WAS 12 YEARS OLD when my dad called me one day. He was sitting on an old chair beside his desk, which were both ancestral heirlooms. I stood near him as he asked, "Do you know that your father is a great man?"

I said, "No," and asked, "What made you great?"

He said, "All great men were born in February," Referring to his February 11 birthday. He then named a few great men who were born in February.

Not long after that my dad had the opportunity to prove that he was truly great. One Sunday I was sitting by myself, nursing an aching tooth. My dad asked my mother why I was looking so unhappy. She told him about my tooth and that I didn't want to go to the dentist to whom we usually go. Though she was my dad's relative, I didn't like her because she was not very gentle. My dad felt sorry for me and asked me if I would be willing to go to a German dentist who treated the governor. My eyes brightened. I was impressed and agreed to go. He made an appointment for me for the next day at 10:00.

We were ushered into a big, posh-looking room. Although there were three dental chairs, there were no patients. Soon the dentist appeared in his crisp white coat and smiled at me. He took my hand and led me to one of the chairs. As I sat down he spoke to my dad, then assured me that I would not feel any pain. He extracted the offending tooth and another small one that was spoiling my appearance. True to his word, I felt no pain and was so relieved. My dad paid the bill—which was higher than he anticipated, as each extraction cost almost a month's salary. (I knew now why there were no other patients.)

Dad didn't say a word about the cost, and I went home happy. I don't know if he ever told Mother how much he had to shell out that morning in order to make me happy. At that time I didn't realize it was a great deed that my dad had done for me. Only after many years did I realize that my dad was a truly great man. It is great to relieve someone's pain without counting the cost.

God is a great God in that He gave His only Son without counting the cost!

Birol Charlotte Christo

Heading Home

In my Father's house are many mansions. John 14:2.

AS PART OF HIS duties as conference youth director, my husband was in charge of summer camps for nine years, something our two boys really enjoyed as they were growing up.

I wanted to be involved, but how? I was not into crafts. I like animals but am not an authority. My swimming consists of dog paddling, so waterfront duty was not for me. I could, however, cook. When I was 9 years old I entered a cake in the county fair and would have won first prize if it had had a fancy frosting—and that was before Betty Crocker!

Of course, cooking for 100 hungry campers, plus staff members, was more than cake baking. It meant three hearty meals a day, but with a good crew and only a few minor disasters, that was accomplished.

One day the cooks decided to take a horseback ride after supper. Now, I had ridden a horse only once and that had been years before, but I went along with the plan. My doubts began when I approached an animal that seemed to get taller and taller as I got closer. With help, I climbed aboard, and then we were off. Being accustomed to amateur riders, the horse ambled peacefully along, stopping now and then to graze, almost causing me to slide over his head as he bent it low to munch the grass. In spite of that, it was so pleasant that after we had turned back toward the corral, we decided to go around the trail again. That's when my trusty steed rebelled. He had been patient and willing to humor me until then, but he had been headed for the barn, and that's where he was going! And go he did—at a full gallop, with me, wild-eyed, hanging on for dear life. My loyal friends laughed and thoroughly enjoyed my plight!

When we have been on a trip and are on our way home, I can hardly wait to get there. I want to push on the car's dashboard to hurry it along! Like the horse, I'm headed home and don't want to take any detours.

There's another home waiting for us. It's not a barn or an earthly home but a mansion in heaven. Are we eager to get there? Are we willing to go against anything that pulls us in the opposite direction? Do we *really* want to go home?

MARY JANE GRAVES

Do It Again, Daddy!

For you are a [daughter] holy to the Lord your God. The Lord your God has chosen you out of all the peoples on the face of the earth to be his [daughter], his treasured possession. Deut. 7:6, NIV.

DEBORAH WAS THE perpetual "Do it again, Daddy!" child. She watched her older brother and sister jumping off the high dive and wanted to do it, too. She was only 4 or 5, but John told her if she went up on the high dive, she had to jump. Up she went to the top and looked down at her father, who looked like a tiny dot in the water. "Come on; I'll catch you," he assured her. Deborah's eyes widened, but off she went, down, down, down to where her daddy waited.

Deborah was the one who cried when the roller coaster ride was all over, "Let's do it again, Daddy." Sometimes they did, and sometimes not.

When he took her up on her first helicopter ride she loved it; she couldn't wait to go flying in whatever plane John was flying or teaching in at the time. Her eyes sparkled with such joy and delight that doing it again made John just as happy.

Then there were the times John would have to say no because they had to be somewhere or needed to do something different. In her own persistent, stubborn way, she would say no, and had to learn to follow Daddy. They both said it wasn't always the easiest lesson to learn, but she did learn and now depends on her dad for advice and for a listening ear.

I visit with the Lord, and He listens while I am driving. There are times I know distinctly that He's answered a problem I've been trying to solve. Sometimes I get an answer I really do not want; but it is the answer, and I need to follow. Only by exercising those spiritual muscles do we get to the point in our lives when we know His voice so precisely that we will not be fooled.

The faith and security Deborah showed as a child toward her daddy is similar to our faith in our heavenly Father, Lord, and Spirit. We trust Him to look after us and catch us when we fall. We trust Jesus to save us and comfort us. We depend on the Holy Spirit to show us the safest way to go through life to avoid dangerous situations. Sometimes we are saying, "Daddy, let's do it again!" and sometimes He's saying, "Follow in the path where I lead."

SALLY J. AKEN-LINKE

Crying in the Hotel

Let him who walks in the dark, who has no light, trust in the name of the Lord and rely on his God. Isa. 50:10, NIV.

I WAS IN THE CITY of Ribeirão Preto, São Paulo, Brazil, together with my only daughter, Rebecca. We were in a hotel in the downtown area, and I felt helpless and desperate with many problems to solve. One day while my daughter played with some friends in the hotel swimming pool, I went to Apartment 512 to pray. I needed comfort. I needed help. I needed God. I threw open the door and collapsed in tears. There I was, weak and defenseless, and although surrounded by friends in that city, I felt extremely alone. I wept deeply for quite some time.

While I was crying and sobbing, I heard whistling that for some reason caught my attention. I stopped crying. The soft whistling indicated the melody of a song, a song I knew! Still in tears, I began to sing. But who was whistling? Who knew this song that I had known since I was a child? In an instant I got up to discover who was whistling. I opened the window. There was no one outside. I left the window and ran to the door. Beyond the door was a wide, empty, lonely hallway that was perfectly empty and in order. I returned to the room. What was happening? What did all this mean? The whistling had stopped! I was puzzled.

I pulled out a piece of hotel stationery and began to write the words of that marvelous melody. But—how did it go? I was so far from my God. I didn't really remember. Little by little, I remembered my parents, my childhood, the family worships offered to God with everyone gathered in the morning and in the evening. I could almost hear the little bell that my father rang to gather his wife and five children. With my eyes still damp with tears, I began again to write the words to that hymn: "He hideth my soul in the cleft of the rock that shadows a dry, thirsty land; He hideth my life in the depths of His love, and covers me there with His hand."

I began to weep again, but this time the crying was different. I had been deeply touched. I no longer felt alone. I was ashamed. How could I have gone so long without Him?

O Lord! Your love, Your indescribable love, compels me! Thank You for loving me and continuing to love me, even when I remove myself from Your company!

FEB STABENOW

How Bold Dare I Be?

Whatsoever ye shall ask in prayer, believing, ye shall receive. Matt. 21:22.

Is it right to pray for something that will definitely inconvenience another person? The following true story will provide my answer to the question.

A group of tourists in Fiji were on a bus heading for the Nandu Airport on the opposite side of the island. Suddenly, when several miles away from their hotel, a couple realized that they had forgotten to pick up their passports from the hotel's safe. There was no time to return and still be able to catch their flight to Auckland. Neither could they leave the country without their passports. What should they do?

At the next town the tour manager phoned the hotel, asking them to select a taxi to deliver the passports to the airport in haste. The bus continued on its way with every passenger praying that the cab driver would arrive in time. Soon the tour group had to board their plane, leaving the couple behind to work out other arrangements. Shortly after all passengers were comfortably seated, an announcement came over the loudspeaker. "I'm sorry, ladies and gentlemen; your flight will be delayed because not all the crew members have arrived."

The Boomerang tour group heaved a partial sigh of relief, praying the delay would be long enough for their friends to get their passports and catch this flight. Time ticked by. Suddenly someone saw two pairs of feet under the plane's wing. Sure enough, the couple entered the plane with broad smiles and passports in hand.

The group couldn't contain themselves and sang, "Praise God, From Whom All Blessings Flow." Their prayers had been answered at the expense of others who would miss their connecting flights. What had God done? Should the Boomerang tour group feel guilty?

Finally the crew members were in place, and the plane took off. After the flight attendants went through all the demonstrations of passenger safety and emergency measures, the pilot's voice came over the loudspeaker: "Ladies and gentleman, we're sorry for the delay, but because of a strong tailwind our flight will arrive in Auckland on schedule."

What a God we serve! He is able to answer two diverse prayers. Trust God to find a solution to your most complicated requests today. Nothing is too hard for Him.

EDITH FITCH

Chosen

The Lord your God has chosen you out of all the peoples on the face of the earth to be his people, his treasured possession. . . . It was because the Lord loved you. Deut. 7:6-8, NIV.

I WAS TRAVELING BACK home to the United States from Fiji after being the speaker at a women's congress there. The women had made me feel special, and I had souvenirs and gifts and happy thoughts to treasure for years to come. I was exhausted, though, having spent a day in airport security lines, waiting for flights, and not sleeping well in cramped airplanes. Not feeling well, I had another day's travel. Now at Honolulu International Airport, the security line wove its way through the airport, out the door, and down the street. I'd been standing in the line for more than an hour and could finally see the checkpoint. I breathed a sigh of relief.

Suddenly, out of nowhere, a female security officer appeared. Peering through the crowd, she looked at me and said, "You! You are chosen!"

Me? Chosen? How wonderful! I chuckled to myself. As I got out of the line, I looked back and cast a smile at the stranger who had been my conversation partner as we inched along in the line. He looked happy for me, I thought. And I was happy because I was chosen.

At the checkpoint the security officer turned and said harshly, "Open your bag!" My happiness instantly turned to surprise. Being chosen had always conjured up feelings of being loved and cherished, of being special. I gulped and opened my carry-on suitcase as people stared. My surprise turned to embarrassment. Several security officers rummaged carelessly through my belongings. My embarrassment turned to anger. Was I chosen because I had made several phone calls during the long wait? Was it because I had paced nervously because of stomach pains? Was it because a previous baggage clerk had mistakenly marked my larger suitcases for my final destination instead of having them accompany me every leg of the journey? Why?

Three or four minutes later the officer spoke again. "You can move on through now." *Chosen,* I thought again. *Humph!* And I gladly moved on.

I am thankful today and every day that regardless of how others may treat me, I really am chosen. Yes, God has chosen me because I am special and because He loves me. That I will never forget, because it is wonderful, and it is something to smile about!

Iris L. Stovall

When Joy Is Gone

Restore unto me the joy of thy salvation; and uphold me with thy free spirit. Ps. 51:12.

DAVID HAD LOST HIS joy. This experience is recorded for our learning in Psalm 51. He lost joy because of his own sin, and in its place he acquired a broken spirit. Not only did he break the seventh commandment, but he violated the sixth as well. I can imagine how David must have felt when he came to himself. He was not only an adulterer, but also a murderer. I think he felt awful. Perhaps he felt like dying. I thank God that He led David to see himself, for when he did he sought God with his whole heart.

David cried to God for mercy, cleansing, and forgiveness. He realized that it was against God that he had ultimately sinned, for all sin is against God. David, a man described as a man after God's own heart, prayed earnestly for a clean heart, a right spirit, and restored joy. He yearned for the experience of joy and gladness in the Lord. God didn't forsake David. He heard his cry, He inclined His ear to him, and He answered him. He gave him peace and restored his joy. What a merciful God we serve!

Like David, we at times lose our joy, too. We may not have committed adultery or murder, but other conditions caused by sin can make us lose our joy. Don't be afraid if this is your case, because a very good time to get to know God better is during difficult times. This is the time we feel weak and helpless. It is at this time we tend to lean heavily on the Lord. What an opportunity to get closer to Jesus!

Whatever it is that has stolen our joy, we, like David, serve a God who is powerful and who is able to restore joy. Yes, God has the power to restore joy and gladness. He is able to renew the right spirit in us. God can deliver us from all ills.

Let's keep on trusting and serving Jesus fully and completely. Let's seek Him with our whole hearts, and just as He did for David, He will incline His ear unto us. Despite our flaws and difficult circumstances, God will supply the strength for us to go on, and in His own time He will restore our joy.

The darkest hour is just before dawn. Let's not give up now, because Jesus is coming, and joy—real joy—will come in the morning!

JACQUELINE HOPE HOSHING-CLARKE.

I Call You Friends

No longer do I call you servants, for a servant does not know what his master is doing; but I have called you friends, for all things that I heard from My Father I have made known to you. John 15:15, NKJV.

WHEN THE CLASS OF 1941 from Mount Ellis Academy, a Christian high school, celebrated its sixtieth anniversary, I took it on myself to get in touch with as many of our classmates and former faculty as possible. One of the people I contacted was Christina Cooper. For some years Mrs. Cooper and I had exchanged Christmas letters. She had been our matron, in charge of the kitchen and the laundry. She and Lester ("Prof Cooper" to us students) came as newlyweds to this Montana boarding school. She was 26, an accomplished violinist and organist; and in her white-trimmed navy suit ornamented with cherries, white gloves, and navy sailor hat, she was our model of style and culture.

She was also the soul of graciousness. She managed the kitchen and the girls who worked for her with patience and good humor. We felt privileged to be on the kitchen crew. Considering the tightness of her budget (this was the tail end of the Depression), she "set a good table," as Montanans say. But she was faculty; we were students. We loved her, but kept our distance.

Now it was the fiftieth reunion of "our" class from medical school, and I wanted to visit with the other wives again from that class. But where could I stay? My budget didn't allow for a motel. Then I thought about Mrs. Cooper. Her husband had passed away three years before, but she continued in good health.

"Yes," she said when I called. "Please come. I shall be delighted to visit with you again."

So I did go. My days were filled with family and class activities, but we spent the breakfast hour and the evenings together. We visited as early and as late as we dared.

During those visits I saw in Christina her love for her family, for her friends, for her God. I saw her paintings and her hobbies. I tasted her hospitality. Now I feel I truly know her. There is no longer any distance between us. She is my friend, and I am hers.

And I learned the difference between knowing Jesus casually and actually being with Him, spending large blocks of time with Him.

RUTHANNEKE EDWARDS

Phone Credit

He shall call upon me, and I will answer him: I will be with him in trouble; I will deliver him, and honour him. Ps. 91:15.

IT WAS ANOTHER OF those rare moments that parents of toddlers come to treasure—being alone together with your spouse, even if it's only a return trip from the city. As I was basking in the beauty of the setting sun, pleasant music, and light conversation, the sound of a sputtering engine changed the mood. In no time the car was dead, leaving us stranded at a lonely spot on the highway. I panicked!

My husband opened the hood and made himself busy, leaving me in the car feeling helpless. As the shadows descended, so did my anxiety and the fervor of my simple prayer: "Lord, please send help."

We both had our cellular phones, but neither of them had credit. *How irresponsible!* I thought. I whispered a prayer, asking God to allow someone—*anyone*—to call so I could get in touch with help, but the phones remained silent. Then I thought that maybe if I tried to make a call in faith it would go through. Slowly I dialed my mother's number and anxiously waited to hear if it would indeed ring. It did. Not trusting my blessing, I asked her to call me back. When she did, I explained our dilemma, and she assured me she would send help.

Just then the car started, allowing us to at least leave the lonely spot. Now I needed to call her again to let her know we would be relocating. Would it work again? It did! I was beside myself with the excitement of an answered prayer. Then I thought that maybe I should try my luck at yet another call—just for the fun of it. Would it work? It did not!

I chuckled to myself as I thought I heard God say, "My credit is for your emergencies."

Do you sometimes grovel with feelings of helplessness or worry about the unexpected becoming a reality? Do you withhold a prayer for help thinking *If only I were more responsible I would not be in this dilemma?* I proved yet again that God is a present help in time of trouble. Trust Him today, and every day, to make the impossible possible.

Patrice E. Williams-Gordon

The "Wild" Fan

The angel of the Lord encampeth round about them that fear him, and delivereth them. Ps. 34:7.

SINCE MY MOTHER IS getting older we have promised to visit her almost every year, but she is about 14 hours away by plane. After the September 11, 2001, attack, traveling and flying has been very scary for me. Living in Europe and flying to Asia is also quite expensive for us. My husband said we would try to manage it because my father passed away when I was 4 years old, and my mother is the only one left. I want to enjoy every precious moment being with her and again feel her love for me.

The time goes very quickly when we visit. It is always hot and humid in the Philippines, but we enjoyed every minute of it, for it was a holiday and family reunion at the same time. My husband left for home ahead of me because he couldn't get more vacation. That night I was praying earnestly, asking God for protection for my husband and my family. As I stood up, the following text came to my mind: "I will lie down and sleep in peace, for you alone, O Lord, make me dwell in safety" (Ps. 4:8, NIV). Peace instantly overwhelmed me.

When I went to bed the assurance and the promises of our Lord in His Word made me feel safe in His care. My 10-year-old niece, Janelle, was staying with me in the same room, sleeping on a mat on the floor. Because of the uncomfortable heat, we let the standing fan blow fresh air on us the whole night long. I was awakened suddenly before midnight. It seemed that someone had touched me, shook me, and awakened me. My heart was pounding! I opened my eyes, and when I looked they focused directly on the electric fan. It had fallen on my niece's face and was still running. She was still sound asleep. I jumped up to remove the fan, and as I lifted it up, the safety cover fell off. One single movement of my niece could possibly have caused severe injury to her face.

I was reminded of my prayer the evening before when the Lord impressed one of His promises on me. I was so thankful that God sent His angel to wake me up in time. I felt so thrilled to know that I can depend and rely on Him. I don't need to worry, for God is still in control, and He will do the same for you—just keep on trusting. LOIDA GULAJA LEHMANN

Angel in a Van

For he will command his angels concerning you to guard you in all your ways. Ps. 91:11, NIV.

I SLIPPED MY HEADPHONES off as I made eye contact with a white pit bull. He eagerly waited, crouching on the sidewalk about 25 feet in front of me. As I began to back up, he inched toward me. I screamed aloud and gave a low-toned "No" command again and again.

A quick look at my watch told me it was 7:00 a.m. I usually took my daughter along in a jogger stroller, but today she had stayed at home with my husband. Now, only one block from home, I found myself in great danger with nowhere to turn. If I turned and ran, surely the pit bull would chase me—and win.

Two children stood across the street, waiting for the bus. They too were paralyzed with fear. I imagined the dog's jaws clamping down on my legs. Between panicked thoughts and yells, I breathed this prayer, "God, please! Please!"

At that moment a white van drove up and picked up the children. I made eye contact with the driver and waved at her. She nodded and pulled up next to me and opened the door. As I jumped in, the dog began to run toward me.

I slammed the door and sat in the stranger's van, legs shaking, mouth dry, and a heart rate that demanded my attention. The fortysomething blond driver said, "I'll take you home now." She drove around the curve into my driveway and dropped me off at my front door. I jumped out, said a quick "Thanks," and ran in the door.

Once inside my house I began to cry, as I once again pictured what could have happened to me had that woman not picked me up. It wasn't until then that I realized that I had never seen her before. How did she know where I lived?

Months later I still find myself occasionally looking for that white van in my neighborhood. I long to thank her for saving my life. For now I'll settle for knowing without a doubt that God has plans for me. I'm looking forward to the day when He will say, "I'll take you home now."

Father, thank You for answering when we call on Your name. We eagerly await the day You take us home. DARLENE ALMEDA SHOWALTER

Trash or Treasure?

Seek ye first the kingdom of God, and his righteousness; and all these things shall be added unto you. Matt. 6:33.

I WAS MOVING AGAIN, but this time was different. I had time to organize. I didn't have to throw things into boxes in a rush, so I took time to go through 40 years of storage, throwing out things that once had meaning but now had no part in my life. I was enjoying some of my finds, and I was finding it easy to classify items as "Trash" or "Treasure." I'd open one box and find things from last year's spring cleaning. The next box would be from 1969 and be full of reminders of my mother and my son when he was a child. There were all my son's report cards! And there were Mama's knickknacks!

Ah, here is a box of books and magazines. Surely these are all "keepers." There is Drew's *Boy's Life;* look at all of these *Adventist Reviews!* We must have saved them all!

And what are these? Mama's horoscope magazines? I'd forgotten about them. My mother had been, for the 10 years before her conversion and baptism in 1973, quite deep into astrology. Once she turned to Christ her subscriptions to horoscope magazines were discontinued, because her greatest joy in those last eight years was reading her Bible.

As I tossed that unexpected find, the thought occurred to me: An occasional sorting of my life's accumulation of possessions is a good thing. I was rediscovering things worth keeping, and I was finding things that should have been discarded a long time ago.

An occasional accounting of my mental storage areas was probably a good idea as well. What have I buried deep in everyday experiences that should be put out where I, and others, can benefit from them like Mama's pretty little knickknacks? And what ideas, thoughts, and practices have accumulated that are no longer of use or value in my present life? Or worse, are there actual sins that I should have turned from and discarded years ago—such as my mother's old astrology magazines?

Lord, help me to sort out my life as I have sorted out my personal possessions. Help me to distinguish between that which is worthwhile and worth saving, and that which is trash. Amen.

DARLENEJOAN MCKIBBIN RHINE

A Little Taste of Heaven

No one's ever seen or heard anything like this, never so much as imagined anything quite like it—what God has arranged for those who love him. 1 Cor. 2:9, Message.

DUNSTER IS A TINY village, almost overlooking the sea, in the southwest of England. My parents had been there once and told me that it was worth a visit; and I really wanted to see the quaint old houses, the castle, the thatched cottages, and the river running past the old mill. My three children weren't quite as excited as I. They wanted to get to the campsite, where we would spend the night and meet some of their old friends.

My husband, Bernie, managed to persuade the children to get out of the car while I wandered into a lovely shop close to the village square. I found some wonderful presents for my friends, a scarf I really wanted, and something I'd been trying to find for ages. I went to pay for them and pulled out my credit card. "I'm sorry; I don't take credit cards," said the woman.

"Oh, no," I groaned inwardly. We had no cash, and there were no local banks in this tiny place. "It's all right," she said smiling, "Just take the things and send me a check when you get home. I'll write your name and address in my book. No one's ever let me down yet." I couldn't believe it! She handed my things to me in a bag, with a handwritten note and her address.

Meanwhile, the children were outside in the lane when an elderly gentleman walked past. "Have you ever seen a goose egg?" he asked, as he brought out a pure white egg, bigger than the children had ever seen. He let them hold the egg as he explained that it was as big as four hen's eggs, and that he was taking it to his wife who would use it to make his favorite cake.

We wandered up to the castle, then down flowery fragrant paths to the old mill, stepping on old stones to cross the stream, and past a woman repairing the straw thatch of a tumbledown house. She stopped to chat and show us what she was doing. It was beautiful and tranquil. Everyone we met was relaxed, smiling, willing to talk and to share. We all felt soothed.

The children reluctantly got back into our car and sat in silent wonder. Finally one of them voiced their thoughts: "Mom, when I retire I want to live here. It's just like heaven."

Yes, I thought, this afternoon was as heavenly as earth could be. I can't wait to experience the real thing!

KAREN HOLFORD

July 1

Message of the Shells

And God created . . . every living creature that moveth, which the waters brought forth abundantly, . . . and God saw that it was good. Gen. 1:21.

I HAVE AN ATTRACTIVE wicker tray in my lounge that displays various types of shells I've collected over many years. I have a great fascination for shells; I can't resist picking up a shell when I see one. Time seems to glide away when you're picking up shells. One gets so absorbed in the pretty shapes and colors. To think that God created all these creatures that dwell in the sea!

The study of mollusks and their shells is called conchology; but I am not a conchologist—I just love collecting them. The word *kohnkho* comes from the Greek word *konkhe,* for "shell."

While I was on vacation, someone gave me a shell with a sponge on top to use as a pincushion. There are many crafts made with sea shells. Just to mention a few: wind chimes, brooches, vanity boxes, coasters, serviette/napkin holders, picture frames, and key rings.

The sea has billions of shells, but we treasure those that wash to the shore. Inevitably, on the beach shells get broken or shattered under our feet as we walk. Do we treasure the broken shells, too? Sometimes when we find a better or a perfect shell, we throw the broken one away.

Is that how we treat people, too? Our friends and loved ones? God requires that we treat them lovingly. One example: You have been in a marriage relationship for several years and have seen each other's flaws. Do you cast him/her away for a more "perfect" spouse? Just as each shell is assessed with appreciation for its beauty, so we should recognize the virtues in our partner and have a tolerant and caring spirit. There is value and beauty even in broken shells. God requires us to stop and fall to our knees and pray with one another before thinking of casting that once-lovable soul away. We all like to be loved, appreciated, and treasured.

The next time you take a walk along life's beach, consider those who are broken, those whose lives lie in fragments because of circumstances. Remember, God loves each one. He created each one beautiful and unique. No matter who or what you are, you are His precious treasure.

PRISCILLA ADONIS

The Angel in Front of the Car

For he shall give his angels charge over thee, to keep thee in all thy ways. Ps. 91:11.

I WAS PLANNING TO get my driver's license. I had put it off for so long that I'd lost all my confidence and had no courage to go through with it anymore. My husband gave me his support and believed that I could do it. He knew that I was more prepared than I thought.

One Sunday afternoon when we were going to visit some friends, my husband wanted to give me a chance to drive our new car. It was only a few blocks away, so he gave me the keys. I knew how to control my speed, how to make my turns, how to accelerate and to slow down when needed. I started to regain my confidence. In the back of my mind I knew that this would be "a piece of cake."

I needed to park in the friends' garage, but instead of entering into the garage, the car headed for the front yard and the house. As fast as my confidence had shot up, it came down. My husband tried to get the car back under control. I knew the only solution to our problem was to call on God. Immediately, I prayed under my breath. All I could think about was my baby, in the back seat (sleeping); my unborn child, who would never get a chance to see the world; and my husband, who would be unable to fulfill all his dreams and goals. I kept praying.

Suddenly the car moved on its own. Out of nowhere it took a detour and headed for a tree that blocked the window in the master bedroom. The impact of the car hitting the tree uprooted it out of the ground. I was so scared; I didn't know what to do. And I was worried about what my husband was going to say, and what my friends were going to think about me. I failed to realize that God had everything under control. No one was hurt; the house was still intact; my husband was able to see beyond the dent in the car. My friends were more worried about me and the babies; and the car only received a dent in the hood. What an awesome God we serve! God used the car to cut down the tree so my friends wouldn't have to pay someone to do it.

My husband and I decided to leave the dent in the hood. It is just a small reminder of how close we came to losing it. It is a lesson in faith. It also serves to remind us of how God takes care of those who love him, by sending His angels to encamp around us. DIANTHA HALL-SMITH

Comfort Those in Trouble

Praise be to the God and Father of our Lord Jesus Christ, the Father of compassion and the God of all comfort, who comforts us in all our troubles, so that we can comfort those in any trouble with the comfort we ourselves have received from God. For just as the sufferings of Christ flow over into our lives, so also through Christ our comfort overflows. 2 Cor. 1:3-5, NIV.

SOUNDS OF MOURNING filled the air as men, women, and children stepped up to the open grave to shovel a little dirt onto the wooden casket. My husband and I were teachers at a Christian college in the Punjab province of Pakistan, and we were learning that disease and death were far too common.

Yvonne, a fellow teacher from Australia, took me by the arm and led me through the campus cemetery to a tiny grave. Then she told me this story:

A foreign family once lived at the police colony down the road from the college. The man and his wife were devastated when their 3-year-old son drowned in his small swimming pool. They were far from home, and they had no faith in God. In their grief they didn't know what to do or where to turn for help.

Dr. Carrie Robbins received word of the tragedy and paid a visit to the grieving parents. During her initial term of service in Pakistan her husband had become ill and died. He was buried in the campus cemetery. She talked to them about God's love and comforted them with the resurrection hope. Then she said, "I can't do much else for you, but I can offer to let your little boy sleep next to my husband."

I looked down at the little headstone snuggled close to Mr. Robbins' bigger one and thought of my own two children. What could be more heartbreaking than to leave your precious child behind as you depart for your homeland with empty arms?

Then I read the words the parents had written on the little tombstone: "I love Jesus."

Because God comforted Dr. Robbins in her bereavement, she could pass on that comfort to this grieving family. We can only hope that experience was the beginning of their journey toward a friendship with the "Father of compassion and the God of all comfort" (2 Cor. 1:3, NIV).

KAREN FISHER

Paid in Return

Give and it shall be given unto you; good measure, pressed down, and shaken together, and running over, shall men give into your bosom. For with the same measure that ye mete withal it shall be measured to you again. Luke 6:38.

THE 1999 MAZDA Protege was packed, and we headed from Atlanta for the Sunshine State of Florida. We three sisters had planned for a month to make the trip to visit one of our brothers who was healing from a viral heart infection and a fractured ankle. After talking with him by phone, one day we decided we would visit him, because the presence of family can boost the spirits of a member who is ailing. One sister had come to Atlanta by plane from New York City; I had driven from Huntsville, Alabama; and a third sister lived in Atlanta.

So it was that early on the morning of July 4 that we packed our luggage and our lunches, and off we went. We were excited because our family had always been—and still remains—very close and communicative. Our mother taught us to love each other and stick together. I remember when a brother suffered a severe heart attack and lay in a hospital hundreds of miles from his home. Brothers and sisters from New York, Illinois, Alabama, and Georgia camped in the hospital to visit and encourage him. I was ushered into his room alone, and while there alone with him, he asked, "Where's Alice [his daughter-in-law]?" When my time was up, I told his son and wife what he'd said. They were shocked. You see, doctors hadn't gotten any response from him all that morning.

The visit with our brother and his wife and family in Florida was greatly appreciated. He perked up and seemed like his old self—bursting into song, fixing breakfast, assisting with the dinner, washing dishes, and entertaining. When we returned to Atlanta and called back to let them know we had gotten that far safely, he told us that he was proud of his sisters. We knew for sure that we had accomplished our purpose.

Sometimes what we do can have serendipitous effects, and those are very good. We know that we will be rewarded in heaven—someday in the future. But we are also rewarded here and now when we reach out in love to others. We give, but we are also paid in return. LOVEY DAVIS VERDUN

July 5

The Culprit

Thy faithfulness is unto all generations. Ps. 119:90.

I WAS VISITING MY parents, siblings, and other relatives and friends; enjoying ourselves, recalling happy memories, and recounting interesting experiences since we were last together. We were having a grand time when a niece, who was about 3 years old, rushed into the room. She was crying at the top of her voice—no, not crying, screaming!

I picked her up and tried to console her. I checked all the places where I thought there might be cause for such an expression of discomfort—her hair, her ears, her eyes, her mouth, her feet, her stomach, and finally the Pampers. No problem! But my niece kept screaming.

Perhaps a change of venue would solve the problem, I thought. So I took her outside, pointing out all the things I imagined would be sure to take her mind off what was upsetting her. We looked at dogs and cats and trees and lizards and birds and flowers. She was distracted for a moment, but kept crying, and I kept trying to console her. I couldn't think what next to do, when all of a sudden my niece flashed her hand in front of my face. There was the culprit, the cause of her distress—a clothespin locked securely on one tiny finger that was now swollen and red.

I immediately removed the clothespin, kissed the finger, and gently massaged it. Then we hurried back into the house and immersed the finger in cold water. As the pain slowly eased, the crying gradually stopped, and everyone was relieved.

As I look back, I think that even if my niece knew what was wrong she probably didn't know what to do about it. I was an adult and should have been more alert at spotting the problem. How could I have checked everything and missed her hands?

I had studied the Bible and had read and memorized several promises relating to various situations in life, and I should have thought of looking beyond myself for direction. I was depending on me, on my ability to solve the problem. I could have turned to God for help. I could have whispered a prayer when I failed to locate the culprit.

So now I try to put into practice the instruction given in Matthew 23:23: "These ought ye to have done, and not to leave the other undone."

Quilvie G. Mills

God's Ways Are Supreme

For as the heavens are higher than the earth, so are my ways higher than your ways, and my thoughts than your thoughts. Isa. 55:9.

HAVE WE EVER SUCCEEDED in identifying the ways in which God could lead us if we were in a tight corner? On most occasions we may not have, because our God is a marvelous God and can lead us in wonderful ways that we couldn't even dream of in our wildest of dreams! Remember how God led the Israelites through the Red Sea?

In July 1998 my husband and I accompanied my brother to a nearby college to seek admission for a degree. We had money enough to pay the tuition fees, but not for the special registration fee. We put our trust in God and hoped that He would speak to the principal's heart to grant him admission. We were in for a rude shock!

Before we could say anything, in a gruff voice the principal asked us to pay Rs.25,000 for the fee and Rs.10,000 tuition fees. We left disappointed and began to pray for some source of finances, as we knew of no other options. We didn't realize that God's ways were far from ours.

Before long my mother told us that she'd found somebody who could influence the principal to reduce the fee. Though we didn't really expect anything to come of it, we gave it a try. My mother and brother took this person along with them to meet the principal.

"How much did you pay?" I asked my mom when they returned.

"Nothing!" she said.

We never imagined that God would work out a way in that particular manner or through my mom (whom we thought didn't know anyone with such influence).

When my brother got his timetable for his final exams his final year, one exam was scheduled on a Sabbath. We prayed again. Nothing happened until the first day of his exams when it was announced that that particular exam was postponed by government order. It was election time, and the exams had to be rescheduled for a date after the elections.

We marveled at what God had done! Indeed, God's ways are as far from ours as the sky is from the earth.

Arul Mary Daniel

July 7

To Know and to Meet

O Lord, you have searched me and you know me. Ps.139:1, NIV.

EVER SINCE I WAS a child I always liked to study languages. But since I always lived on a farm, I didn't have the opportunity to study them in specific language schools until I was an adult. Recently, God spoke to my heart through my study of the English language. I had read stories of people who heard God speak to them through simple things, but deep within I didn't believe that this could happen to me. I didn't believe that God could teach me lessons through daily happenings or even through secular study.

One day, returning home by bus, I was reading a book about frequent errors that Brazilian students commit as they learn English. The author made a distinction between the use of the verb "to know" and "to meet," both *conhecer* in Portuguese. Both are verbs used with the meaning of "to know" in Portuguese. However, "to meet" is generally used when one refers to having been presented to someone. The verb "to know" reveals a profound knowledge about someone or something, and not a superficial knowledge. As I thought about the difference between the two verbs, I thought that it's comforting to know that God "knows" us, and that He wasn't just introduced or didn't just "meet" us. However, just knowing us, He knows us profoundly.

The second lesson came when I arrived home. I enjoy music, so I put on an English CD. Two phrases stood out in one of the songs: "God knows the broken places" and "God heals the broken places." I didn't know the meaning of the word "heals," so I went to the dictionary. "To heal" is to make or become well or healthy again, "to cure." Then, God cures and makes healthy what is wounded or broken in us. What a marvelous God we have! Besides knowing us profoundly, He cures our wounded heart. And it is through the fact of knowing us so well that He knows exactly where the wound is and what medicine will cure it. He never makes a mistake.

That night I prayed, *Thank You, Lord, because You know me as no one else. Thank You because You cure and heal my emotional wounds. I want to know You more each day.*

IANI LAUER

Promises, Promises

For all the promises of God in him are yea, and in him Amen, unto the glory of God by us. 2 Cor. 1:20.

THERE ARE VERSES IN the Bible that you hear again and again throughout your life, yet you remain unaffected by the words until you really need them. At least that's the way it seems to work for me. Some of the Scripture texts I've known verbatim since childhood are just now making inroads in those proverbial "fleshy tables."

Last night during midweek service, the pastor read 2 Corinthians 1:20 toward the end of his presentation. Actually, it was a rousing discussion, and I was blessed. I couldn't get my mind off that particular text, so this morning I read verses 20-22 in the New King James Version: "For all the promises of God in Him are Yes, and in Him Amen, to the glory of God through us. Now He who establishes us with you in Christ and has anointed us is God, who also has sealed us and given us the Spirit in our hearts as a guarantee."

Beautiful! His promises are "Yes, ma'am, I mean it," and "So, there it is," and "That's what I said," and "You heard Me and I love you too much to let you down." These promises are nothing like the ones you and I make—to Him or to one another, for that matter.

Years ago, part of the credo of my personal parenting platitudes was: "Never promise the kids anything—that way they won't be disappointed when you don't—or can't—come through, and you won't be caught in a lie." You see, that way I kept myself covered. When they said, "Please, Mommy," I said, "We'll see." No commitment—one way or the other.

But God has the audacity to make approximately 4,000 promises in the Bible—and means to keep every one without fear that He will be caught in a lie. On top of that, our text says that the Father, the Son, and the Holy Spirit are in this together. All of these promises are backed by the Godhead with no apologies, backpedaling, or clauses—unless you consider our lack of cooperation a type of inherent disclaimer. But even then God always keeps His side of the bargain. It is always we who renege.

Thank You, Abba-Father, adoring Son, and comforting Holy Spirit for Your provision, Your patience, and Your promises. RENEE VERRETT-DOOLEY

I Do, I Do

Not that we are competent in ourselves to claim anything for ourselves, but our competence comes from God. 2 Cor. 3:5, NIV.

EVERYTHING CAMERON DOES comes from a heart full of joy. He is equal parts determination and exuberance as he carelessly bounces through days that seem far too short to accomplish all he wishes. Fiercely independent, he struggles with tasks beyond his grasp.

Cameron has a walk all his own, strutting around with a swagger of importance, knowing no limits to what he can achieve. And he believes he can achieve it all on his own.

The other day he clomped along—determined to be helpful—in his shiny rain boots, anxious to water spring flowers just returning to life. The water sloshed over the edge of the bucket, causing a sudden torrent of water to spill onto the innocent buds. Wiping his muddy hands with satisfaction, he quickly moved on to his next endeavor.

"I do, I do" is his constant childish refrain, endlessly echoing throughout the house. One morning not long ago I chuckled as I listened to his repeated cry of independence. Reaching for his white tennis shoe, I watched as he wrestled in vain to cram his small foot backward into the shoe.

Undeterred, he next reached for the appealing white laces, pulling and tugging without success. Keeping with his theme of "I do," Cameron soon moved on to the other shoe, determined that this attempt would meet with different results, unaware that he couldn't do it on his own.

This is often how we relate to God. When life is easy, God seems the perfect fit. But when difficulty strikes, we stubbornly exclaim, "I do, I do," still determined to fix our problems on our own. We pull and tug at the laces of life, determined to achieve different results the next time when things go wrong.

Yet just as we let God have control during the smooth times, so we must know that He is in charge during the tough times when we are convinced we can do everything on our own.

Dear God, thank You for being in control through both the easy and difficult times in our lives. Help us to know and remember that You are Lord of all. Amen.

LORI L. MANTZ

Wartime Experience

Nothing bad will happen to you; no disaster will come to your home. He has put his angels in charge of you to watch over you wherever you go. Ps. 91:10, 11, NCV.

WE RECENTLY WENT back to our homeland, England, and visited the town where I was born and lived the first few years of World War II. One incident from that childhood is vividly in my memory to this day.

It was a Friday afternoon. My mother was preparing food and didn't have one of the ingredients in the recipe. She asked me (then 6 years old) to run to the corner store two blocks away to get the necessary item. I had gone one block, turned right at the corner, and was halfway up the second block when I heard a noise that sounded like the whistling of a falling bomb. But it couldn't be! We had never had daylight air raids before, although night raids were common. And there had been no air raid warning siren. Then I heard it again—nearer this time—and it ended in an explosion. I turned to run home but then I remembered the drill: "Always go to the nearest air raid shelter." Seeing a couple with a toddler in a stroller going into their house, I asked if I could accompany them to their backyard shelter. There we waited out the raid. Then came the very welcome "all clear" siren, and I thanked the couple and ran toward home.

At the corner where I had turned on my way to the store there had been an English pub. Now there was only a pile of rubble. I ran on home. My parents and brothers were very relieved to see me, and had a story of their own to tell me. A large piece of shrapnel from a bomb casing had come through the kitchen roof just moments after they had passed through the kitchen on their way to our shelter in our back garden.

We learned later that a large land mine had been hurtling toward our area, but it had caught in the tall trees across the road from us, exploding into many pieces, one of which had ruined our kitchen roof. But for those trees, that bomb could have fallen right on our home, and I would have lost all my family. But for the friendly couple who took me, in I could have been right at the corner when the bomb hit the pub.

I learned a lesson of God's protecting power that day that has never left me.

RUTH LENNOX

The Washing Machine

Take heed that ye do not your alms before men, to be seen of them: otherwise ye have no reward of your Father which is in heaven. Matt. 6:1.

DEAR LORD," I PRAYED when I noticed the agitator wasn't turning and water still remained with the load of clothes in the machine. "You know I can't afford to buy a new washing machine right now."

I pushed and pulled on the agitator in the direction it would normally go if working properly, then gave the on/off knob a few spins in between. I also continued to pray about how much I needed the machine to function.

Suddenly it hit me. *You ungrateful child!* I thought to myself with much guilt, remorse, and shame. I raced to get the receipt, booklet, and contract that came with the machine. It was purchased in September 1983, and it was now 2001. That made the machine 18 years old. A replacement of the timer was the only repair made throughout its lifetime. The only time the machine got a break was on Sabbaths and when we went on vacation. I used it daily for uniforms, bedclothes, curtains, throw rugs, and towels. I frequently used every cycle. If it was washable, I washed it.

Now I was crying out, "Lord, You know I . . . and I need . . ." "I, I, I" instead of thanking God for having the ability to purchase the machine in the first place. According to the receipt, I put $100 down and paid $331.34 upon delivery. Installation was free. Replacing the timer five years later cost $150. In addition to that, it would not spin for a while at two different times—once in 2002 and again in January of 2003. I had left the machine and waited overnight before turning it on again; then it was business as usual until February 2003.

Having received an answer to that prayer, God even blessed me financially. I returned my tithes and offerings as usual, and I also returned a thank offering. Within two days I was given a 2-year-old washing machine that looks and runs like new. It was installed on the day my old machine would no longer run again. I was not charged an installation fee.

Lord, please help me recognize and be more appreciative of Your wonderful blessings.

Cora A. Walker

My Deliverer

And call upon me in the day of trouble: I will deliver thee, and thou shalt glorify me. Ps. 50:15.

WE WERE WORKING IN one of our boarding schools in northern India where summer is extremely hot. Just to be out of the house and in the open somewhere was all I could think of one hot summer night. I felt miserable in the heat, miserable in my fifth month of my first pregnancy. My husband, my mother, and I walked to our school farm area with our faithful dog trotting along like a bodyguard. It felt pleasant to be out, though it was late in the evening. Before returning home, we sat on the low boundary wall that separated the school campus and the farm. I got off the wall first and went to play with our dog and gave him a pat.

"Something pricked me," I told my husband as I jumped up and looked closely. "It was a snake!" I yelled. My frightened mother and husband rushed me to a lighted area. He checked my leg and found fang marks just below my right ankle.

Medical help was about two and a half miles from our campus; and the only person with a vehicle in those days was the principal, so we asked him to drive us to the hospital. At the first hospital all the doctors on night duty were out at an accident spot, so I was taken to a small clinic. But they had no medicine for me. Our next alternative was to go to a civil hospital. While in the hospital I knew my husband was worried because I heard him say to the doctor, "Save her; it is all right if you are unable to save the baby." My mother kept crying until she was sure that I was out of danger and we knew there was no poison spreading through my body. I recall that I wasn't frightened or worried while the others around me were anxious.

I did not want to lose my first baby. What saved us? Who saved us? People wondered and said, "Maybe it wasn't a poisonous snake." We do not know—all I saw was a snake. Someone (not a medical person) said, "Poison works slow on people with O-positive blood [my blood type]." I don't know how true that is; but one thing I know for sure is that I'd been praying throughout the ordeal, and the women on the campus cried and pleaded with the Lord to save me and my baby. He is my deliverer.

It doesn't matter what kind of trouble you are in. Pray! My favorite text has always been today's text. Today my first daughter is 20 years old. We continue to glorify God.

A. (Molly) Bara

Summer Sprinkles

I will sprinkle clean water on you, and you will be clean; I will cleanse you from all your impurities and from all your idols. I will give you a new heart and put a new spirit in you; I will remove from you your heart of stone and give you a heart of flesh. And I will put my Spirit in you and move you to follow my decrees and be careful to keep my laws. Eze. 36:25-27, NIV.

WHAT A BEAUTIFUL piece of writing this text is! It touches my heart. I was raised in an alcohol-affected home where, as the oldest child, I didn't feel free to be a child. My child's heart I locked away in a safe place so it wouldn't be totally destroyed. No love entered that stronghold where my heart was kept for "safekeeping"—and no pain or hurt entered it, either. As I grew into adulthood, that box stayed closed—even after marriage, children, divorce, and remarriage.

One day, when the trees were renewing their foliage, I read these verses. My life felt dirty, unworthy, unlovable, untouchable. Then I read, "I [God] will sprinkle clean water on you." Sprinkle gently, no "chuck a bucket" of water on me. "I will clean you." So I will be clean, rid of all the filthy history that I had. "I will give you a new heart and put a new spirit in you;" a new heart, a soft, gentle, loving, caring heart for myself and for others. Not an untouchable heart, but one that is soft, smooth, and reflecting gentleness. He will take away my stony heart, the one that was put away for safekeeping to protect it from pain and hurt.

This heart had become stony because it received no love or nurture while locked in the safe box. But God promised that He would change all that. I took Him at His word; I gave Him permission to open the locked safe box and breathe life and love back into my heart. It wasn't easy, the removal of fear and hurt. But now I have journeyed along the path of renewal, praising God daily for teaching me to love gently, to receive love gently, to give love gently. God is good.

When the summer rains came and sprinkles fell from heaven my heart rejoiced as I remembered what He had done for me, remembered from where I had come and the endless possibilities afforded to me now that my heart was open to be filled with His Son's light.

Father God, bring the summer rains to renew my dry thirsty land. Cleanse me, O God, and know my heart today. Thank You. JULIE NAGLE

Summer Camp Blues

"For I know the plans I have for you," declares the Lord, "plans to prosper you and not to harm you, plans to give you hope and a future." Jer. 29:11, NIV.

ARE YOU HOMESICK?" I asked. Misty's blond head nodded. It was the first day of camp, and I held the position of counselor to six preteen girls. The tears stopped for a while, but in the middle of song service the uninvited guests started again. Several hours later I crawled into my sleeping bag, eager for dreamland. My ear caught an unmistakable sniff and half-stifled sob. Reluctantly, I emerged and tiptoed over to Misty. Again I went through my routine of trying to comfort the homesick child. Eventually, I heard the sound of deep breathing.

The next morning she was sick from the previous night's crying. I attempted to get her excited for the day by describing all the fun activities planned. By the time my meager attempts started working, I had to head off to staff worship. During prayer requests the director asked how many counselors had homesick campers. I raised my hand.

The rest of the week continued much like the first day with my homesick one. She didn't want to eat, didn't want to be there, didn't want to do anything. I did what I could to make the moments as merry as possible. I tried to make the campers laugh, asked them questions about their day—anything to keep them happy. Nevertheless, at least once a day Misty cried for home.

"I need to talk to you." It was Thursday night, and Misty's voice warned of what was to come. "I hate it here! It wasn't worth my parents' money to send me. I'm not coming back ever again!" A short time later the girls' director came over to us and insisted that Misty join the evening activities. The homesick girl begrudgingly followed orders.

"Every year!" the girls' director stated to me after Misty had left. "Every year she does the same thing and still comes back!"

Sometimes in life we act like Misty. God places us where He wants us; yet we complain and cry, fuss and fume, at being there. No matter how much He tries to comfort us, we still miss where we came from or even where we could be. We want to go "home," and we neglect to see that where God has put us is right where He wants us to be. KRISTI GERACI

A Matter of Timeliness

Let us therefore come boldly unto the throne of grace, that we may obtain mercy, and find grace to help in time of need. Heb. 4:16.

YOU'RE ALWAYS ON TIME, aren't you?" a sister greeted me when I walked into church one Sabbath morning.

"It's a matter of principle," I told her, smiling. Another sister wanted to know the story behind the principle.

In the late 1940s, when I was a very young, trusting woman, I was supervisor of a confectionery shop, specializing in designing flowers of hard icing. A coworker, Evelyn, invited me to attend a gala affair with her husband and herself at 10:00 one night.

That evening as I walked the block to my apartment to meet the couple, I was startled by a movement in the bushes. A figure jumped out from the darkness. It was William, Evelyn's brother. He invited himself to my tiny walk-up for a soda. Uneasy because I did not know him very well, I let him in. Then I found I couldn't get him to leave.

At 10:15 the doorbell rang. From my window I could see Evelyn and her husband standing below. "It's late. Are you still coming?" they wanted to know. Minutes later the doorbell rang again. My cousins, visiting from Florida, had decided to find out why I was so late. Then William came out of my kitchen to suggest what he could do with the ice pick in his hand.

By then it was clear that he was up to no good. I was so thankful that everyone knew that punctuality was my watchword. It had saved my life.

In the 1970s I moved back to Florida. A kindly old gentleman invited me to a meeting at his church that evening. "I can't," I told him sadly. "I'd be too late. I would have just finished my tennis lessons then, and I wouldn't have a chance to go home to change before the meeting."

"Wear your tennis whites," he said, as tennis outfits of that day were suitable street wear.

I was there on time that evening, and no one questioned my dress. Those evangelistic meetings and the warmth of the people convinced me that this was a church I had to attend, so I went to every meeting after that. God had used timeliness and caring people to save my soul.

Thank You, merciful Lord, for using timeliness to save my life and grace to save my soul. G. G. (Geneva Gwendolyn) Taylor

I Can Do All Things

I can face any situation with Christ who gives me strength. Phil. 4:13, Clear Word.

NOT LONG AGO I was struggling to write a thesis for completion of the requirements for an academic degree. I would go to bed at night thinking about this project and would frequently say, "I just don't think I can do this." The next morning I would arise and attack it once more, energized and able to handle it until late in the day when I would be tired and return to the I-can't-do-this attitude. My moods alternated between utter despair when I was stuck to soaring elation when the paper was going well. Sad to say, my poor family suffered right along with me.

One week at church I assisted with the children's Bible school class. During the program they were repeating the Bible memory verse they had learned during the week, Philippians 4:13, where we are assured that we can do anything with Christ's help. Suddenly a light went off in my head and I realized that I hadn't been relying on the only thing that truly strengthens me—my God.

I once attended a motivational seminar in which the speaker was telling us how our messages—even to ourselves—could influence us positively or negatively. She illustrated this by calling a volunteer onto the stage, and asked the man to hold his arms straight out from his body on either side. She then told him to repeat after her three times: "I am a bad person, I am a bad person, I am a bad person." Then she instructed him to resist her pushing down on his arms. He resisted, but she easily pushed his arms down.

She then instructed him to repeat three times, "I am a good person, I am a good person, I am a good person," and then tried to push his arms down again. This time, try as she might, she couldn't get his arms down. She encouraged us to try it at home, if we didn't believe what we had seen. I tried it on my son, and it worked just as she had said it would.

We are stronger when we give ourselves encouragement and positive messages. As Henry Ford once said: "Whether you believe you can, or whether you believe you can't, you're absolutely right."

When you are faced with situations that seem beyond your abilities, remember that you are strongest when you give your abilities to Christ and let Him solve the problems.

FAUNA RANKIN DEAN

Wedding Feast

When you are invited by anyone to a wedding feast, do not sit down in the best place, lest one more honorable than you be invited by him. . . . But when you are invited, go and sit down in the lowest place, so that when he who invited you comes he may say to you, "Friend, go higher." Then you will have glory in the presence of those who sit at the table with you." Luke 14:8-10, NKJV.

CHRISTIAN WEDDINGS ARE some of the happiest occasions my husband and I enjoy. I also believe that weddings are very beautiful. Not only that, but weddings become an occasion to meet friends and old acquaintances whom we haven't seen for ages. The occasion becomes a time to renew friendships and catch up with all the news of our respective families.

My husband was asked to be one of the officiating ministers at one particular wedding. The other officiating pastor was the bride's father, who flew in from the Philippines. This special occasion brought the bride's relatives and loved ones from all over the United States. What a joy to see those who knew us from the mission field when we were together as missionaries in Thailand. As my husband and I were ready to leave for the reception, we offered to take the bride's parents in our car. Because the officiating ministers were the last to have their pictures taken with the newly married couple, we were almost late to the reception. Since there were almost 500 guests, it looked as if there was no place for us at the tables. The person in charge of the reception said, "You and Pastor will sit at the head table with the couple and their parents."

I replied, "Oh, no, please! We don't belong at that table." I also thought, *What if someone told us to leave the head table. I would certainly die of shame.* I said we could sit anywhere; I even saw some empty seats. However, since my husband was an officiating minister, we were designated to sit with the newly married couple. What a privilege and an honor it was for us to be at the head table!

When Jesus comes to claim His bride, the redeemed, there will be a greater and more impressive wedding banquet where hundreds of thousands will sit with Him. I am looking forward to that grand occasion.

Ofelia A. Pangan

Shingles That Tingle

God shall wipe away all tears from their eyes; and there shall be no more death, neither sorrow, nor crying, neither shall be any more pain: for the former things are passed away. Rev. 21:4.

ONE MORNING I LOOKED in the bathroom mirror. The scar on my chin was still pronounced, but the redness and the swelling were gone. I was happy and thankful to God to be able to wipe my face again with a towel.

Have you ever had shingles, shingles that tingle? Those of you who have had shingles will agree with me that it is a very painful ailment. Shingles is a sweet-sounding name for a terrible disease.

One evening I felt a funny sensation on my face. Later a red spot appeared on my chin. At first I thought it was an insect bite. The sore got bigger and became very painful. The next day more red spots appeared on my face. Someone said they were cold sores. I doubted they were, for I've had cold sores before, and they weren't as painful. Then my neighbor, a nurse, said, "I think you have shingles, Mrs. Christo." And shingles they were! The biggest sore was swollen with a cluster of transparent pimples in the middle.

I read all about shingles in the books at home. My head throbbed. My ear had a series of excruciating pains. Painkillers didn't help. Each time the pain came I stopped whatever I was doing and prayed, "Lord please take this pain away because I can't bear it. Anything, Lord, but this pain."

One morning, when looking in the mirror, I felt so sorry for myself that I cried. I told myself, "This too shall pass." In time I got over this bout with shingles and was happy to be free from pain once more.

God never intended for us to have pain. Pain is a result of sin. Jesus has promised to be with us always. It's comforting to know and to experience God's presence when we are in pain. I look forward to heaven and the new earth where pain does not exist. Take heart, all of you who have had shingles, or any other painful condition. Let's plan to be there. God wants us to be there.

BIROL CHARLOTTE CHRISTO

The Sun . . . Long Awaited!

For the Lord God is a sun and shield; . . . no good thing does he withhold from those whose walk is blameless. Ps. 84:11, NIV.

IT WAS A GRAY MORNING. The sky, heavy with dark clouds, predicted that the day would be one of those that no one likes when they're at a beautiful beach on vacation after months without feeling the benefits of the sun and without having had the liberty to walk barefoot in lightweight clothing.

While observing the people on the seashore, I saw a family arriving. They were all happy, chatting, and carrying all the necessary beach equipment to face a day with lots of sun. It seemed as though nothing had been forgotten: comfortable beach chairs, beach umbrella, a thermos of water, juice, food, and suntan lotion.

Just look at those people, I thought. I felt like laughing because there was no chance that we'd have the sunny day they had imagined. However, this family was certain, even though they didn't see the sun, that it was there behind the dark clouds and at any minute would come out and make them happy with its shiny rays. They had a faith that I did not have.

After a few hours they were delectably enjoying the solar benefits, and I had to leave so I wouldn't get sunburned.

Jesus is our sun. Even when we can't see Him, when the cold, dark clouds of trials involve us, He is present and always ready to warm us when we must travel the frozen paths of this world.

Even when the burden of life's sadness is too heavy, we can rest peacefully, believing that at the right time He will give us the relief and comfort we need, because beyond the thick dark clouds, the Sun still shines. We can say with confidence that "no good thing does he withhold from those whose walk is blameless." I know I want to be counted among that group, ready to enjoy the Sun.

Regardless of the weather today, won't you join me in walking in the Sonshine?

EDIT FONSECA

Hospitality

Be not forgetful to entertain strangers: for thereby some have entertained angels unawares. Heb. 13:2.

SUMMER WAS HASTENING to an end. *We must eat on our deck one more time,* I thought, *before fall comes and the cold winds blow.* And with that in mind, I invited the pastor and his wife and another couple to come home with us for dinner after church.

But as I sat in church, I noticed there were visitors again this day: a group of three young men, one of whom had been a former student of mine. I sat there pondering, *Shall I, or shall I not, invite them? I know I can always extend my food, but I had it all planned so nicely for the number of guests I wanted to invite.*

I remembered again the story I'd read recently in the weekly church paper. It seems this woman hesitated about inviting a guest to her house. But she did do it, and it had been an important invitation for the guest that day because of circumstances in her life. I knew it was something I could graciously do, and I needed to do it. (And I guess secretly I thought to myself that they might very well say no, but that I would have done my duty.)

David was glad to see me and eagerly accepted my invitation for the three of them. The sun shone brightly on the flowered placemats and added color to the curry, rice, and fruit salad. We had a pleasant afternoon, eating and visiting on the deck. And there was plenty of food for all.

Later, as they were leaving, the young man from one of the poorer countries in our hemisphere, who was working in a restaurant to help pay for his education, had a hard time expressing his gratefulness. Finally he burst out, "That was just the most wonderful meal I have ever had in a home."

I quickly responded, "I am so glad you could come." I was glad. It was just one of my usual company menus, but it was "wonderful" to him.

Surely God has blessed my home—and probably yours as well. Is it too much for us to make the effort to share them with others around us? God shared all He had with us; soon we can share new homes and eat with Him in heaven. Now, that will really be a wonderful meal!

DESSA WEISZ HARDIN

God Preserves His People

The Lord shall preserve your going out and your coming in from this time forth, and even forevermore. Ps. 121:8, NKJV.

WE ALWAYS PRAY BEFORE we leave home and ask God to guide us and protect us from all evil. One morning three of us planned to visit churches and schools in Dasuya. Before we started, we asked for God's mercies and for Him to be codriver with my husband.

The day was rainy, and the road was very rough. Near Khanpur we saw a big traffic tie-up ahead of us. My husband stopped the car and got out to see if we could get through. The rain had stopped by then, and the sun was very hot. Seeing the long queue, one of our passengers said, "Sir, I think an accident has taken place, and we have to wait for at least an hour—and we are already late." Meanwhile, I started praying in my heart: *God, please help people to clear the way soon as you know that we're already late—and it is very hot. Please, God, help us. Amen.*

As soon as I opened my eyes a police van came from behind, and one of the police officers waved his hand for us to follow his van. Without any hesitation we followed. Nobody stopped us, and within a few minutes we were out of the backup.

As we went a little further, I saw three young boys from our church going on a scooter along the road. We stopped and greeted each other. Suddenly one of the boys pointed at the back tire of our car and said, "Padre Sahib, I think your car's back tire is punctured."

My husband asked, "Is there a repair shop close by?" The boy said there wasn't, but if we had a tool kit he would change the tire, and we could pick it up from his home when we came back. So the boys changed the tire, and we thanked them and again we set out on our way. Thinking of those boys and the help they rendered to us, I repeated this verse quietly in my heart, "God is our refuge and strength, a very present help in trouble" (Ps. 46:1).

When we reached home, we knelt down and thanked God for the rain and for saving us from the accident. We also thanked God for sending those boys and the officer to help us.

My prayer is: *Lord, please help us to remember that You are always watching over Your children and are ever ready to deliver Your children in times of trouble.*

KAMLA MASIH

Thank You, Lord, for Saving!

The angel of the Lord encamps around those who fear him, and he delivers them. Ps. 34:7, NIV.

IT WAS JULY 14, 2002. I was traveling with the family of Pastor Raimundo, returning from Maceió in the direction of Aracaju. During the day we'd held a beautiful meeting for senior citizens in the capital of the state of Alagoas. It was rather dark and late by the time we reached the city of Maruim, near Aracaju. Suddenly, before us lay a dead horse on the highway in our lane of traffic.

There was no time to brake or to swerve to the other lane. It was a terrible crash! Because of the speed we were traveling, the car went airborne when it hit the animal, then turned over. While still on its side, the car slid more than 325 feet (100 meters) without stopping, heading directly toward a sharp drop off. *Lord, stop this car. Stop this car, Lord,* I prayed silently. God heard my simple prayer, stopping the overturned car right on the shoulder of the highway. The Lord prohibited our falling to the depths below the edge of the road. And no fire broke out.

A truck driver, who was apparently following right behind, stopped to alert other cars about the accident; and many people stopped to help us. They encircled our car, which was naturally somewhat damaged.

We thanked God because we felt His angels had protected us. No one broke any bones, nor were there any serious injuries. At that moment we felt Jesus had held us in His arms of love. I am grateful to God for His constant protection in my life. I feel that it was the power of continual prayer that saved our lives.

In the difficult moments of life, when we think we are alone, we are not. It is exactly at those times that the power of God acts most abundantly.

Each day we should be in communion with our beloved Jesus. As the Bible verse states, "Search me, O God, and know my heart; test me and know my anxious thoughts. See if there is any offensive way in me, and lead me in the way everlasting" (Ps. 139:23, 24, NIV).

May we walk each day on the eternal paths without fear, without wavering.

JÔNIA O. A. MENEZES

The Broken Sunflower

The flower fades, but the word of our God stands forever. Isa. 40:8, NKJV.

IT WAS IN THE late 1980s. The community hospital, my employer, was deep in financial crisis. Bent on keeping the hospital solvent, the new administration began downsizing, giving my quality assurance title to a new employee. Shortly thereafter the head of the medical records department resigned. Being a registered record administrator, I hoped I'd be asked to fill the vacancy. Instead, the administration employed a new graduate and asked me to do medical transcription, in addition to being secretary to the medical staff. I was also to assist in their committee functions, regular meetings, and ongoing retrospective patient-care review. The drop in my pay to that of a transcriptionist came hard. I asked the Lord to handle my life.

While tending my organic garden, I felt free to pour out my heartaches to Him who made the plants grow and the birds sing. One day I saw a sunflower seedling growing between the tomatoes. In spite of the fact that my *Organic Gardening* magazine warned that sunflowers inhibit other plants' growth, I left it alone. It grew like a weed; soon a large bud appeared. Before long, yellow petals unfolded, and the blossom kept its face to the sun.

On my way to work every morning, I visited it for moments of inspiration. One day, however, I found the stalk broken. I completed the break and took the long-stemmed blossom with me to the office. I set it in a water-filled container, centered it on the windowsill, drooped blossom facing in. As the afternoon sun rays came through the windowpane, the blossom gradually turned to the sun. I shared this awe-inspiring response with my coworkers. Though broken, the sunflower lives up to its name. My heart warmed to the promise in Romans 8:28 that "all things work together for good to them that love God."

Not long after that I lost even the transcriptionist job; but after attending a workshop I was offered a job with a salary three times that of my lost one, plus benefits galore. The workshop and experience working at the largest military hospital in the world broadened my horizon.

Lord, I praise and thank You, for in acknowledging You in all my ways You did indeed direct my path (Prov. 3:6). CONSUELO RODA JACKSON

The Boat Ride

Then the waters would have overwhelmed us, the stream would have gone over our soul. Ps. 124:4, NKJV.

THE TINY LOG CABIN nestled among the pines along the St. Croix River. It was sunny and hot, and this promised to be a relaxing, wonderful weekend. Along with the cabin came the use of a boat. We had come there with our friends and agreed to share expenses. Each of us had a small baby with us, and this promised to be a fun getaway.

Nancy's husband had a small motor, so we planned a boat ride down the river in the afternoon. After lunch we left to go exploring. Everything went well for a while. It was great fun with the wind blowing through our hair. The two babies, Dixie and Sandi, seemed to enjoy the ride, too.

We were out in the middle of the river channel when suddenly the motor sputtered and stopped. Wayne pulled the starter rope many times, but there wasn't even a spark. It wasn't going to start! Here we were in the middle of the river, caught in a swift current, and drifting rapidly. Our husbands grabbed the oars and tried rowing, but we were drifting with the current so rapidly we began going in circles. That wasn't the worst of it. We were headed straight for Taylor's Falls—and they were close! What began as a pleasant day was turning into a nightmare.

Nancy and I began to desperately pray that the Lord would spare all of us. As we drew closer to the falls, we prayed harder. All the while Wayne worked feverishly to get the motor going. By now we were getting close to the warning rope strung across the river. The current was so powerful, I could scarcely breathe. "Please, Lord, help us," I said out loud. Just then the motor sputtered and started. Praise the Lord! The boat began to move, but we could gain only inches at a time because the current was so strong. Finally, much to everyone's relief, we got far enough away from the falls and to the side of the river, out of danger.

Without a doubt, the Lord had saved us.

Thank You, Lord, that You were there to rescue us, and that You continue to rescue us.

DARLENE YTREDAL BURGESON

Walking on the Water

And Peter answered him and said, Lord, if it be thou, bid me come unto thee on the water. And he said, Come. And when Peter was come down out of the ship, he walked on the water, to go to Jesus. Matt. 14:28, 29.

WHEN I WAS LITTLE I loved listening to the weather forecast—a strange thing for a little girl to enjoy, but I liked to hear how the sea was doing. You see, small islands like Trinidad and Tobago depend a lot on commercial and subsistence fishing. So the weather forecast includes the condition of the sea. On nice days the forecast might be: "Seas calm, waves 1.5 meters [5 feet] and 1 meter [3.3 feet] in sheltered areas." During bad weather it might be: "Seas choppy, waves 2 meters [6.5 feet] and 1.5 meters [5 feet] in sheltered areas." God would use these forecasts in a special way to help me.

Several years ago I faced several personal storms. I had been in the United States for only a short time and was still adjusting to a new culture and new accents as I worked and attended graduate school. My uncle had died of cancer the year before, and I had just received news that my grandfather—the only real father to me—had the same cancer and had only a few months to live. I had little money and was frantically trying to get money for a plane ticket so I could see him. I had recently been through a violent experience and was trying, with the help of my family, friends, and a Christian counselor, to overcome the resulting shock and depression.

I became so overwhelmed during my devotion time one day I did nothing but cry. God led me to Matthew 14. As I read the story of Jesus' walk on the waves, I remembered the weather forecasts in Trinidad. I imagined what the forecast might have predicted for that night: "Sea turbulent, waves 2.5 meters [8 feet] and no sheltered areas!" I appreciated the courage it took for Peter to step out onto those waves that were perhaps six feet (1.8 meters) high. But as long as he focused on Jesus, Peter walked on top of the waves, too. I prayed, *Father, help me to stop sinking. Help me to trust You enough to walk on top of my storms.* As peace filled my heart that day I began the process of really learning to trust God. It didn't happen all at once, but God brought me to a place of faith. Nowadays when a storm appears I hold my head high and step out onto those six-foot waves with my hand securely in my Savior's.

KAREN ABDOOL

Doing It My Way

Trust in the Lord with all your heart; do not depend on your own understanding. Prov. 3:5, NLT.

PLEASE STAY OFF THE highways unless it's an emergency. Don't go out unless you absolutely must. It's very dangerous to be out on the roads and beaches."

These were advisories from the media after a tropical storm passed through our area. Even during the storm they were encouraging people to stay inside: "Don't go out to see how strong the winds are!"

But we are curious people. When it's announced there is high surf, we go to see it. When there's an accident, we slow down to figure out what and how it happened. The site of a crime scene becomes a pilgrimage for people to flock to with flowers and other remembrances.

Ever notice how we as humans just hate being told what to do? What not to do? It's like we want to be free to do anything we want, when we want, where we want. When someone says we should or shouldn't do something, we feel it's an infringement on our personal freedom. Some respond by saying, "Nobody is going to tell me how to live my life. It's my life."

Cities encourage people to carpool or take public transportation. Most cities struggle with too many cars on the road at certain times of the day. But people don't want to give up the freedom that comes with driving their own car. There are special lanes provided for three or more persons traveling together, but people who drive alone abuse even that.

So it's understandable that when we ask people to give up one day a week totally to the worship of God, they balk. God says in His Word to come aside and rest, "Spend 24 hours with Me and My family—your church family. Develop a deeper relationship with Me during those 24 hours through worship and relating to others as I would." We are to take the time to reach out to others who need our love, patience, forgiveness, mercy, and grace.

We can do this only by allowing God to work through us, by being His channels. We have to surrender ourselves to what God asks of us, to give up our I-know-better attitudes, and humbly accept His wisdom and guidance in and for our lives. "Pay attention to my wisdom; listen carefully to my wise counsel" (Prov. 5:1, NLT).

LOUISE DRIVER

The Blessed Doorkeeper

For a day in thy courts is better than a thousand. I had rather be a doorkeeper in the house of my God, than to dwell in the tents of wickedness. Ps. 84:10.

THE WORDS OF OUR text came from the depths of David's heart, for he had missed church for many, many weeks. David was in hiding from Saul. He was an exile from home in his own country. Out there in the wilderness, among rocks and the deep recesses of the caves, he found refuge. Even though deprived of a normal, peaceful life, his main desire was to attend church. He longed to worship with God's people and to take his offering to the altar. He felt that even to be just a door-keeper in the temple courts would be great.

In Psalm 84 David mentions both the sparrow and the swallow, common birds in Palestine. Perhaps David had seen these birds having free access into the sacred precincts of the temple many times (verse 3). David, as an exile, was unable to attend church. In verse 4 he said, "Blessed are they that dwell in thy house."

I've just learned of a modern-day doorkeeper of a church. It seems that at one church there was a problem between the members and the pastor that they weren't able to reconcile. So the members stopped coming to church, and the pastor locked the church and left. But there was one member who wouldn't give up. Week after week she faithfully went to church with her Bible and songbook. She had no key to open the church, so she had her worship alone on the doorstep. She sang, read her Bible, and prayed. The nonbelievers mockingly told her to hire day laborers for one day a week to fill the church for her. Nevertheless, she continues this practice to this day as I write this story.

Another member was denied entry to her church because the members did not approve of her marriage. She felt rejected by God himself for decades. Later, she found another church that allowed her to enter but denied her membership. She said that even if they allowed her to be a door-keeper in God's church it would be a blessed experience. I am happy to say that after a long wait she was accepted into the church as a full member.

Do we consider it our privilege to go to church? Each hour of sacred Sabbath worship is for our blessing. It is to prepare us to dwell in God's house forever. Consider yourself blessed!

BIRDIE PODDAR

Miracle at the Fabric Store

The grace of our Lord was poured out on me abundantly, along with the faith and love that are in Christ Jesus. 1 Tim. 1:14, NIV.

THE NEATEST THING happened to me at the fabric store the other day. I'd been working all afternoon on a new dress for church when I got to wondering whether some flowered trim I'd bought for another project would look nice on it. It was a perfect match; however, there was enough to go around the neck but not completely around the hem. I considered just trimming the neck and leaving the hem plain, but when I modeled the dress for my husband he said he thought it'd look better with matching trim at the hemline. So I took his advice and drove over to our local fabric store. They didn't have any of the trim, so I got back into my car and started over the mountain to Frederick—a half hour away.

The Frederick store has a much bigger selection of trims, but after twice searching all four aisles from top to bottom, I was ready to give up. I knelt in front of a row of trim on the bottom shelf that had rolls of similar design but none of the same color. I told myself that if they had any it would be right here. I started to stand up and walk out when I heard a voice inside my head ask, "Have you prayed about it?" I wasn't sure if I had or not, so I bowed my head and made my simple request: "God, if it's here, please help me find it." I opened my eyes and looked down at the row of trims again, noticing how crooked and crowded the rolls were. *H'mm,* I said to myself, *I wonder if a roll could get pushed out of line and fall to the back of the shelf?* I bent down and peered behind the rolls of trim. There was one roll sitting sideways behind the others. Could it be the one I was looking for? I reached in and picked it up. Hallelujah! It was! My vision blurred a bit as I knelt there holding God's answer in my hand.

The sales clerk asked me how much I needed and I told her I'd take all of it. I decided as long as I was being blessed, I might as well be blessed abundantly. And I was. Not only was there enough trim on that roll to finish trimming the hem of my dress, there was more than enough left over for the first project. Isn't that just like God?

Maybe it was just another answered prayer in God's busy day, but to me it was a miracle; I know I would've walked out of the store empty-handed if I hadn't asked God to help me look.

TOYA MARIE KOCH

The Power of Prayer

They that wait upon the Lord shall renew their strength; they shall mount up with wings as eagles; they shall run, and not be weary; and they shall walk, and not faint. Isa. 40:31.

I WANT TO TELL YOU about my best friend's mother, Mrs. Zita, and what her life has taught me. Though widowed, she was determined to take care of her three young ones. Life was not easy, but she managed to educate her children in Christian schools by sacrificing and doing without a car. At the same time she studied university courses through correspondence and attended classes at night.

She sacrificed much for her children, teaching them the love of God and the power of prayer. I remember visiting her home—it was filled with warmth and love. During prayer time she would ask each of her children to recite a memory verse. She led a simple life, and I know that caring for the children alone wasn't easy for her.

She was young and beautiful, and I think could have married again, but she didn't. As time went on she finished her studies and graduated. At her graduation, she thanked God for all He had done for her, how He had taken her from nothing to where she was. Little did she know, but God had a lot in store for her.

Mrs. Zita cared not only for her children but also for her relatives. She encouraged her younger sister to go to school and offered financial help. She encouraged her niece, who was working in a factory, to go to school. Now she is a doctor. She encouraged me to continue with my studies after I finished my diploma in teaching, and I am pursuing further studies. She was also a dedicated mother in church.

Two of Mrs. Zita's daughters completed their college education—one is a doctor and is my best friend; the other is a lawyer. A third daughter is busily studying medicine. Two of them are married. She is blessed with a job as principal in a higher primary school. When she is 55 she plans to retire and begin selling Christian books from door to door.

Mrs. Zita was a living testimony to me. I learned several things: that the tears we experience in life will one day be washed away, and to never to give up because there is power in prayer. She waited on the Lord and received her strength. We should do the same. DEBORAH MATSHAYA

Judging

Judge not, that ye be not judged. Matt. 7:1.

MY GRANDDAUGHTER, ASHLEY, works for a woman who lives around the corner from us. She has horses of her own, as well as boarding horses. As I drop Ashley off to work, I always go to the barn to see the horses. I love to talk to each one and pet them all.

One day when I went to pick up Ashley, she had a horse in the hall in cross-ties, brushing her. Ashley was telling me what a sweet horse Lea was and that she really liked her. I approached the horse and reached up to pet her, but she laid back her ears and pulled away. I tried to reassure her that I was no threat; but every time I tried to pet her nose or face, she acted up. Different times when I went to the barn I'd try to pet her face, but she never wanted me to.

I love horses, and usually they respond to the attention; but I gave up on Lea, even though Ashley told me she was such a great horse. I didn't think so. Yes, she was in beautiful color and form, but what an attitude! Every time I came I visited all the other horses who were glad for my attention, but I left Lea alone.

One day as I was talking to the owner, she told me a story about her horse, Lea. One day when Lea was young, she was in her stall, her head leaning over the half-door. Someone came up and grabbed her. She reared and hit the top part of the door, ripping her face and forehead open. Since then Lea has been wary of people coming up and petting her head.

Now I understood why Lea was acting as she did—seemingly so unfriendly. She had a good reason. I had a little talk with Lea and discovered that she is very friendly if you just don't touch her face. Sometimes we prejudge others before we know all the facts. How we need to know people better and not jump to conclusions!

When we prejudge, we are unable to interact with others as we should. If I had found out the facts about Lea earlier rather than judging her, I would have approached her differently. ANNE ELAINE NELSON

The Sunshine State

Trust in the Lord with all thine heart; and lean not unto thine own understanding. In all thy ways acknowledge him, and he shall direct thy paths. Prov. 3:5, 6.

THE TIME HAS COME," I told my husband one day. "The children are all grown now. After nine years in England and 19 here in Brooklyn, I think it's time to relocate to a warmer climate." The more we thought about it and prayed about it, the stronger the urge grew. But we hadn't heard from the Lord. So we waited.

One weekend we decided to take a trip down south. We wanted to see what Palm Bay was like. We loved it! That Sunday I asked God to send us $4,000 by Wednesday if He wanted us to move. That's how much we needed to send to the contractor to start building our house. I wrote the check but didn't mail it. By early that Wednesday morning I had the funds. He had spoken.

But I needed another sign. "Lord, I want to be absolutely sure that this move is Your will. Please send me another $4,000."

Everything was going well as we made plans to move. My husband's cousin, who owns a moving truck, stopped by to visit. "You are moving us to Florida," I told him in no uncertain terms. "And you are moving us in August." His surprise at my certainty was obvious. "You're moving our things to Palm Bay, and we're giving you $1,000."

His astonishment grew as he flopped back in the chair. "Wait a minute here!" he remonstrated. "I can't move you for that price. It will cost you at least $2,000."

Undaunted, I responded, "Don't forget the date."

My heavenly Father was summoned again. Some months later our cousin, the moving man, called. "Guess what?" He sounded unbelieving. "I have to move a woman from Queens to Miami; she wants to leave on the same date as you do. I'll load her things in the truck first, and then I'll take yours." Jubilant, we praised the Lord again.

But where would we find the $1,000? Again I approached my Father, who promised to hear and answer. And guess what? He did just that. I received a check just in time!

"The Lord is my strength and shield; my heart trusted in him, and I am helped: therefore my heart greatly rejoiceth; and with my song will I praise him" (Ps. 28:7). ELIZABETH MCINTOSH

Thank You, Aubrey

And Jesus increased in wisdom and stature, and in favor with God and man. Luke 2:52.

THE BABY HAD THICK, black hair and deep, brown eyes that occasionally opened to gaze at the wonder of the new world around; a perfect little nose; perfectly formed red mouth that was constantly moving; changing expressions; yawns so big that it looked like it hurt; and a tiny little chin that quivered when the mouth unsuccessfully searched for milk. The features were set in a smooth, light-brown face with fat, pink cheeks.

I was sitting on the couch one lovely August morning admiring my week-old granddaughter, Aubrey. As I memorized each feature I realized I could also have been describing the baby Jesus, and the wonder of His sacrifice overwhelmed me once again.

I think Aubrey is just perfect, of course, but sometimes she is obviously uncomfortable and lets us know that she wants something changed: her diaper, her feeding schedule, the light, or her position. And I know that in spite of her loving parents and grandparents who would do anything for her, things will not always go perfectly for her. There will be pain, and there will be discomfort. We just don't know when or where or perhaps why. That's life.

But when the Trinity decided that part of the Godhead would come to this earth as a tiny baby, God knew that little Baby would be a long way from the perfection of heaven. God knew precisely the kinds of taunts, struggles, and wants that this child Jesus would have to endure. What's more (and most amazing), the members of the Godhead knew the temptations that would be faced, and the horror, the pain, and ultimately the death on the cross that this Child would endure as an adult. But Jesus decided to come as this little Baby anyway. For you and for me. He was willing to come to a suffering world that is often unfair. For you and for me. No other reason. No personal benefit for Him, other than a relationship with us.

Thank you, Aubrey, for reminding me of this great mystery. It is more than I will ever comprehend. Never would I want to think of such things happening to you.

Thank You, heavenly Father, for Your willingness to think such thoughts, for taking such risks—for me. ARDIS DICK STENBAKKEN

Flashlight Fish

The Lord is my light and my salvation. Ps. 27:1.

MY WALK THROUGH A southern California marine science museum felt a bit like snorkeling without getting wet. The beautiful exhibits included hundreds of fish and other sea life. Children especially enjoyed the human-made tide pool because they could reach in and touch the ocean creatures.

Rows of large display tanks treated curious onlookers to a variety of fish. I saw lumpy ones and flat ones. Some sported stripes, while others were adorned in polka dots. There were beautiful fish and ugly fish, comical fish and ferocious looking creatures. Some looked like rocks, others like snakes. They came in every color of the rainbow, and all were fascinating to see.

One display looked empty and dark. I almost passed it by until I saw a sign: "Flashlight Fish." I pictured fish with little batteries strapped to their sides. A small window in the tank offered a view of these special little fish. When I tried to locate them, though, I couldn't see anything but black. After waiting for what seemed to me to be a reasonable length of time, I still saw only darkness. I had almost given up when I noticed a small beam of light that shone for only a fraction of a second, but it was enough to see that fish were really there.

The Bible tells us that God has a plan for our lives—even if we don't always see what it is. Sometimes it's as though we're peering into total darkness. Even when we pray and wait for what seems to be a reasonable length of time, we may still see nothing.

But every now and then the Lord seems to flash a signal to us through a Bible verse, a prayer, or a person in our lives. It may be small and of short duration, but it sends a beam of light to penetrate the darkness of our souls. It is enough for us to know that there is light, and then we begin to see the direction of His leading.

Then, no matter what happens, it's OK, because that little light tells us that God is really with us, even though we can't see Him. The good news is: He always will be.

MARCIA MOLLENKOPF

Summertime Surprise

In the midst of the street of it, and on either side of the river, was there the tree of life, which bare twelve manner of fruits. Rev. 22:2.

SUMMERTIME IS PEACH time in the Carolinas, and once again I've done some canning and freezing so we'll be able to enjoy the fruit after the season is over. As always, I remember the long ago summer of 1950.

I was looking forward to my wedding day and decided to surprise my groom with home-canned peaches. Back then there was a wonderful orchard only a few miles from my home in Tennessee. I thought that picking the peaches would make my offering even more special, as well as saving money—which was scarce. So my mother and I went to the orchard and plucked the luscious ripe fruit from the trees.

Mother's canned peaches were always artistically packed, so I did the same with mine. How proud I was of those jars of golden, rosy-tinged peach halves! What I didn't know until much later was that Ted was highly suspicious of any home-canned fruit or vegetable.

Actually, he had good reason for feeling that way. His grandmother had canned green beans without using a pressure canner, and the jars, tucked behind a trunk in her bedroom, had exploded, one by one, spewing green beans all over the room.

Strangely enough, my grandmother had done the same thing. In spite of Mother's warning that green beans could not be canned in a hot water bath the way peaches can be, she was sure it would work. Her rude awakening came quite literally when the jars stored under her bed gave way, making quite a mess and doing away with our winter supply of green beans.

During the more than 50 years we've been married, Ted has learned that home-canned food, if done right, can be perfectly safe and good to eat. But I picture a day when it won't be necessary to go through the process of preserving. In heaven there will be the tree of life offering a different fruit every month. No doubt there will also be other trees with fruit hanging in clusters, ready to be picked and eaten. I can imagine wonderful varieties that we've never had before, with taste beyond anything this earth has to offer. There will be no more wondering about the safety of the food or dealing with exploding jars of green beans. Sounds good to me! What about you?

MARY JANE GRAVES

The Stain

Though your sins are like scarlet, they shall be white as snow; though they are red as crimson, they shall be like wool. Isa.1:18, NIV.
These are they who have come out of the great tribulation; they have washed their robes and made them white in the blood of the Lamb. Therefore, they are before the throne of God and serve him day and night in his temple. Rev. 7:14, 15, NIV.

WHILE PREPARING ONE of our favorite meals of spaghetti and tomato sauce, I made extra, just in case. My husband put away the leftovers in a clear plastic container. Over the next two days when spaghetti was desired, some was removed and the remainder returned to the refrigerator.

After a few more times of serving, the sauce was gone—except for the red stains on the bowl. After days of soaking, scrubbing, and bleaching the container was clean but the stains were still there.

I was later doing a load of laundry and carefully sorting out the colors from the whites. Upon removing the clothes from the washer, I noticed that the entire wash was a very vibrant shade of pink! I searched diligently for the culprit, which turned out to be a tiny, red baby sock. That one little baby sock had ruined my wash!

Likewise, one unforgiven sin can stain our lives forever. Sin is so ugly. In our daily Christian walk we see the evidences of sin and its ugly web. God has a chemical laboratory of redemption that will take my sins, wash them in the Blood of the Lamb, and make my heart whiter than snow.

We have all sinned. We've tried to clean ourselves up and make ourselves right; but the more we try to make it appear all right, the bigger mess we make of the situation. However, we have an Intercessor, One to whom we can go to confess our sins and be assured of forgiveness. The Lord can still use us in His service if we are willing and obedient, allowing Him to order our steps.

Dear Lord, thank You for another day. Please wash away the stain of my sins and order my steps to Your will. Thank You. Amen. BETTY G. PERRY

Overcorrected

O Lord, you are my God; I will exalt you and praise your name, for in perfect faithfulness you have done marvelous things. Isa. 25:1, NIV.

I HAD SIX PATIENTS TO visit, so I began with the one who lived farthest away. I had completed my first assignment and moved toward the next one. The road, a busy two-lane highway, had a ditch on each side. My speed increased as the speed limit allowed, and I was soon traveling between 50 and 55.

Suddenly my car veered to the left, putting me on a collision course with an oncoming vehicle if I hadn't quickly turned back to my lane. But I overcorrected. The next moment I found myself on the other side of the ditch, my car "turned turtle." I was hanging head down by my seat belt. My right pointer finger was bleeding—apparently from broken glass. My right hand was turning purple, possibly from getting twisted in the steering wheel.

Fifteen minutes later a man in a navy-blue uniform was squatting by my left side, looking up at me. "Hi; how are you?"

"I'm OK!" I responded. "Get me out of here!"

A few minutes later other officers and two ambulances arrived with equipment to cut away the driver's door. In a few moments I was fastened on a gurney and away we went, headed to the trauma center. Intravenous fluid was started in the ambulance. After one liter of IVF was infused and all the X-rays were completed at the hospital, I was released.

That evening was an agape feast prepared by the women's ministries of our church. My testimony was one of thankfulness. Even though I overcorrected, God made sure that His correction was just right. He sent an angel to protect me at the exact place and at the right time.

For the sake of His children, God never leaves us alone, especially in precarious places. He is the perfect "Corrector." His amazing love cannot be overestimated. He will be there for those who trust Him.

"Blessed is the [woman] whom God corrects," Job says (5:17, NIV). And Proverbs 29:15 declares, "The rod of correction imparts wisdom" (NIV). And finally, Psalm 32:10 says, "Many are the woes of the wicked, but the Lord's unfailing love surrounds the [woman] who trusts in him" (NIV).

Esperanza Aquino Mopera

A Family Picture

And a little child shall lead them. Isa. 11:6, NKJV.

THE SUMMER THAT MY youngest granddaughter was 2, she and her mother visited me from their home in Maryland. We had a happy time getting reacquainted. We drove to the farm for a few days so Katherine could become familiar with the home in which her mother had been raised. We visited cousins, aunts, and uncles; and the weeks sped by. Too soon it was time for them to return home.

I drove them to the airport. We arrived a little early, so we picked up a snack and sat at a table in the lunch room. At a table diagonally across from us were four airport employees enjoying their coffee break. We could tell who they were by the logos on their jackets. A fifth young man arrived, pulled up a chair, and joined them. There was welcoming laughter, and they seemed happy to be together.

Katherine watched them curiously—as children will—and then she said one word: "Family." In her baby voice she began to sing, "I wuv you; you wuv me; we a happy famiwee." The look on her face told me that what she saw represented the words she had sung. The openness, the camaraderie, the smiles, and the laughter are really what love is all about—what family should be all about.

If we adults could get past our hang-ups about color or creed, wealth or poverty, and all the other mountainous molehills that attend our days, we could be what our Creator intended us to be: His children, His family. People are watching us to see if we are reflecting God's character. One time the Pharisees said to Jesus, "We know you are a man of integrity and that you teach the way of God in accordance with the truth. You aren't swayed by men, because you pay no attention to who they are" (Matt. 22:16, NIV). So we, too, must accept people as they are and become a family.

"Out of the mouths of babes," you've heard it said, and "except ye become as little children . . ." Thank you, Katherine, for helping us to understand.

EVA ALICE COVEY

Embracing the Light

For God, who commanded the light to shine out of darkness, hath shined in our hearts, to give the light of the knowledge of the glory of God in the face of Jesus Christ. 2 Cor. 4:6.

THE REPUBLIC OF PALAU has become the Pacific Ocean center for coral reef studies and reef conservation for the twenty-first century. Not long ago that country opened a national aquarium on the 129-square-mile island of Babeldoep, with an accompanying museum full of living exhibits that display live coral and other sea life.

"Look at those darling things!" I exclaimed to my husband, pointing to one of these museum exhibits. We looked at what appeared to be myriads of satin-covered, golden-white Victorian lampshades gliding past one another in slow motion behind the glass of a smaller aquarium. The nonscientific name for these creatures is nonstinging jellyfish. A write-up near the exhibit stated that other than this museum these unique sea creatures live in only one other location: a fresh water lake high atop one of the mountains in the Palaun archipelago.

Early each morning these exquisite creatures congregate on the eastern side of the lake, waiting for the sun to rise. As the sun climbs into the sky and moves across the heavens, the jellyfish follow the source of the sunbeams, feeding on algae as they go, and playing in the sunlight. By evening the sun has led them to the western shore.

Here's something else I found fascinating about these jellyfish that follow the sun: they never do harm to other creatures, as do most other species of jellyfish. The freshwater jellyfish are too busy following the sun. When darkness comes at night, the jellyfish somehow "remember" where they last saw the light originate. They make their way back across the lake to patiently wait for the sun, when they can embrace the light once again.

Likewise, the more we embrace the light God desires to shine into our hearts, the less harm we will do to others—and to ourselves. We, too, can follow His light from early each morning until we lie down to sleep at night. God has promised that when we live in His light we will experience, personally, His glory through our relationship with the Son of Righteousness.

CAROLYN RATHBUN SUTTON

A Serendipity

I will comfort them and exchange their sorrow for rejoicing. Jer. 31:13, NLT.

I HAD BLOWN IT! The can't-wait problems on my desk had delayed my departure to my son's house more than 100 miles away. When I called to tell him of the delay, his wife informed me that the surprise he had planned for my birthday would no longer be available.

I was heartsick until he called back and invited me to go with him to another concert in San Francisco the next evening. My excitement mounted during our fast trip to the concert hall. Suddenly we stood in front of the building, but nobody was around. Something was dreadfully wrong. My heart sank again as I read the sign about the 3:00 matinee. Why was my son's loving gesture turning out so wrong? Why did we have to be disappointed again? I felt truly heartbroken that I had spoiled my son's initial plans, and now it seemed that the new plans were down the drain, too.

Across the street men and women in formal dress were entering another hall by a side door. With my curiosity piqued, I suggested we go across the street and see what was happening. My joy knew no bounds when we discovered it was a recital given by Kiri te Kanawa. Her vocal solo at Princess Diana's and Prince Charles's wedding, plus her recordings in my possession, had given me a deep appreciation for her music.

All along, God knew what He was doing with our disappointments. He provided the most amazing serendipity, which Webster defines as the faculty of making fortunate and unexpected discoveries by accident.

It was one of the most memorable concerts I've ever attended. The rapport between the artist and the audience was electric. Every number brought unbounded applause. With encore after encore, it seemed she was as reluctant to end the recital as the audience was to let the magic of the night die away.

God understands our pain, our heartaches, our trials and disappointments. He's just preparing us for a very special surprise. No serendipity this time. The long-hoped-for joy, excitement, and ecstasy beyond our wildest imagination will never die but only grow more glorious with each passing moment. *O Jesus, come quickly.* DONNA LEE SHARP

Unspoken Messages

When you talk, do not say harmful things, but say what people need—words that will help others become stronger. Then what you say will do good to those who listen to you. Eph. 4:29, NCV.

THE QUESTION WAS HOW do you like it? After studying the girl's hair, Melissa said rather diffidently, "It's fine." But one eyebrow arched toward the ceiling, and one shoulder lifted ever so slightly. The person who posed the question walked away.

Later, as we were cleaning up after the summer potluck, the opportunity presented itself for a little chat. "Angie says I hurt her feelings," Melissa began, a stack of paper plates in her hand. "I told her it was fine!"

"But she knows you didn't like the cut," I mused. Melissa was silent. "Well," I persisted, "did you like it?"

"It was absolutely abominable!" (Melissa was into alliteration at the moment, and I suppressed a chuckle.) Her words were accompanied by a rather unladylike snort.

"The spoken message was 'It's fine,'" I pointed out, "but the unspoken message said the opposite. A mismatch between the spoken and the unspoken messages is often the basis for misunderstandings, especially since 75 percent of the content may be portrayed through nonverbals!" Melissa's face curved into a question mark, and I continued. "The unspoken message generally reflects what we really think, and the listener often reacts to that."

"H'mmm," Melissa mused. "What could I have said?"

Fortunately, I had my mother's example of canning compliments. It suggests the benefits of preplanning compliments that are genuinely affirming. This can be especially critical when we need to say something and our own personal tastes differ. For example, Melissa might have said: "The texture of your hair works well with that style," or "That's a great time-saving cut for summer," or "Kool." It was, literally.

A horn tooted out front. "'Bye for now," Melissa called, and ran for the car. A fragment of conversation drifted toward the front porch: "Guess what, Mom? I'm starting a journal of preplanned compliments."

ARLENE TAYLOR

Cowboy Wisdom

Keep me as the apple of the eye; hide me in the shadow of thy wings. Ps.17:8.

CARL IS A COWBOY. At 74 he's still tall and lanky with sun-leathered skin. Always a gentleman, he rarely speaks and quietly ends each response with "ma'am" or "sir." He spent his life riding horses and rounding up cows. Now he suffers from lung and heart problems caused by years of countless cigarettes—which he still can't completely give up. He's unable to walk more than 10 feet without stopping to catch his breath.

Carl severely injured his left leg a month ago and requires daily wound care. He's unable to do this for himself, so for the past four weeks I've been changing his dressings almost every day. The procedure is complicated and sometimes painful. Carl patiently endures what has to be done as I talk about the weather, the football games, my family, or anything else to keep his mind occupied. Sometimes during the dressing change the pain is evident in his eyes or by the stiffening of his arms or legs. "I'm so sorry, Carl; I don't want to hurt you," I gently apologize; and I pause for a few moments until Carl says, "OK, ma'am."

At the close of each visit I shake his hand and tell him it was a pleasure to see him. Carl always just nods his head and says, "Thank you, ma'am." That is, until last Friday. That day as I put my hand on the doorknob to leave Carl slowly said, "Ma'am, is your husband proud of you?" As I stood there trying to figure out how to respond to a question like that, he quietly added, "He should be."

Do you ever tell someone in your family or circle of friends that you're proud of them? That they are doing something well? Do you ever feel as if no one could possibly be proud of you? Do you have days when you feel totally worthless? Do you thank people for what they do for you? Don't ever forget that there's Someone who's incredibly proud of you. No matter what you've done (or haven't done), you are still the apple of God's eye! He loves you more than life itself. Bask in the sunshine of His love!

SUSAN WOOLEY

If Your Problems Persist

In my distress I called upon the Lord, and cried unto my God: he heard my voice out of his temple. Ps. 18:6.

ON AUGUST 11, 2002, I woke up early to the sound of someone coughing and sneezing. Not surprisingly, it was 8-year-old Elwin, the elder of my two sons. He'd had a terrible cough for some time, but this time I began to panic as he coughed and sneezed uncontrollably. I couldn't bear the sound of my son in such agony.

From the time he was 5 Elwin had not had good health. Though it was just a common cold and cough, it was persistent enough to make us worry. We consulted several doctors who performed all possible tests on him, only to show that everything was normal. He took medication for a few months and was even restricted from playing outdoors or having oil in his bath. He was constantly remembered in our prayers, yet he only developed more complications. We were in and out of all the hospitals in town, but all our efforts proved futile.

Months went by, but his trouble still remained. Years rolled on, and our one request to God didn't change. More importantly, our faith in God remained firmly grounded.

Just when it seemed as if we might have to endure the problem longer than we could stand, August 11 dawned unpleasantly. It was unbearable for me to see my son suffer from this recurring illness; I wept and prayed for him with a broken spirit. A short while later I switched on the TV, and as I scanned through the channels I found a powerful morning prayer session. As I watched them pray earnestly, my heart opened to the Lord. I was determined to get His healing hands placed on my son. I made two requests to God: Elwin's healing should be instantaneous, and he should not suffer from the problem anymore. I cried for God's help for a long time; I don't know how long, because when I opened my eyes I saw my son resting—peaceful, quiet, and serene, with no cough or sneezing to disturb him.

The Lord heard my prayer and granted both my requests, for from then on Elwin never developed even a mild cough or cold. I continually called upon the Lord, and He answered me. I praise His name for His love and grace.

If your problems are persistent, let your prayers be so too.

ARUL MARY DANIEL

August 12

Flavor of the Day

This is the day the Lord has made; let us rejoice and be glad in it. Ps. 118:24, NIV.

WE WERE EAGER TO explore our new neighborhood. Our previous home had been located south of town, and we had to drive many miles to go to a grocery store or even get gas. We were stuck out in the middle of nowhere with no conveniences in sight. Now we were within two minutes of just about any kind of service we desired.

Only a couple blocks from our home we discovered our favorite place: a restaurant/ice cream parlor called Culvers. Their claim to fame was the famous custard they served fresh daily, along with their standard vanilla, chocolate, and lemon ice. This custard is so creamy it melts in your mouth. Every day the marquee indicates the "flavor of the day"—caramel brickle, candy commotion, chocolate symphony, hershey kiss crunch, trufflicious, M & M swirl, really Reese's, strawberry bon bon, cookie dough craving, and hundreds more. It makes you want to try all of them! My kids and I even started to make up our own flavors of the day. You can see why this place was so much fun!

The daily marquee got me thinking about how God can flavor my day. He says, "If anyone is thirsty, let him come to Me and drink." He offers this to anyone, every day. When I get out of bed in the morning and spend my quiet time with Him, He knows what my day is going to be like. He knows if it will be a great day with the works—syrup, whipped topping, nuts, and caramel. He knows if it will be plain and routine—simple vanilla. He knows if the day will be rough and challenging. We can taste His flavoring and trust His will to guide us through any situation. He also knows how the outcome is affected if I don't make it a priority to spend time in Bible study and prayer. For you see, Satan is out to flavor our day also. He can make concoctions that will make us sick emotionally, mentally, physically, and spiritually. They may seem to sound and taste good initially, but they always make you sick eventually.

What will be your choice today? I know that I want only the best the Savior has in store for me.

KAREN PHILLIPS

Seeking the Son

My heart says of you, "Seek his face!" Your face, Lord, I will seek. Ps. 27:8, NIV.

I HAD DRIVEN TO Valley Agri to pick up the special dog food we feed our arthritic dog, Buddy. As I drove up in front of the store, my eyes were drawn to an appealing array of potted plants that had been placed near the entrance. The large flowers on two of them were approximately six inches across and were a delight to behold. One was a deep pink with a purple center, and the other was white with a dark-pink center. I hadn't seen flowers so lovely since we were in Hawaii celebrating our anniversary several months earlier. Since I'm not a gardener, I asked the manager what kind of flowers they were. He said they were Hardy Hibiscus and were newly arrived. I bought the dog food and decided I just must have the pink one for my husband to plant in the yard of our country home. I put it in the passenger seat for the trip home and steadied it with my right hand as I drove. I didn't want to damage the blossom or the three remaining buds. I carefully placed it in the center of our kitchen table to surprise my husband.

The next day was Sabbath, and I decided to share the beauty of my plant with our church family. We arrived early, and I placed it on the altar, where it brightened the sanctuary. I felt the Lord was pleased to see such an offering of praise for the services. We then returned home with me carefully holding my precious plant. My husband suggested that the plant probably needed warm sun, so we placed it by the front porch steps for the afternoon.

Sunday morning I arose early, put the leash on Buddy, and walked through the garage to go for our usual two-mile walk. As I came around the corner my heart was made glad as yet another pink blossom was in full bloom. The sun was bright, little birds sang, the breeze gently caressed the wild flowers that bloomed along the way. We returned home refreshed. I glanced over at my pink flower before entering the house. To my amazement I couldn't see it anywhere. I made my way across the green lawn for a closer look. My precious flower was still attached to the plant all right, but its face was looking straight upward to the warm sun.

If only I will keep my eyes more directly on the Son, He will be found more fully. How much more peaceful and happy our lives will be if we always keep Him in full view!

Rose Neff Sikora

An Angel in the Lock

For he shall give his angels charge over thee, to keep thee in all thy ways. Ps. 91:11.

WASHINGTON, D.C., IS A beautiful place with lots of places to tour. There's something for everyone. However, there's one thing about Washington—some locations aren't so safe. Even though we lived in a good location, we were not far from the red light district of town.

Early one morning my roommate and I were rushing to get out for work. I realize that God should always be first, but sometimes I'm short of time. Nevertheless, I've learned that it is always best to never forget my Friend. So I took time to pray, and as always I asked Jesus to go with me. I asked for protection throughout the day. Sometimes I take a little extra time and ask Him to send His angels to protect our house, and *please don't let anyone break in.* I always feel anxious, never wanting to meet a stranger in my house.

We went off to work, having confidence that God would take care of us.

After a good day at work, I returned home. Something was wrong! I paused for a moment. *Oh, no! The door was broken!* The lock that was supposed to be the best dead bolt lock had been completely taken out. The regular doorknob lock area was battered.

Please, God, what should I do? Is he looking at me? Where should I go? It seemed as if God said, "Calm down, My child. Go to your neighbor next door; she is home most of the time." I knocked on my neighbor's door, and she came right away. *Thank You, Jesus.* I explained what had happened, and we called the police. When the police arrived and assessed the situation, they decided that no one was in the apartment. They said I should call a locksmith, and they'd return when they thought I was ready to go inside.

When the police returned we all went in. We discovered that the lock people can usually open with a credit card had jammed, and the thieves hadn't been able to open the door. They had no problem getting the secured lock out, and they left a big hole in the door. The police and the locksmith were amazed and couldn't understand why the thieves couldn't get in.

Thank You, heavenly Father, that You sent Your angels to stop the thieves and jammed the lock. You have proven that You will protect me in all my ways.

Odessa S. Gentles

Wooing Gilda

How often I have longed to gather your children together, as a hen gathers her chicks under her wings, but you were not willing. Luke 13:34, NIV.

THE POPULAR BELIEF IS that when you rescue a sick animal they are so grateful that they will be a friend for life. I guess my cat Gilda never heard of that, because she thinks she's entitled to everything I give her.

When I found Gilda, she was a kitten living in a feral colony. She was hiding under a dumpster when I coaxed her out with some food. One eye was swollen shut from an infection, and she was anemic from flea bites. She eventually got healthy, but she never got very big. Gilda fit in very well with my family of dogs and cats. My cats, Gilley and Gilah, became surrogate parents for her. As far as she was concerned, she had simply moved from one colony to another.

The only problem was that Gilda never really warmed up to people. She followed the lead of the other cats and learned where the litter box was and that the food came out of the big white box in the kitchen. She even learned her name, coming whenever I called her five or six times. But she had trouble learning how very much I love her.

After 14 years together, I've made a little progress. At age 8 she got up on the couch with me for the first time. Now she comes near me every day, although she's only crawled into my lap a total of three times. She likes having her tummy rubbed and will lie down near me and flip over.

She also has a penchant for hiding and getting stuck. One memorable Thanksgiving she crawled underneath my mother's seven-foot-high kitchen hutch. We ended up taking every single dish out of the cupboard so that we could move it a few inches to let her out.

Whenever I feel discouraged about Gilda, I think about my relationship with Jesus. Can He tell by my actions that I love Him, or does He have to guess? Do I talk to Him because I enjoy His company, or do I just seek Him out when I need something, the way Gilda always shows up at mealtimes?

When I think of how patiently Jesus waits for me to demonstrate my love, 14 years doesn't seem like a long time at all to woo Gilda. I'm even starting to suspect that maybe Gilda's loved me all along.

GINA LEE

Just Like in the Cartoons

As a father has compassion on his children, so the Lord has compassion on those who fear him. Ps. 103:13, NIV.

I WAS 7 AND MY sister 5 when late one summer evening (dressed only in little girl nightgowns) we decided to venture outdoors and see how our neighborhood looked after dark. Buildings, trees, and shrubs—all familiar to us in the light of day—somehow seemed much larger and more threatening at night. So our evening stroll didn't take us nearly as far as we had planned, and I soon found Kathy's small hand creeping a bit nervously into mine. Rounding the back corner of our garage, we heard a low moaning sound coming from somewhere nearby, and we both froze in our tracks—barely able to breathe, let alone move.

Then, as the sound became louder and turned into a ghoulish *Ooooooh,* we reacted, as if shot from a cannon, and raced for the back door, screaming in terror!

If you've ever watched cartoons, I'm certain we looked just like the animated characters who, in a state of panic, keep pulling and pushing each other out of the way in a scrambled attempt to be the first inside. Hearing our frantic cries, our equally frightened parents met us and literally dragged us through the door. Our father's next reaction was to grab a flashlight and run outside—barefoot and in his undershirt—to try to locate the terrible "who" or "what" that had so traumatized us, while our mother was left inside to deal with our hysteria.

After several minutes of searching, our father came back inside and declared all was safe. He had found no trace of the horrible "thing."

I chuckle now, but there is a comparison between our earthly and heavenly fathers.

With no regard or thought for his own safety, Dad was out the door and searching for whatever it was (real or imagined) that had threatened the very lives of his two young daughters. And as the Bible tells us, though our earthly father loved us so much that he was willing to risk his own life to protect us, our heavenly Father has risked much more so that we might have eternal life with Him.

PAULETTA COX JOHNSON

The Blackout

The love of Christ constraineth us. 2 Cor. 5:14.

I'M NOT ONE WHO is in love with traffic lights. In fact, they can be a plain nuisance when I'm running late for work. One red light can hold me up for 60 seconds—that's a whole minute. Oh, I respect them all right, not out of love and appreciation but out of fear—fear of a traffic ticket or an accident. I obey, but my heart's not in it.

Then on Thursday, August 21, 2003, I entered a department store to pick up a couple of items. I noticed that the lights were very dim, but shoppers were still going about their business. Soon I was in my car and headed home, a drive of a few minutes.

As I dashed down the street I soon realized that all traffic had come to a halt. The traffic lights in that area were out. In my impatience I made a U-turn and headed in the opposite direction. In less than three blocks it became clear that those lights were also out. Now I was stuck and annoyed. Where were the traffic lights when I needed them? Finally, I turned on my car radio and learned that we were in a blackout. In fact, all of New York City and major portions of the northeastern and midwestern United States and Canada were without power. Millions were without electricity, and many had no water. I knew my husband was home and concerned about me, but I couldn't get any signal on my cell phone.

As I sat in my car, literally inching along a path that would eventually take me not 10 minutes but 100 minutes to get home, I had time to do some thinking about this traffic light business. I found myself longing for them to work again. What chaos there was without them! Police officers stood in the middle of many intersections directing traffic. *Oh, for a traffic light,* I thought. The power in our area was finally restored 12 hours later.

Traffic lights. Now I have a deeper appreciation for them. I respected them, but out of fear. Is this the kind of respect I have for God? Do I follow His "rules" because I'm afraid of getting a "ticket" that will assign me to eternal damnation? Out of a fear of being eternally lost? Or do I really, really love Him? Is my obedience a willing outflow of that love?

Lord, help me to submit to You fully every day. Please give me a total surrender that will cause me to obey You simply because I love You so much and want to please You. Then I know my heart will be in it.

GLORIA STELLA FELDER

Going Home

Go home to thy friends, and tell them how great things the Lord hath done for thee. Mark 5:19.

MY HUSBAND AND I looked forward to going home in the summer around the same time every year. We moved from a Northern state to a Southern state about 12 years ago. Although we enjoy the countryside, we believed "there's no place like home."

To return home, our usual mode of transportation was the bus, airplane, or car. Several times we flew, but most of the time we rode the bus (which is enjoyable to me).

I begin packing our luggage six weeks before our planned departure. I start a countdown on the calendar and on my job. With anticipation, my husband and I both begin to discuss whom we are going to visit and which special treats we are going to purchase. Oh well, there's only so much you can do in seven days.

Finally, departure day is upon us. At the bus station we see hundreds of people anxiously waiting to get to their destinations. Some are going home; some are leaving home; others are just going on vacation. I enjoy people watching! Some have large bags, some small. Some even have plastic bags or none at all. Some are very friendly; others are very rude. Because of my husband's vision we had the opportunity to ride "priority seating," up front next to the driver. It was a long 19 hours, but very pleasant and educational. We even had a praying bus driver. He wouldn't move his bus before having prayer with his passengers.

Finally, home at last! But wait—we notice a change in our city. New homes have been built in my old neighborhood. Old familiar buildings have been torn down! People are not as friendly. There's a vast amount of sickness; classmates are deceased! What's happening? Home is just not the same!

Don't despair! One day we'll be going to another home! It won't be a long bus ride. We'll always travel by air. Preparation takes a lifetime. This is a home where there are only new mansions. No death, no sickness. We'll even be able to see some of our loved ones and friends we haven't seen in years.

Pack your bags for an eternity. You can never start too early for going home.

ELAINE J. JOHNSON

Dare to Dream and Do

Upon the handmaids in those days will I pour out my spirit. Joel 2:29.

HOME-BASED BUSINESSES ARE common today, but in the late 1940s and early 1950s home businesses were almost unheard-of. That's what makes my mother-in-law, now almost 98 years old, so remarkable. She had a card/gift shop in her home in Vermont. This town of about 500 people had only one tiny grocery store, one small gas station, and an elementary school.

Her neighbors and other townspeople would come to her shop to get cards—birthday, anniversary, wedding, baby shower, Christmas, and thank-you cards. She also carried small gifts, such as exquisite embroidered handkerchiefs. Sometimes the handkerchiefs would be embroidered with a letter of the alphabet, a flower, or a dog or cat. Since she also crocheted, sometimes there were wee baby gifts for one to purchase, or doilies to put on a stand. It was just a small shop in part of her living room, accessed from the porch by its own door. Even though it was limited in its goods, it was an interesting place to visit.

At age 15, when I first met my husband, it seemed to me that she must be rich to be able to afford to buy things to sell. I didn't know anyone else who could afford to have a shop in their home. I only saw things for sale in regular stores, so I was in awe of my future mother-in-law. I realize now that she was far ahead of her time. She had a home-based business before the term was coined. She dared to dream and to do something no one else in her town or area had done before.

Do we dream and dare today? Many times I think we have stifled our creativity to the point that we've forgotten how to dream and dare to do for the Lord. John the Baptist may not have been a dreamer, but he certainly was a doer; and he dared to do and be something different. He eventually lost his head over it, but he counted for something before that happened.

I often think of the song "Dare to Be a Daniel." Daniel dared to "have a purpose firm" and dared to "stand alone." My prayer for you today is to take up the cause of John and Daniel and many others (and don't forget Deborah and Dorcas, either). Dare to dream and do for God—just for today.

LORAINE F. SWEETLAND

The Race

Let us run with perseverance the race marked out for us. Heb. 12:1, NIV.

YESTERDAY WAS MY eldest son's first field day at school. He's in kindergarten now, so he's no longer a "little kid," he had reminded me quite proudly. Of course, Mom had to be there for the momentous occasion.

He hadn't known that I was coming, so he was surprised when I was the person in charge of the beanbag toss—the event his class started with. Everyone was given four tries. When it was his turn, he made the first one easily and got 10 points. But he missed the others. The first-place finisher had 80 points. No, he wouldn't come in first in my event. Next stop was the spoon-and-golf-ball race, a more economical version of the traditional egg-and-spoon race. No, he wasn't one of the top three winners there, either. Then on to the sponge race (you just had to be there to see that one), potato-sack race, three-legged race, and 50-yard dash. His shoulders sagged with each successive race, and the tears—just one or two at first—became a sad wail. He had started out with such confidence. He'd been sure that he'd win in everything. My heart ached for him. I knew all too well how he felt. He had tried so hard; why couldn't he win?

Mom, the cheerleader, to the rescue: "You did your best." I tried hard to comfort. "You're a winner just for trying and for staying in the races. Don't give up; I'm very proud of you," I assured him.

It took everything I had to convince him to participate in the last event, the scooter relay. "Come on, Brandon!" I cheered, prayed, and held my breath.

The starter yelled, "On your mark, get set, go!" He zoomed past me, and I squealed with delight. "Come on, Brandon! You can do it!" And he did—he came in second!

Lord, I'm glad that with You there are no first-, second-, or third-place slots. At times You alone know how hard I've tried. Help me to remember when I'm faced with setbacks in this life that with You I am a winner.

MAXINE WILLIAMS ALLEN

My First Day of School

In all your ways acknowledge him, and he will make your paths straight. Prov. 3:6.

I HAD MY MIND SET on being the best kindergarten teacher I could be. With no experience in the education field (I was a biology/pre-med major) after taking a student missionary class at college, and going through orientation in Hawaii and again in Chuuk, I thought I was ready to conquer the world—well, the small part that I would be responsible for.

As the beginning of school crept closer, I prepped further and spent hours cleaning and decorating my classroom. I reviewed my lesson plans for the first day again and again and reminded myself that this first day of school would decide if I would have a "great" or "horrible" year, as the people in orientation had put it. I was determined to make this first day the greatest!

On August 21, 2002, I chose my most teacher-like outfit. I was ready to face the day. Thirty minutes before class started I sat in my classroom trying to rub the sweat off my hands. Confident and well prepared, I was still nervous. At 7:45 I opened the door and, one by one, met pupils and parents. As I looked at the little faces gazing so innocently at me, I was comforted. *This will be easy,* I thought, *they all look like perfect little angels.* Before long the quiet little angels had turned into screaming little "monsters." For three and a half hours I had a chaotic classroom of 20 energetic kindergarteners over whom I had absolutely no control.

By the end of the day I was tired, frustrated, and very discouraged. I wanted to pack my bags and leave. Maybe teaching wasn't meant for me. Maybe this wasn't God's will at all! Then I did what I should have done first—I got down on my knees and pleaded for God's help. I told Him that the only way I could mold and shape these children was if He held my hand. He showed me that the only way I would succeed as a teacher was if He would teach with me.

The next day I faced my children again. This time I wasn't nervous. I introduced classroom rules and respect for each other and took time to listen to each child. The day turned out great, not because I was well prepared or had improved my classroom management skills, or because my children became perfect little angels again. This time Christ, the greatest teacher of all time, had entered with me.

Cristine Jeda Orillosa

Pray Without Ceasing

Know that the Lord has set apart the godly for himself; the Lord will hear when I call to him. Ps. 4:3, NIV.

WE LIVE IN A wonderful age—space travel, e-mail, computers, and cell phones. Speaking of cell phones, I've had three. When the first one was in the right place at the right time, it was a joy to use. But more often than not, it either needed the battery charged or was in a roaming area, which costs many more dollars. Then it got too old to operate properly and had to be replaced.

The Sprint phone was serviceable on the road where we traveled frequently, but refused to make connection on the mountain where we spent most of the year. Therefore, the Sprint was retired. Someone advised me to give the old phones to the police department where they were re-serviced for battered women to use.

The third time a Cingular was activated. But it is much the same as its predecessor, except that it can be used up on the mountain—if you are outdoors. That seems to be the secret of using cell phones—you need to be outside and somewhere in the proximity of a tower. Otherwise, you experience "breaking up" and lose your connection with your party.

Recently, when I was suffering from a broken left arm, the doctor cautioned me not to drive. But I felt that I was as safe a driver as all those people on the freeway using their cell phones while moving at 80 miles per hour! This is one of the real dangers of the cell phone. A friend of mine had a bad wreck and ended up in the hospital with a broken leg and hip and chest injuries sustained while she was using her cell phone on the road.

My experience with cell phones had given me a new appreciation for prayer. My Father in heaven is always ready to listen to my petitions wherever I am. There is no special place or special time when He is more accessible. He never "breaks up" or "drops off" when I am talking to Him. There are no roaming charges. I don't have to worry about running out of minutes on my plan. I can talk to Him as often as I like, in the day or at night and even on the road. According to Psalm 4:3, "the Lord will hear when I call unto him." And He has promised in Isaiah 65:24: "Before they call, I will answer. While they are still speaking I will respond" (Clear Word).

Rubye Sue

God Will Move That Mountain!

Cast your cares on the Lord and he will sustain you; he will never let the righteous fall. Ps. 55:22, NIV.

I JUST HAVE TO SHARE this incredible experience with you! It was an hour past midnight on a Friday night, and I was awake. Why? Thanks to my "neighbor from hell" I was again disturbed from sleep as she and her friends arrived back from clubbing. The peaceful silence was broken by loud music as they turned it up to full volume. Often this lasted until 6:00 or 7:00 in the morning. As you can imagine, the lack of sleep meant that my son, Michael, and I were so exhausted Sabbath mornings that sometimes we missed going to church.

I tried to talk to my neighbor, and each time she promised that it wouldn't happen again. But once Friday night came around again, so did the old problem. When this had happened for several weeks, I asked the Lord, *What should I do? I don't want to aggravate the situation by calling the police.* So I tried a different approach. I called a number of my dear, God-fearing friends who put the problem to the Lord in a prayer session.

On Thursday I felt impressed to knock on my neighbor's door and try to reason with this most disagreeable young woman. She opened the door and immediately took a defensive stance. "I'm not here to complain," I said quietly, "but to talk to you, because I would really like us to get along and to try and find a solution to this problem." As I talked I prayed in my heart for the Lord to move upon this young girl's heart. As she listened to what I said, her face started to soften. She apologized and promised to keep it down.

Friday night arrived, and my son and I retired early because she always had broken her promises before. This time, however, she arrived back from the club and there was no loud music. No loud, drunken brawls and arguments. Just hushed, quiet talking.

I gave God thanks and praises as my son and I dressed in the morning for church. But would she continue to keep her promise? Sure enough; when Friday night rolled around again there was not a peep.

God can surely move mountains and make the "neighbor from hell" into the neighbor converted.

CAROL BRYANT

We Are All God's Children

Judge not, that ye be not judged. Matt. 7:1.

I WAS ON MY WAY home from work when I decided to stop at a fruit vendor's to buy some avocado pears. I thought that they would add color to the salad I was going to prepare for supper. They didn't look too good. Some were bruised and others looked overripe. So I thought I would buy them elsewhere The vendor, however, insisted that they were delicious and persuaded me to buy a few. I was anxious to catch my train, so I paid for them and hurried on.

As I sat in the train I was certain the vendor had cheated me. The fruit looked unappetizing, and I was sure most of it would be thrown away. At home I prepared the ingredients for the tossed salad, then reached for those disappointing avocado pears. Some resentment at being cheated still lingered as I sliced them open. To my utter amazement, they were as fresh and tasty as any I'd had before.

We often look at people in the same way. The outside may look bruised, damaged, and spoiled, and we are quick to judge. We base our negative opinions and erroneous assumptions on what we see, not what is under the skin. We may not realize that the bruising is a result of the hurt that people suffer, the trauma of life. The outside may mask the inner pain and turmoil that someone is experiencing. I'm thankful that God doesn't look on the outside, but on the heart.

I immediately murmured an earnest prayer that God would help me not to judge anyone until I have walked in his or her shoes. Satan is pleased when we are quick to point out the weaknesses and faults that we see in others. We don't realize that our faults may be more grievous in the sight of the Lord. Let's find the good in others, encourage the development of these traits, and strengthen one another in the Lord.

Lord, help us always to be sensitive toward the next person's feelings and not judge their outward appearances. May we always reflect Your character and be a blessing to those with whom we come in contact.

CORDELL LIEBRANDT

White-Water Trouble

God is our refuge and strength, always ready to help in times of trouble. Ps. 46:1, NLT.

WE'D GONE WHITE-WATER rafting the previous year toward the end of summer in a slow river where there weren't very many rapids. This time my husband, Roger, and I decided we wanted more excitement and signed up for a more technical river trip.

When we arrived at the rafting tour guide company, we were given a safety talk and were fitted with wetsuits and helmets for protection. The group was loaded into the van and taken to the section of the river where we were to raft. That section was called The Numbers because there were six rapids, one after the other. Olympic kayak tryouts were being held around the first rapid, so we went down the river and set up to put in above the second rapid. The river was high and flowing swiftly.

We loaded into the raft and started paddling. Seconds into the trip the raft started to high side on the right. The group was able to correct it, although the next instant the raft overturned and everyone was thrown into the river. Half the group was thrown to the river's edge and reached safety without difficulty. Roger and I weren't as fortunate. The water was freezing, and I was in the center of the river. The current was too strong to swim to shore, and I was not a strong swimmer. *Lord, help me,* I prayed. The sleeves of my jacket were filling with water, making it difficult to swim. I watched for downed trees and tried to avoid the boulders in the riverbed. Out of the corner of my eye I saw Roger get to shore; he was safe. Later, he told me it was with his last ounce of strength that he grabbed hold of the tree root and crawled to shore.

There was a huge boulder ahead, and I was heading straight for it. What should I do? As I was getting closer to it, I noticed the current wasn't quite as strong. I felt impressed to grab hold of the boulder. After a few seconds of clinging to the side, I was able to catch my breath and regain the strength to climb on top. The guide company employees at the river's edge about 20 feet away threw a rope to me and pulled me to shore.

I know that Roger and I are alive today because of the Lord's protection and help in a time of trouble. LINDA DOMENY

Blow Me a Song

All things are possible with God. Mark 10:27, NIV.

EXHAUSTED FROM CHILDBIRTH, the young mother stared at the ceiling of her hospital room. She was alone, for another woman had taken her place in her husband's heart. Weeks ago she had taken away their two little boys and separated from him at his request. Now the divorce papers had been served to her in the hospital where their baby girl lay in the nursery.

Enveloped by a cloud of fear, uncertainty, and rejection, she struggled to concentrate on a plan for the future. Her mind was a whirl of despair and guilt, for her mother had strenuously disapproved of her marriage in the first place. Off and on in recent years she had made feeble efforts to embrace wholeheartedly the faith of her parents, but the effort to make her marriage succeed had pushed her away from them and, she felt, from *their* God. She could expect no help from any of them. As life swirled about her, she was overcome by the hopeless situation she was facing. No answer came to the problem tumbling in her mind. Where was God? She didn't know. And she wondered if He knew where she was. But she felt that if anyone would and could help, it was He. She believed that much. Weak from crying, she prayed to *her* God—more out of desperation than of faith.

At last she fell into a restless sleep and dreamed that she was standing beside a turbulent stream. Snow, melting in patches here and there, ran off to join the whirling river. Suddenly her attention was drawn to a leaf floating and bobbing on the tumbling water. Sitting on that leaf, barely keeping dry, was a butterfly—hanging on for dear life. She couldn't take her attention from that tiny creature, clinging so precariously on its journey downstream. It couldn't attempt to fly for fear of being washed away if it let go. Its only safety was in clinging to the leaf on which it was perched. Then, while she watched, the leaf floated into a quiet pool at the side of the stream, and the butterfly flew away.

When she woke, she was calm inside. If God could protect a little butterfly, she need not fear the future. Life could not swamp her, either, if she clung to Him.

"Blow me a song on a wisp of wind, encourage my heart, rekindle my heart, . . . awaken my soul, call my consciousness home, help me back to my task, to reach out with my faith."—Ila McClenahan.

BETH CARLSON

The Little Person's Dilemma

Treat everyone as you would like them to treat you. Luke 6:31, Clear Word.

JAMIE WAS A 6-YEAR-OLD victim of abuse from a home where little was known of love and care. For several years he'd been moved from one foster home to another, and on this day I was called to collect Jamie from such a home.

On arrival I noted the well-kept place with its nice surroundings overlooking the sea, and I thought it a pity he had to leave this. However, the door opened and my thoughts changed somewhat as I was greeted by a well-dressed couple, eager to pour out a list of problems Jamie had brought to their home.

I stood for a moment as they hastened to get his bags and berate him for his misbehavior before a chilly farewell. I took Jamie's hand and headed for the door, not wanting to prolong the ordeal. Pausing, I whispered to him to say thank you, and we left. I felt sad; what I had witnessed spoke volumes.

Sketchy instructions had been given to a place two hours on the other side of Adelaide. With darkness and a storm approaching, I was anxious to reach our destination. However, the rain started and the weather deteriorated so that I could barely see ahead or pick up any signs along the dirt track. It was wet and slippery, and I was growing concerned as I didn't know where we were.

Jamie, huddled in the seat beside me, suddenly spied my flashlights and said confidently, "I'll shine the torch, Lyn, and you can see where to go." I prayed earnestly to myself that his confidence be rewarded for both our sakes. He shone it out of his window while I strained to see the road. After some time Jamie yelled excitedly, "Lyn, look!" Sure enough, it looked like an entrance. So with uncertainty we followed along this narrow track through the trees for a mile and, finally, into a farmyard.

I made my way to the door, and once again a couple greeted me. I relaxed. We were at the right place. "Oh, yes, please bring him in!"

It was warm inside the old home, but the hearts that took us in were even warmer. This time it was I who said thank You—to my heavenly Father who loves and cares for us all.

Jamie was taken in—and there he stayed.

LYN WELK

God's Agenda

Thou wilt keep him in perfect peace, whose mind is stayed on thee: because he trusteth in thee. Isa. 26:3.

AS AN ELEMENTARY school teacher in the middle grades, my life often becomes hectic and stressful. There always seems to be more grading, more supervision, more programs to plan, more parents to contact, and more adolescents with raging hormones to handle than I can comfortably deal with. This often sent me to the Lord in my morning devotional time with my wish list and agenda.

My prayers used to go something like this: *Dear Lord, it's me again. Thank You for everything You do—especially thank You for dying for me. Today I lift up my problems to You.* And then I would enumerate all the worries and hassles I was facing and ask Him to handle them for me. It was a good prayer life, or so I thought.

But one morning the Holy Spirit caught me up short by asking: "Why are you bothering with the list? Don't you realize that My agenda is a lot shorter and simpler than yours? I'm concerned with only this moment. From a cosmic perspective your current trials, problems, annoyances, and worries are completely insignificant in the light of one core question: Who is in control of your life at this moment?"

If your answer is unequivocally "God is in utter and complete control of everything I am and everything I do and everything I say right now," then you are at peace. God says, "No matter how wild and crazy things get around you, you are in the 'eye of the storm' that is the center of My will. I am training you to surrender to the uttermost part of your being so that you will be a joyous participant in My eternal kingdom of selfless love.

"When your priorities have been merged with My priorities you have complete peace and assurance that everything is going as planned in the universe."

My prayers are different now. Now I pray that whatever happens to me today that I will face it in God's strength. I pray that I will remain so centered and focused on Christ that none of "me" will show through to my students—only Him. And I pray that if there is anything in me that would hinder His work, He would take it from me. From now on, it's *His* agenda, not mine.

LOIS WADE

A Change in Plans

Weeping may endure for a night, but joy comes in the morning. Ps. 30:5, NKJV.

IT HAD BEEN A lovely Friday morning in August, but then I got some very sad news. One of my former pastors, a beloved man of God, had passed away in Connecticut. I knew immediately that I wanted to attend the funeral service. Even though it was going to be held in New York (1,000 miles away) in just a few days, I wanted to go.

The phones began to ring. A few church members planned to travel to New York by car. "Would you like to join us?" they asked. Pleased, I accepted the invitation to ride with them.

But when the time came to finalize my travel plans, a score of problems started to show their ugly faces. First, my supervisor couldn't grant me the time off because she herself would be on vacation. Though she tried to arrange it so that I could go anyway, other little things started to happen, such as several changes of date and time of departure and return.

Then I decided not to make the trip. The next day when one of my coworkers asked me if I was disappointed about missing the trip, I shook my head. "No; maybe I'm needed here more than I'm needed in New York." I didn't know it then, but my response was Spirit-filled.

Friday, when I made a regular visit to my beloved sister in Christ who had been ill for a while, I found a drastic change in her condition. She was declining speedily. That Sabbath afternoon her husband called and asked me to come to their home to check on her breathing. Rushing to her bedside, I found her very close to the end. Though she appeared comatose, I prayed with her. I left the house very sad. At 10:40 that night I received the call. She had fallen asleep. Now, although I mourned the loss of both a brother and sister in Christ, I realized that God had a plan for me. He knew where I would be most needed, and He nudged me in that direction.

I was so happy that I had stayed home and could minister to the family close by. God taught me a lesson during that stressful week. Everything will work out just the way it should if I trust Him.

Please help me stay very close to You, Lord. Remind me that You are leading in every aspect of my life. Help me never to be disappointed when things do not go the way I plan them.

GLORIA P. HUTCHINSON

The Beltway Accident

He has put his angels in charge of you to watch over you wherever you go. Ps. 91:11, NCV.

IT WAS A BEAUTIFUL afternoon. Traveling home on a beltway, my husband and I were in the middle lane. All at once we felt—and heard—a big thump. Not knowing what had happened, and hearing another loud thump, I screamed. Our sport utility vehicle had been hit by a BMW that was in the outside lane and, as it turned out, was being driven by a pregnant woman who was two days overdue. The impact from her car caused us to hit the front fender of another vehicle. Everyone around us began using their cell phones to call the police for assistance. We later learned that someone in a vehicle with an out-of-state tag had hit the BMW in the rear, causing her to lose control and hit us. That driver stopped for only a minute, then left. There was nothing anyone could do.

When the emergency vehicles arrived, the paramedics looked after the pregnant woman. Although there were no apparent injuries, she was unable to contact any of her family members, so they took her to the hospital.

Neither my husband nor I was injured—not even a scratch. Talk about thanking God—we did! Even the witnesses recognized how blessed we had been. Had we not been in the heavy vehicle that we were, we really would have had serious injuries. Our angels were protecting us.

We realize the accident could have been so much worse. Other cars and people could have been involved with serious bodily injuries and, possibly, even fatalities. Arriving home safely, we thanked God again. Expecting trauma afterward, we each took a hot bath before going to bed.

When we awakened the next morning, we thanked God for a new day; then I asked my husband how he felt and if he was sore. He was fine. Then he asked about me. Neither of us had any soreness or bruises of any kind. Each time I think of that accident I feel special in the sight of the Lord. So many have had accidents that tied up traffic during rush hour, or in which they were thrown out of the car, or had broken bones—or were even killed. The God who shut the lions' mouths so they wouldn't harm Daniel, the God who kept the fire from burning the three Hebrew boys, is the same God who kept us safe that day.

Marie H. Seard

A Little Bit of Heaven

Now the Lord God had planted a garden in the east, in Eden . . . And the Lord made all kinds of trees . . . that were pleasing to the eye and good for food. Gen. 2:8, 9, NIV.

I SIT IN MY GARDEN this morning, writing. It is midmorning in southern California. The late-summer sun gently warms the dew from the grass. I'm reluctant to leave.

Finishing a breakfast of pancakes with fig jam, fresh figs stuffed with cheese and honey, melon, and fresh orange juice, I contentedly rock back in my outdoor chair. *A little bit of heaven,* I think as I observe my garden. Crape myrtle trees are in deep-pink bloom beside a large blue flower bush. A rustic fence protects one side of the garden, and a brick wall the other. On my porch sit ruby and white flowers in terracotta pots.

I enjoy the warm peacefulness and watch a yellow-and-black butterfly leisurely sample the blossoms. A hummingbird flits nearby. I hear chirping from the fig and orange trees.

Again I think, *A little bit of heaven.* The peacefulness doesn't exist outside my garden, though. The nations are talking war again. Almost a half dozen children have been kidnapped within the past few weeks. The forest trees are beginning to die in the mountains from lack of water and a devious kind of beetle.

I'm on vacation, weary, tired, trying to renew. A friend is in the hospital and not expected to live; other friends are trying to stabilize a troubled marriage.

No, this isn't heaven, I'm starkly reminded. Yet I put an oasis of peace and beauty in my life that provides strength for service—the moments that I spend in my garden reading or writing, or at my grand piano playing Beethoven, Mozart, and other classical favorites, or contemporary hymns. Moments that I spend with my Savior talking, praying, listening for His inspirational encouragement from the Bible, and gathering ideas from life around me.

I'm also reminded that heaven isn't even in my garden, as I notice the rust on a pole and a piece of steel jutting sharply from the bottom. Several patches of weeds poke unsightly seed heads among the flowers. In the corner is a dead patch of grass that needs water. Heaven is not yet, but God lovingly gives us reminders that heaven begins here with a relationship with Him as we savor moments of beauty.

EDNA MAYE GALLINGTON

September 1

Sunrise With Jesus

His great faithfulness is new every morning, as refreshing as the dew and as sure as the sunrise. Lam. 3:23, Clear Word.

IT OCCURRED AGAIN THIS morning as we were on our early-morning walk. My husband and I were about to turn a corner when our eyes caught a glimpse of an awesome sunrise. Amazed, we stopped to take another look at God's handiwork that lit up the skies, ushering in the miracle of a brand-new day. Another day to be thankful and to contemplate God's goodness and abundant blessings we so often take for granted. A song we used to sing long ago instantly came to mind: "For the beauty of the earth, for the glory of the skies, for the love which from our birth over and around us lies; Lord of all to thee we raise songs of gratitude and praise."

We continued our walk but the beautiful picture remained with me, and I began to hum the tune to "New every morning is thy love/Our wakening and uprising prove;/Through sleep and darkness safely brought,/ Restored to life and power and thought./New mercies each returning day,/Hover around us while we pray,/New perils past, new sins forgiven;/ New thoughts of God, new hopes of heaven."

How blessed we are to be able to enjoy the sunrise! To listen to the birds chirp their musical tones; to be able to walk briskly and enjoy the crisp early-morning breeze. To offer a prayer for my wonderful family, my workplace, the world church, and for the people and leaders of our nation. My heart overflows with joy and gladness for these magnificent gifts that remind me of God's faithfulness to us every morning.

As I reflect on the beauty of that gorgeous sunrise, my mind envisions the great sunrise soon to take place when our beloved Jesus, accompanied by His angelic host, will burst the azure skies and every eye shall see Him. What a day of rejoicing that will be! There'll be no more sadness, no more sickness, no more crying, no more pain, no more doctors or hospitals, no bills to pay, no more anguish of soul and spirit, and no more death—just sunrise with Jesus for eternity. I want to behold Him face to face on that grand and glorious day. What about you? Until then, let's be faithful.

Shirley C. Iheanacho

The Prayer Piano

But my God shall supply all your need according to His riches in glory by Christ Jesus. Phil. 4:19.

HOW WERE WE GOING to find a piano? Our 7-year-old daughter was asking to take piano lessons, and we had two other daughters we wished to have music lessons as well. My husband's family had several gifted musicians among them, and I had a grandmother who had been a music evangelist in the early 1900s. It seemed important to keep the blessing of music going in our family. The problem was that we had no money for a piano; a new one was out of the question. We went from farm to farm, looking for old uprights. There were two or three we could afford, but they needed much costly repair. Plus, we also didn't have the ability to transport a large piano, and it was costly to hire it done.

Every day our daughter prayed, "Dear Jesus, please send us a piano." School started, and we still had no answer.

Grandma and Grandpa Burgeson helped with the school lunch each day, and one day while they were getting lunch ready two men came and began hauling out the piano that stood at the far end of the kitchen. They had been told to get rid of it as the school had purchased a new one. Grandma Burgeson immediately caught them and cried, "Please stop! Don't take that piano to the dump! We need one for our granddaughter." So the piano stayed. It was a smaller upright, and because it had been used regularly for music at school it was always tuned and kept in good working order. It wasn't long before Grandma and Grandpa secured a truck and brought the piano to our house. Our prayers had been answered. Now the girls could start music lessons.

An even greater surprise was that it was the same piano I had taken lessons on years before. That was a special sign to me of God's love.

Many years later it survived a bad house fire in one of our daughter's home. All of our girls learned to play that piano, which is still in our family. It's a constant reminder of our answer to prayer and of a faithful, caring grandmother who in the right place and at the right time caught it on its way to the dump.

DARLENE YTREDAL BURGESON

September 3

What a Friend We Have in Jesus!

I will never leave you nor forsake you. Heb. 13:5, NKJV.

WHEN I WAS A CHILD and a teenager I never had a special relationship with my parents. I was the middle girl, the one who felt ignored and totally unimportant in my parents' eyes. My parents both worked and provided for us very well, but I was lonely in the middle of the family—insecure and floundering. I argued and pointed out what I perceived as blatant favoritism toward my sisters, but I was never on the receiving end of it.

In the eighth grade I became involved in candy stripers, a hospital volunteer program for young people. I spent time at the hospital greeting visitors, taking dinner trays to patient rooms, feeding the elderly, and consoling lonely little children. I was appreciated by the patients and staff—it was a wonderful feeling to be needed! For the first time in my life I felt valued. My self-confidence grew, and I looked forward to becoming a registered nurse one day.

I had always liked to go to church when friends would invite me, and it was there I learned the most basic memory verses. I began to go to church with a high school friend and her mother each Sunday in a little white church on a corner of a shady street in our town. I gave my heart to the Lord and was baptized one Sunday. When I came home after that service my mother asked, "Why is your hair all wet?" When I told her I'd been baptized by immersion, she got a surprised look on her face.

When I finally went off to college, my parents wrote often and paid all my bills. I couldn't have done it without them. My mother wrote one day and asked that instead of going to the nondenominational church on Sunday that I go on Saturday to White Memorial (across the bridge in Los Angeles). Reluctantly, I agreed. It was there I felt the hand of the Lord guiding me through the ministry of pastors who cared enough to come to the dorms and visit. Bible studies opened the Word of God as never before. I began to read and study my Bible several times each day; and the more I read and studied, the more I trusted the Lord. When I began dating, I always asked God to send me the man He wanted me to marry. And He did!

Life doesn't always treat us as we hope. We may still feel rejected, ignored, and slighted by some of those we love; but throughout our lives we can be secure in the knowledge that our Lord loves us. He never leaves us nor forsakes us. For that reason I rejoice!

CHERYL HURT

Inside Out

Martha, Martha, you are worried and distracted by many things; there is need for only one thing. Mary has chosen the better part, which will not be taken away from her. Luke 10:41, 42, NRSV.

IT'S NO SECRET THAT many women are overworked and stressed beyond their limits because of the demands of balancing work, home, and family. The multiple roles we play dictate that we multitask, and it's so easy to fall into the trap of juggling more than we can humanly handle. Women focus on "doing" because we can't stand to waste time. Nike's slogan, "Just do it!" resonates well with us. Don't just stand there; *do* something!

In working with women's ministry groups around Southeast Asia, I've found that women are enthusiastic to do what they can for God, based on what they see as their spiritual gifts. They plan a list of programs with a focus on numbers to report to their boards at the end of the year. This used to be my own thinking, too. Over time, though, the good Lord has taught me that women's ministry isn't what I want to do for God. It's not a list of programs planned for women to keep them busy in the Lord's vineyard—even though this may be the result of it. After reflecting on the following paragraphs taken from *Experiencing God,* by Henry Blackaby and Claude King, my whole perspective changed.

"Sometimes individuals and churches are so busy doing things they think will help God accomplish His purpose that He can't get their attention long enough to use them as servants to accomplish what He wants. We often wear ourselves out and accomplish very little of value to the kingdom.

"I think God is crying out and shouting to us, 'Don't just do something. Stand there! Enter into a love relationship with Me. Get to know Me. Adjust your life to Me. Let Me love you and reveal myself to you as I work through you. This relationship with God MUST come first'" (p. 30).

God opened my eyes to see what Jesus meant when He gently chided Martha. God was telling me that the primary focus should be on a relationship with God, our Father. That has to come first in all ministry. According to Blackaby and King, when we get to know our Father, the Holy Spirit gives us the desire to adjust our lives so that we desire to do what God wants us to do.

SALLY LAM-PHOON

Am I Ready?

Therefore be ye also ready: for in such an hour as ye think not the son of man cometh. Matt. 24:44.

WHILE AT SPICER MEMORIAL College in India, training to be a teacher, I had to do directed teaching in the elementary school. Our efficient supervisor and teacher, Noelene Johnsson, told us she could come at any time to inspect our classes.

On the first day I had to teach the class for the first standard students. It was my first time seriously teaching a class. I didn't have the slightest idea how much pandemonium 6-year-olds can cause in a classroom. I was supposed to teach five new words from their reader. So I had written down the steps carefully and made pictures and flash cards for each new word. More flash cards were made to drill them at the end of the lesson.

Grabbing my materials, I went to the elementary school. After introducing myself, I presented the new words, one by one. All the children were very attentive for the first 10 minutes. I wanted to assess how much they had grasped, so I looked for the flash cards I'd prepared. They were nowhere to be found. *What will I do without them?* I asked myself, realizing too late that I'd forgotten to bring them. Suddenly a girl from the back of the classroom shrilled, "Miss, this boy is calling me funny names." Turning to reprimand the culprit, whom did I see but my respected supervisor, standing at the door of the classroom. By that time numerous complaints and requests were pouring in from all over the classroom. "Miss, this girl is grabbing my pencil." "Miss, that boy's head is blocking my view of the blackboard." "Miss, this girl is copying my notes." "Miss, that girl is taking my book." Within seconds the class was in chaos. I couldn't respond to all their complaints at once. I stood still, not knowing what to do. I felt ashamed for forgetting to pick up all the materials. Seeing my pathetic condition, the supervisor took control of the class for the rest of the period. After the class she made many valuable suggestions that would help me to become a better teacher.

How much more should I be preparing and be prepared for the coming of the Lord. Will I be ready to meet Him? Will I forget to talk to Him in the hustle and bustle of life? Will He find me wanting?

SOOSANNA MATHEW

Where's Greggie?

Can a woman forget her sucking child? . . . Yea, they may forget, yet will I not forget thee. Isa. 49:15.

EMGEE WAS SO PROUD of her 3-week-old firstborn when she brought him to meet his grandmother. Emgee lived in Ontario, California, and her mother lived a two-hour drive away by freeway in Compton. Her mother enjoyed her visit with her first grandchild, and then Emgee started for home.

Before she got to the freeway she saw a department store advertising a sale. She stopped and, carrying Greggie in one of those plastic baby carriers that were so prevalent in the 1960s, went into the store. She set Greggie in the middle of one of the low tables, piled high with soft lingerie, so she would have her hands free to inspect the dresses. She found several she liked and took them into the dressing room. Choosing several, she took them to the checkout stand, paid for them, then got into her car and drove home.

About 10 minutes from home she was thinking, *Mike won't be home for a while. I'll have time to start dinner and feed Greggie—*

"Greggie!" She reached over and swept the department store bags off the seat. No Greggie. She pulled off the freeway and checked the packages in the back seat. No Greggie. In a panic, she got back onto the freeway and headed back to Compton, two hours away.

When she got to the store she drove the car up onto the sidewalk by front of the door, jumped out of the car without even closing the door, and dashed into the store. She spotted a group of salespeople and several patrons gathered around the lingerie table, smiling and saying, "Isn't he cute!"

Greggie had slept the entire four hours he'd been on the lingerie table, watched over by salespeople who assumed his mother would be coming back for him as soon as she realized she had left him behind.

The Bible says that though a nursing mother may forget her suckling child, God will not forget His children. He gives us protecting angels to guard us until He returns for us. "For he shall give his angels charge over thee, to keep thee in all thy ways" (Ps. 91:11). What a blessing—and what a reassurance!

DARLENEJOAN MCKIBBIN RHINE

He Knows

I am the good shepherd, and know my sheep, and am known of mine. John 10:14.

EVERY WEEK YOUNG people were joining the church to make their public commitment to give their hearts to the Lord. A new pastor had come to our medium-sized church in the Midwest. When he learned that most—if not all—of the young people in his congregation who attended each week had not been baptized, he was greatly surprised and determined that these fine young people would give their hearts to God and be baptized.

Week after week I watched as young people—some older and some younger than I—gave their hearts to the Lord, while I remained firmly if not comfortably in my seat. Baptisms followed. This happened again and again.

One Sabbath I listened to the appeal yet again with no intention of responding. While singing along with the congregation to the appeal song, "I Surrender All," I found myself suddenly on my feet. It was as though I'd been lifted out of my seat by the power of the Holy Spirit. I didn't resist this assistance; I was just surprised. I walked down the aisle and gave my hand to the pastor and my heart to God. I didn't want to join just because everyone else was joining—I simply had no earthly reason not to. The Lord knew my heart. He couldn't wait any longer. So He lifted me, unresisting, out of my seat.

I was baptized with others that April at the age of 14. In spite of my sinful nature, I haven't turned my back on the Lord. I grew up in a home that believed in God as our Creator and Savior. Well do I remember us children on our knees while mother prayed for us before we left for school each morning. Dad had already had his breakfast and gone to work. I remember how all of us piled into the family car, with lunch packed, to go to church, beginning with Sabbath school and ending with young people's meeting or sunset vespers. How we enjoyed the services and the fellowship! We learned about the Bible characters and God's care.

Thank God that He knew my heart and lifted me to my feet at an early age. He knew before I realized it that I do love Him and need Him in my life forever. I have the assurance that He loves me, too. What a wonderful feeling to know that the great God of the universe knows me, loves me, and will be with me even unto the end of the world.

LOVEY DAVIS VERDUN

Little Giants

Faithful is He who calls you, and He also will bring it to pass. 1 Thess. 5:24, NASB.

I'VE BEEN WATCHING THE changing face of the university campus from my nearby apartment, and it's been fascinating. What had been several streets of housing is quickly changing into parkland as homes are being torn down or moved.

One block from my apartment sat a beautiful two-story brick home (probably built in the late 1940s or early 1950s). Someone cares enough for this home to go to the expense of having it moved rather than allowing it to be torn down. What an experience to watch as the workmen dug around the foundation, tore down old basement walls, pulled in huge steel beams, and prepared the house for moving! The preparation appeared to be carefully done without hurry or shortcuts.

Finally the big day came when two large tractor-trailers arrived carrying several sets of wheels. I waited for several days, eager to see how these two large semis would move this lovely old home, and wondering, too, if they would have enough power to move it safely. Much to my surprise, when all was ready, the house moved across the fields and down the road, towed by a little Payloader that had been used to dig out the basement! The semis' only job had been to bring in the wheels.

That little Payloader reminded me of a line attributed to Hudson Taylor: "All God's giants have been weak men who did great things for God because they reckoned on His being with them." We are able to do what the Lord calls us to do, no matter how large that task seems to be, when we allow God to do the preparation.

In the process of being moved, the home didn't appear to be under any stress or strain. I expected to hear creaks and groans from the structure as it was moved from its moorings over rough terrain. Instead, it traveled solidly and with dignity. When our foundation is secure in the heavenly Father it doesn't matter what our situation may be. We can be lifted out of our comfort zone (and perhaps actually moved to another territory) without being fearful. We can travel this earth with surety and dignity, knowing God will prepare us for whatever He asks us to do. JUDY-ANN NEAL

Mixed Feelings

You, O Lord keep my lamp burning; my God turns my darkness into light. With your help I can advance against a troop; with my God I can scale a wall. Ps. 18:28, 29, NIV.

AS I GOT OUT OF my car to buy a melon, a man in a wheelchair rushed over to me with a smile. I hid my surprise and asked for the produce seller. "I am," he said. After I chose a melon and paid him, he quickly moved to the back of the heap of melons, where another man with a disability sat on a mat, smiling. The first man gave the money he had gotten from me to his friend, who wrote the amount in their little book. He then shouted, "We have made 100 *dalasis.* God is good."

Can you believe this? Two persons with disabilities running a melon business. I turned around to hide a tear of mixed feelings. Yes; joy for their achievement with determination, and sadness for their disability and the struggle.

Normally people with disabilities in this country depend on their relatives or the government to help out and provide for all their needs; others sit and beg or live in care homes. Amazingly, these two are on their own, with mutual understanding and trust for each other. They have accepted their fate and have decided to struggle, with God's help, for their survival.

That's what we should do—trust in God and move on in faith. Often, when we have problems, we look only at the bad side and brood—forgetting that God is in control. But these cheerful men showed me that every problem has more than one side. Because of their disabilities they attracted more buyers than the other sellers. As children of God we have to look at the brighter side of issues and move on. As the saying goes: "When God closes the door, somewhere He opens a window." Where there's a will, there's a way. With faith we can conquer mountains.

Thank You, Jesus, for Your promise that one day You will come and change our bodies, take us home, and dwell with us. There will be no pain nor disabilities there—only joy. I know that there the melon sellers will be on their feet; they will pluck apples, coconuts, oranges, and pears; and children will pick melons and the strawberries on the ground.

I can't wait to be there. See you there! MABEL KWEI

Divine Love and the Ministry of Presence

A voice of one calling: "In the desert prepare the way for the Lord: make straight in the wilderness a highway for our God." Isa. 40:3, NIV.

I LET IT BE KNOWN through our church prayer chain that I desired work for the hours Sonny attended school. Within a couple days I had a job at Costco as a demonstrator. I was scheduled to begin work on a Thursday. At 3:30 that morning I was awakened by the Holy Spirit with these thoughts: *Ask the Lord's blessing on the product that you are promoting, because without it you'd not have a job. Ask the Lord's blessing on everyone who comes to your work station. Look for at least one amazing spiritual blessing every day you work, and record it in your new work journal.*

Wow! I was given my assignment before my job began. I understood—love was to flow from me in absolutely everything I said and did, for Jesus' sake, because I sincerely believe that He is coming for His people any day now.

Before noon a young woman came to my table. She was very friendly and asked if I liked my job. I told her yes, and that this was my first day at Costco. She inquired about the type of work I did before getting this job. I told her that I have a special needs son, and I hadn't worked outside my home for many years. "I'm so sorry," she said softly, then she lowered her head. When she looked up, she repeated, "I'm so sorry."

Then she shared from her heart. "I've been married for eight years, and I desire to have a baby." Our eyes met, and I whispered, "Let's pray." Bowing my head, I prayed, "Dear Jesus, You have heard my dear sister's prayer request. Thank You for hearing our prayers. Amen!" Our prayer was perhaps 15 seconds long.

When I opened my eyes she was glowing! "Thank you," she said—twice. Still smiling, she turned and walked away.

If you know Jesus intimately, He'll empower you to impress others with Himself. He will give you His boldness when needed. As it says in 1 Corinthians 15:58: "Always give yourselves fully to the work of the Lord, because you know that your labor in the Lord is not in vain" (NIV).

DEBORAH SANDERS

The Small Voice of God

And after the fire a still small voice. 1 Kings 19:11, 12, NKJV.

WHO CAN POSSIBLY FORGET Tuesday, September 11, 2001? Most of us can vividly recall where we were, whom we were with, and what we were doing when we heard the news. I had a 10:00 appointment with the orthodontist. Often I don't turn on the television when I'm home in the daytime, but I do like to listen to the radio. For some inexplicable reason I didn't even turn on the car radio as I traveled the less-than-10-minute drive to my appointment. I didn't have long to wait before I was ushered into the exam room. The assistant commented on the horrible news coming out of New York, but it still didn't register, not until I was seated in the chair and looked up at the overhead television screen. Like millions of people around the world, I too looked on in shock and disbelief when the second plane struck the twin towers. Even then I had no comprehension of the enormity of the tragedy that was unfolding.

For the rest of the day, into the night, and during the next few days I became transfixed by the television. When I could absorb no more emotionally, I sobbed uncontrollably for some time, then decided not to watch or listen to any more reports. I knew no one personally involved in this tragedy, yet it impacted me severely. I just can't imagine what it must have been like for the new widows, widowers, orphans, heartbroken siblings, parents, friends, coworkers, and rescue workers whose lives were changed forever by this senseless act of violence. I felt tremendous anger toward the perpetrators; and yes, I even questioned the presence/absence of God.

In the end, I took comfort in knowing that though the storms of life may rage around us, God is still in control. The heartache and pain leveled on the world by the prince of darkness on September 11 will not soon be forgotten. God will grant healing. His still small voice was heard through the reports of many selfless acts that occurred during that time.

Dear God, I know not what today will bring. This one thing I do know: You are in control. Please make me a blessing to someone today.

AVIS MAE RODNEY

Promises to Live by Today

Under His wings you may seek refuge; His faithfulness is a shield and bulwark. Ps. 91:4, NASB.

IT'S GOING TO BE ANOTHER orange weekend," the radio announcer intoned. Knowing what he meant, I turned the radio off. Orange, the next-to-the-worst color on the scale of "imminent danger" to our country from terrorist attack. My thoughts went to Psalm 91, an old favorite I'd memorized years before (and was now rememorizing).

From the words of this psalm and many others, I know that we can live our days in the peace and rest of the shelter the Most High provides within His shadow. In our hearts and minds we can say, "He is my refuge and my fortress, my God, in whom I trust." We can know that it is He who rescues us from those who would entrap us—even from any deadly pestilence their chemical and biological weapons can devise.

We don't have to live in fear, for He covers us with His "feathers," and we are safe under His wings. Safeguarded by His faithfulness, we don't fear the terrorists by night or missiles that fly by day, or pestilences that may stalk us (smallpox or anthrax) or bombs that spread destruction at noon.

A thousand might fall at our side, or even 10,000 at our right hand, but it won't approach us. We have only to look with our eyes and eventually see the reward of terrorists. Because we've made the Lord our refuge and our dwelling place; no evil will befall us, no plague will come even near our homes. Because He gives His angel charge over us, to keep us and bear us up, we are safe from injury. We may even have to tread on "lions and cobras and serpents" and trample them!

Because we love Him, He will deliver us and set us securely "on high" because we know His name. We can always call upon Him; and He, our wonderful Father in heaven, will answer us. He'll be with us in trouble and rescue us and honor us.

I don't know if these promises are literal, but I do know from experience that we can trust Him; He never fails us; and He never leaves us or forsakes us. He will satisfy us with long life—even eternal life—and we will have the joy of being together with Him.

Father, thank You for Your Word and for the comfort and guidance it gives us. We love You.

MARILYN KING

Listening

I love the Lord, because he hath heard my voice and my supplications. Because he hath inclined his ear unto me, therefore will I call upon him as long as I live. Ps. 116:1, 2.

SEPTEMBER 11, 2001, LEFT me devastated. I lost my son-in-law. Only those who have lost someone in a similar situation can know the agony I experienced.

I needed to talk, to tell people what he was like and what a special person he was. My church family and friends listened, encouraged, hugged, and prayed for me.

As time went by, their listening ear became less available. They had their own lives and problems, and I didn't want to add to them. But thank God! He is never too busy to listen. Night and day, moment by moment, I poured out my heart to the Lord and found comfort. Sometimes I still want to tell someone how I'm feeling, but I think they will think it petty. Thank God I can tell Him anything, and He will not think so.

One Sabbath morning I was feeling very sad and low in spirit. I decided not to go to the early-morning prayer meeting, deciding to go just in time for Sabbath school. About 15 minutes later it was as if someone pushed me. Before I knew what was happening, I was up and dressed. I was at the church in time for prayer meeting, and I felt much better. "This morning I was feeling low and didn't plan to come to prayer meeting," I told a friend. "In fact, I went back to bed. Suddenly—"

She seemed to be listening, but halfway through she said, "You know, I wanted to tell you . . ." And she began to tell me something that was not relevant at the time, totally disconnected from what I was telling her.

I was crushed. But thanks be to God, He heard me. The singing in Sabbath school buoyed my spirits up, and I rejoiced that I have a loving and understanding God.

Thank You, Lord, for being there for me, for listening to my praises, my thanks, my gratitude, my heartaches, and even my complaints. Because You always listen, I will call upon You for as long as I live. ENA THORPE

Are Our Names Written There?

No one who is impure will be allowed to enter that city, nor will anyone who is wicked or dishonest, but only those whose names are written in the Lamb's Book of Life. Rev. 21:27, Clear Word.

IT WAS THE WEEKEND after the September 11, 2001, attacks on our country. All of us were still reeling from the overpowering grief that had consumed us. Our wounds were still very fresh. The media reported that they hoped to find survivors. Weeks before, one of my new coworkers had invited my husband and me to his wedding. The ceremony itself was set to take place in a large, very beautiful Catholic cathedral; but the reception after the service was to be held on a local Air Force base. We had looked forward to being alone together as husband and wife, as our 6-year-old son usually accompanied us. After the initial shock of the attacks began to clear, our next thoughts were whether or not we'd be able to attend the elaborate reception that was scheduled to follow the wedding.

The Air Force base was on high alert, as were all military bases in the rest of the country. Soon word traveled through the grapevine that those of us who planned to attend the wedding and reception would be allowed to proceed as planned with one small requirement: Upon entering the base, we'd have to go immediately to the visitors' center, where we were to make sure our names were on the "approved clearance list." Besides several hundred guests, the bride had a very large family, many of whom were traveling from New York for the wedding. This meant the list would be very long. I must admit I was a little nervous that our names might have been overlooked or inadvertently left off the list. We walked into the visitors' center, unsure if we'd be allowed to attend the festivities.

Our names *were* there! No one had been left out. I breathed a sigh of relief. Had my name not been there I would have only missed a friend's reception. He and his bride no doubt would have been sorrowful had everyone not been allowed into the reception to celebrate their new marriage. But one day we will wait to hear our names read from another, more important, list. Live each day as Christ would have you. My prayer is that our life's priority will be living to hear our name read from that great list.

MELISSA DAUGHETY MCCLUNG

Order in the House!

Commit to the Lord whatever you do, and your plans will succeed. Prov. 16:3, NIV.

KING HEZEKIAH, ILL AND dying, was told by the Lord, "Put your house in order." He cried out to God, and God not only healed him but added 15 years to his life. As a sign, the Lord gave the king a choice: the clock could go forward, or it could be turned back. Hezekiah replied, "It is a simple matter for the shadow to go forward ten steps. Rather, have it go back ten steps" (2 Kings 20:10, NIV).

Many of us want to make the clock move back so we have more hours in a day. Time gets away from us. We mean to get our house in order; but before we realize it, a day, a season, or a year has passed, and we're still talking about getting organized.

It isn't possible to turn the clock back, but we can do something about the time we have before us. Whenever we lose control of our time, we are malfunctioning. We become like the pilot who announced to his passengers, "We're lost, folks; but cheer up—we're making excellent headway." Many of us function in a mediocre manner because we have no plan. A sense of direction can make the difference between responsible living and simply surviving. Having a plan puts us in control.

Sometimes we don't know where to start to bring order out of the chaos that sometimes surrounds us. But whenever we feel overwhelmed by all our responsibilities, a plan will help us handle it all. It takes determination, but it can be done—not overnight, but step by step. As we master small skills we are developing habits that can last a lifetime.

Fatigue and time pressure are two of the greatest problems facing women today. But just as money makes money, so does making a wise use of time create more time—the one thing most of us have so little of! Developing a plan, then, is really an investment in our future.

Best of all, a feeling of success and achievement will pervade. We'll know that we are women of excellence in process. As we get our time and homes under control, we are becoming admirable managers of the time and talent God has given us. We can look forward to hearing God say, "Well done, good and faithful servant" (Matt. 25:23, NIV).

NANCY VAN PELT

It Is Important to Remain Near

If you are willing and obedient, you will eat the best from the land. Isa.1:19, NIV.

I'VE HAD MARVELOUS opportunities to travel and get to know beautiful, interesting, historic, and exotic places. When I was young I never thought that one day I'd have the opportunity to go to Germany, the land of my ancestors, and there interact with people who speak the language of my family. My heart filled with joy when one Sabbath morning I praised God with church members of my same faith in Russia. Although I didn't understand their language, our feelings were one—gratitude and praise to God for His goodness to all of us.

When we travel it's very important to remain near the tour guide. If we are far away, we can't understand what we're seeing or visiting. It was so interesting to hear the explanations from our German guide who took us to the mosques in Istanbul. I didn't want to miss one word about the history of the persecuted Christians when we visited the catacombs in Rome. The guide in Honolulu, in addition to having a thorough knowledge of the culture of Hawaii, was very happy and funny, making everyone feel at ease.

On trips my motto is *learn.* I'm curious to learn everything about the location we're visiting. There's one trip on which I especially want to be open to learning from the Guide.

On the great trip we're making toward heavenly Canaan, we're in a large caravan that has Jesus Christ as our guide. We've passed through difficult locations, but it's necessary to continue on to reach the most important objective—arrival in heaven.

On this trip I've attempted to remain as near as possible to the divine Guide. He has so many things to tell me that I don't want to miss one single word. If I'm late and wander about, seeking my own interests, I'll miss the words of the Guide; and I'll not hear what is important for my spiritual life. Only when I remain as close as possible to Him can I be certain that I'm hearing all He has to say.

Father, thank You very much for being the guide in my life. Give me the certainty that I will always be as close to You as possible. I don't want to miss any of Your instructions on this great trip that we are making to the heavenly Canaan.

Ani Köhler Bravo

Why Us, God?

For he hath not despised nor abhorred the affliction of the afflicted; neither hath he hid his face from him; but when he cried unto him he heard. Ps. 22:24.

G*OD, WHY ARE YOU doing this to us? It's not fair!* My heart was filled with sorrow and grief after passing the long night at my mother's bedside, impotent to alleviate the excruciating pain she had from her terminal illness. Being the oldest of six girls, I had to pretend to be strong and all together for my sisters and my father. But I couldn't hold it anymore. I realized my mother would die that day. We'd been convinced that God would perform a miracle for her. She was a devoted Christian; she loved God, and taught us to love Him, too. So many people were praying for her recovery, I just couldn't believe God would take my mother away from us when we needed her most. I was in my early 20s, and my youngest sister was only 13 years old. Mother was the center of our world in every sense.

I went to my room and burst into tears. I cried and cried, pouring out my anger against God. I was angry because I thought He didn't care for us. We loved and needed our mother, and she was dying; and He didn't seem to care. How would the six of us survive without her? I couldn't deal with all the responsibility I had on my shoulders—the household, my sisters, the bills, the university, and everything else—because my father was home only on weekends. It wasn't fair.

Suddenly, in the midst of my misery, I stopped crying and closed my eyes. In my mind I saw a clear image of Jesus with tears in His eyes—He was suffering along with us. He was feeling our pain. He understood our grief. I was ashamed; how could I do this to God? How had I doubted His love for us? Calm and peaceful, I felt assured. If He would not heal my mother, He would give us strength to get through this ordeal.

Four days later our mother died. It was painful and difficult, and we miss her terribly, but God never left us alone—not for a moment. He was, He is, and He will be at our side.

My mother's last wish was to see all of us in heaven. She died with this blessed hope. With God's help, we will meet her there.

I can't wait to go to heaven!

HANNELORE GÓMEZ

Ready?

And while they went to buy, the bridegroom came; and they that were ready went in with him to the marriage: and the door was shut. Matt. 25:10.

I WAS BOOKED ON A flight to Barbados on a work assignment. I made sure I packed all the papers that had been sent to me to review prior to the meeting. I made sure that along with my personal belongings needed for the trip, I included my ticket. Since I was leaving from an airport that was closer to my workplace than to my home, for my Monday morning trip I'd be traveling 100 miles to the airport. I left home very early to be ahead of the peak-hour traffic, and got into town four hours ahead of my scheduled time of departure. Two hours later I was ready to check in. Alas! I didn't have my passport. It was safely at home, and the authorities insisted that although I was traveling only to another Caribbean island, an ordinary identification card was insufficient for this journey.

The only other flight from Jamaica to Barbados would be leaving in six hours, and I could board only if I had my passport. I had to travel the following day, and although I missed the first hours of our meeting, I was still welcomed.

There is a more important trip I'm planning to make. There's no way I can forget my passport because it is being kept for me by my host, Jesus. I must make my booking now, however, by accepting His free gift of salvation. There can be no change of plans on departure day, and there will be no opportunity for a late arrival at this meeting of persons of all ages from all nations.

There are documents I must review in preparation for this trip. They contain all the instructions for getting ready. There's no need to worry about packing the documents for the trip, as no baggage is allowed. Only a special garment described in the document will be necessary for that trip. I now have the opportunity to understand and apply the instructions that will prepare me for the journey.

Lord, please make me ready—and keep me ready until that day.

DESMALEE NEVINS

A Hollow Branch

Be on your guard; stand firm in the faith; be [women] of courage; be strong. 1 Cor. 16:13, NIV.

THE MORNING DEW WAS still on the grass when I walked out of the driveway for my morning exercise. As I turned around the bend I was confronted by an unusual sight: a huge branch from my favorite mango tree had fallen off. *It must have broken in the heavy storm we had last night,* I thought. Its branches and leaves blocked off the entire road, scattering the juicy mangoes all over the ground. Since I couldn't go forward, I had to turn around and jog the other way.

After completing my jogging, I stopped by that broken branch again to examine it carefully. Of course I picked up quite a few of those yummy mangoes from the ground, too! As I looked up at the section of the tree that had been severed, I made an amazing discovery. The fallen branch was actually hollow inside. Some termites must have eaten through it, and diseases within had also resulted in the decomposition of its interior. So when the storm came, this branch couldn't withstand the strong winds that beat on it with tremendous force.

Aren't we so much like this branch? We look good and strong, as Christians should be. We're busy with church work, organizing potlucks, running errands, rushing to choir practice—termites eating into our spiritual lives—all the while thinking we're doing all right. But looking good on the outside is not sufficient to carry us through the storms and trials of life. We're simply hollow inside. Only when we fill our lives with prayer, time with Jesus, listening to His leading, stretching out our hands in loving-kindness to those in need, will we build stronger characters. When the storms of sickness, financial difficulties, or family crises come upon us, we will then have the strength to trust God with the outcome.

Dear Lord, help me to develop inner strength each day. May I make time with You, learn from You, grow in strength and depth with You, that I may be strong enough to go through the storms of life. LINDA MEI LIN KOH

What I Can See From My Window

Open my eyes that I may see wonderful things in your law. Ps. 119:18.

THE BEGINNING OF THE afternoon was special—it couldn't have been better. It was the second council meeting of Just for Wives, a meeting for pastors' wives from all over Brazil. Imagine the congestion in the hotel lobby as women reunited with friends, filled out identification sheets, looked for others to form a group of three, and found room numbers, stairs or elevators, suitcases, or pillows! There was lots of laughter, hugs, and kisses; finally, I found myself in room 304.

The open window invited me to look at the scene outside. To my disgust, all I saw were houses with dirty patched roofs and unkempt backyards. *What a horrible view!* I thought. *I should have taken a room on the other wing. Perhaps there would be something better to see.* I closed the window and pulled the curtain closed.

Sunrise the following day, Sabbath, invited me to look out the same window that my roommate had already opened. Without remembering what I'd seen the previous day, my eyes automatically went in the direction of the horizon, far above the roofs to the edge of the city. What a lovely countryside! Lining the banks of the Madeira River, the jungle made up a hem of green lace along the gray-blue sky, mixing with the rays of the sunrise. Closer, a few city lights still twinkled.

Before such a magnificent scene, I praised the Creator. I couldn't hide my tears of joy. I whispered, "Lord, thank You for allowing me to see the river instead of fixing my eyes on the ugly rooftops below this hotel room."

How magnificent it will be to see the crystal-clear river of life on a beautiful Sabbath morning in the new Earth. But before that day arrives, let's stop looking at the "rooftops" in the evening of our life. Let's lift our heads and look a little beyond, to the river, at the dawning of new blessings each morning.

Why look at rooftops—the vicissitudes and anxieties of life—if we can contemplate the river?

Lord, thank You for such marvels that bring joy to the dawning of my day. I can hardly wait, Lord, for the day all of us will be together at the margins of the crystalline river!

MARLY G. OLIVEIRA

Giants

What time I am afraid, I will trust in thee. In God I will praise his word, in God I have put my trust; I will not fear what flesh can do unto me. Ps. 56:3, 4.

MY FAMILY BACKGROUND consists of two extreme genes: very tall and heavy built, and very small and petite. I belong to the latter. As a child I was often cuddled by huge uncles and tall aunties. My young sister hoped that she would one day look like them, while I thought it was ridiculous to be so big. I feared hugging them sometimes.

Sometimes we're faced with giants in our daily lives—things we don't wish to face. These could be giants of financial stress, giants of terminal illnesses, abuse, violence, and even poor relationships. Most of the time these giants seem so huge that we think we can't win the battle. We often have fear and doubts as we face them, thinking they will crush us under their feet. Don't be deceived! Big or small, God loves us all, and He promises that there is a way to win the battle.

The case of David and Goliath will never be forgotten in the entire history of the earth. Size was not the determining factor in that battle. Only God's power prevented disaster, and the giant Goliath was slain by the "giant" David with only a sling in his hand. David knew exactly to whom the credit belonged.

The giants of discouragement and despair may be lurking around you. In the truest sense, the shields they carry are but for a moment, and they shall not harm you. The sling and stones in your hand are more powerful than the shield in the enemy's hand, for there is One who holds your hand and shows you the direction in which you should aim. The forces of evil still send out giants to defy God's people, and they seem invincible. But remember David's decision to do battle with the best the enemy had to offer.

God can still topple any giant, anywhere, any place. He is a winning God, and we're part of His team. The enemy, on the other hand, is a perfect failure, and we must have no collaboration with him. The real issue here is to resist the satanic suggestions to make our own demands of pride. God's tool for our success could be the simple sling that we have rejected, thinking we will be a winner if we go for Goliath's shield. Instead, use the sling when He says to do so.

BERYL ASENO

What Makes the Difference?

Blessed are those who trust in the Lord. . . . They shall be like a tree planted by water, sending out its roots by the stream. Jer. 17:7, 8, NRSV.

ON THE HILLS AND mountains around our southern California home, thousands of pine trees are dead. The once-green slopes are reddish brown. The cause? A massive bark beetle infestation. These trees constitute a serious fire hazard.

During a visit to the San Bernardino Forest, a ranger turned over a piece of bark to show us how the damage was done. On the underside of the bark the beetles had eaten out a maze of tunnels in the growth layer, where capillaries carry the nutrients from the ground up the tree. The beetles had thrived and reproduced, but their digging cut off the circulation of sap. The situation, we were told, was aggravated by the long drought. If it had had enough water, the tree could had withstoodd the onslaught of the beetles. Without water, death had ensued.

On another trip to the mountains, we noticed something else. Not all pines were dead. Some remained verdant and vibrant. We noticed that the green trees grew in places where the ground seemed to hold more humidity. They got more water. Some green trees, however, stood next to dying, or dead, ones. The explanation was simple: their taproot was longer, grew deeper, reaching the water supply and assuring the tree's survival.

Our spiritual life is also under attack. Just living in this world exposes us to the beetles of sin. Their attacks are subtle—often hardly noticeable. But their depredation cuts off the feeding of the soul. Our spiritual growth is stunted, and the tree is weakened.

On the other hand, a tree whose taproot sinks deep finds the water of life. Thus invigorated, it survives and thrives. This tree is the one who trusts in the Lord and sends out its roots by a stream. Such a person fears neither heat nor drought and never ceases bearing fruit (Jer. 17:8). For a similar picture, see Psalm 1:1-3, where the verdant believer delights in God's law, producing fruit in season.

Lord, I want to dig deep—deeper into the riches of Your Word—to drink the water of life. Thank You for promising to make me a beautiful and fruitful tree!

NANCY JEAN VYHMEISTER

In His Image

So God created man in his own image, in the image of God he created him; male and female he created them. Gen. 1:27, NIV.

SEPTEMBER 23 IS MY mom's birthday. It was the first time she would celebrate it with us, her children, here in the United States. I was so excited as I looked forward to her birthday. My sister and I planned to do something special for her. We decided to bring her to New York City to celebrate.

On Friday morning we left our home in Maryland for the three-hour drive. The September weather couldn't have been better. We could feel the fresh air blowing in our faces from the open car windows.

It was almost time to have our lunch when we arrived in New York City. We checked into the hotel and headed out on our adventure/celebration. I learned from the hotel's receptionist that it was only three minutes by cab to the bus stop, and the bus would take us downtown within 15 minutes. Soon we were walking on the bustling streets of Manhattan, packed with people from everywhere—local people and tourists. We stopped by a restaurant to get our lunch and had a really memorable time before joining the crowd outside again.

As the day was ending and it was beginning to get dark, we decided to get back to the hotel. While walking to the bus station, we passed by a portrait painter. I sat on the small chair while the artist began to draw my face on the paper. I could see he was trying very hard to get the best angle. As he painted, I thought about the greatest Artist Creator, our God.

"So God created man in his own image . . . ; male and female created he them." Suddenly my heart overflowed with joy and happiness. To be created in His image made me feel so special.

Yes, we are all so special in God's eyes; each one of a kind, each special and unique yet like our Creator. *Lord, help me to be more like You!*

LANNY LYDIA PONGILATAN

Call Him Up

And it shall come to pass, that before they call, I will answer; and while they are yet speaking, I will hear. Isa. 65:24.

TRAVELING IS ONE OF my favorite adventures. Being single, I have the freedom to go whenever the opportunity presents itself. At first my travels were part study, part sightseeing. Later, I traveled mainly for sightseeing. On one of these trips I invited two of my nieces to come along. I looked forward to us being together on a 15-day cruise to Europe.

My niece, Linda, and I live in Florida. Helen lives in New York. Because the plane to Europe would be leaving from John F. Kennedy Airport in New York City, various connections had to be made. Trouble began the day of departure from Orlando. The flight was scheduled to depart at noon. As we approached the airport, I got a call reminding me that I had forgotten my medication. So we headed home to collect it. By the time we got back, the plane had taken off.

Another flight was due to leave soon, but was fully booked with 11 passengers on standby. The next possibility would be at 3:00 p.m., with a definite flight at 6:00 p.m. The flight from JFK to Europe was due to leave at 8:00 p.m. The only solution, I reasoned, was to turn to the Lord in prayer. This I did. *Lord, You know how much I need Your help so that my niece can see the incredible power of prayer. Let us get on the next plane.* Since it appeared that we'd be waiting for several hours, my niece left to get something for us to eat. I kept on praying. While I was still praying, I heard my name called to go to the ticket counter.

To my delight, I was told we'd be able to get on the first plane. The problem was that my niece wasn't around, and I couldn't leave the luggage to go looking for her. Passengers had already boarded, the gate had closed, and I was about to lose out on God's miraculous answer to prayer.

I continued praying, this time that my niece would show up soon. Even though it seemed hopeless, I still watched for her. I finally spotted her at a distance and began waving my arms frantically to get her attention. Fortunately, a supervisor was passing by, and I told her my plight. She unlocked the door leading to the aircraft and phoned ahead, asking them to hold the aircraft door open. We made it! I thanked God for another answer to prayer.

Dolores Smith

Basking in the Father's Love

And he said to them, "Come away by yourselves to a lonely place, and rest a while." Mark 6:31, RSV.

GOD GAVE MY HUSBAND and me a special Christmas gift—a visit to the Holy Land. The circumstances leading to the trip and our experiences clearly indicated that this treat had been carefully planned for us by Providence for this particular time. Some years earlier, we had thought of doing this. Nothing worked. But now an unexpected check had arrived that was sufficient to cover expenses.

At this time we needed some cheering up. In March my husband had suffered a stroke that changed our lives with such suddenness we had no time to be stunned. We left our work in Africa and returned to our homeland, the Philippines. He recovered, but had to retire to avoid any stress. I returned alone to the Congo to pack our things. Thinking of my husband in frail health and aiming to be back to the Philippines by early June if I was to find a teaching job, I worked feverishly and finished in three weeks flat. The prayers—mine and many others'—sustained and helped me during those days.

A teaching job opened for me in Thailand; but 21 years in Africa, away from Asia and out of the classroom, had taken a toll. I was adjusting poorly to a new country and to my new roles. I became aware that I was building up tension the day that I began dreading meeting anybody on the way home from school because I could not smile.

That was when we got this vacation opportunity. Oh, the wonderful, unfathomable love of our heavenly Father! We felt blessed to see the place where His Gift to the world had once lived and worked. Four months earlier, war had broken out between Israel and Palestine, so there were hardly any other tourists at the time of our visit. When we went to Bethlehem, our guide said that if there had been no war we'd have had to stand in line for hours to see the spot they said was Jesus' birthplace. That would have been stressful. At the Dead Sea we had it all to ourselves—and almost didn't know what to do with it! Every day of those three weeks our hearts overflowed with gratitude and amazement at how God could be so lavish with His love. We returned home fully refreshed. May you too turn to Him for refreshment for your every need.

BIENVISA LADION-NEBRES

Manila Hotel

Come unto me, all ye that labour and are heavy laden, and I will give you rest. Matt. 11:28.

BRENDA AND I WERE en route to Guam, where she planned to enjoy her grandchildren while I spoke at a women's retreat. In Manila we had an 11-hour layover.

In the immigration hall we spent more than an hour on our feet in stifling conditions before transferring to a different terminal for our next flight. At the departure terminal we discovered our airline desk would not open for seven hours. All waiting lounges and restaurants could be accessed only after we checked in; so we had no place to sit, our feet ached, our stomachs growled, and we longed for a cool resting place. We decided to try the "affordable" hotel suggested by the woman at the information podium.

We climbed marbled steps where the doorman bowed to us as though we were royalty. The spacious lobby was dazzling with mirrors and chandeliers. A porter took our luggage and placed it behind the counter.

"How much is your cheapest room?" I asked the clerk behind the carved desk.

"Two hundred forty dollars," she said. "It is very nice."

Brenda and I gulped and shook our heads, whereupon the clerk turned her back on us.

Now what were we to do? We didn't want to go back to the airport and sit on our suitcases and sweat, so we headed for the air-conditioned coffee shop. There we sat in luxury and took a very long time to decide what we wanted for lunch. We actually had only two choices of vegetarian dishes, but we had to stretch our stay in such a comfortable spot as long as possible.

Fortunately, the cooks took a long time to prepare our food, and we took even longer to enjoy it. Then we waited as long as possible before ordering dessert. That good meal stretched over three wonderful, relaxing hours in air-conditioned comfort. Then we explored the tourist shops and took a taxi back to the airport, our afternoon rest having cost us very little.

Sometimes, Lord, I feel as tired out spiritually as we felt physically that afternoon. At such times I long for the coolness and comfort of Your presence. How thankful I am that I don't have to pay for such rest, nor do I have to pretend even to be wealthy to enjoy Your comfort. I simply need to "come."

Dorothy Eaton Watts

September 27

God's Watch Care

Look at the birds of the air; they do not sow or reap or store away in barns, and yet your heavenly Father feeds them. Are you not much more valuable than they?" Matt. 6:26, NIV.

ONE SEPTEMBER MORNING as I was eating breakfast, my eye caught a flash of red outside my patio window. A male cardinal, sitting on the arm of the glider, seemed to be eating something; and then he flew away.

Then I heard a persistent chirping that was definitely not a bird song. Out of the corner of my eye I saw a tiny, sparsely-feathered ball against the leg of the glider. A brown, speckled baby bird had fallen from its nest. Worried that my neighbor's cat might decide to visit, I stood by the window, wondering just what to do. I've always had a fear of birds, so picking it up wasn't an option. I continued to watch the wee creature as it struggled along, trying its best to flap its undeveloped wings. Soon, still chirping, it made its way onto the grass; then grew very still when the scarlet cardinal suddenly flew down. The baby opened its mouth, and the daddy cardinal fed it! He quickly flew away, and the tiny bird again began its awkward journey toward the fence, still chirping. Every so often it would become quiet, and Papa Cardinal would fly down with another morsel.

At last the baby bird reached the trellis gate that leaned against the fence and tried to hop onto it. It would try and try, fall, and begin again. I was cheering it on when Papa Cardinal alighted on top of the fence. He looked down on the little bird but never made a sound. At one point Baby Bird made it almost to the top; then alas! It fell back down. When Papa Cardinal flew down to it, I wondered if it might be hurt, but soon he flew away. The baby bird continued to hop and finally made it out the gate. Soon I could no longer see it.

As I watched this little nature drama unfold, I thought: *This is how our heavenly Father watches over me.* Repeatedly I stumble and fall, but my heavenly Father never leaves me.

Thank You, Father God, for Your loving care. Mary Cerovski Reinhold

Baby Steps

Continue to love each other with true brotherly love. Heb. 13:1, TLB.

AUNTIE, GET HIM DOWN!" my nephew Brenden urgently begged as Cameron took several steps in his direction. Three years old, he wasn't impressed by his 1-year-old brother's newfound mobility. Cameron, on the other hand, was fascinated with his sudden ability to walk. Careening cautiously, he wobbled toward his adored big brother. Brenden leaped out of his way.

"He's out of control! Make him stop!" Brenden cried, sprinting across the room. Climbing into a chair beyond Cameron's reach, he surveyed his brother's progress. "Catch him!"

Relying on the age-old technique of turning problems into learning experiences, I suggested we all play a game. Lifting Brenden down from his defiant perch, I said, "How about this? You stand in front of Cameron and let him walk with you. Keep moving, and I'll wait with my arms open to catch you. See who reaches me first, OK?"

Giggling, Brenden raced to the edge of the caramel-colored carpet. Delighted at the challenge, he helped Cameron to his feet. "Hang on, Cammy! Let's walk to auntie!" Slowly, they started out, Cameron's little bare feet stepping into the imprint of Brenden's larger feet. "He's walking!" Brenden laughed.

Step by step they continued on, Cameron trusting Brenden to steady him, never letting him fall. Cameron's eyes grew big as saucers as he neared my waiting arms. Seconds later the boys were wrapped tightly in my warm embrace. Kissing their boisterous little faces, I said, "See? It wasn't a race! You leaned on each other and made it!" Brenden, the experienced walker; Cameron, the novice.

Who have we helped today? Who have we allowed to lean on us when they're unsure of their next step? We all start our Christian walk in different places. Some of us grew up in this lifestyle, while others are only beginning. Just as Cameron relied on the assistance of his wiser, more experienced big brother to get him to his destination safely, Jesus offers us a loving hand and warm embrace to keep our feet walking. Every time we stumble, He is the one who picks us up, dusts us off, and helps us resume our life travels. It doesn't matter how quickly we walk, for God is the God of baby steps.

LORI L. MANTZ

A Pattern for Good

Moreover we know that to those who love God, who are called according to his plan, everything that happens fits into a pattern for good. Rom. 8:28, Phillips.

O*H, NO! I COULDN'T have,* I said to myself as I sped down the interstate, already late for an appointment with my doctor in the city an hour away. *Surely I didn't forget the diagnostic films,* I told myself. But I had indeed neglected to pick them up from the hospital. And that was 15 minutes in the opposite direction. Bringing them to the physician was the reason for the trip.

Sheepishly I called the doctor's office and explained my faux pas. The receptionist promised to reschedule an appointment for me as soon as I could get to the office with films in hand.

Still irritated at myself, I turned the car around and headed for the hospital, inching along a very busy commercial vein of highway. Suddenly I heard a loud *ping.* Checking the rearview mirror, I saw a small black object fly behind me across the highway.

"I hope that wasn't anything important," I muttered. But no sooner had that thought crossed my mind than I noticed a sudden loss of power and absolutely no steering control. I tried veering the very stiff wheel to the right. Fortunately, the car moved from the center lane to the right lane before coming to rest beside a business parking lot in a somewhat questionable part of town.

It took several prayerful seconds before I realized not only that I had safely negotiated an exit from the busy road but also that I knew the owner of the business. God had provided a known and safe haven for me. Grabbing my cell phone, I dialed AAA. Within the hour they towed the car and took care of the mechanical problem.

That evening as I was searching for material for a devotional for my Pathfinder group, I paused at the conclusion of an article on how to find a pearl. "The outer covering belies the inner beauty." I knew that sentence described my day's experience.

Thanking God for His innumerable blessings, I started counting. Turning around that morning had brought me into town before the car broke down. AAA towed me free of charge because I was not on the interstate. I had a working cell phone. And now I had a testimony with a wealth of interest and excitement to share with my Pathfinders. God does transform inconvenient situations into beautiful shells through His care, mercy, and love!

Janet M. Greene

The Vetkoek

Can that which is unsavoury be eaten without salt? Job 6:6.

ON SUNDAY WE WOULD leave the weekend women's retreat to travel back home. The kombi was already loaded with our luggage when our group of women took a long walk along the beach.

It was nearing midday when we returned to join the other women at the meeting place. I was getting hungry, and we still needed to attend the farewell meeting. When would we finish? We had many hours to travel, and wouldn't reach home before evening.

As I neared the supermarket on the beachfront, I decided to buy something to eat. The vetkoek looked so appetizing. (Vetkoek is a bread dough that's allowed to rise, after which pieces are pinched off, flattened, and fried in hot oil. It puffs up in the hot oil and is removed when it turns a golden brown. When cooled, it is sliced through, and a savory filling is sandwiched inside.) Oh, the vetkoek, with vegetable curry filling, *really* looked good wrapped in plastic wrap. It was a bit pricey, but I was hungry.

I found a seat and took my first bite. Ugh! No salt! Tasteless, horrible—*yuck!* But I was so hungry that I struggled to eat on. I felt like throwing it away in the nearest bin; but I had paid for it, and there was nothing else to eat.

Salt—what is it? Just a common, white, fine, grainy substance used to flavor or preserve food. You need only a little to enhance your food; too much spoils it and can make you sick.

Salt is used for many other things. Before the advent of refrigeration, meat was salted down to prevent spoilage. Many years ago when our family went camping, Mother preserved her eggs (immersed in salt) in a shoebox. A teaspoon of salt can be used as a gargle in a glass of warm water. Roman soldiers were paid with salt, hence the saying "They are worth their salt."

"Ye are the salt of the earth; but if the salt have lost his savour, wherewith shall it be salted? it is thenceforth good for nothing, but to be cast out, and to be trodden under foot of men" (Matt. 5:13).

I don't want to be like that vetkoek that looked so appetizing yet was so tasteless. I want to be like the pinch of salt in society, modeling goodness, kindness, and reliability.

PRISCILLA ADONIS

October 1

Showers of Blessing

I will send down showers in season; there will be showers of blessing.
Eze. 34:26, NIV.

IT RAINED TODAY. That may not sound particularly noteworthy; but I was happy to lie awake at 4:30 this morning, listening to the gentle rhythm on the roof. Later people at church looked out at the gray skies and exclaimed, "Praise the Lord!" New South Wales, along with other parts of eastern Australia, has been in the grip of the worst drought in 100 years and has recently suffered some of the worst bushfires on record. So the sight, sound, and smell of rain was something to gladden the heart.

In our yard grass that was crisp and brown has turned green—literally overnight. Flowers that usually close as soon as the sun goes down have stayed open—seemingly to drink the refreshing moisture. Even the birds sound happier. We've been watering as much as the water restrictions allowed, but using sprinklers and hoses simply can't compare with a good downpour.

We city dwellers have been the lucky ones, however. Out in the rural areas farmers have had to watch their livelihoods destroyed as dams dried up, crops failed, and livestock died. There has been no water to spare for gardens. Even drinking water has had to be brought in by truck.

But it rained today right across the state, and the weather report says there's more to come. Many times in the past weeks the skies have promised much, but given little or nothing. So now that the farms—which had been reduced to dust bowls—are turning into vast lakes of mud, the children are out playing in it.

As I watch the life-giving drops falling, I can understand why water is such an important metaphor in Scripture. Jesus spoke of living water which, within the recipient, becomes "a spring of water welling up to eternal life" (John 4:14, NIV). That precious water is freely available, but do I sometimes neglect to drink? God promises, "The Lord will guide you always; he will satisfy your needs in a sun-scorched land and will strengthen your frame. You will be like a well-watered garden, like a spring whose waters never fail" (Isa. 58:11, NIV).

Lord, let me not be content to live a drought-stunted existence when I can be like a flourishing garden, watered by Your love; a source of refreshment for those who are thirsting for something more than this world can give.

JENNIFER M. BALDWIN

An Answered Prayer!

Ask, and it shall be given you; seek, and ye shall find; knock, and it shall be opened unto you. Matt. 7:7.

WE HAD JUST ARRIVED at a meeting for pastors and their wives. When one of our colleagues arrived with his wife and small children, we learned the sad news that they had just been held up and their car had been stolen. Later we learned that the entire year had been very difficult for them. Their home had been robbed; their newborn daughter was in treatment for a serious health problem—and now this episode. And it was exactly one week before their planned and much-deserved vacation. The question everyone asked was: "Where were God and His angels?"

The pastor's wife and I decided to go to the meeting while a group went with her husband to the police station to report the robbery. When we reached the meeting location, the women gathered to share pleasant experiences in their ministries; however, instead of continuing with the experiences, one of the women suggested that we kneel there and ask God for guidance and assistance. Even if the car were not found, we should ask for His will to be done.

Few times have I felt such great union, warmth, and fervor as in the two prayers that were offered sincerely from the heart. Our colleague's wife went out to take care of her children and to wait for her husband to return with good news. When she returned to the meeting room, she had a different look on her face and marvelous news in answer to our prayers. A few blocks from our meeting location the car had been found—with all of their belongings. This was truly a miracle, considering that only a few blocks away was a very dangerous area of the city that isn't accessible even by the police. In this location thieves can hide with the fruit of their robberies, certain that no one is going to bother them.

I would like to share with you the words of the Christian writer Ellen White: "Keep your wants, your joys, your sorrows, your cares, and your fears before God. . . . There is no chapter in our experience too dark for Him to read; there is no perplexity too difficult for Him to unravel. No calamity can befall the least of His children, no anxiety harass the soul, no joy cheer, no sincere prayer escape the lips, of which our heavenly Father is unobservant, or in which He takes no immediate interest" (*Steps to Christ,* p. 100).

MERCEDES ALMIRON DE TAPIA

Lost at Sea

This is what the Lord says: "Maintain justice and do what is right, for my salvation is close at hand and my righteousness will soon be revealed." Isa. 56:1, NIV.

RECENTLY I READ *Adrift,* by Grenville Lee Dunstan, in which he tells the story of six men who got lost when they sailed to an island to visit their relatives. They knew the way very well because they made this trip frequently. But this time they were carrying too much fruit, and the boat was overloaded. This was enough for them to make an error in their route and get lost for nearly three long months that were filled with peril and hunger.

The author mentions several other instances, and in almost all of these cases the people survived using creativity and trust in God; although they experienced hunger and thirst, and withstood storms and scalding sun for a very long time. But on the very last day, the day before these people would be saved, someone gave up on living.

How many times have I felt like giving up on everything and taking care of things myself, when salvation could be tomorrow? Tomorrow is exactly 24 hours from today; and it's possible to put up with these 24 hours, no matter what comes, when one knows that at the end the much-desired salvation will be here.

Therefore, no matter what you are going through or whatever may be breaking your heart, remember that, as bad as your problem may seem, you could be exactly 24 hours away from salvation. Don't stop fighting. Don't give up on living. Don't surrender; remember all the victories that you've won by experiencing hunger and thirst; holding on through storms and the burning sun; being denied comfort, health, or being with your dear ones. It doesn't matter what your problem may be; do not give up!

Salvation for those lost at sea was not a plateful of food, as they may have dreamed. If they'd eaten that much food in their weakened condition, they could have died. Perhaps for you salvation will not come in the manner you wish or the package you've been dreaming about. Perhaps salvation will be just a warm, reinvigorating broth so that you may recover your strength until you're able to receive your favorite dish prepared especially for you!

Waiting is worthwhile! It's only 24 hours! KÊNIA KOPITAR

Grow New Leaves

Happy are those who reject the advice of evil people, who do not follow the example of sinners or join those who have no use for God. Instead, they find joy in obeying the Law of the Lord, and they study it day and night. They are like trees that grow beside a stream, that bear fruit at the right time, and whose leaves do not dry up. They succeed in everything they do. Ps. 1:1-3, TEV.

I LOOK OUT AND ALL I see are falling leaves. But if I keep an eye on those trees, in a few months they'll grow new leaves. Trees must be persistent. You don't see them giving up because the weather got cold and they lost their leaves. No; they simply wait until it warms up, and they grow more leaves!

So I'm thinking that I need to grow more leaves. Why should I let the seasons of my life keep me from doing things that I need to do, that I want to do, that I can—and maybe should—do?

At this particular season of my life many would think that I should be thinking about slowing down—maybe even retiring in a few years. Certainly this is not a time to be thinking about starting new things, achieving new goals, right? Wrong!

When I turned the big 5-0, I felt as if I had been set free! Since that time I have done many things that I never thought I'd do. Writing poetry, for instance. I didn't think I even liked poetry! I've written songs, words and music, and even made a CD with them. I've learned to understand and enjoy a computer.

I also find that the older I get, the bolder I get. I'm not as afraid to speak up and say what I think or feel. I'm not afraid to try new things. When someone asks, "Can you do this?" I think to myself, *Sure I can!* That doesn't mean that I really can, or am good at it; but I'll give it my best, and many times I find that I really can do it.

So I'm growing new leaves. I'm persistent. The winds of life may try to blow them away, but not before I've tried them out. But it's OK; I'll just grow new ones! I'll be persistent. Furthermore, our text says that these people find joy in obeying the law of the Lord, and they study it day and night. That is probably why "they succeed in everything they do."

Donna Sherrill

Bringing Trophies to God

For Christ also suffered once for sins, the just for the unjust, that He might bring us to God, being put to death in the flesh but made alive by the Spirit. 1 Peter 3:18, NKJV.

MY SON, HIS WIFE, and I anxiously awaited the arrival of their first grandchild and my first great-grandchild. When we heard that a baby girl had arrived October 1, we were elated! Of course we wanted to see her as soon as we could arrange to drive the 150 miles to where she and her parents lived.

My daughter-in-law left work and drove straight to the hospital the day the baby was born. But it was two days more before my son and I were able to go see her. By then she was 3 days old and home from the hospital. What a perfectly beautiful baby girl she was! We took many photos and stayed there the whole day.

All my granddaughter's friends at our church also wanted to see this new baby and had gifts to present to her. It was two and a half weeks before the proud parents could drive all those miles to our area to show off their beautiful baby girl to their friends. How happy the people were to see—and even hold—the baby of their friend; some friends and family had even held the new mother when she was a baby! It was a wonderful reunion.

The next time my granddaughter brings her baby girl to see her parents and me, I'll be thrilled even more to see the growth that has taken place in this small person.

Greater than this reunion will be the reunion in heaven when Jesus can bring His children whom He has saved from this sinful earth through the spacious universe and present them to His Father in heaven. What a joy and thrill it will be for Jesus to do that! This will fulfill His prayer in John 17:24: "Father, I desire that they also whom You gave Me may be with Me where I am, that they may behold My glory which You have given Me; for You loved Me before the foundation of the world" (NKJV).

Dear Lord, I pray that we all may be there, just as You prayed to the Father when You were here with us! Bessie Siemens Lobsien

Flesh of My Flesh

"This is now bone of my bones and flesh of my flesh." Gen. 2:23, NIV.

AS I WAS REVIEWING my Sabbath sermon early that October morning, I received a phone call from our son, Benjie. He said in passing, "Kartini's been in labor during the night, but she thinks it was Bracksden Hicks labor pains. I'll keep you posted, Mom, so don't worry."

I'd just given my first presentation Friday night at the women's retreat in Chicago and had three more presentations in the series. After the second presentation, I turned on my phone. It rang immediately, and with excitement Benjie reported, "Mom, we've taken Kartini to the ER; I hope you can be here."

Realizing this was *the* phone call, the retreat director immediately said, "Mary, you go; you need to be with your family. We'll take care of your presentations."

In total shock, I asked my friend Paula to pack my equipment while I ran up to the motel room to call American Airlines to see if they could find me a seat on the next flight. While on hold, I grabbed clothes from the closet. Finally the reservation attendant said, "We have a seat for you on the 5:58 p.m. flight that arrives in Baltimore at 8:30 p.m." I booked the flight.

Paula arrived in my room and began packing the rest of my clothes while I made other phone calls. My husband had already left to be with Benjie and Kartini.

While rushing to the airport, Paula and I prayed that the baby wouldn't come until I arrived, so that I would have the honor of "coaching" my grandson into the world, upon the request of my precious daughter-in-"love." "What a selfish prayer," I mused.

Out of breath, I arrived at the hospital at 10:00. Saturday night was a long night, as Benjamin Edward decided to come the following morning. Praise the Lord, he was healthy enough to go home safely three days after birth.

Flesh of my flesh. Bone of my bones. That text has a different meaning to me now. As I renewed my commitment to Christ as I saw that new birth, I was reminded of the new-birth experience Jesus wants with me every day. Hearing that first cry of the newborn, I reflected on my gasping for the breath for eternal life—a new beginning. How Jesus longs for that intimacy with you and me—a new-birth experience every day!

MARY MAXSON

October 7

How Bright Are You?

For God, who said, "Let light shine out of darkness," made his light shine in our hearts to give us the light of the knowledge of the glory of God in the face of Christ. 2 Cor. 4:6, NIV.

DON'T WORRY; I'M NOT talking about your intelligence quotient. What I am talking about is the light of God's love shining in your life.

A group of friends and my husband and I were camping in the fall in Colorado's mountains to see the glorious display of aspen. We arrived shortly before sunset on Friday and quickly set up camp. After securing our tents, we fixed dinner, and of course that required a campfire, though all the cooking was actually done on our camp stoves.

There was a definite chill to the air, so we all gathered around the fire and began to talk. Subjects varied, and time passed. It was getting rather late when Paul, a young Canadian friend of ours, happened to notice that it was a full moon. As we watched, the moon seemed to develop a halo. It was faint at first, but as we watched it became clearer. We all watched for a few minutes, then went back to our conversation. Soon, however, our attention was back on the moon, because Melinda noticed that the halo had changed—it had become a pale rainbow.

We couldn't really believe it ourselves, but it was true. A clear, soft rainbow circled the full moon that night. We thought it must have been a miracle, as the moon doesn't produce light, but only reflects it. So that night there must have been some moisture between us and the moon, because it was reflecting so much light that it caused a rainbow.

When you think about it, we're a lot like the moon. We don't produce light either, but we can—and do—reflect it. Our text demonstrates this idea completely: "For God, who said, 'Let light shine out of darkness,' made his light shine in our hearts to give us the light of the knowledge of the glory of God in the face of Christ."

I encourage you to read the entire passage of 2 Corinthians 4:4-11 and to meditate on this concept of reflecting, or revealing, the love of Jesus Christ in your life. Then, when someone asks you how bright you are, you can say: "I'm so filled with the love of Christ I shine even in the night."

May God bless you today as you brighten your world with His love.

Juli Blood

Misery Loves Company

For the Lord your God goes with you; he will never leave you nor forsake you. Deut. 31:6, NIV.

I KNEW MY BACK HURT when I had to pick up books from the bottom of the book cart, but that wasn't unusual. With arthritis in my back and knees, it was always a painful stretch; but my job at the library required it. This time, however, my back went into spasms, and a couple hours later the pain was so bad that I had to go home.

Driving myself home was painful, and climbing the stairs to my trailer took true grit. Once inside I was greeted by my tribe of hopeful kitties, who assume that any time I walk in the door they'll get fed.

"No supper tonight, guys," I announced. "Mama's dying."

I made my way over to the couch and lay down. What could I do to help myself? I'm allergic to aspirin and other pain relievers, so there was nothing I could take for it. Getting a heating pad or an ice bag would require actual movement on my part, so I decided it would have to wait until I was better—or braver. My only options were to cry and pray, both of which I did. Poor me. By now the pain was shooting through my side into my neck, and I couldn't move my arm. The worst of it was that I was all alone. No husband, no roommate—not even a neighbor to come to my rescue! Poor, poor Gina.

I should have known I wasn't really alone. God sent His angels in feline form. My cat Gilley curled himself around the top of my head. Gracie got on my chest. Gilah, who can best be described as a big-boned gal, decided to squeeze her ample self into the space between Gracie and my chin. I was taking big breaths of fur, but all three began purring, and we fell asleep together.

God is not limited by our idea of angels who have wings and halos. He can use anybody who's willing to be a comforter to the hurting. Angels come in all shapes and sizes. Sometimes they come in fur.

With what kind of angel has God met your needs? Remember that even in your misery, God will never leave you nor forsake you. GINA LEE

Joy of Serving

I tell you the truth, whatever you did for one of the least of these brothers of mine, you did for me. Matt. 25:40, NIV.

IT WAS EXACTLY 30 days until the commemoration of Children's Day when my son Marcos, other young people, and I met in our church to plan for what would be done for needy children. We didn't have any project in mind, but we wanted to do something different. We ended the meeting without knowing what we would do; but we'd promised each other to pray, asking God to help us.

In the middle of the week my son called me. "Mother, let's give the children some toys, but let's also give a basic food basket to their families." I accepted the challenge. Because we had little time, we began to pray and make ourselves available to God to carry out this project.

We visited the families in the surrounding areas, registering each one and recording how many children were in each house. We wrote letters and personally visited some commercial establishments, requesting food, toys, and clothing.

The day before Children's Day we packaged 136 bags of food, clothing, and toys to benefit these families. The next day a large number of people came to the prearranged location to receive the bags, and each smile rewarded and compensated us for our exhausting work.

When I think of the little time that we had, I remember the words of the apostle Paul in Philippians 4:13: "I can do all things through Christ who strengthens me" (NKJV).

We can never do anything if we don't first ask our God for His help. We are small as human beings, but giants if we place our lives in the hands of our God in order to be useful to our fellow human beings.

Today, when we see people giving their lives to Jesus through that project, I thank God for His infinite kindness; He helped children and youth change their lives through a simple project with the slogan "Make a Child Smile." According to today's text, when we do something for one of these little ones, we have done it for the Lord Jesus.

NICÉIA TRIANDADE

Junk-free

If we confess our sins, he is faithful and just and will forgive us our sins and purify us from all unrighteousness. 1 John 1:9, NIV.

IT WAS ANOTHER OF those busy Sundays when I begin the task of cleaning a room and, partway through, feel completely overwhelmed, wishing I'd never started. If you can't relate to this experience, you're above average. If you can, however, you are one of about 90 percent of normal homemaking women, I'm sure.

Just at the peak of frustration, the doorbell rang. Lucky for me, it happened to be one of those real girlfriends who knows you have junk in the closet and still don't mind being your friend. After a quick chat, it was back to business, only this time there were two pairs of hands. Things were going well until she moved toward my bed. Kneeling down, she attempted to clear under the bed.

"Oh, no!" I protested. "Not there! We'll never be finished if we attempt that mess!"

The job of cleaning soon came to an end, leaving me to bask in the comfort of a clean space. I was, though, bothered by the untouched "junk" beneath my bed, so I got up to clear it out. To my surprise, I found a clutter-free space. Then I remembered that a few weeks before I had cleared the junk. I could enjoy my truly junk-free room without reservation.

How many times do we live with reservations, thinking that God has been so good to us; but we have so many mistakes lurking just beneath our consciousness? This is one of the tools the evil one uses to swell his ranks. He makes us forget that Jesus has forgiven us of past repented sins, making us reluctant to accept the blessings of a forgiven life. He causes our past mistakes and sins to loom high before us, making it seem presumptuous to even think about approaching the throne of grace. The very gift of forgiveness—given so freely and undeservedly—is traded for guilt and despair.

This is contrary to God's plan of love and intention. Isaiah reminds us in Isaiah 43:18: "Remember ye not the former things, neither consider the things of old." Why? God responds, "For I will forgive their wickedness and will remember their sins no more" (Jer. 31:34, NIV).

So the next time you're haunted by the past and tempted to shun the inviting presence of our loving heavenly Father, remember: you are junk-free!

PATRICE E. WILLIAMS-GORDON

October 11

Rainbows

I do set my bow in the cloud, and it shall be for a token of a covenant between me and the earth. Gen. 9:13.

I WAS RUNNING LATE with supper preparations. Since I was busy at the kitchen sink washing, peeling, and chopping vegetables, I didn't look outdoors to see the pelting rain. But I could hear it quite distinctly on our roof. "Thank You, Lord, for that generous rain shower," I said.

All summer we'd had no rain, and drought had taken its toll. I was grateful for the rain. "Now I won't have to water the garden until tomorrow!" I joyfully mused.

Suddenly the downpour stopped as I returned to the sink to clean up. I glanced out of the window and, amazingly, saw dark clouds rolling eastward toward the mountains even as the sun shone brilliantly and a perfect rainbow hovered in the sky! I was awed by the rainbow's distinct, colorful beauty. As I admired it, I suddenly discovered a second rainbow higher in the sky (not as vivid as the initial bow, but composed of the same beautiful, distinct colors).

"Awesome! Beautiful!" I exclaimed as I stood for a few moments admiring God's artwork. "Your beautiful rainbows have made my toilsome day worthwhile, Father!"

Then I thought of God's promise to Noah in Genesis 9:11-15, that He would never again destroy the earth with a flood. He gave Noah a rainbow in the sky to seal His promise. Though that promise was made thousands of years ago, even today God puts that beautiful arch of colors in the sky to remind us that the promises of His Word are eternally binding and sure.

"Thank You, Lord, for giving us such an awesome promise as the colorful rainbow!" I said as I stirred the simmering vegetables. I thought of a number of my favorite Bible promises. John 14:1-3 is one. Another is Isaiah 41:9, 10, which became my mainstay throughout high school and college: "Thou art my servant; I have chosen thee, and not cast thee away. Fear thou not; for I am with thee: be not dismayed; for I am thy God: I will strengthen thee; yea, I will help thee; yea, I will uphold thee with the right hand of my righteousness." NATHALIE LADNER-BISCHOFF

Full of Good Works

In all things shewing thyself a pattern of good works. Titus 2:7.

I HAVE A FRIEND WHO often says, "If you need anything, just C-O-V [Call on Von]." Many seniors have benefited from her availability and generosity. She takes them to church, doctors' appointments, grocery shopping, special programs, dinner in a restaurant, or to visit friends. Some longer trips may entail overnight stays in a hotel when she takes seniors to Calgary, a distance of 100 miles, for cataract surgeries. She crochets afghans for those who want to give one to their daughters, or she knits sweaters for someone's new grandchild. The yarn is provided, but her time is free. Yes, Von exemplifies the Bible text: "Let us consider one another to provoke unto love and to good works" (Heb. 10:24).

I'm not one of those needy seniors, but she frequently does something special for me and won't accept payment for it. These special gifts don't fall on my birthday, Christmas, or any other Hallmark day. She says she gives because "you're my friend."

My latest gift was an "Around the World" afghan made of 725 granny squares. "If you like it, you can have it," she said. The afghan has special meaning to me because she and I have traveled around the world together. Another time I was the recipient of two lamps because she insisted, "I don't need them anymore." On four occasions she saw beautiful patterns for sweaters and knew I'd like them, so she made them just for me!

I count myself fortunate to have her as a friend. She's not only generous but obliging. I'm grateful for her willingness to accompany me to visit Iceland, my mother's birthplace, no matter what the cost. Nothing can surpass the value of a good friend.

Her generosity and kindness remind me of the numberless gifts God has provided for our enjoyment. He bestows His goodness on us even when we don't feel a need and even though we are unworthy. "He maketh his sun to rise on the evil and on the good, and sendeth rain on the just and on the unjust."

Lord, I'm grateful for a friend like You. Thank You for the many blessings You provide before I ask and when I ask. Help me to be a friend to someone today.

EDITH FITCH

God Is Our Present Help

God is our refuge and strength, a very present help in trouble. Ps. 46:1.

THROUGHOUT MY LIFE God has been my strength and refuge, but most of all He is my Father. He has been so generous toward me. As my Father, He has forgiven and loved me unconditionally. He is my teacher; He uses my mistakes, accidents, and mishaps for my good. I know that I'm not worthy of such care, but He constantly reminds me that I belong to Him, and all my sins are at the bottom of the sea. He has no remembrance of them, and He wants me to do the same. He urges me to come to him so that we can reason together. He has a special plan for my life that involves giving Him my complete being.

When my husband and I decided to leave New York and move to Virginia, we had no idea what God wanted from us. We left the comfort of family and a steady job to move to the unknown, where I probably would be out of work for a while. Yet God had a master plan for us. He unfolded His plan for our life little by little, not giving us too much leeway so that we would think the plan or the success came from our own efforts. In just a year we were living comfortably in a home, with two beautiful children and a car in the driveway. He provides for our needs on a daily basis. We have met other couples who are also preparing themselves for the return of our eternal Father.

It is only by His grace and mercies that we are at this fascinating point in our lives. We aren't considered to be rich by society—not even close, because we're still living on a one-person salary. Yet we are wealthy because God keeps on blessing us. Don't get me wrong: we still have bill collectors calling and writing to us; there are the everyday mishaps and unexpected occurrences. Nevertheless, God is a present help in our time of need.

Yes, Lord, it's obvious to me that You are our refuge and strength. I thank You for being there to always help in our time of trouble. Today I want to pray for those around me who also need to know the assurance of Your presence.

DIANTHA HALL-SMITH

The Child Within

But Jesus said, Suffer little children, and forbid them not, to come unto me. Matt. 19:14.

HAVE YOU EVER FELT scared, lonely, lost, and forsaken? I guess many of us have, at one time or the other. What do you do with such feelings? Most of us try our best to hide them from others. Feelings of such insecurity are best kept inside. At least that's what we tell ourselves.

The world in which we live is intolerant of weakness and frailty. Sometimes we find that same attitude in the church. How many times have I wanted to be vulnerable, to unburden, to stop the pretense, and just be me. To allow the "little, frightened girl" inside to surface and be comforted. But among the "brethren" that's not always possible. That is, until I got involved in women's ministries.

I've found that being with women, whether at a retreat or a training program or even a small group meeting, can do much to nourish my soul. Women are just wonderful! (Of course, being a woman means that I'm somewhat prejudiced.)

I've discovered through the years of working with women that God uses our hands, our arms, our feet, and our voice to love, nurture, and support each other. Once we're in an abiding relationship with Him, He lives in us and works through us.

In Matthew 19:14 Jesus told the disciples not to stop the children from coming to Him. I can almost feel the joy the children felt. Jesus thought they were important and wanted to spend time with them.

So when my feelings of insecurity and loneliness surface, when I feel that little girl within crying for attention or nurture, I come to Jesus, and He welcomes me with open arms. Each time I feel the arms of my sisters around me, each time I hear their words of encouragement and their prayers on my behalf, I know that Jesus is holding me and blessing me through their love.

There's no need for any of us to suffer alone. We can meet in small groups for prayer or Bible study, and by so doing we can support each other and nurture our inner child. There is strength to be shared among Christian women. Let's not let anything stand in our way. Come to Jesus. Let Him lay His hands of love on you and bless you, too.

Heather-Dawn Small

A Cat in the Sun

I have learned to be content whatever the circumstances. Phil. 4:11, NIV.

DRIVING INTO OUR YARD, I looked at the flower bed in front of the house. A killing frost had put an end to the growing season. Sitting in the middle of the drying flowers was a cat, her feet tucked under and her tail curled around her body. She faced into the sun, eyes closed, drinking in the warmth. This moment of her life was being lived in the sun. Warm, cozy, and at peace with the world, she epitomized the picture of contentment.

I thought of our opportunity to bask in the warmth of our Savior's love; to sit in the light of the Son and drink in the nourishing rays of joy and peace. His protection gives us perfect contentment. Life can't get better than that!

Contentment is not a characteristic that most of us possess. We always seem to want more—more material possessions, more time, more money are only a few of the things we want. To learn to be content with what we have and where we are is a state of mind to be desired.

The tranquil feelings that are ours when we're content bring blessings to others with whom we associate. When feeling upset and anxious, I like to find a friend who will look at the situation from the viewpoint of a contented person. From such friends I've received blessings untold simply being in their presence. The words they speak, the manner in which they approach solutions is calming. The contented person shares an element of peace that is greatly needed by all of humankind.

Instead of being content, we humans often worry, stew, and fret about every little thing that comes along. We think we must come up with the solutions to all of life's problems. Unfortunately, our solutions are not always the best.

Even when we pray we lack the patience to wait for the answer. Our thoughts lead us down various paths and to possible solutions. Then we rush ahead of the Lord and act upon our own solutions. If we basked in the Son a little longer and waited for the Lord to lead us in our decisions, the outcome would be entirely different—and it would be the best answer.

I believe the cat has set a good example for us. Basking in the Son brings contentment.

Evelyn Glass

Reflections of a Centenarian

Make a joyful noise unto the Lord, all ye lands. Serve the Lord with gladness: come before his presence with singing. Know ye that the Lord he is God. Ps. 100:1-3.

WEEDING MY GARDEN one sunny morning, I took the time to praise my God for His loving-kindness over the years. With every plant I tended, I thanked Him for His goodness. Moving to the sweet potatoes, I thanked Him for life. Going to the cassava plants, I thanked Him for shelter. Pulling the weeds away from the yams, I thanked Him for food and family.

My mind wandered to one Monday in Jamaica more than 80 years before. I was young and newly married then. Money was very scarce, so I boosted the family income by taking in sewing. I had learned to sew by the time I was 4, and people thought I was very good at it. Orders for new clothes came pouring in. Because I knew we could make more money if I had a machine, my husband and I arranged to buy a sewing machine on credit.

Then calamity struck: my husband became very sick. We had no money. We had no food. The storeowners sent someone to take back the sewing machine. I don't remember what we did for the next few days, but I do remember sitting on the bed, crying out to the Lord. I knew He could help us.

God answered me right away. My husband's cousin, who lived 25 miles away but had not heard about his illness, hitched a ride on the bread delivery van all the way to our doorstep that Friday. We were glad to see him and the £1 note (a lot of money back then) and the bag of food he brought; but I was even more moved by another gift he brought—a sewing machine!

Now I could sew clothes much faster than I'd been doing by hand. Now I could make more clothes. Now we could get medicine. Now we could buy food. Now my husband would grow stronger. And he did!

Sitting under the orange tree one day last week, I turned again, in my mind, to Psalm 100. It seemed as if every verse of that psalm was written just for me. I know I have to make a joyful noise of thanksgiving because my Savior always watches out for me in merciful love.

Heavenly Father, Your mercy overflows. Your goodness is everlasting. I have to thank You for my 100 years. I have to praise Your name. Help me share the story of Your love with all the generations around me.

GROTEL HUTCHINSON

In the Small Things Also

I love the Lord, for he heard my voice; he heard my cry for mercy.
Ps. 116:1, NIV.

IT WAS ONE OF THOSE busy days at work. The hospital overflowed with patients, and the beds were all full. I was in my office supervising the admission of patients and trying to put my desk in order.

A man came in and handed me a paper, a statement in reference to an amount that had been given to an employee. It was payment of the health plan connected with the health institution. In a flash I remembered that a few days before, an employee had given me a statement and a receipt of payment clipped together. The big problem was that I didn't know where I had placed the papers.

I asked the man to wait, and I returned to my desk. I looked in file after file but found nothing. I asked the man if he were going to have some type of procedure done. He told me that he was going to the emergency room to have a bandage changed. I arranged with him to return to my office to get the payment receipt when he finished in the emergency room. I sank down at my desk in despair. I simply couldn't remember where the documentation was that the client needed. So I prayed, *Lord, You know where those documents are. I don't know. So I'm going to ask for two things: first, that that man doesn't return from having his bandage changed until I find his papers; and second, that You show me where the papers are.*

Having finished my prayer, a thought came immediately, and I knew the exact location of the documents. On top of my desk I had a large calendar. In addition to being a calendar, it contained various large sheets on which to make notes. I had placed the receipt between the sheets of that calendar. I went to the emergency room and learned that the man had not yet been attended to. As I gave him his receipt, great joy filled me for having solved that problem. But my greater joy was realizing that I could count on God in all situations—even to help with small problems at work.

Don't you just love the Lord and the way He meets our needs when we cry to Him! *Thank You, God, for listening and responding.* IANI LAUER

The Lost Child

In the same way your Father in heaven is not willing that any of these little ones should be lost. Matt. 18:14, NIV.

WE LOST THE CHILD on the ferry from Sweden to Finland. These ships are so huge that you wonder how they can navigate the narrow waters between the islands of the archipelago. I was traveling with my parents and my 2-year-old daughter. We had ordered seats for the noon meal, planning to go to the restaurant at 12:00. When we arrived, we realized that it was noon in the Eastern European time zone, or Finnish time, while our watches still showed the Swedish time. We were an hour too late, and our places would soon be given to others.

Many people were leaving the dining room while we were discussing what to do about the situation. In this hassle I lost sight of my little girl. She was so small that you could not see her above the tabletops. My first thought was that she might have left the dining room and gotten lost somewhere on the large boat. So I ran out and dashed through the whole ship, hoping to find her—to no avail. I pictured her climbing the railings and falling into the water. Perspiring and panting, I returned to the restaurant, but she hadn't been sighted there, either. I ran out again, still looking for my lost daughter, frantically praying that God would help me find her. When I finally came back to the dining room, she had been found. She had been standing at one of the large windows on the other side of the room—oblivious to the fact that we were looking for her. She didn't even know that she had been lost.

The panic that had seized my heart dissolved, but my appetite was gone. I was now shaking in relief. How happy I was to have my little girl back, safe and sound! God had known where she was all the time and had taken care of her so that she hadn't even started to cry.

Sometimes we are lost and don't even know it. But God knows where we are, and He wants us to find our way back to Him. Let's listen to His voice today, calling us back home, saying, "Come to me, all you who are weary and burdened" (Matt. 11:28, NIV).

Gracious God, I thank You for helping us find my daughter unharmed. Today I want to pray for the lost around me. Most don't know they are lost. Bring them to safety, I ask. HANNELE OTTSCHOFSKI

The Hand of Hope

Before I formed thee in the belly I knew thee; and before thou camest forth out of the womb I sanctified thee, and I ordained thee a prophet unto the nations. Jer. 1:5.

A FRIEND SENT ME AN interesting story by e-mail, along with a picture entitled "Hand of Hope." It was about little Samuel, an unborn fetus who suffered from spina bifida. Correction could be done only while he was still in the womb. There was no other way to save him. The doctor made a small incision on the mother's womb and performed a successful surgery. When the repair had been done, a tiny hand emerged through the small incision and grasped the doctor's finger, as if to say, "Thank you, Doctor, for saving my life." A picture was taken, and the little hand was tucked back inside and the incision closed. The doctor said it was the most emotional moment of his life. Four months later a healthy Samuel was born.

Samuel survived because of that hand of hope. We can certainly say the same of ourselves. It's the divine hand of hope that made us, sustains us, and destines us to be saved. God knew Jeremiah before he was conceived. He was called before he was formed; he was sanctified and ordained to be a prophet. David recognized that it was God who formed him: "By thee have I been holden up from the womb: thou art he that took me out of my mother's bowels: my praise shall be continually of thee" (Ps. 71:6).

Though God called Jeremiah and ordained him from the womb itself, it didn't mean that he was free from suffering. He and Job suffered so much that they cursed the day they were born. Jeremiah prayed, "O Lord . . . remember me, and visit me, and revenge me of my persecutors; . . . know that for thy sake I have suffered rebuke" (Jer. 15:15). The Lord assured him that "they shall fight against thee, but they shall not prevail against thee: for I am with thee to save thee and to deliver thee" (verse 20). Though Job felt he didn't deserve to suffer the way he did, he declared, "Though he slay me, yet will I trust in him" (Job 13:15). David prayed, "But I am poor and needy: make haste unto me, O God: thou art my help and my deliverer; O Lord, make no tarrying" (Ps. 70:5).

Our only hope is in that hand of hope. Like little Samuel, take hold of that hand, grasp it, and thank God for deliverance. Hang on to that hand and never let go!

BIRDIE PODDAR

God Cares About Washdays, Too!

Call unto me, and I will answer thee, and shew thee great and mighty things, which thou knowest not. Jer. 33:3.

THE SUN SHONE BRIGHTLY, as if in favor of my washday. We in the Caribbean enjoy drying our clothes outside on the clothesline in the sun. It's not only more economical; we like the clean, fresh smell the sun seems to give the laundry. I had gotten up very early that Sunday morning while my children still slept, and started the washing machine. As usual, it worked faithfully while I prepared the family's breakfast in the adjoining kitchen.

Sometime during the first washload I heard an unusual sound coming from the laundry room. The strange sound from the washing machine did not suggest progress. I was discouraged.

By now my children were up, and we all agreed that it wasn't an encouraging sound. Five more extra-large washloads waited to be done, and the first wasn't even halfway through. It sounded very much as though my faithful machine was about to stop working.

Minutes later the feared thing happened—the washing machine stopped. We tried everything we could think of to restart it, but it just wouldn't go. Now I was really frustrated. Then I remembered it was just about time for morning worship. I called the family to worship, telling them that perhaps this worship service would make the washing machine work again, if we asked God for His help.

We had a very meaningful worship experience, and we told God all about our concerns—including the washing machine. Toward the end of the worship session we heard a familiar sound. Everyone was startled; we looked at each other. Yes, it was the washing machine! It had started to work again, all on its own. And the strange sound was gone. Now I was joyful! Such faith in God that gave me!

I was able to complete my wash—yes, all six loads were done, problem-free. Isn't God good? Isn't He wonderful? God still hears, and He still answers prayers. Yes, Jesus cares—even about washdays. O for grace to trust Him more!

JACQUELINE HOPE HOSHING-CLARKE

Lessons in Growing

Give to him who asks you, and from him who wants to borrow from you do not turn away. Matt 5:42, NKJV.

TODAY IS THE anniversary of my mother's death, and I've been thinking of the many valuable lessons she taught us as we were growing up. One thing in particular comes to mind that has had a positive influence on me over the years.

This particular incident happened the first year we moved to our little farm in the country. We were living in Canáda at the time, and my folks had planted a large garden with every kind of vegetable you could think of. The weather was perfect, and consequently our garden produced an abundance of everything. We had a wonderful root cellar where we stored our potatoes, carrots, onions, and other assorted vegetables. We had apples packed in barrels from our own trees, and Mother canned everything she could think of. We wouldn't go hungry, because of the hard work my mother did for her family.

One day a woman, with two small children in tow, came to our door. She asked Mother if she could spare a few small potatoes. Mother invited her into the living room and offered her a cup of tea and fixed a cup of hot chocolate for the children. Then she told me to go into the cellar and bring up a basket of potatoes. The woman had asked for some small potatoes, so I picked out the smallest potatoes I could find and brought them to the kitchen. *At least I won't have to peel these,* I thought, as I eagerly called my mother into the kitchen to show her how generous I was. To my dismay, she dumped them into a bin for me to peel later.

"Now," she said, "go back to the cellar and pick out the biggest and best potatoes you can find and fill the basket full. When someone is in need, we always give our best!"

I was so happy that the woman was in the living room and not in the kitchen where she could have seen what I'd done. It was a lesson I never forgot and still practice to this day.

On this anniversary, and every year that passes, I want to remember the valuable lessons I've learned, and I hope I can pass them on to my children and grandchildren.

Thank You, Lord, for blessing us with a godly mother and for the many lessons she taught us over the years. Amen.

MARGARET FISHER

The Chandelier

The angel of Lord encampeth round about them that fear him, and delivereth them. Ps. 34:7.

THE CRASHING OF SHATTERED glass rudely interrupted my quiet concentration on a dinner menu. I'd been sitting at the dining table checking students' papers when I decided to take a break to prepare dinner. I'd not been in the kitchen more than five minutes when I heard the dreadful sound. Rushing into the dining room, I discovered the chandelier hanging dejectedly from its socket, and molded glass lying in a hundred pieces all around the room.

As I took another look at the shattered remnants of the beautiful chandelier, my eyes caught sight of something unusual—a big gash on one side of the lamp corresponding to another big gash on the opposite side. Looking directly from the lamp to the drapery opposite the front porch and the street, I noticed two holes—actually bullet-blackened, yawning gashes.

Someone had tried to shoot me.

I was horrified! Metal-blackened holes were plainly visible in the drapery, on the walls, and in the windowpane. I grabbed the phone and dialed 911. The police arrived immediately and asked the usual questions. From the apertures visible in windows, woodwork, and plaster they estimated that exactly six bullets had been fired. They also found other evidence—a hole in the outside wall, a dent in the metal grating, and a hole in the roof.

My neighbors' reaction? "Mistaken identity!"

My reaction? "The angel of the Lord encampeth."

Why was someone trying to kill me? Could a student have done this? Was someone trying to get back at me for a failing grade I'd given? Whatever the cause, I couldn't find enough words to thank the Lord for shielding me from those bullets.

Had the bullets been intended for me, or someone else? What's the difference? If any one of those six bullets had hit the target, would I have been ready?

I regretted the loss of the gold-emblazoned chandelier, prized but not priceless; but I praise the Lord for His Holy Spirit and the presence of the angels who delivered me, who is prized and priceless, covered by the precious blood of the Lamb.

QUILVIE G. MILLS

The God of Little Things, Too

Is anything too hard for God? Gen. 18:14, TLB.

LATELY I'M BECOMING something of a collector of watches. Some are gifts; some I purchase. Two weeks ago I lost one of my watches. It wasn't just any old watch—it was one of my favorites that I liked wearing to work. It wasn't an expensive watch; it actually cost only $7. But it was special to me.

It could have fallen off anywhere between the office building where I work and home, but I noticed it was missing from my wrist when I got home that evening. I retraced my steps from the car to the house; and the following day I checked my office, but didn't find it. I didn't think it was worth pining over or losing any sleep over; after all, it only cost me $7, and I did have others.

Nevertheless, standing over the sink in my kitchen that same evening, I prayed: "Lord, I know it's not a big deal, and I'm not going to make an issue of it, but I really would like to have my watch back." I didn't think about it much more after that.

Three days later, as Laverne, my friend and prayer partner at work, was ending our Friday morning prayer, there was a knock on the door. It was Pastor Brown, holding my watch in his hand and asking, "Do either of you know who may have lost this?"

In excitement I hugged him, and then shared the story about my little watch with him and Laverne. Pastor Brown told me that he'd found it several days before in the office parking lot. He'd made an announcement over the public address system, but got no response. He said he was impressed to come to my office that morning to see if I might know to whom it belonged. Miraculously, it hadn't been stepped on or rolled over by cars coming in and out of the parking lot.

Afterward, I called my husband and told him that my watch had been found, and we rejoiced together over this "small" blessing.

Thank You, Lord, for giving such thoughtful things big and small.

GLORIA STELLA FELDER

I Still Like Psalm 119

Seek ye the Lord. Isa. 55:6.

JUDYE! PENNY!" our mother called. "Let's have worship."

"It's almost 7:30," I protested. "I'm going to watch ———"

Now, many years later, I don't remember just what I was so set on viewing, but until the day I die I'll remember what happened next. You see, parent-approved TV programs were few and far between in our home. "Lucy tells a lie and everyone laughs," my mother was fond of saying. "You don't need to be watching that." So seeing this program was really important.

Mother called us again, adding that we'd just read a few Bible verses, but I remained in the living room near the TV. "Penny, what shall I read?" she asked cheerfully from the doorway.

With the sarcasm of a 13-year-old I responded, "Why don't you read Psalm 119?"

"That's a *good* idea," she responded, calling my sister and grandmother. "Judye! Mama!" I'd done it. There was no one to blame but myself. I dragged myself into the room and accepted the Bible my mother gave me. "We'll go around the circle, reading one verse at a time," she instructed, as though I hadn't just sealed my own fate. And so beginning with verse 1, "Blessed are the undefiled," on through "It is good for me that I have been afflicted; that I might learn thy statutes" (verse 71), to, at last, verse 176, "I have gone astray like a lost sheep," we read the entire psalm.

Do you want to know how long it takes to read Psalm 119? I'll tell you. It takes a full 30 minutes!

Early on in this marathon I started to giggle when it was my turn to read. And now when this family legend is retold, I laugh louder than anyone else. Oh, how I treasure this memory and value my mother's love of God's Word. In my own Bible I've written her name—and Mama's—by verses they held dear. "The angel of the Lord encampeth round about them that fear him, and delivereth them" (Ps. 34:7) was Mother's favorite. Mama I associate with Isaiah 55: "Ho, everyone that thirsteth, come ye to the waters, and he that hath no money; come ye, buy, and eat. . . . Seek ye the Lord while he may be found, call ye upon him while he is near" (verses 1-6).

This is a good heritage. Riches beyond price! PENNY ESTES WHEELER

Whom Do You Worship?

Come, let us bow down in worship, let us kneel before the Lord our Maker; for he is our God and we are the people of his pasture, the flock under his care. Ps. 95:6, 7, NIV.

SINCE I WAS A LITTLE girl I longed to be a mother. God was so gracious in granting that wish in four lovely children. Then one day disaster struck; and our oldest son, Matthew, age 14 at the time, was diagnosed with acute myelogenous leukemia—a very deadly form of leukemia. We did everything possible, and the doctors and nurses were great; but 14 months later we laid our precious son to rest.

We worked through the grieving process, as one must do when you lose a child. Several months passed, and I *thought* I was doing OK with accepting God's leading in my life. I'd been sleeping better and dealing with family matters in a more positive way. Then the month came that would have been Matthew's birthday. The week before his birthday a fresh wave of grief spread over me. It was so hard! I prayed for acceptance and pleaded with God to be close to me. I was still finding it hard to sleep; I kept waking up in the middle of the night with memories of Matthew, of how I had longed for his birth, and memories of his early years, and tears would flow anew.

Then three days before his birthday I awoke at 2:00 a.m., as usual. I was weeping silently so as not to wake my husband. I cried out, "Lord, help me!" and heard a voice—not audibly, but nonetheless I knew it was His voice! God said, "Nola, we worship Jesus, not Matthew!" My tears were instantly dry, and I felt the hair on my arms standing on end. I was so ashamed! I crawled out of bed and fell on my knees to plead for forgiveness.

In the moments that followed, God impressed upon me that yes, it's OK to grieve, but there is a limit. Jesus needs to be uplifted in our lives. Jesus should be our central focus. If we let anything other than Jesus take that central focus, we aren't in harmony with God's will. He must be first, and He will take care of our grief, as well as our needs.

I knew from that moment on that God really does care! NOLA THOM

In the Dark

I am the light for the world! Follow me, and you won't be walking in the dark. You will have the light that gives life. John 8:12, CEV.

TREES SWAYED IN A frantic dance in the early-evening light before hurricane force winds. Rain falling steadily on the rooftop made me glad to be inside, in my living room, watching a kids' video with my three young granddaughters. Bianca, Kali, and Ariyah and their parents lived with me, and I looked forward to spending time with them each day after work.

Before long the storm worsened. When the lights flickered and the TV clicked off occasionally, the girls wondered what happened. But the electricity returned within seconds, and they settled back down.

Then the electricity went off and stayed off! *It won't be long,* I thought. *The lights will come back on.* To pass time and keep the kids occupied, their parents and I sang songs and recited nursery rhymes. Before long, boredom set in, then crankiness, and it was impossible to explain to the toddlers that no electricity meant no lights, no videos, no TV, no music. A half hour passed; then an hour. I pulled back the curtains to catch a bit more light from the outside, then gathered matches, candles, and a hurricane lamp, which I soon had to light. The girls' endless questions about why we were in the dark wore me out—but even I wondered. Would the lights ever come back on? I vowed to buy packs of batteries for my mini TV-radio so we would have more entertainment options the next time. Bedtime finally came.

The next morning, there was still no electricity. Nor that evening. Nor the next day. The girls grew more bored and became crankier, and so did I! Finding enjoyable things to do during the day was challenging, and stumbling around in the dark each evening was no fun. We all yearned to have lights again, to have life again! When would it happen?

Reflecting on that experience and my spiritual life, I'm thankful I no longer have to walk in darkness, bored and cranky. I don't have to stumble around. I don't need temporary light to illuminate my path or guide me along life's way. Jesus, the light of the world, beckons me to follow Him and have the light that gives life. I am following. Won't you follow too?

IRIS L. STOVALL

October 27

Is Anything Too Hard for the Lord?

Is anything too hard for the Lord? Gen. 18:14, NKJV.

WEDNESDAY'S BATHWATER was too cool. I couldn't warm it up by turning the faucet toward the hot side, either—it only got colder. Then I forgot about it until it was almost time for Thursday's bath. At that time we discovered that we were entirely out of propane. My husband took a small propane tank off our trailer, and we had hot water, temporarily.

I dreaded calling the propane company; I knew what they'd say, and I didn't want to hear their lecture: "It is the responsibility of the homeowner to notify us when the tank is 30 percent full. Without advance notice, it can take 10 days to put you on our schedule. Call back on Monday morning. That's when we do our scheduling."

I called other propane companies and got similar replies: "We must get an application for service and do a test. It could take 10 days." The dispatcher from our propane company offered one thread of hope. One of their trucks was in our area that day and might have enough extra propane and the time to deliver to us if he could first take care of the needs of the people on his list. Otherwise, we'd have to wait a week or more. I started to pray for the driver and asked that he'd have plenty of gas and enough time to take care of all the other customers and also serve us.

I thought of recent blessings. When our daughter's vacuum cleaner had suffered a total burnout, friends at the church rallied to the need and smuggled a new vacuum into the back of her truck with no evidence of the identity of the givers. Her best friend received much better news after a medical test was repeated (the first test had been very questionable). Our brother-in-law was given a new pair of work boots by a woman whose husband had passed away before he was able to use them. There were more blessings than I could name, and I thanked the Lord for as many as I could remember. I asked myself out loud, "Do I dare to hope, to pray, for the propane delivery to arrive today? God is good, but am I pushing it?"

Then I heard a large truck coming down the street. I shouldn't have been amazed. It stopped at our gate. The driver unrolled the hose, went to the propane tank, and filled it.

Thank You, God, for all Your blessings. Nothing is too hard for the Lord!

LILLIAN MUSGRAVE

The Ministry in Your Lap

They shall still bear fruit in old age; they shall be fresh and flourishing. Ps. 92:14, NKJV.

DURING THE LAST TWO years of her life my mother chose to reside in an assisted-living residence only two miles from our house. Though legally blind, she wanted to be as independent as possible. She had always loved being surrounded by youthful minds, thriving on the give-and-take of the classroom. However, a cataract surgery gone awry had forced her to resign at the beginning of what was to have been her forty-fourth—and final—year of teaching. To help fill the void, she learned how to make greeting and condolence cards. Sometimes she'd even pretty up a teddy bear with a bow and send it along with the card.

Then came the day when she couldn't see well enough even to tie a simple bow. Her unavoidable choice was to embrace either hope or despair. No decision in her life ever required more faith and courage than that one. She chose hope—pursuing a ministry that, she said, "God dropped into my lap." Though she could no longer see well enough to tie bows around the necks of teddy bears, she could feel to dress them. That's how her personal "burden bear" ministry came into being.

In just three and a half years, she sent off a burden bear, with an attached poem of encouragement, to some hurting heart on the average of one every 7.3 days. One day I pointed out to Mother that she was almost to burden bear number 200! She replied, "That's nearly 200 times God has given me an extra-special blessing."

One of the greatest lessons Mother taught me in those two years before she died is that no matter what befalls me, I can still "bring forth fruit" for the kingdom by discovering what God has "dropped into my lap."

Are you ill? Then you have a lapful of prayers that can ascend to God on behalf of a hurting world. Do you have a disability? So does my friend Lucy, confined by a surgical tubing tether to the pole that holds her "feeding bags" for abdominal tubal feeding. Yet she praises God that she can donate her former food budget to feed starving orphans in developing countries! Are you aged? Then God has specifically appointed you to "bring forth fruits" throughout your sunset years. Whatever our challenging situations, why not resolve to discover—and then pursue—the customized personal ministries God has dropped . . . into our laps?

CAROLYN RATHBUN SUTTON

October 29

Needy Parent

O taste and see that the Lord is good; how blessed is the man who takes refuge in Him! Ps. 34:8, NASB.

AFTER 21 YEARS OF being a very busy mom, the last two months have been strangely quiet with our boys now away at college. There is no green computer glow emanating from Travis's room; no half-eaten spoonfuls of peanut butter sticking out of Austin's light switchplate, and there's a pleasant, almost clean, smell in the boys' bathroom. I had always thought that my days would be achingly empty when our boys went away. Well, they are quieter—and frequently teary—but certainly not empty.

Yesterday was typical, with sick patients to be taken care of, church responsibilities to handle, an early evening meeting to attend, and almost running out of gas on the way home. Now it is 6:50 in the morning, and I have 10 minutes before I must dash out the door to make it to work on time. I've been up for an hour and a half and have showered, dressed, made lunches for Steve and myself, had my morning devotions, and fed the bird. Now I need to have my breakfast, and I'll be on my way.

Then I remember a good friend who is going through a very rough time. I'd made a mental note to call her last evening but never had the chance. I know that she checks her e-mail every morning and would really appreciate an encouraging note. It would take every second of my 10 minutes to get to our computer and write her even a short note, and breakfast is very important to me. I use up one of my minutes vacillating between what I want to do and what I know God wants me to do. Finally I go to the computer and type out something that I hope will make her day a little bit better.

It's 10 minutes later now as I dash through the kitchen on my way to the garage, grabbing an apple, and thinking how very hungry I'll be without my usual morning cereal. As I'm backing the car out I turn around to look behind me, and lying on the back seat is a bag from the convenience store where I had stopped for gas the night before. I'd gotten an eight-pack of little cereal boxes and forgotten to take them into the house when I got home. Tears came to my eyes as I praised God for His unspeakable kindness! I think we've given our boys what they "need," but God provides for us even before we know we have needs. What an awesome Friend!

SUSAN WOOLEY

Sand Flies and Mosquitoes

No temptation has seized you except what is common to man. And God is faithful; he will not let you be tempted beyond what you can bear. But when you are tempted, he will also provide a way out so that you can stand up under it. 1 Cor. 10:13, NIV.

LAST SUMMER MY HUSBAND and I went to Australia to visit his brother and sister-in-law, who live right on the coast in Queensland. We'd lie in bed at night, listening to the waves breaking on the nearby shore. It was an idyllic spot—except for the sand flies, those annoying little creatures that seemed to get everywhere. We smothered ourselves with cream and spray, wore long sleeves, and generally went into protection in a big way; but we still had the occasional bite that itched for days.

Sudan, in Africa, is part of the territory I work in. I try to avoid visiting there in the rainy season because of the number of mosquitoes buzzing about. They just don't leave me alone. Cerebral malaria is a very real threat that can be fatal, so I take a number of precautions: anti-malarial medicine starting a week before I travel and taken regularly all the time I'm away; mosquito netting; anti-mosquito creams and sprays; and coverall clothing. Despite all the precautions, I still get the occasional bite.

Mosquitoes and sand flies are actually small, insignificant insects, yet we take enormous care not to let them bite us because of the very unpleasant side effects. Preparing for a recent trip, I got to thinking about all this care so as not to be bitten by a mosquito! Do I take the same care to ensure that I don't get "bitten" by Satan? Am I giving enough time to personal prayer and Bible study? Am I able to respond to Satan's temptations with an "It is written," as Jesus did? If it is important for me to protect myself against insect bites, isn't it *much more important* that I protect myself against the attacks of Satan?

The effects of sin are all around. There will always be temptations, but I can be fully prepared to resist. If I'm honest, I have to admit that sometimes I'm more conscientious about my anti-malarial protection than about my temptation protection. Today I want to focus on God and His Word. I want to be fully protected. I want to use today to be more in tune with my God and His will for my life. Then Satan can "bite" all he wants—I'll be protected!

Valerie Fidelia

October 31

Firestorm

Daniel, for your request has been heard in heaven and was answered. . . . But for twenty-one days the mighty Evil Spirit who overrules the kingdom of Persia blocked my way. Then Michael . . . came to help me, so that I was able to break through these spirit rulers of Persia. Dan. 10:12, 13, TLB.

CAN YOU PICTURE THE blanket of evil covering the Persian Empire and blocking the angel? Finally Jesus Himself came to break the power of evil.

We live in the beautiful Okanagan Valley of southern British Columbia, Canada. For generations residents of Kelowna have felt satisfied, smug, to live in Canada's most pleasant climate. We enjoy long, hot, dry summers; sandy beaches; fruit-laden orchards; and forested hills. Winters are short and mild in the valley, but a short drive takes us to beautiful ski mountains.

Several events in the summer of 2003 led to a change in our comfortable lifestyle: temperatures up to 110° Fahrenheit (44° Celsius); no rain for more than 75 days; and then—fire! At one point more than 900 forest fires were burning in British Columbia. For years the media has reported wildfires in faraway places such as Australia and California, but now it was touching our lives. Kamloops, 100 miles (160 kilometers) away, was fighting a stubborn fire that destroyed a community, cut off power, and closed major highways.

Then, during the night of August 15, lightning started a fire on the border of our city. Suddenly radio, TV, newspapers, and residents began talking about prayer. By August 22 heavy smoke filled our valley, and 30,000 people were evacuated as the fire roared into town, consuming 258 homes. Where was God?

As we watched it nearing one of our churches, suddenly the flames were gone. A single cloudburst extinguished that part of the fire. That's where God was! Officials realized their efforts were insignificant and futile. "Nature started this, and nature will have to put it out," they said. Finally, on September 8, the angel with the answer to our prayers was able to break through, and we awoke to rain.

The smoke of sin separates us from God and blocks His angels. If God protected us from all consequences of sin, we wouldn't be motivated to finish His work. This firestorm motivated me; what will motivate you?

ELIZABETH VERSTEEGH ODIYAR

When the Lights Went Out

But the path of the just is as the shining light, that shineth more and more unto the perfect day. Prov. 4:18.

IT WAS NOVEMBER 1. The clocks had gone back to standard time a few days earlier; and this was the first long, dark Friday evening, a time I especially enjoy. Taking my Bible and lesson book, together with a couple of church magazines, I climbed into bed and settled down for a cozy evening of study.

Suddenly the lights went out. I could see nothing. My mind wandered to Jesus, the light of the world. When He is our friend, our spiritual eyesight is sharpened; the light of His love fills our hearts, and our lives become a source of light and blessing.

Not wanting to leave my warm nest under the covers, I continued to sit quietly in the darkness. Before long a pinpoint of light appeared, growing brighter as my husband approached, holding a small flashlight. Just one tiny light, but what a difference it made to the darkness! Even if smaller details were still invisible, large objects were now clearly outlined. Such is the impact of one humble Christian life shining faithfully in the darkness of our sad old world.

My husband quickly disappeared, only to return a few minutes later with a large plate on which he had stuck a half dozen candles—all alight and burning brightly. Now, that was light! I could see well enough to continue reading and even make out the details of the room, which a few minutes earlier had been virtually invisible. One tiny light dispels some darkness, but several small lights shining together in harmony can make a significant difference.

Suddenly the electricity came on again. It blinded us for a moment until our eyes adjusted and the darkness was gone. But where were the candles? They were still burning steadily, but were almost unnoticeable in the now brightly lit room. So in the presence of Him who is the true light our tiny sparks of reflected light are hardly noticeable. Until He comes, though, these millions of tiny lights play an important role in scattering the darkness.

Jesus said, "Let your light so shine." He is our indwelling source of light; and if we don't obstruct His rays, love and salvation will shine out from us.

REVEL PAPAIOANNOU

Bloom Where You Are Planted

I have learned the secret of being content in any and every situation, whether well fed or hungry, whether living in plenty or in want. Phil. 4:12, NIV.

THE HOT, DRY SUMMER had passed, and although the fall months had come, there hadn't been any rain for a long time. So as we started our trip on the highway that signs proclaimed "The Loneliest Road in America," we didn't expect much in the way of scenery, and certainly we weren't looking for any wildflowers. Once in a while another car or truck would pass; but mostly we had the well-paved road to ourselves, and we agreed that the highway had earned its name.

And then we noticed them. While looking for something to relieve the monotony of the trip, we began to see golden clusters of flowers. Sometimes they were growing on the dry, arid roadside; other times they were clinging to rocky outcroppings. As we climbed higher, we saw them marching up boulder-strewn mountainsides amid the scrub pines. At times the plants were very small; then there were huge clumps of gold several feet high filling an entire field. There were other flowers also: pinkish and lavender and not quite as showy, but a welcome sight nonetheless. For several hundred miles they brightened our trip.

The flowers weren't complaining because they didn't have good soil to grow in or because it hadn't rained for a long time. They were simply growing where they were planted, in good soil and bad, with or without rain, and blessing the countryside with their beauty.

Sometimes I'm tempted to complain because I don't have the talents of my friend, or as much money as someone else so that I think I can't do much to help others. But God has given each of us strength and wisdom for each day. He has supplied friends to help us. Even if they are the showy ones, we can use our lesser talents to be an added blessing to those around us.

As mothers, grandmothers, aunts, cousins, or friends, our actions each day—wherever we are "planted"—can help to show our love and brighten the lives of our families. And we have an advantage over the flowers because we have the same promise Paul depended on: "I can do everything through him who gives me strength" (Phil. 4:13, NIV). I know too that He gives me strength to bloom wherever I am planted.

Betty J. Adams

Shelving Assumptions

Do not judge, or you too will be judged. For in the same way you judge others, you will be judged, and with the measure you use, it will be measured to you. Matt. 7:1, 2, NIV.

WE MANEUVERED OUR WAY carefully across the treacherous parking lot, cart piled high with holiday groceries. At the car we'd just begun the process of transfer when Melissa uttered an exclamation, gestured toward the nearby filling stations, and cried, "She's smoking!" In a flash she was skittering toward the woman. The words "I have to tell her it's dangerous" floated back over her shoulder.

I groaned. In this day and age that might not be a brilliant choice! Throwing the last of the bags into the trunk, I stowed the cart and hurried toward the drama I feared was unfolding—only to meet Melissa coming back. Arms folded across her chest, eyes on the ground, she was the picture of . . . despondency. Surely not embarrassment! Melissa? My arm draped itself over her little shoulders as we wended our way back to the car and headed for home. In silence.

Eventually I risked asking, "Ready to debrief?" (That word had proved to be a bit less threatening than some others.) She was. The words tumbled out pell-mell. Not a cigarette . . . stick candy . . . just her breath in the frosty air . . . assumed she was smoking . . . can't believe I was going to give her advice!

I suppressed a chuckle for two reasons. One, to avoid trivializing Melissa's experience (there'd be plenty of time to laugh later, and I knew we would); and two, because of my own actions of the day before. Oh, not for assuming someone was smoking. Related rather to a misunderstanding between outward appearances and my perception of what was going on in the woman's heart. Ouch! I sighed a big sigh.

"Guess you've done it too, huh?" Melissa commented almost hopefully. "Assumed incorrectly?"

"Yep," I admitted, "although I'm not proud of it!"

She swiped at her eyes. Our hands met across the seat. Her young-vivacious-just-starting-life hand, and my been-on-the-journey-awhile hand. We made a pact, the two of us, as we drove into the deepening twilight. It was time to shelve assumptions.

ARLENE TAYLOR

God Will Not Abandon Me

Though my father and mother forsake me, the Lord will receive me. Ps. 27:10, NIV.

MARTA AND ALEJANDRO heard Francisca's heartbreaking cry from three blocks away. A live-in maid, Francisca had given her baby up for adoption because her employer had prohibited Francisca from keeping her little daughter. Three-month-old Maria was malnourished and unkempt. Now in her new home with Marta and Alejandro, there was nothing she would need.

When Maria became a teenager her desire to find her biological mother increased. She set out on a diligent search that resulted in finding the address of her biological mother. At 45 years of age and having established a lovely home, Maria traveled alone to San Luis, Argentina, to find her mother. When Maria arrived, she got a room in a hotel near the address that she carried. She was able to sleep little; and the next morning, very early, she awoke, opened the window, and looked toward the street. Maria checked the address she had. Questions whirled through her mind. "Is she still alive? Will she believe me? Will she reject me? Do I have brothers and sisters?"

Reaching her destination, she knocked at the door. When the door opened, a light dizziness came over her. She took a breath and quickly uttered, "I need to see Francisca."

"Yes, that is I," the woman at the door answered.

Maria regained her composure and asked the woman, "Do you remember your baby who was born on November 4, 1949?"

Francisca's face turned white. Maria smiled. There were no more words. Francisca learned that Maria would not accuse her. There was a long embrace and the beginning of an enduring and beautiful relationship.

Even during their first conversation, Maria remembered that since she was small, she had thought, *Is it possible that my real mother has forgotten me?* But she also remembered her mother, Marta, who many times quoted Psalm 27:10: "Though my father and mother forsake me, the Lord will receive me." So she was able to live happily with the parents who had lovingly raised her, and she could also love her biological mother.

God does not abandon us in the difficulties that come our way either. He seeks us out so that we may be together permanently with Him.

ELMA BERNHARDT DE CARDINALI

No More Pain

He will wipe every tear from their eyes. There will be no more death or mourning or crying or pain, for the old order of things has passed away. Rev. 21:4, NIV.

OUR DAUGHTER, LISIE EVELYN, was not yet 3 years of age when she was diagnosed with acute lymphocytic leukemia. This news fell like a bomb on us. There was an enormous emptiness and many whys. The only answer could be found through God.

As nurses, my husband and I had experienced much pain and death related to many children; now we felt it touching home, because our daughter, who we had been waited for with such expectation, who was so full of life, had such a frightening prognosis.

Our lifestyle suffered a complete turnaround, and not only ours but that of our youngest daughter, who was only 7 months old, as well. We moved to São Paulo, Brazil, where more advanced treatment could be given. There the physicians gave us a 70 percent chance for a cure. We were supported by family members and friends with whom we shared our sadness and our anxieties. After beginning the treatment with chemotherapy and corticoids that brought many undesirable side effects (such as vomiting, loss of hair, weight gain, and others), Lisie Evelyn responded well to the treatment and entered into remission.

However, 11 months later the illness returned, and this time it was much more severe. The treatment had to be much more aggressive; unfortunately, our little one didn't respond to the treatment. We prayed a great deal that God would perform a miracle and cure her. Some weeks before her death, she very tranquilly spoke of the resurrection that Jesus promised, and asked that we pray for her.

In spite of all the suffering, we were assisted by our loving heavenly Father. Even though we didn't understand His plan, we placed our little daughter in His hands. We know that "we have nothing to fear for the future, except as we shall forget the way the Lord has led us, and His teaching in our past history" (*Life Sketches,* p. 196).

One year after being diagnosed with leukemia, our daughter rested in the Lord and the hope of Jesus' promise. We too await that day in which "the trumpet of God will resound and those who died in Christ will be resurrected first." And then all things will be made clear.

Aucely Corrêa Fernandes Chagas

Toppling the Trees

At least there is hope for a tree: If it is cut down, it will sprout again, and its new shoots will not fail. Job 14:7, NIV.

OUR HOUSE STANDS BESIDE a school, which we own. The space dividing the two areas is small, but there were several coconut trees, orange trees, guava trees, and others in the space. The patio, where the children had their recess, was also small, and since there had been an increase in students, we needed more area for them to play. Finally it was decided that the trees must be cut down for the expansion of the recreational space.

My heart was heavy with great sadness at the thought of the toppling of the trees, because those trees were my friends. Long before, I had learned to love them. Early every morning I awoke with the affectionate song of the birds in the leafy crowns of the trees; praising the Author of nature. What joy I felt as I praised and thanked our loving Lord and asked for guidance!

My husband said, "Look; there's no other way. You must accept the decision!" But I prayed without ceasing that there would be another way to solve this situation.

Finally the day arrived for the toppling of the trees. However, the young man in charge of executing the work said there would be no necessity of sacrificing the trees—a play area could be made in the space between the trees. Everything worked out, and I was immensely content, without words to express my joy as I enjoyed the melody of the birds and this marvelous blessing that the Lord provided for me.

The children were also enthusiastic because now they have a large space for their recreation period—and in the shade, as well. They are excited and truly enjoy the park.

I believe that these incidents that take place in our lives are to test us so that our faith in God may grow more and more. This experience helped me to better understand that when things seem impossible to us, for God they are possible. God has plans for our life that are being accomplished each day.

Lord, thank You very much for having created the trees that are such dear friends! Thank You also for being present in our daily life, filling us with special blessings.

Maria Sinharinha de Oliveira Nogueira

The Payoff

Let us not become weary in doing good, for at the proper time we will reap a harvest if we do not give up. Gal. 6:9, NIV.

HE WAS LIKE A RAY of sunshine, his broad smile and upbeat attitude completely transforming a drizzly, damp morning. Client Ted Knott slipped into a chair in the Community Services Center and asserted, "This is the last time I'll need assistance. I'll complete my course in three weeks. Isn't that just cool?"

I glanced at his record. "It's two years since you first came, Ted."

"Yeah, and everything's really neat now. I've taken every class in the entire course." He beamed. "I can cut and style your hair, give you a perm, a facial, a manicure; and I have a good job!"

Even his appearance radiated enthusiasm—smart, perfectly styled hair, demure mustache, tidy beard. Such a change from the bedraggled, despondent young man of two years ago. That day he had fidgeted restlessly while I, with a prayer for guidance, assembled information, counselors, and schools that might enable Ted to develop marketable skills. As he returned for provisions, I encouraged him, affirmed his achievements—even cajoled him occasionally.

Similar gratitude had been expressed when Pat came in and told me, "I'm now employable!" An immigrant and a licensed pharmacist in her former homeland, she needed further study, examinations, and licensing to be employed in America. Pat needed direction as to where and how to make professional contacts. She would need to spend endless hours studying the challenging English language. She too periodically received commendations and reassurances. Pat has persisted. She now thanks God that she is employable!

It is satisfying to assist the needy with necessities. But there is an added plus that comes when their energy is directed into the avenues that provide greater self-esteem and provide independence to break the continuing circle of poverty.

With God's help, Ted, Pat, and I, in our own ways, have persisted. Now we are experiencing the payoff. We're reaping our harvests. And it is gratifying!

LOIS E. JOHANNES

An Experiment Gone Bad

God saw everything that he had made, and indeed, it was very good. Gen. 1:31, NRSV.

AS I WALKED INTO the women's restroom in the convention center, I heard someone say: "I think she was an experiment that went bad." The two women continued to talk, and I could tell from the conversation that the first woman had been talking about her daughter. I left the lounge feeling sad—no, it was more like distressed and depressed. What must that young woman think of herself if her own mother felt she was an experiment gone bad?

I thought about the women I've met and those I've read about who believe that's the way God created woman—an experiment that went bad. I've even heard women say exactly that, but it's not true. When God finished His creation, even the creation of woman, He said "It is good." Actually, He said it was *very good* (Gen. 1:31)! You've probably heard the saying (terrible grammar but good theology): "God don't make no junk."

Through the centuries some have taught that woman is inferior to man, that she was not created equal with man. In an ancient rabbinical prayer the men thanked God that they weren't created a woman. But Mary, the mother of Jesus, had an entirely different perspective. We find her saying in Mary's Song, "My soul glorifies the Lord and my spirit rejoices in God my Savior, for he has been mindful of the humble state of his servant. From now on all generations will call me blessed, for the Mighty One has done great things for me—holy is his name. His mercy extends to those who fear him, from generation to generation" (Luke 1:47-50, NIV). I believe her attitude had something to do with how Jesus treated women.

Sometimes we joke that God created man and then said, "I can do better than that," and created woman. But it wasn't that way, either. The New Revised Standard Version puts it this way: "Then God said, 'Let us make humankind in our image, according to our likeness; and let them have dominion over the fish of the sea, and over the birds of the air, and over the cattle, and over all the wild animals of the earth, and over every creeping thing that creeps upon the earth.' So God created humankind in his image, in the image of God he created them; male and female he created them" (Gen. 1:26, 27).

That was no experiment gone bad! ARDIS DICK STENBAKKEN

1741 Hill

Show me the path where I should walk, O Lord; point out the right road for me to follow. Ps. 25:4, NLT.

LOOKING IN THE MIRROR one afternoon I knew that it was time to take advantage of the 20 percent off coupon my stylist had sent, inviting me to visit her at a new location. I had to make a series of presentations and couldn't allow my unruly hair to distract the audience.

Checking the address for the new salon, 1741 Hill, I departed. The after-work traffic was just beginning to build up as I turned onto Hill Street. Slowing down to search for the number, impatient people in a cavalcade of cars began honking their horns behind me. So I moved on.

Doubling back, I looked for the number once more, to no avail. Parking my car in an office parking lot, I reached for my cane, determined to find the salon on foot. Hobbling down the road, I checked the numbers on the block. There was no such number. Finally I went into an office. "Can you tell me where to find 1741 Hill?" I asked the gentleman behind the desk.

"Oh, madam," he said courteously. "You must be looking for 1741 Hill *Avenue.* It's about two miles down the road. This is Hill *Street.*"

An hour later, with hair neatly coiffed, I collapsed on my sofa. I realized that I'd made one major mistake. I'd not put first things first. I didn't have the complete address before I left. I didn't know where I was going and had wasted both time and energy.

Perhaps it had only been because I felt intimated by the pressure of impatient strangers behind me or the ache in my tightening muscles that I finally asked that one vital question. But I was so glad that I eventually asked. A line from John Newton's often-sung hymn came to mind. "I once was lost, but now am found." And I had been totally unaware that I was lost!

As the spiritual connection between that experience and my spiritual journey became clear, I fell to my knees. "Merciful God, I will make You first in my life. Help me to begin every journey with Your directions engraved on my heart. Point out the way that I should go. Remind me that I am totally lost without You."

Had the expedition been worth it? The mirror suggested that it had been. And so much more did my thankful heart. GLENDA-MAE GREENE

The Washed-away Prayer

Wash me, and I will be whiter than snow. Ps. 51:7, NIV.

I'VE BEEN WRITING A book about creative ways to pray, and my husband and I put together a "garden" of creative prayer that we take to different churches and seminars. We cover the tables with white cloths and arrange all the items needed for each creative prayer in an attractive setting. Every prayer idea has beautifully designed and laminated instruction cards placed next to it for people to pick up and read. After a brief introduction to the idea of finding new and multisensory ways to pray, we invite people to wander around the room, visiting the tables, and praying the different prayers.

One prayer that is particularly powerful is the "washed-away prayer." A pile of white fabric squares is placed on the table with a few special fabric pens and a large bowl of water. The special pens are used to mark fabric for sewing, and the ink "magically" disappears when a little bit of water is sprinkled over it. People take a piece of cloth and write a word or a symbol on the fabric that represents a particular sin. Then they submerge the cloth in the water as they ask for forgiveness. When they've finished their prayer, the fabric is perfectly white again. Children are especially fascinated by this idea and want to watch the miracle again and again.

At one of the seminars an elderly woman stood at the table with tears in her eyes. "I did something wrong 40 years ago," she said, "and I prayed for forgiveness. I kind of knew in my mind that I was forgiven; but it wasn't until today, when I saw my sin dissolve, that I really understood what forgiveness is all about. It's gone, isn't it? Jesus has made it disappear forever. I'm all clean and fresh again."

Yes, it's gone. Jesus takes all our sins, our messy stains, our marked clothes, and dips them in the water of His loving forgiveness. In a moment, as we pray, they are all washed away and our clothes come out purest white, as if there never was a stain. As we see the difference He has made in our lives our hearts are filled with an amazing peace and joy. We're clean and fresh again! We're strengthened for a new beginning.

Thank You, Jesus, for the washed-away miracle You provide for the messy laundry of our lives.

KAREN HOLFORD

Ordinary People

Lord, through all the generations you have been our home! . . . Teach us to number our days and recognize how few they are; help us to spend them as we should. Ps. 90:1-12, TLB.

IT SEEMS TO ME THAT coming to terms with being ordinary is one of life's many challenges. The thought came to me recently when a friend showed me a photograph of the castle in Ireland that her forebears owned until a few decades ago. As far as ancestral homes are concerned, my own family research has revealed a small weatherboard farmhouse and an even smaller brick terrace-house—but no castles. Although it would have been exciting to find connections to famous or important people (even to royalty), my ancestors appear to have been mainly farmers, tradesmen, or laborers—very ordinary folk indeed. Or were they?

Many of the family members I have known or met through old photographs and documents, or via the memories of elderly relatives, confronted challenges that would certainly make me shrink. I think of my great-grandparents having to cope with the loss of both their young sons on the same day when the boys accidentally drowned in a creek on their way to school. I picture my grandfather, still only a teenager, leaving England on his own to seek his future on the other side of the globe.

Then there was my shy grandmother who went to teach at a little country church school a long way from home and was credited with influencing students who later became prominent church workers.

I consider the struggles my maternal grandparents went through to raise a family during the Depression years. I try to imagine what it must have been like for my father as an 18-year-old, called up to join the Army at the height of World War II; or for my mother, a young wife, with four children under the age of 7, one of whom had a severe disability.

That these "ordinary" people not only survived poverty, war, sickness, and loss—as well as many other challenges—and managed to pass on a legacy of faith surely makes them noteworthy. After all, being a member of God's family is more important and a far greater honor than being able to boast blood ties with any so-called nobility. What an extraordinary blessing it is that whatever our human heritage, "we really are God's children" (Rom. 8:16, TLB)!

Jennifer M. Baldwin

Angel in the Storm

God is our refuge and strength, an ever-present help in trouble. Ps. 46:1, NIV.

OUR OFFICE WILL BE shut down within 10 minutes because of the thunderstorm. All employees should leave their office station immediately." As I heard the announcement from the intercom, I panicked and immediately packed my stuff.

I walked as fast as I could to the parking lot. "I'll be safe at home within another half hour," I whispered to myself.

It started getting dark. The wind got stronger, and I could see the leaves on the trees swaying mightily. As I passed the supermarket I remembered that I didn't have any more groceries left at home. There weren't many cars in the parking lot as I parked my car and walked briskly into the store.

The wind blew even stronger.

Suddenly I heard a man's voice screaming behind me: "Miss, Miss! Your car is rolling back!"

I quickly turned around and saw a man struggling to hold my car with his hands while it rolled back, blown by the strong wind of the thunderstorm. I quickly ran to my car; turned the engine on, and managed to move it forward. I was so frightened! I turned the engine off and set the brake. I stepped out from my car, wanting to express my thankfulness to the man who had helped me, but I couldn't find him. I could only imagine what would have happened if he hadn't been there—my car might have hit another car. One thing I know for sure: It was no coincidence that he was there at that moment. It was God who sent him to the specific place and at the right time to help me.

I thanked and praised God for His help. As Psalm 46:1 says, "God is our refuge and strength, an ever-present help in trouble." The promise is true and alive, especially in my experience. *Thank You, Lord, for Your unfailing help and mercy toward me,* I prayed.

My faith is getting stronger day by day as I experience God's help in my life.

LANNY LYDIA PONGILATAN

I Told Jesus

I love the Lord, for he heard my voice; he heard my cry for mercy. Because he turned his ear to me, I will call on him as long as I live. Ps. 116:1, 2, NIV.

MOMMY, CAN YOU PLEASE send money for my twenty-first birthday party?" That was our May on the phone.

"Sorry, love. I wish we could; but we cannot afford a party. Daddy and I are low on funds." I said it with pain in my heart, but it was the honest truth. Sending our two daughters to England for studies had affected our savings. But when I was leaving them in September, I'd gotten some presents for their birthdays and hidden them.

November 12 came and I called Abbie to wish her a happy birthday and told her where to find her present. I did the same for May two days later. The girls were very happy because they weren't expecting gifts. But deep down, I knew that May was a bit low-spirited because she didn't have the party she so much wanted.

I was very worried, so I asked Jesus in a prayer to help our May to understand that we love her very much but we just couldn't afford all her needs and wants. What made it worse was that we were thousands of miles apart so we couldn't talk face to face. But one thing I knew: "In all their distress [God] too was distressed" (Isa. 63:9, NIV), and He makes sure we aren't distressed. My prayer was answered more than I expected. The Wright family, who are the guardians for our girls, organized a surprise party for both Abbie and May on the Sabbath after their birthdays. Isn't God *awesome?*

I was so happy when I got that news that I cried. This reminded me of a hymn written by Elisha A Hoffman: "I must tell Jesus all of my trials./I cannot bear these burdens alone/ In my distress He kindly will help me,/ He ever loves and cares for His own. I must tell Jesus, Jesus alone."

Yes, I realized that when I poured my heart out to Jesus He helped just as the song says. In His own way. Are your hearts burdened? Why carry it? Tell Jesus. He can help.

Dear Jesus, thank You for Your help. Please bless the Wrights for being there for my daughters. Teach me to keep on reminding others to tell You everything. Amen.

MABEL KWEI

A Message From Ruth

Since we have now been justified by his blood, how much more shall we be saved from God's wrath through him!" Rom. 5:9, NIV.

THE PHONE CALL SHOCKED me! Her husband was telling me that Ruth had just passed away that morning. Only last Sabbath we'd been having a good chat together, and I had been impressed once again by her joy, her gracious Christian manner, and her insight. But now I was happy for her that she had died peacefully in her sleep.

We'd known of some illness as she had confided in me some time before, and recently she'd needed blood transfusions to stabilize her condition. But she never complained, and happily lived with her limitations. After her last blood transfusion she told me how this giving of blood symbolized God's gift to her; how He gave His blood—and even His life—so that she could live.

This beautiful thought was something she wished to share to help her family understand, so she included the following in their Christmas cards: "After my last blood transfusion a wonderful thought came into my brain, and I'd like to share it with you:

"Someone has given blood, and I've been the fortunate recipient of that gift in order to give me a better quality of life here on earth. Jesus Christ, my Savior, gave His life blood that I may have eternal life—surely the greatest gift! May you, too, find:

"Hope in the birth of Jesus and His promise to come again,

"Peace in the life God has given,

"Joy in accepting the love that Jesus brought, and

"Eternal life when Jesus comes the second time to claim those who have accepted Him and been faithful to Him.

"My desire is that each one of you will share in the greatest Gift of all!"

This beautiful message from Ruth Wilkinson was read at her funeral, where hundreds of people were touched by its poignancy.

O Ruth, we can't wait to see you again, healthy and whole, redeemed and rejoicing, at Jesus' second coming. What a hope! What a Savior!

URSULA M. HEDGES

Election

Give diligence to make your calling and election sure: for if ye do these things, ye shall never fall. 2 Peter 1:10.

I WAS IN BED BEFORE 8:00 the night before the national Election Day. I wanted to be in the polling area before anyone else would get there, hoping to be the first voter. I also needed to get this responsibility out of the way.

I arrived at the polling place at 6:00 the next morning. When I got to the entrance, there were hundreds of voters already in line ahead of me. Another voter who was on my left side had had the same train of thought, I gathered. While we were conversing, the line of people slowly moved toward the table where the voter registration was verified.

My conversation friend and I thought of backing out, of waiting for a better opportunity when the crowd thinned down. We stuck it out nevertheless. It took almost one hour to complete the process, whereas in the previous elections five minutes was sufficient to finish such a task.

The result of the election was a tremendous success for the president. It was an overwhelming popular vote by the people of the United States. Each team had involved families, extended families, friends, and political parties nationwide. The election returns came in amazingly fast, too.

Then I thought of the election that Jesus has arranged for us individually. In this election, we don't have to work as hard as those national candidates admitted doing. They spent months on vigorous campaigns, many sleepless nights, and endured mental anguish from slanders by their opponents. They also spent millions of dollars to advertise via television, radio, newspaper, websites, and posters. They traveled to 50 states, met Americans far and near, and appealed for their votes. But for us, Jesus has already done and paid for everything.

In this election we are all candidates. But we don't have to work as hard as those candidates, and our election is sure. His invitation does not need to be hooked to electronic devices. We do not have to travel far. We do not have to suffer the ridicule of those whose trusts are based upon material promises. God has everlasting positions for every believer who will accept His offer to be elected. May we make the right choice.

ESPERANZA AQUINO MOPERA

Bethesda

I will give them eternal life; and they shall never perish. John 10:28.

NEVER GROW OLD, never grow old, in a land where we'll never grow old."

The words of this beautiful chorus have never meant so much to me as when I heard them the last time I visited my parents at Bethesda Retirement Home. The years came and went with such rapidity that suddenly there was the realization my parents could no longer cope with the day-to-day living in their own home. Age had caught up with them! So came the family discussion with Dad, Mom, and my siblings, followed by selling property and packing and the inevitable scaling down of furniture.

There was sadness when they moved into the retirement home, but there are so many blessings. There is the blessing of their church friends. Though they are my parents' friends they bring back childhood memories to me. I remember Mr. and Mrs. Cobb from camp meetings (she's in a wheelchair now). Mr. Cobb is a little man with a beautiful, big singing voice. With the passing of years his voice is perhaps a little frailer but still a joy to hear. Mrs. Cobb has the sweetest smiles. Then there's Mrs. Ligget. My sister and I went to stay with them once during school holidays, and I just hated the dessert I was given one night. She said, "Sit there until it is eaten, Leonie." I can still see that kitchen scene in my mind. I had burst into tears, and all I wanted was my mother! Mrs. Ligget and I laughed when I reminded her of the incident. Mr. and Mrs. Anderson . . . she made the most marvelous scones. Now a severe stroke had put Mrs. Anderson in a wheelchair.

Another blessing is the fact that my parents don't have to go outside in the wet and cold of winter to go to church. A beautiful chapel is part of the institution and, week after week, the elderly—but oh-so-faithful—congregation attends. After the service there is quite a procession back down the passageway for lunch—dear old people with their walkers, other in wheelchairs, gray-haired women with walking sticks, carefully making their way. I push my father, now in a wheelchair, with Mom beside us.

"Never grow old, never grow old." I long for Jesus to come. No more wheelchairs, no more walking canes—eternal life with our Lord. What a glorious promise!

Leonie Donald

Faxed!

Show me your faith without deeds, and I will show you my faith by what I do. James 2:18, NIV.
Now faith is being sure of what we hope for and certain of what we do not see. Heb. 11:1, NIV.

RECENTLY I CALLED A merchant concerning the absence of a receipt. I asked if it could be faxed, and he said he'd fax it at once. After a time I called back to see when he would send my receipt. He said that he already had, but cheerfully agreed to send it again. Again I waited and received nothing. Again he was called and agreed to resend it.

Then, after consulting my fax machine manual, I learned that in order to receive a fax the start button has to be pressed. So I pressed the start button and received the requested information. I had to act on faith by getting up and trying to receive it.

The eight natural health remedies available to us are pure air, water, sunshine, rest, exercise, proper diet, and trust in divine guidance. If you are physically sick, your trust in divine guidance will lead you to seek appropriate health-care professionals. You act in faith when the offered treatments are accepted. Divine guidance will lead you to the right persons for what is needed. The enemy will use our lack of faith to our detriment to inflict doubt.

In our daily Christian walk we pray for certain blessings, then get up off our knees and sit and wait—sometimes impatiently. We have to listen to the promptings of the Holy Spirit by acting on faith. Maybe there's a certain task to be done to be the receiver of the blessing. If you feel your request hasn't been granted, maybe you're not ready to receive it. Our all-wise God will grant it in due time.

Our heavenly Father is all-loving and caring and wants the best for us. When asking for a blessing, we need to be ready to receive it. Sometimes during the delivery process we can't seem to see or press the start button so that we can receive the blessing. The Lord doesn't send us facsimiles; He blesses with the exact blessing we need.

Dear Jesus, please prepare me to be more open and receptive so that when blessings are poured out I can be a recipient. Thank You.

Betty G. Perry

November 18

The Wall

But one thing I do: Forgetting what is behind and straining toward what is ahead, I press on toward the goal to win the prize for which God has called me heavenward in Christ Jesus. Phil. 3:13, 14, NIV.

SEVERAL TIMES A YEAR we attend weekend family retreats at a local Bible camp. One of the favorite activities there is the 75-foot rock-climbing wall known to the kids simply as "The Wall." My son has been especially intrigued with that challenge. After three failed attempts, he told me that this time he was determined to climb that rock wall! As he stepped into the climbing harness and the ropes were attached to the camp counselor who would belay him up the wall, he told her, "I'm not coming down until I make it to the top!"

And so his climb began. The first 25 feet were easy. He accomplished that in no time. The next 25 feet were a bit harder. He stopped from time to time, holding fast to the bits of rock that had good hand holds. The counselor and I shouted encouragement: "You can do it! Remember, 'I can do all things through Christ who strengthens me'! Don't give up; keep going!" As my son reached the final third of the wall, he stopped and rested frequently, looking up at the next rocks. When he stopped, the counselor told him, "Go ahead and grab the next rock. I've got your belay rope. I won't let you fall!" And so he continued on, one small step up the wall at a time, until at last he was at the top. I quickly snapped a few pictures before he began his excited descent, eager to tell his friends, "I climbed The Wall!"

Later we talked about his climb. I asked why he paused when he was so close to his goal. "Well, Mom," he answered, "there are some places on the wall that are comfortable. Reaching out is scary. Sometimes I just wanted to be where it was comfortable."

In my walk with God I know there have been times when I've stopped climbing. I've stayed where it was comfortable instead of moving up the climbing wall into a closer, deeper relationship with Him. Then in my mind I see Jesus attached to my belay rope, my anchor, firmly securing me against a fall from the spiritual wall I'm climbing. He calls out encouragement to me: "Don't give up; keep climbing! Don't be afraid; I've got your rope!"

SANDRA SIMANTON

Nasty Stains

"Come now, and let us reason together," says the Lord. "Though your sins are like scarlet, they shall be as white as snow; though they are red like crimson, they shall be as wool." Isa. 1:18, NKJV.

MY GRANDSON WAS A week old when I arrived by plane. This was our first grandson but second grandchild, so I had come prepared to help. I remembered with fondness my mother coming to assist me at the birth of my sons. Cooking, laundry, and babysitting the 3-year-old granddaughter were things I was prepared to do. Weekends would be spent with my 89-year-old aunt.

After returning from one of these weekends, I learned that a pen had exploded in the dryer, causing ink to go everywhere. I had put those clothes in the washing machine before leaving Friday and had somehow missed seeing the pen. As I looked at my son's two shirts and several items of baby clothing, I felt sick. How does one remove ink from clothes? For berry and cherry stains my mother had taught me to use boiling water poured over the stains. Bleach was out of the question. My hairdresser suggested toothpaste, but I could foresee having to use many, many tubes to clean up this mess.

Then I remembered my niece using hairspray on ink stains. What did I have to lose? I sprayed every stain on the shirts, as well as the stains on the baby outfits. Now what? I rubbed the spots, but there was no sign of fading. I went off to bed feeling defeated. Why had I been so careless?

Next morning, the first thing I checked was the baby's red outfit. Where were the ink stains? They were gone—not a trace left! I rushed to find the shirts. There were no stains on them, either. I was excited to announce to my daughter-in-law that the stains were gone. I hadn't ruined the clothes after all.

Sin leaves dreadful marks on our lives. Nothing we do of our own efforts can remove those stains. There is something, however, that works every time—it is the precious blood of Jesus Christ. We need to apply it liberally and let Him do the rest.

VERA WIEBE

Promise Renewed Through a Rainbow

I have set my rainbow in the clouds, and it will be the sign of the covenant between me and the earth. Gen. 9:13, NIV.

DURING VACATION WE visited a family of friends who were also spending their vacation on Ilha Bela (Beautiful Island) on the northern coast of the state of São Paulo, Brazil. It was my birthday, and also the birthday of one of the daughters of our friends. Their hillside house is completely surrounded by palm trees, the front facing the ocean and a boat harbor. To reach the boats, one has to go down several steps.

After a delicious lunch I decided to get some exercise and walked down the steps, breathing in that wonderful sea air, feeling the wind in my hair, taking advantage of the scene to engrave on my mind that beautiful picture of the green sea, palm trees curving in the wind, and the deep-blue sky sprinkled with clouds that seemed like tufts of cotton.

All this beauty made me think of all that God has done for me, a humble sinner. Looking closely at such blue immenseness, I imagined that just beyond this sky was God, so I began to talk with Him about my projects and desires—especially my desire to be there with Him. My desire to live forever in a place where I would never again cry, never feel sadness, discomfort, or frustrations was the topic of my conversation with God.

Then right before my eyes I saw a beautiful rainbow. Stunned by such beauty (and at that moment, on my birthday), once more I felt the truth of the divine promises. Through that rainbow God said to me that He is real. Very soon the struggles of this life will come to an end and Jesus will return. I felt such a great peace fill my heart, because I felt that God was there and had not forgotten me. At His side I will be safe. He is El-Shaddai, "the almighty God." He is the covenant-making and -keeping God, the God who has promised us eternal life, as well as the assurance that He is beside us each day in our projects and plans. All we have to do is accept Him.

I thank You, loving God, for the magnificent promises that You made so long ago and still fulfill today. I trust in You, and I know that by Your side I will overcome the battles of this life. ANI KÖHLER BRAVO

The Waiting Wheelchair

And it shall come to pass, that before they call, I will answer; and while they are yet speaking, I will hear. Isa. 65:24.

WE LIVE IN AN AGE of questioning. When a child begins to talk, he or she wants to know why, when, where, and how; and the answers have to come from someone, somehow, somewhere. Children have always asked these questions. Now I find myself asking the why, where, when, and how questions, and I'm sure other women do also—whether it be on their job, at school, at church, or at home.

When I ask myself why, I start counting the many blessings I receive day after day, and the why question doesn't dominate my life. The song advises, "Count your blessings, name them one by one; count your many blessings, see what God hath done." Knowing God, I don't dwell on the whys of life. In 1982 my husband came in from working in the yard not feeling well. He decided to relax, but didn't feel any better, so we knew it was time to seek medical attention. As we were driving to the nearby hospital, he began having chest discomfort. Anxiety mixed with questioning. *Why is this happening on Mother's Day? How am I going to get him out of the car when I get to the hospital entrance?* Then a text came to me: "Before they call, I will answer; and while they are yet speaking, I will hear."

As I drove up to the emergency entrance, a nurse was standing outside with a wheelchair, even though no one knew we were coming. As I stopped the car, she pushed the wheelchair up to the car and helped my husband inside.

I'm still thanking God for answering before we could call. Although my husband had had a heart attack, with blessings he was able to resume working in the church for 19 more years. The songwriter is right: "Count your many blessings, name them one by one, and it will surprise you what the Lord hath done." Knowing God is much better than asking, "Why?"

God, I have other questions as well, but I will wait for the answers. You have already shown that You will take care of me even before I ask.

Annie B. Best

Prosperity

And he shall be like a tree planted by the rivers of water, that bringeth forth his fruit in his season; his leaf also shall not wither; and whatsoever he doeth shall prosper. Ps. 1:3.

BLESSINGS UPON BLESSINGS. Can you count all of yours? I really don't think so! Revelation 5:12 declares: "Saying with a loud voice, Worthy is the Lamb that was slain to receive power, and riches, and wisdom, and strength, and honour, and glory, and blessing." That's a blessing beyond measure!

Have there been times when you've had to scrape pennies together to buy a loaf of bread or to buy some milk or to put gas in your car to get to work? Have there been times when you received shutoff notices for lights, gas, and phone—all at the same time? Have there been times when you simply didn't know how you would survive? Those who have never experienced poverty—or just coming up short financially sometimes—have something to be thankful for.

When I lived in downtown Detroit, I watched people dig in garbage bins and beg for quarters on the street for food. I've seen young children, 12 and 13, going from table to table in restaurants, begging for leftovers. They were either homeless or family circumstances were such that they were raising themselves.

Someone has said, "Homelessness is only one paycheck away." We should praise the Lord and say "Thank You, God" if we have a home! Psalm 106:1 says, "Praise ye the Lord. O give thanks unto the Lord; for he is good: for his mercy endureth for ever." Let's be thankful for the blessings we are receiving and have received. We should always try to help others, remembering how we'd want to be helped should our situation change.

Lord, help me remember that situations do change, especially when You are involved! You have turned the most difficult situations into victory for me. Help me to trust You, regardless of what I see or feel during difficult times. I may have wept through the night, but my morning is on its way! I will rejoice in You, for You will not leave me or forsake me. Help me to be thankful for the blessings I've received, and continue to bless me so that I can always be in a position to help others. In Jesus' name, amen. HATTIE R. LOGAN

Thanksgiving Guests

If I have found favor in your eyes, . . . do not pass your servant by. . . . Let me get you something to eat, so you can be refreshed." Gen. 18:3, 5, NIV.

MY IMMEDIATE FAMILY was not with me. Friends were out of town, or had families of their own. For the first time I was facing a Thanksgiving alone. Yet Thanksgiving or Christmas is never "alone time" for me. I love the holiday season—the aroma of home-cooked food, spicy scents in the air, the glow of fireplace and candlelight, cheery music wafting on the air. People seem just a little friendlier, and I look for people with whom to share the holidays.

My neighbor, a widow I had known since childhood, wouldn't be spending Thanksgiving with her son. "Would you like to have Thanksgiving dinner with me?" I invited. Would she! She was so happy that she told her neighbors, a couple newly arrived from Australia.

"Can we come too?" they asked. Of course they could.

Then the couple next to them heard about my Thanksgiving and asked if they could come. Again I said "Yes." And the news spread.

On Thanksgiving Day a friend came over to help me cook dinner. We baked cracked-wheat rolls that came fresh and warm from the oven. We made dressing with walnuts, cranberries, raisins, celery, and other aromatic delicacies associated with Thanksgiving. We decorated the house with arrangements of Indian corn, striped squash, autumn leaves—even candles. I put music on the stereo and warmed spicy apple cider to cast a welcome aroma across the rooms.

We welcomed 10 people to my home; each brought a favorite dish for a late afternoon dinner. That was one of the best Thanksgivings in my memory!

Christmas came, and one of the couples held a Christmas party and invited the neighbors (25 of us).

That was the only year we all got together as a neighborhood for Thanksgiving and Christmas. In later years we went our separate ways with family and friends. It was a memorable year, all because I hadn't wanted to spend it alone.

Dear reader, if you find yourself alone on a holiday, invite someone to share it with you. You never know what special blessings God has in store.

EDNA MAYE GALLINGTON

Sweet Somethings

And we know that all things work together for good to them that love God, to them who are the called according to his purpose. Rom. 8:28.

THIS IS JUST ANOTHER sweet story that proves that Romans 8:28 (one of my favorite texts in the Bible) is still true.

Thanksgiving Day has come and gone, and my memories will be pleasant ones. This year my husband and I decided to participate in our church's annual community Thanksgiving dinner. Our "neighbors," whether homeless or just hungry, are invited to share a satisfying holiday meal and afterward may take any of the many cleaned and donated items of clothing away with them, courtesy of the church's Community Services department.

I was asked to purchase and season two large cans of green beans. *Where do I find them?* I wondered. Wayne and I had recently moved from a city in which we knew where to find a warehouse store that didn't require membership. I decided to ask Freddie, a friend who lives in our new home town, to direct me. The store she suggested required membership, and I advised her that I didn't have one. When I explained that I needed green beans and had to prepare them before Thursday morning, she agreed to pick up a couple cans for me, as she had some shopping to do there the next day.

Wayne went to get the cans for me and returned with a great story. Freddie had totally forgotten to get my green beans as she completed her own shopping. As she made her way to the checkout counter, she approached the end of an aisle and saw someone giving out free food samples. Yes, you guessed it—the woman was offering tiny cups of green beans! Now, when is the last time someone offered you anything but cheese, beef stew, pizza, or salsa? Vegetables? I never heard of it. Freddie told my husband that all she could do was laugh and praise the Lord. And so did I!

I am always blown away when I see how God provides that great parking spot in an otherwise crowded lot, or I finally find my favorite fragrance and it's the last one on the shelf! Our heavenly Father works it all out for us because He loves us. We love Him, and we are His called-out-and-chosen ones. I marvel at His consistent provision—teeny-tiny, as well as "exceeding abundantly" (Eph. 3:20) given.

RENEE VERRETT-DOOLEY

An Amazing God

Now to him who is able to do immeasurably more than all we ask or imagine, according to His power that is at work within us, to him be glory in the church and in Christ Jesus throughout all generations, for ever and ever! Amen. Eph. 3:20, 21, NIV.

YOU WOULD THINK THAT by now I'd have learned that God always does more than I ask or can even imagine, but I must be a slow learner because I'm invariably taken by surprise.

For many years my husband has been the volunteer transport manager for Adventist Development and Relief Agency in the United Kingdom, and his dedication is a source of inspiration to me. Hearing that a children's orphanage was in need of $20,736 for a project to provide clean water and sanitation, I decided to organize a festival of flowers to raise funds so ADRA could begin the work. A previous festival had raised $12,000 for a children's hospice, and this time I set myself a private goal of $16,000.

As always, flower-arranging friends from church and flower clubs were tremendously creative, supportive, and generous; and the resulting 40 floral displays, depicting the work of ADRA throughout the world, were stunning. The public who came to view the flowers were greatly impressed and responded with generous donations. Church members gave of their time and talents to create beautiful music and wholesome food, and the result was "immeasurably more" than we had ever imagined. We not only exceeded my private goal; we exceeded the amount needed for the project—a staggering sum of $22,584! In addition, we had collected more than a thousand shoe boxes filled with goodies for children in orphanages throughout Albania. It was a tremendous privilege to visit that country to initiate the distribution of the boxes and to see firsthand the needs in the orphanages.

I wish you could have been there as those children opened the shoe boxes we brought in! The joy on their faces was wonderful to behold as they exclaimed with delight over sweets and coloring pens, pencils and hats, T-shirts and toys—and even over toothbrushes and toothpaste. It was a joyful—and humbling—time!

We now have a list of projects needing our aid, but we're confident that as we give God all the glory for what has been accomplished, we can rely upon Him to give us "immeasurably more than we can ask or think" in the future.

AUDREY BALDERSTONE

Wake Up With the Birds

Have no fear; you are worth more than any number of sparrows.
Luke 12:7, NEB.

WAKE UP WITH THE birds, listen to their singing, and join them in praising the Creator. Your day will be blessed." This was the sweet admonition from my mother when we were young. I was fortunate to have been born and brought up in a countryside where waking up with koel, parrots, sparrows, kingfishers, ravens—listening to and joining them in praising God—was the most thrilling experience I had.

The atmosphere of the boarding school I attended was no different, situated far away from the city on a beautiful hillock surrounded by evergreen valleys. The grounds, an extensive estate of mango and cashew trees, provided shelter for a variety of birds throughout the year. I enjoyed waking up with the birds.

In the later years I missed these wonderful mornings when I migrated from village to towns and cities in pursuit of higher studies and employment. I thank God that after many years I finally had the privilege of living with my husband and three children in a house far away from the business of city life. After a tiresome day of unpacking and setting up the house, I went to sleep late at night. How soothing it was when the silence of the night was broken by the melodious songs of the birds in the bushes at the dawn of the day. Old memories flooded my mind. Remembering the sweet admonition of my mother, I tiptoed to my children's rooms and whispered for them to wake up with the birds, to listen to their singing, and join them in praising the Creator. "Your day will be blessed," I promised, using my mother's words.

How thrilled they were to listen to those wonderful singing birds! I saw it in their eyes. How they loved to wake up with the little creatures each morning! We made it a point to wake each other up to that beautiful experience all the days we lived in that house. It soothed our hearts and uplifted our spirits to be with the Creator and Sustainer of the universe.

Thank You, Lord, for creating me with eyes and ears to enjoy the singing of one of Your wonderful small creations. It makes a difference in my day.

MARGARET TITO

Sparrows and Kittens

Are not two sparrows sold for a penny? Yet not one of them will fall to the ground apart from the will of your Father. Matt.10:29, NIV.

FOR AS LONG AS I can remember we always had animals in our home. We had cats, dogs, monkeys, turtles, parrots, parakeets, and even an armadillo. When any of the animals was sick, all of us became very concerned.

On one occasion our cat was going to have kittens, and she was sick. My mother took her to the veterinary clinic where it became necessary to perform a Caesarian section, followed by a tubal ligation so that she wouldn't become pregnant again. Six kittens were born. One of them had to go into the oxygen tent because its respiration wasn't good. On the weekend I went to see the little babies at my mother's house. I noticed one of the kittens had a large cut on one of its paws. My sister told me that the kitten had been accidentally cut by the surgical knife during the surgery. We put a bandage on that paw; however, it became worse during the week. The kitten (or its mother) ended up removing the bandage, and the wound didn't look good. On Friday I called my sister for an update. She said that my brother-in-law had decided to have the kitten put to sleep since its paw hadn't improved.

I prayed intensely that night that God would save a small animal He had created. The following morning I called, anxious to find out the kitten's fate. He replied that the wound was almost completely healed—he wouldn't have the kitten put to sleep. I couldn't keep quiet! "Do you know why the kitten's paw has healed? I prayed to God so that He would salve it, because if He cares for sparrows, He also cares for little kittens."

That night I learned two important lessons. First, God cares about the creatures He has created. Second, as we pray we need to leave everything in God's hands. He simply had to cure that kitten. At first, when this idea came to my mind, I wasn't able to have serenity; but I felt peace as I put everything in His holy will. After all, that kitten was a creature of God, and God protected it. As wonderful as having the prayer answered was learning such a valuable spiritual lesson.

IANI LAUER

Man's Extremity—God's Opportunity

And my God will meet all your needs according to his glorious riches in Christ Jesus. Phil. 4:19, NIV.

WE WERE IN A financial crisis, and I was ill and terribly depressed. I had read our text for a devotional several times during our morning worship: "And my God will meet all your needs according to his glorious riches in Christ Jesus." I knew this was true because God had promised, but somehow I couldn't shake off the depression.

The day before I had spent a substantial amount of money for examinations and laboratory tests and was scheduled for more X-rays and testing the following day. We had depleted the funds allotted by our insurance plan; therefore, we had to finance our medical costs. As I lay on the rug in the living room, I lifted my thoughts in prayer, asking for divine help.

The ringing of the telephone interrupted my prayer for help. The voice on the other end said, "Sister Lindo, you've been in my thoughts all morning. I know you have always been helping others, and now that you are ill I think you could use some help. I would like to make a contribution to you." I tried to say something, but I had no voice, no words, humbled that I had been faithless to the point of depression. God in His love and mercy had fulfilled His promise to supply my need.

"Hello? Hello? Sister Lindo, are you there?" said the caller.

"Y-e-s, y-e-s, hello, Sister Bishop," I stammered, "I'm sorry. I was just overwhelmed that God had answered my prayers so dramatically, and I'm so touched by your kindness that my voice left me temporarily. Of course, I'm very grateful," I continued, "but I would be embarrassed to take money as a gift; however, a loan would be an answer to prayer."

As I hung up the telephone I knelt right there and gave praises and thanksgiving to God. He never fails. All His promises are true, and He supplies our every need. Many times, when every avenue seems closed and there appears to be no way out, the circumstances are just the opportunity God uses to show His great power to the honor and glory of His marvelous name.

Dear friend, whatever your need might be today—be it financial, social, spiritual, physical, or emotional—remember, God has promised He will supply that need.

OLGA I. CORBIN DE LINDO

Rejected

The gift of God is eternal life through Jesus Christ our Lord. Rom. 6:23.

WEEKS BEFORE CHRISTMAS I'd been busy sorting recipes and getting them into the computer in sections, proofreading them, and doing everything I could to make a cookbook of all our family's favorite recipes. I thought this would be a really nice gift for each of our children, grandchildren, brother, nieces, and a very few friends. Now that all the pages had been put together professionally, I wrote a personal note in each book. I was *s-o-o-o* excited to be able to give each such a personal gift, and truly hoped each recipient would be as excited to receive my gift as I had been to put it together.

About five days after they were mailed, one came back. The notation on the outside of the package said: "Return to Sender." But somehow I knew that the person had refused the gift because it was from me. I had agonized over whether to send her the book and had made a last-minute decision to do so. And now she was returning it unopened. It was like a slap in the face. It hurt!

Then I got sensible and decided that maybe the post office had returned it without her ever having seen it. The address looked perfect to me, but I had to know. So I called her on her cell phone and got the answering machine. When she didn't return my message I was more sure than ever that she simply didn't want my gift. Then I decided to send an e-mail and ask her, telling her that if she didn't, I would respect that; but if she did want it, I would resend it.

To make a long story short, she assured me she had not returned anything at all to me and couldn't figure out why it had been returned. She made sure I had the correct address, and when I checked the address again, I discovered that I had written WA for Washington rather than CA for California. So the post office returned it.

When I think of how hurt and rejected I felt over nothing, it made me realize again how terrible it must make my Savior feel when He gave the ultimate, His very life, in order that we might have eternal life through Him, and it is rejected. Let's determine to never refuse the greatest Gift of all.

ANNA MAY RADKE WATERS

My Life Changed

Unless you are converted and become as little children, you will by no means enter the kingdom of heaven. Matt. 18:3, NKJV.

SEVERAL YEARS AGO I attended church on Sunday with my only child. I was not a Christian then, but felt quite comfortable attending religious services. My friend, who attended a church on Saturdays, kept inviting me to attend church with her; but I always found a good reason not to go. She changed her strategy and began asking if my daughter could go with her. I finally consented, with the understanding that my daughter and I would continue to attend services together on Sunday.

This routine continued for months until my daughter became reluctant to attend church with me; she felt more comfortable among the children at the new church and was having a good time participating in services. When she was 8 years old, she insisted that she wanted to be baptized. I thought she was much too young, but I finally gave in when others convinced me that it was a good decision that required my blessing.

I couldn't believe the rate at which my daughter was growing spiritually. She wouldn't miss any church-related activity and found every opportunity to witness to us at home. I had no thought of attending church with her, but my cuuriosity got the better of me as I attended some programs to see her perform. I kept asking myself if this was really my child—so self-confident and open as she played her various roles at church. Without realizing what was happening, I began to attend her church more frequently so I could enjoy watching her in her happiest moments as she participated in the various activities. It was in the midst of this participation that I met the Lord for myself.

My daughter had found a good thing and lured me to come and see. In return I got much more than I expected—a saving knowledge of Christ. There was no turning back for me.

My daughter is even happier as we worship together. We are both praying that my husband will also discover this good thing we have found, and that one day we will all be together in heaven as part of a bigger family.

Lord, help me to tell others of the joy to be found in You and be as convincing as was my child. Carol A. Williams

Best Friends

I have loved you even as the Father has loved me. . . . You are my friends.
John 15:9-15, NLT.

IT WAS AN UNUSUALLY mild December day unfolding under a bright sun and a clear-blue sky streaked with beautiful cloud formations. Walking along the footpath at the edge of the field, I noticed the broken fence post with the inscription in neat schoolchild handwriting:

Becky	Claire	Fallon
+	+	+
?	?	?

I stopped to ponder awhile—three young girls on the verge of womanhood, dreaming about a romantic future. With whom would they meet and fall in love? Who would be a Prince Charming—a Mr. Right for each of them? Would they live happily ever after? I'm sure this was how each one saw her dream ending. Or would one or more of them end up another statistic in the broken homes/abusive relationships/multiple partner tables?

Then my thoughts turned to another question. Did they—would they ever—know the most important relationship that any of us can know? Had anyone introduced—would anyone ever introduce—them to their best friend Jesus?

I did not know Becky, Claire, or Fallon, the three friends who in an idle moment with indelible felt marker had written their questions on the fence post. The chances were I'd never meet them, but as I continued my walk I said a silent prayer for them, that they would one day meet Jesus and find true happiness in Him.

Again I wondered how many Beckys, Claires, and Fallons there are—young women, older women, and their male counterparts—looking for that special relationship? How many of them do I meet every day? Am I introducing them to my Best Friend, and theirs?

Lord, help me today to be a friend to someone who needs to know You, and to show them by my life and example that You are the best friend they can ever have, that You love each of us, even as Your Father loved You. Amen.

ANTONIA (ANN) CASTELLINO

The Me I See

I will praise thee; for I am fearfully and wonderfully made: marvelous are thy works; and that my soul knoweth right well. Ps. 139:14.

I'M LOOKING AT MYSELF three years later, and the transformation is amazing. Today I am celebrating God's creation of me! Tall. Dark. Natural. I am His daughter, and I look like my Daddy! I am made in His image, and His image is good (Gen. 1:27).

For the first time in my life societal standards of beauty do not limit or hinder me— after all, I look like my Daddy! The decision to allow my hair to grow natural is a part of my celebration of God's creation. I had always disliked my hair, so I often altered it and then rejected it; but now that I look at myself through God's creative eyes I know that everything about me—from head to toe—is good. Twists, braids, up-dos, and puffs—what beautiful, soulful expressions!

I really like the me I see. My dark, smooth covering was designed just for me. My thick, natural kinky hair was neatly and intricately woven just for me. I like the me I see. We women are often too critical of ourselves!

Today I want to challenge you to look in the mirror and see the wonderful creation you are. You look like your Daddy! You are fearfully and wonderfully made. Don't let *Vogue* and *Ebony* define how you should look. Instead, look at the "true" beauty book that tells us to have beautiful lips that speak words of comfort and encouragement to others; a beautiful heart that loves unconditionally; beautiful hands that serve God and our brothers and sisters; and beautiful characters—for that is all we will take with us to heaven.

My sister, hear me loud and clear: Red and Yellow, Black and White, we are all precious in His sight. We all look like our Daddy, and if we should meet we'll see each other with eyes of understanding and a heart of joy. We'll see each other with a deep sense of knowing that it is in God's plan for us to look in our mirrors and love the reflection of our Daddy that we see! And that others will see our Daddy in us as well.

Yes, I love the me I see. TERRIE RUFF

Reflections

When a [woman's] ways please the Lord, [she] maketh even [her] enemies to be at peace with [her]. Prov. 16:7.

I NEVER LEARNED TO SWIM. That hit home one day, and it made me sad to realize I've lived almost eight decades and can't swim a stroke. It made me wonder: *What else have I missed out on all these years?*

Well, for starters, I've never flown in an airplane—unless you count that short spin we made over our house in a small Cub two-seater back in the fifties. I don't own a computer. I took crash courses in typing and organ years ago but never became proficient in either. I get by with my typing, but I eventually sold the organ. I can't play tennis, and I never learned to knit. I've never been on a cruise to the islands or visited the Holy Land. Only on video or in magazines have I seen beautiful English gardens and thatched roof cottages with the window boxes all in bloom.

Just about the time I became immersed in my own little pity party I decided to try to recall some of the things I *have* accomplished through the years. Not much to write home about, but I did go back to school at age 38 and became a nurse. I can prepare a tolerable meal and bake my own bread, and I've written a few songs and poems. I've been fortunate to have had some articles and stories published. My main project is sending cards and letters to shut-ins and those who need some encouragement.

I learned to ride a bicycle; I can drive a car, and I've traveled to both coasts. I rode on the back of our motorcycle on our trip to New York. I made it to the top of the Empire State Building and had the pleasure of visiting both neighbors to the north and south of us, Canada and Mexico. I survived a lengthy illness, and I'm still able to do some walking in spite of a less-than-perfect knee.

As I reflect on it, I guess I haven't really missed out on so much after all. I never had great aspirations to begin with, so I guess I'm about up to par for my league.

As long as I can spend quality time with my family, perform my duties at my church, pray for those who need my help, and do what pleases my Lord—well, that's what counts! Clareen Colclesser

The All-knowing God

Casting all your care upon him, for he careth for you. 1 Peter 5:7.

ONE COOL AFTERNOON about six years ago I was deeply absorbed in reviewing the activities of the day as I walked home from work. In the distance I saw a smartly dressed, middle-aged man coming toward me.

"Good afternoon," he greeted me. "I usually appear on television, and I have healed many people with different ailments. Have you ever seen me?"

I looked at him keenly and replied, "No."

Suddenly a woman appeared from the opposite direction. "Hello, sir," she said. "I am very excited to meet you today. I want to extend my cordial thanks to you once again for assisting me in recovering my lost items recently."

The man smiled, but his eyes stayed on me. "Nothing is impossible," he said. "I do all through God's power." I stood there, wondering about this man who was able to find lost items. "Do you need help?" the man asked the woman.

The woman relayed the nature of her sickness and her desire to be well.

Then the man turned to me and said, "It has been revealed to me through the Holy Spirit the events that will befall you and your family. You will be promoted soon, but you will die within six months."

Die? The idea of death struck deeply in my mind. Then the man said that he wanted to pray for us and that he would bless us and multiply our money. He then asked how much money we had with us and in the bank. The other woman responded, "Two thousand Kenyan shillings with me, and 20,000 Kenyan shillings in the bank." I said that I had 50 Kenyan shillings with me; then, fearing they were robbers, I began praying silently: *God, help me get out of this situation. You are an all-knowing and all-seeing God.*

Another well-dressed man appeared, thanking the man for healing his mother. Fearing these were indeed robbers, I told them I had to hurry home, and started walking. My heart was beating rapidly, and I was shaking and trembling. I continued to whisper a prayer in my heart.

When I arrived home I shared this incident with my family, and we praised God for caring for and protecting me. Yes, God really does care. Depend on Him all the time.

NYARANGI M. BUNDI

Crystal, Gold, and Silver

For where your treasure is, there will your heart be also. Matt. 6:21.

FOR FIVE YEARS I'VE been cleaning house for a couple who are antique collectors. I spend untold hours polishing silver, dusting valuable furniture, and shining up their expensive crystal. Countertops are covered with very valuable, collectible ornaments; and antique furniture and pictures fill every space. There's lots of expensive jewelry in drawers. The china cabinets are full of crystal and silver items. It all just sits there; and I clean it—again and again.

The basement contains shelves and shelves of boxes packed with valuables that are taken out maybe once a year, and everything upstairs is replaced with collectable Christmas glass, candles, and icons. One day I accidentally broke a large glass globe. It cost $60; I was more careful after that.

These people are always shopping and buying more and more glassware; nearly all of it stays in its box; most I've never seen and never used in day-to-day life.

One morning a friend called to tell me that the couple's house had caught on fire. The four lovebirds and the family's lives were spared, but almost everything else was either wet with water, black from smoke, or melted from heat and fire. The first time I entered the now-black-and-stinking house, I cried.

The next day I stopped to reconsider the priorities in my life. Is my money or idle time spent on the wrong things? Do I hoard away stuff I cannot bear to part with just for the satisfaction of owning it? Do I consider the difference between what is a *need* and what is a want? Are my things more important to me than my relationship with Jesus?

When He comes to take us to heaven, all will have to be left behind, and it will end up being nothing more than a melted, blackened heap of expensive and collectible "nothingness."

About a month after the fire I ran into my friend in town. In her shopping cart was more unnecessary stuff. She felt she had to replace everything she had lost, and she talked about making a trip to the United States to buy some more jewelry. I think of that song that declares, "I'd rather have Jesus than silver or gold, I'd rather be His than have riches untold." So would I, wouldn't you?

VIDELLA MCCLELLAN

Pain and Joy

Now the God of hope fill you with all joy and peace in believing, that ye may abound in hope, through the power of the Holy Ghost. Rom. 15:13.

IT WAS LATE IN the year of 1999, and I was in the hospital, sitting by my mother's bed. I'm not quite sure what time it was. My mother couldn't sleep because of the pain, so she'd stay awake, but only for a short while; and I'd read to her or talk about silly things or wonderful family memories.

I prayed every day that she wouldn't have pain, or that she would be healed. What was truly amazing to me was that the closer she got to death, the more she comforted me and those around her. I expected something different and thought it was supposed to be the other way around. My mother had always had a great sense of humor. She was always finding funny ways to keep from being so sad and trying to stop the pain. She used the humor to manage all the stuff that was going on around her—from the bedpan to the tubes that seemed to run everywhere over her body and arms. Laughter is sometimes a great way to feel better—sometimes better than medicine, and certainly better than tears of sadness.

God is good. He helped get our scattered family together to see her before she died. She had time to talk and pray with all her grandchildren, which blessed us all. Because she'd been a missionary for 40 years in India, she'd always been far away from her own family; and then we here in the United States were away from her.

She asked to go home the last week of her life. The last worship we had together will be a memory that God gave us all to keep until He comes again. We sang, shared, and enjoyed our time together. Mother had a wonderful voice, and we got to hear her sing one last time. She lived for six more days, but was asleep most of the time. *Thank You, God!*

Through all the pain God reminded all of us that He is life. He showed us all in big ways how much He cares, and in small ways what it will be like in heaven. *Come soon, Lord!*

SUSEN MATTISON MOLÉ

Sermon in Shoes

How beautiful on the mountains are the feet of those who bring good news, who proclaim peace, who bring good tiding, who proclaim salvation. Isa. 52:7, NIV.

THE OTHER DAY, I bought a new pair of shoes. It had been a long time since I last went shopping and when I found that perfect pair I was delighted—inside and out. Inside, because they didn't cost much—the $10 price tag tickled my heart. Outside, because they were so comfortable and cute. Cute doesn't often accompany comfortable these days.

The first week I wore them, I stepped ankle-deep into a mud puddle just as we were about to visit someone, and my perfect shoes were tested with Georgia clay. I was upset with myself for not noticing the mud puddle just below the car. How was I going to visit these friends with mud on the same feet that would be stepping on their fine carpet? To my relief, my eyes locked on the garden hose just below the front steps, and to my delight, I found out that my perfect shoes could also be rinsed!

Lately, I find myself taking special notice of other people's summer foot attire. Some wear precariously high heels to adorn their feet—in spite of the pain. Others wear shoes that must be pampered and avoid any brush with dirt, grass, or grease for fear that they would be damaged permanently. Each pair of shoes reflects the tastes and needs of its owner. Each one touches its occupant in some way. Whether luxurious slippers or shoes with simple straps, they all tell some sort of story.

Many summers ago I remember singing a song about shoes at summer camp. There we were lined up, a dozen guitarists strumming away to the catchy campfire tune: "Do you know, O Christian, you're a sermon in shoes? Do you know, O Christian, you're a sermon in shoes? Jesus calls upon you to spread the gospel news. So walk it, and talk it, a sermon in shoes . . ." My dad loves the song and has asked several times for me to sing it again. I can see that it reminds Him of something beautiful, the beautiful feet of those who bring the good news of Jesus Christ. You may want to study Isaiah 52:7-10 too, to see what it says to you.

This is my prayer: *Lord Jesus, wash my feet with the peace of knowing that nothing can happen to me today that we cannot handle together.*

NANCY NEUHARTH TROYER

Lack of Faith

Commit thy way unto the Lord; trust also in him; and he shall bring it to pass. Ps. 37:5.

STUDYING ENGLISH IN THE United States had always been something that my husband and I wanted to do. We applied for a scholarship, and after some time we were very happy to receive a positive answer. The next step was to obtain a student visa to the United States. We began preparing the necessary documents and filling out forms. I was very uneasy and nervous because the U.S. consulate was denying visas to many people, and I thought that our application would be denied also. My husband—calmer and more trusting in God—was certain that if it were God's will everything would work out.

Two days before our scheduled interview at the consulate, I was a bundle of nerves. One night I dreamed that I had gone to the consulate and a very kind and considerate woman attended to us and easily granted us the visa. Although I had dreamed that everything would work out fine, I continued to be very nervous and suspicious.

When we actually arrived at the consulate in São Paulo, we faced an enormous line. Many people who had waited in line with us demonstrated through their facial expression the disappointment of having been denied a visa after their interview. There were only three individuals granting visas—two men and a woman—and we waited in line to see which of these individuals would interview us. When it was our turn, the woman waited on us; it was only then that I remembered the dream, and I said to my husband, "This is the same as my dream; we are going to receive our visa." She was very nice and granted us the visa without many questions—which is not common. I realized then how weak my faith had been. I asked God to forgive my lack of faith, because even though He had sent me a dream to help calm me, I had not trusted Him.

We obtained the visa, and the trip to the United States was a wonderful experience that contributed a great deal to our lives. Today I am very grateful to my Lord for every little thing in my life because I know He provides the answer when I trust Him with all my heart.

Lord, thank You. We can trust in You when difficult moments arise in our life. Thank You because You forgive us and understand our weaknesses. Dear Jesus, help us to have faith in You and to trust in Your ways without doubting.

ISABELA SALLES

Hannah

Then Jesus called a little child to Him, set him in the midst of them, and said, "Assuredly, I say to you, unless you are converted and become as little children, you will by no means enter the kingdom of heaven." Matt. 18:2, 3, NKJV.

HAD I KNOWN I'D meet Hannah today, I might have dressed for an encounter with a princess. But I didn't know. My trip to the small hospital lab had been rushed. I dropped my requisition into the wall basket and found a waiting room seat. Hannah first caught my attention as she swung her little booted feet, looking back and forth from me to the adult beside her.

The adult beside her turned out to be a very young grandma who acknowledged Hannah's observation that my boots were just like hers. Then Hannah came over to the table and picked up a book on piggies. She stood there, holding it, looking at me. Her straight, dark hair framed a lovely face with awesome brown eyes. "Would you like me to read it to you?" I asked.

She nodded, and wiggled into the chair beside me. Grandma wandered down the hall.

I'd barely started reading when a lab technician came and called for Hannah. The little 3-year-old trooper got up and silently followed the woman into the lab.

When Grandma returned, a couple exclaimed how the small child was so polite and well-mannered. Grandma just smiled and said she'd tell Hannah's mother. She added that it was only by the grace of God that they could raise Hannah that way.

I was called to an adjoining lab, and when I returned to the waiting room the lab technician was just coming back with Hannah. I didn't know what they'd done, but Hannah was calm and composed. The technician was telling Grandma what an exceptional child Hannah was—so independent and polite. Grandma smiled again, taking it in stride.

Suddenly I wished we could go back and finish the piggy story. There was something very special about Hannah. She was beauty, poise, and graciousness all wrapped up in one tiny bundle. And she was oblivious to it all.

The Pharisees would have been most uncomfortable around Hannah. But Jesus would have taken her on His lap and told the rest of us we needed to become like her to enter His kingdom. Except I become as Hannah, Lord.

DAWNA BEAUSOLEIL

Come Soon, Lord Jesus

When Jesus heard it, He said to them, "Those who are well have no need of a physician, but those who are sick. I did not come to call the righteous, but sinners, to repentance." Mark 2:17, NKJV.

JOE JUST DIED." The nurse spoke softly on the other end of the phone line.

"I'm coming." I pulled myself off the sofa in the doctor's lounge where I'd been sleeping. *Why do these things always happen when I'm on call?* I thought to myself. For 18 days Joe had lain on the hospital bed becoming increasingly yellow and confused as his tired liver refused to function. Almost 30 years of consistent alcohol use had taken its toll.

I listened for heartbeats or breath sounds. There were none. I looked down at the handsome face. His brown skin was now bronze with the yellow jaundice caused by his failing liver. I looked at the nurse who had quietly tiptoed into the room behind me. There were tears in her eyes and voice. "I went to school with Joe," she said. "He was so smart. What a waste."

I couldn't get my mind off Joe's useless death. He and his two cousins were homeless alcoholics. George had died only weeks before as Joe, Jim, and I stood at his bedside. I had begged Joe and Jim to give up alcohol, warning them of the consequences that awaited them.

Although he was an unregenerate alcoholic, I still never heard anyone in town say anything bad about Joe. They all had a memory to share—mostly about Joe in his earlier days, dressed in a white shirt and bow tie, driving the local bread truck. Everybody agreed he was smart, handsome, and likable.

Stories are supposed to have happy endings. This one doesn't—at least not now. I thought about Jesus. The Bible doesn't talk about it, but there must have been alcoholics among the scores who came to Jesus. Did He touch them and heal them of their addictions as He healed the blind and lame? Once Joe had told me he was a believer. My husband, Joe's usual physician, had spoken to him of Jesus as he lay dying. What had his response been? Did he see the healing hand of the Savior and a life beyond the grave that was free of alcohol? I don't know.

I do know that now I pray even harder for Jesus to return soon; to return and end the needless death and pain that sin has dealt our sickened world.

Please, Jesus, take away the hurt in the lives of so many of Your children. "Even so, come quickly, Lord Jesus."

SHERRY SHRESTHA

Waiting for God

Be still before the Lord, and wait patiently for him. Ps 37:7, NRSV.

SOMEONE ONCE SAID THAT the most popular word in the Old Testament is the word *wait.* And it is probably the least popular word in today's world. Who wants to wait? We want everything instantly!

My husband hates to wait in traffic. Two minutes longer behind a red light or a line of traffic than is acceptable to him and out comes the map to find another route. He hates waiting. I have to admit that I don't tend to have a problem waiting for traffic, but I do find it hard to wait for God to work when I need an answer to a problem now!

And yet part of trusting God is to wait for Him to act. Think of some of our Bible friends. Noah had to wait until God was ready to open the heavens to experience the flood. Abraham waited until he was old enough to be a grandfather to become a father. Simeon waited all of his life to hold the baby Jesus.

Waiting is hard, isn't it? The Bible tells us people have always had to wait for God to act—He acts only when the time is right. The Bible also tells us that those people who waited for God were never disappointed, but those who got tired of waiting always walked away empty.

There's a Bible passage that helps me when I become tired of waiting for God to act on my behalf: "I waited patiently for the Lord; he inclined to me and heard my cry . . . and set my feet upon a rock and gave me a firm place to stand. He put a new song in my mouth, a song of praise to our God" (Ps. 40:1-3, RSV).

It's so comforting to know that as well as hearing my cry, God turns to look at me. He gives me His full attention. He cares about what is going on in my life, and He will answer my cries in such a way that I will want to sing and praise Him. Surely that's something worth waiting for!

Trust God. Be patient. Wait for Him to turn to you and put a new song in your heart. You can rely upon Him to do just that!

MARY BARRETT

Of Course He Loves Me

Ask the Lord your God for a sign, whether in the deepest depths or in the highest heights. Isa. 7:11, NIV.

I FACED A NEW PHASE in my life and felt very sad and alone as I considered the many difficulties I faced, and those that I would have to confront. I prayed to God, asking that He show me in some way that I wasn't alone, that He was with me. In my prayer I told Him that I needed something different and unusual, and I promised Him that I'd pay close attention to everything that I came in contact with during the following day.

The entire day I was attentive, but nothing happened. I was disappointed. As I looked out my kitchen window at some trees, remembering my prayer from the previous night, I said, "No, Lord! I see Your handiwork there, but this wasn't what I asked for. I want something special for me. I need this!" Night fell, and as I was eating dinner the doorbell rang insistently. Frightened, I ran to answer the door. It was my nodding-acquaintance neighbor. She was euphoric, inviting me to her apartment right then. I accepted her invitation without question.

"Look what happened!" she exclaimed. "This plant only blooms once a year, and when it does there is only one flower. Look here! I have seven flowers!"

I thought the flowers were beautiful, and I'd never seen flowers that bloomed on the end of the leaf. It was really amazing! Still euphoric, my neighbor said, "Climb up there and see what is in my fern!" I obeyed, and came face to face with the two attentive eyes of a mother bird. She seemed to say, "I am in my house. Do not dare to bother me." I climbed down.

Not wanting to be impolite, I forced a smile and thanked my neighbor and returned to my apartment. I felt too frustrated to enthusiastically appreciate all that she had shown me. After all, God seemed to have forgotten me and had not answered my prayer. I prayed and fell asleep.

Suddenly something woke me. *O Lord! Forgive me for not having noticed You! My prayer has been miraculously answered in two different ways, and I did not recognize the answer. Please forgive me. O marvelous, eternal God, You are real! Give me sensibility to perceive You, even though my sins insist on obscuring our relationship.*

FEB STABENOW

Too Late

Later, when the other five returned, they stood outside, calling, "Sir, open the door for us!" But he called back, "Go away! It is too late!" So stay awake and be prepared, for you do not know the date or moment of my return. Matt. 25:11-13, TLB.

THE BIONUTRITIONIST WAS in town for the weekend, so I decided to consult him. I called for an appointment and was told by the receptionist that I should be there by 6:30 on Monday evening.

Monday sped by so rapidly that before I realized it, 6:30 was not far off. I hastened my preparations; but one of our cars needed some attention that would delay me, and the other one required a trip to the gas station. Also, I'd promised to pick up a friend who also needed a consultation. Needless to say, when I arrived at the doctor's office it was after 6:30. There were lights inside and I could hear movements and voices, but the door was locked. I knocked tentatively at first, and then more loudly. I thought of finding a telephone to call and say, "My name is on the list, and I am just outside the door."

Just as I was about to leave, the door opened to release the one who must have been the last patient. Hope sprang up in my heart. I didn't think they would turn me away; after all, the doctor sometimes works as late as 11:30 some nights, but the attendant told me that they were closed and that I should have been there at 6:30.

Like the foolish virgins, I had come too late. I thanked him and left, forcing myself to feel nonchalant about it. However, nibbling at the edge of my mind was the disturbing thought that I was shut out because I had not done what was required of me. I remembered an old hymn: "Just outside the door, so near and yet so far." It really bothered my mind. What if that had been the gate to heaven? I would be outside now. I thought of all the things I could have left undone during the day, but now it was too late.

Dear Lord, help me to be aware of the times in which I live so that heaven's gate will not close with me outside. CANDACE SPRAUVE

Can't Change the Past

Can the Ethiopian change his skin, or the leopard his spots? then may ye also do good that are accustomed to do evil. Jer. 13:23.

AS I LOOK BACK over my life, all I can say to God is "I'm sorry." I see how I have let Him down time and again, yet He keeps forgiving me and allowing me to live another day to get closer to Him. If only I'd been faithful to my baptismal vow. If only there was a time machine I could step into and undo the wrongs and make things right. If only I had listened to the Lord when He said that sin is pleasurable for a season (Heb. 11:25). The only thing I can say now is: "If only."

I read a book that spoke of the remorse Adam and Eve felt when the Lord told them that Eden would no longer be their home. In essence they told the Lord they were sorry and would never disobey Him again if He would just let them stay in Eden, but the answer was no. The Lord had forgiven them their sin, but they had lost the special blessing He had wanted them to have. Ishmael, the first son of Abraham, turned away from the Lord and his father's teachings. He later repented and came back to the Lord, but the stamp of character given to his posterity remained.

What can I say to those whom I've led astray by my influence, even though I've repented and come back to the Lord? I see where my actions have caused others not to believe the message I was presenting. Adam and Eve's sin affected others. Ishmael's sin affected others. And my sin affected others. The only thing I can say to those in my past is "Please forgive me."

I'm sure I'm not the only one who has something in their past needing to be erased or forgotten. God in His wisdom allows us to remember what we've done so we can see how He has brought us out of the situation. "Old things are passed away; . . . all things," the Bible says, "are become new" (2 Cor. 5:17).

Now all I can say is: *Thank God!*

I cannot change the past, but I have a new future. So do you. By God's grace I can begin again, for I am a "new creature." So can you.

TRUDY DUNCAN

Glorious Reward

But as it is written, Eye hath not seen, nor ear heard, neither have entered into the heart of man, the things which God hath prepared for them that love him. 1 Cor. 2:9.

EARLY ONE COLD DAWN two friends, their three small children, and I left for a rural area to stay for several days. In just a few hours we reached our destination. After settling in, someone suggested a hike that would lead us to an area where various types of fruits and vegetables were grown. That suggestion really filled me with enthusiasm.

It was still very early when the six of us left, walking one behind the other along the path. After walking for some time, we talked about when God's people left Egypt and continued through the desert in the direction of the Promised Land. I mentioned that I expected to receive a reward at the end of our journey—a recompense for the effort that I was making, because the wind was blowing and it was very cold. Wet, tall grass whipped our legs. We faced anthills, jumped large water puddles, and stepped on thorns. Really, it was not so easy to reach our destination.

At a certain point we stopped on top of a very high hill and looked behind us. Off in the distance the sun shimmered on the horizon in all of its beauty. "Oh, how marvelous!" I exclaimed. An extensive green area spread out before us, but it began to take on a golden glow through the strong influence of the sun.

I called again, "How many marvelous things our God offers us!" It was an incomparable, majestic, indescribable color! We remained there several minutes, observing that scene. Finally someone broke the silence. "Behold, a glimpse of our 'reward'!"

Sometime later we could clearly see our reward from a distance. What an abundance of fruit and vegetables given generously by the Lord, Creator of all things!

I've never forgotten that scene. I compare it to our Christian life. We step on thorns, we hurt ourselves, we are whipped by difficulties and struggles. However, we know that at the end of this journey is a glorious reward: a crown, and a beautiful country where there will be no more crying or tears of pain, and we will live forever with the Lord.

Lord, I praise You for Your love, for Your marvelous works, and the beauty that enchants our eyes and gives joy to our life. All of these blessings come from Your hands.

DIVONETE DE SOUZA RAMOS LIMA

The Conveyed or the Conveyance?

Do not love the world or anything in the world. If anyone loves the world, the love of the Father is not in him. For everything in the world—the cravings of sinful man, the lust of his eyes and the boasting of what he has and does—comes not from the Father but from the world. 1 John 2:15, 16, NIV.

IT WAS MY TURN to speak on stage at our school Christmas program, and the poem I'd carefully memorized had been rehearsed perfectly for the teacher. I wanted to be perfect again. All eyes were on me, dressed in shiny blue satin, as I stepped lightly to my place beneath the bright lights.

The memorized words flowed beautifully from my young voice with all the fervor of emotion they portrayed. I was the center of attention for seven glorious minutes, and I bowed as I left amid a thunderous applause—proud of my performance.

It was my secret desire to be a "star" like some I'd seen in pictures and magazines of those late thirties. But in this school program I had reminded the audience of the greatest event in history, the greatest gift ever given, our Savior's birth; and I was taking all the credit for simply repeating the beautiful old story in a poem. It was the message, not the "me"-dium, they had applauded. And it took me a few years to realize that.

Jesus rode the dusty roads on a young donkey to old Jerusalem on His triumphal entry. Some people in the crowd spread their cloaks on the road, and others cut branches from the trees to spread before Him. They shouted, "Hosanna to the Son of David! Blessed is He who comes in the name of the Lord!" (Matt. 21:9, NIV).

I wonder if the donkey might have thought that all that excitement was attention for him, not the Son of God on his back. The donkey simply carried the good news to the people. And I, too, had only been the donkey, not the rider.

I still love to tell the old, old story but in a more humble way, without taking the credit for the results it brings forth. That credit belongs to God through His Holy Spirit.

Dear Lord, I pray for humility as Thy humble servant bringing the gospel to others in whatever way is assigned to me today. BESSIE SIEMENS LOBSIEN

It's Whom You Know

[God] has spoken to us through his Son to whom he has given everything, . . . he made the world and everything there is. . . . He regulates the universe by the mighty power of his command. He . . . died to cleanse us . . . and then sat . . . beside the great God of heaven. Thus he became far greater than the angels. Heb. 1:2-4, TLB.

SOMETIMES WE PICTURE Jesus as the loving Man who healed the sick and blessed the children, but in the verses above, His position and power are being described. He created the world and all that there is, and rules it by the power of His command. Yet He died to save me!

Often we fail to see or be in awe of the power of Jesus. Sometimes we make Him too common—too much like us. Other times we fear Him and place Him so far above ourselves that we can't approach Him. Our text made me think of this example in my life.

I was a few grades behind a fellow who, in his eleventh year, made this statement in the year book: "Rome wasn't built in a day, but I wasn't the foreman on that job." That truly captured his outlook on life. He went on to "high" positions in our denomination. To many church members his name would conjure up a picture of "top leadership," someone with "power" to get things done, someone above their realm of friendship or acquaintance.

After 25 years of living abroad, he has brought his family back home. He still talks to his friends from way back. We socialize together, exchange meals, and celebrate family occasions. His job requires decisions, power, and authority. But when he comes home he is still just like us. He works on the family farm, his kids argue about who will take out the garbage, the housecat has kittens, the dog wants to be among the guests as they eat under the shade tree. While sharing time with this family we don't tremble and think about their position and power. It's the same way with Jesus. We need to be aware of and respect His position. We need to remember that He made our world. He commands the stars, the wind, and even the demons. But He is just one prayer away. We have a Friend in high places, someone who can help us. So often, though, we fail to maintain the friendship or don't trust Him enough to ask for the big things—such things as faith, courage, and a desire to share salvation with someone each day. Today let's ask for the big things, including His power!

Elizabeth Versteegh Odiyar

The Greatest Gift

There is no greater way to show love for a friend than to give your life for him. John 15:13, Clear Word.

THE CONFERENCE CONVENTION that was taking place in South Australia provided an affordable day trip to Kangaroo Island. Several small planes were chartered to fly the group there and back, and cars were hired to tour the island's scenic countryside. It was all an exciting prospect for adventure!

I've never had a desire to go on a plane; however, I was greatly tempted to share in the trip with my friends. Before I knew it, I had paid my fare and with nervous anticipation and a prayer for protection waited the time of departure. In no time the plane, a six-seat, twin-engine Piper, swept off the ground into the sky where I had no chance to change my mind. Before long, we touched down safely.

We had a great day investigating the island's rugged coast and contrasting landscape. There were kangaroos, koalas, and flocks of Cape Barron geese in plenty to enjoy, as well as the thrill of walking close to the seals lying along the beach.

All good things come to an end, for we had to be back at the airport at a set time. Everyone chattered happily about their experiences of the day while awaiting the planes' arrival. My friend and I were talking to those leaving on the next plane. When it came time to go, two brothers in that group offered us their seats; they didn't mind waiting for the next flight.

As we approached Adelaide, the lights looked magical from the air. Although I was relieved to touch ground, I was glad I had participated. However, very sadly, the next plane never arrived, and all aboard died in a crash. I lost dear friends and two brothers who gave not only their seats but their lives for me. Because of this my four small children still have a mother.

Only the Lord has answers. He gave His life for us all, and I look forward to the day when I can thank Him and the men who gave me the opportunity to rear my children.

Certainly they are awaiting their next flight, which will be heaven-bound. Christ will be the pilot, and I pray I'll be with them. Won't you join us?

LYN WELK

Things I've Learned in a Retirement Complex

Finally, brethren, whatsoever things are true, . . . honest, . . . just, . . . pure, . . . lovely, . . . of good report . . . , think on these things. Phil. 4:8.

FOR THE PAST FIVE years I've lived in a comfortable retirement apartment complex. Included are three delicious vegetarian meals, furnished linens, and a weekly housekeeper. The 115 residents are pleasant and congenial. We eat together in the dining room; ride together on our private bus; and enjoy exercise, vespers, and much more together. But even in this cheerful setting there are residents yearning for love and a sense of belonging. As I've thought about them, I've begun searching for things I should learn. Here are 13, and my list is still growing:

1. Think of some good quality in every person I encounter—and share it.
2. Do not try to see through others; rather, see others through.
3. Focus on the other person with your heart. Pay attention.
4. Remember that God has a special purpose for me that no one else can fulfill.
5. The task ahead of us is never as great as the Power behind us.
6. God is not so much concerned with my ability as with my availability.
7. I am only responsible for the effort, not the outcome.
8. If we begin to weave threads of caring around someone, God will give us the thread.
9. We can give without loving, but we can't love without giving.
10. Charm is the ability to make people like you—and like themselves better when they are with you.
11. Our arms are the only ones God has to hug His children.
12. Learn the magic three-word formula for peace of mind: "It doesn't matter."
13. Balance each negative thought with a positive one, and repeat it often.

On his deathbed Oscar Hammerstein wrote a short note to Mary Martin just before she went on stage in South Pacific. It simply said: "Dear Mary, a bell's not a bell until you ring it. A song's not a song until you sing it. Love in your heart is not put there to stay. Love isn't love until you give it away."

After all, isn't that what the sacrifice of Jesus is all about?

LORRAINE HUDGINS-HIRSCH

Peace on Earth, Goodwill Toward Men

Glory to God in the highest, and on earth peace to men on whom his favor rests. Luke 2:14, NIV.

CHRISTMAS IS ONLY days away, and the noise and bustle of activity are reaching a crescendo. People throng the pavements, cars jostle for parking spaces, checkout queues take forever. Inside, the huge shopping complexes reverberate with the sound of red-coated Santa's "Ho-hoing," babies crying, and excited children screaming to be heard above the canned Christmas carols.

Minor mishaps occur by the minute. A woman pushing a loaded supermarket trolley collides with her counterpart coming from an opposite direction. A harassed father knocks over a display when trying to control a couple of whimpering toddlers. Meanwhile, their mother makes secret purchases. Somebody else's child clutches at my freshly dry-cleaned skirt with ice-creamy hands.

Out on the sidewalk scarcely audible through the noise, young celebrators optimistically sing, twang, or tottle "Jingle Bells." Brazenly jaywalking pedestrians escape death by inches.

If there is any time of the year when the whole populace should be stressed to death, it is Christmas. Yet there is surprisingly little ill-temper displayed at this season. Even though most people scarcely know what they are celebrating, there is a general air of good fellowship abroad.

"Oh well, it's Christmas," our usually dour neighbor shrugged at 7:00 a.m. when he found that the paperboy had not made his usual delivery.

"The post office must be handling millions of items right now," Granny said when her pension check failed to arrive on time. "I can manage until next year!" She cackled at her little joke.

"It's simply gorgeous, and I wanted it so badly." The teenager beside me grinned when the person three places ahead of her bought the last top of its kind in the shop. "I guess she's going to a party too."

Wouldn't life be wonderful if we carried this spirit of goodwill throughout the whole year?

GOLDIE DOWN

Shame on Bethlehem

And she brought forth her firstborn son, and wrapped him in swaddling clothes, and laid him in a manger; because there was no room for them in the inn. Luke 2:7.

THE EVENING WAS DARK and cold as we drove across Boston to the south side. Throughout the city the heavy traffic roared and groaned as streets were filled with workers and shoppers, all fighting for space on the expressway. We were on our way to a church Christmas concert, looking for peace.

We slipped into the colonial-style church festooned with holiday decorations. Garlands and wreaths were attached high up along the ceilings. A 10-foot pine tree stood grandly to one side of the platforms. The music and spiritual words caressed our hearts.

The next soloist on the program—one of my favorites—composes her own songs. She stood up with her guitar and sang, "Shame, Shame on Bethlehem." The haunting refrain took us back to the story of the man leading his donkey on which sat his pregnant wife, ready to deliver. He arrives in Bethlehem and looks for room. None is available. Everyone said, "No room in our inn," ignoring the distress and needs of the young couple. Finally, one innkeeper generously offers his stable, filled with straw and animals. We often sing "O Little Town of Bethlehem" and read Luke 2 from the Bible, becoming incensed that not one person could find room somewhere for this important couple. How could they be so indifferent to this wonderful birth soon to take place?

It was a sad state of affairs in Bethlehem. Listen: now she is singing about us. Christ comes knocking on the door of our hearts again and again, and sometimes we don't open the door. . . . We may share Bethlehem's shame. We too may have no room, filled as we are with our activities, work, and goals. There is no time to open the door, no room for Christ within. He knocks and waits at the door of our hearts.

Will our answer be "I have no room" or "Come in, Lord Jesus, and abide with me"? Shame, shame on Bethlehem. May it not be shame, shame on you or me.

DESSA WEISZ HARDIN

Lessons From a Pine Tree

Help us to understand how short our lives really are so we may fill our hearts with wisdom. Ps. 90:12, Clear Word.

SHE STOOD IN ALL her grandeur in a corner of the backyard of our vacation home. As in years past, she produced her long green needles and bulbous cones. Of all the pines around her, she was the tallest and most symmetrical.

Notwithstanding all her good qualities, she had a few that were annoying. Her dead needles littered the yard, as did her cones, some dropping into the swimming pool. During pollen season she excreted a yellow substance that floated seemingly everywhere, leaving a yellow residue and reeking havoc with those allergic to it. But when everything was said and done, her positives far outweighed her negatives.

In November we returned to our vacation home. Several days passed before either my husband or I looked at the pine tree. What a shock! She was dead! When we left in April she appeared to be robust and healthy—and now she is gone. Others who live in the area feel sure she was struck by lightning, since this is an area of frequent lightning strikes. Because she stood so close to the fence, we couldn't see all the way around her to tell if there was a split in her trunk to confirm our suspicions.

The unexpected death of our pine tree brought home in a vivid way my own mortality. Death often comes unexpectedly. I learned from the pine tree that it could happen to me also.

Each day is a gift from God. I have determined that every morning I will open my mind and my heart to my Creator, Sustainer, Redeemer, and Friend, greeting the day with eagerness. I will drink deeply of the joys of life and contend courageously with those issues that puzzle or grieve me. Treasuring each relationship, I will focus on being the best friend possible. May I also forgive easily, laugh much, sing God's praises often, and share my blessings unselfishly.

Father, thank You for this day You have given me. May I live it to the fullest, making You the center. May I share it with those within my sphere of influence in such a way that their lives may be enriched too. Amen.

Marian M. Hart

A Gift at Christmas

For God so loved the world, that he gave his only begotten Son. John 3:16.

WHENEVER THE CHRISTMAS and New Year holidays come, people are generally excited. According to popular beliefs in my part of the world, however, some people think that during this time all kinds of accidents may happen, and that it's natural that people die.

In December 2002 I went on furlough to Cameroon, my native land. For 13 years I'd not been with my relatives during the Christmas and New Year's holidays to give thanks to the Lord for His blessings. I was looking forward to a wonderful time.

I was happy to arrive in Douala, the business capital, but I had to go to Yaounde, the political capital, where most of my relatives live. To reach there, I could travel by train (which I don't like for personal reasons), travel by plane (which I find too expensive for such a short journey), or go by bus. This choice seemed more reasonable because the fares are not expensive, and I would have the opportunity to gaze at the wonderful scenery and the villages. Oh, how I miss them when I'm away!

I decided to take a bus belonging to a transportation company known for its trustworthiness. Breakfast and snacks are offered, and newspapers also. The drivers aren't supposed to speed, but I soon noticed that our driver seemed nervous, and he was speeding. He even passed another vehicle illegally. The host came to sit next to me. I started a conversation with her and told her about my concern. When I asked her what was wrong with the driver, she told me that the previous day he had spent his own money to pay a certain fee, thinking that he would be refunded by the owner since the payment was compulsory. To his great surprise, the owner refused to pay him back. The poor driver found himself penniless and couldn't afford a taxi to go back home. So he decided to drive anyway and was very unhappy.

I asked the host to tell him that there was a passenger who wanted to make reparation for the wrong. When the driver was informed of my good intention, his face brightened up, and he immediately started to behave differently.

It was a small gesture on my part, Lord, but at Christmastime that is all we can do. You gave the big Gift, and for that we give thanks, especially at Christmastime. ANGÈLE RACHEL NLO NLO

So This Is Christmas

Make a joyful noise unto the Lord, all the earth: make a loud noise, and rejoice, and sing praise. Ps. 98:4.

I ABSOLUTELY LOVE Christmas! I love the season, the bright lights, the decorations, the music, the sheer delight of the spirit of Christmas. Maybe it's my imagination, but people seem so much kinder and gentler at Christmastime. Even in the hustle and bustle of large shopping centers we see the display of unusual courtesy. Complete strangers smile and nod at each other in passing. Doors are held open when ordinarily they would be allowed to swing in your face.

Now it begs the question: why can't the spirit of Christmas live on throughout the year? Most people consider it quite tacky to leave Christmas lights up too far into January—at least to have them lit. If we sang Christmas carols in March and April, folks would consider us quite strange. But if we displayed the good graces of Christmas courtesy, kindness, happiness, and generosity throughout the year we would essentially be testifying to the true meaning of Christmas.

There is a Christmas carol that speaks of putting Christ back into Christmas. It seems that is the prescription this sin-sick world needs. I'm aware that many Christians do not celebrate Christmas because of its pagan connections; but I believe it is profitable for us to take the good things of Christmas and celebrate the joy they bring, while discarding the commercialism and other negative symbols.

One of my fondest childhood memories of Christmas is of a time I was a young girl living in my island home. My father had gone ahead to England. My mother was alone with five children, all under age 10. She became ill and was hospitalized. There were no relatives to care for us, but a neighbor came to our rescue. Although it was Christmastime, our hearts were very sad. I felt like an orphan until an aunt who lived some distance away heard of our predicament and came bearing gifts. The realization that we belonged to someone—that we were remembered and especially loved—brought overwhelming joy to us. In remembering the gifts now, I've concluded they were quite inexpensive, but what tremendous joy my aunt's visit and gifts brought! That single act of love endeared her to me. Thank you, Aunt Maud.

Thank You, God, for giving us the ultimate Christmas Gift—Your dear Son, Jesus Christ.

Avis Mae Rodney

The Best Gift

Eagerly desire the greater gifts. 1 Cor. 12:31, NIV.

IT WAS CHRISTMAS, and in our family it's usually a time when all members of the extended family are together—with no one missing. The only exception would be the years during which one sister and her family spend Christmas Day with the in-laws. At those times we are almost certainly all together for Boxing Day.

This year was going to be different. Our son, Mark, was working as a student volunteer with Adventist Development and Relief Agency in Albania and wouldn't be home for Christmas. We'd miss him as much as he would miss us. We spoke to him on the phone, but of course it wasn't the same.

On Christmas Eve our daughter, Emma, went out, saying she was driving into town to do some last-minute shopping. While she was out the phone rang. It was Mark. We chatted for some time and told him how much we were missing him. I told him Emma had been gone a lot longer than we had expected her to be.

Shortly after the phone call, we heard Emma at the door. She came into the living room, grinning mischievously. I noticed that someone else was obviously behind the door; but my husband, Frank, couldn't see this from where he was sitting. He almost fell off his chair in shock and surprise when Mark walked in!

What laughter, what joy there was in our house that day! When Frank was finally able to speak again he said, "This is the best Christmas present I could ever have! I don't want any ties or aftershave now!"

Isn't that what Christmas is all about? Two thousand years ago God gave Himself as the best gift ever! Humble shepherds, the aged Simeon, the prophet Anna, and Wise Men from the East were among the few who recognized Him as God's gift or rejoiced at the giving of this gift!

He gives us the same gift of Himself today, and all He wants us to do is accept and give Him our hearts in return. ANTONIA (ANN) CASTELLINO

With Gold, Frankincense, and Mirth

And when they had opened their treasures, they presented unto him gifts; gold, and frankincense, and myrrh. Matt. 2:11.

THE MORNING DEVOTIONAL speaker was serious, and the morning Scripture reading was done in all seriousness, too; but I clearly heard "And when they had opened their treasures, they presented unto him gifts; gold, and frankincense, and mirth." As he expounded at some length about the gifts we should bring to Christ at Christmas, I couldn't get the "mirth" out of my mind.

I wondered how much mirth there was for Mary, having to walk some 90 miles (150 kilometers) at the end of the third trimester of her pregnancy. (Or ride, if they even had a donkey. I think walking would have been more comfortable.) And where was the mirth in having no place to stay, and strangers attending the birth, and placing the new Baby in a manger—even if it did have clean straw in it.

I thought about this young mother looking down at the tiny Baby as she nursed him in the months that followed. What fears and concerns might she have had for this Child who was so different! What was going to happen when the neighborhood children taunted Him about being illegitimate? And what about the looks she had probably already endured as she went to the marketplace and the town well? She might have wondered where the "peace on earth" was.

And there certainly was no mirth a week later when they went up to Jerusalem to have the Baby dedicated. They didn't even have enough money for a regular sacrifice—they had to give the offering allowed for the poor people. And then Simon told her that "a sword will pierce your own soul too" (Luke 2:35, NIV). Scripture tells us that Mary "treasured up all these things and pondered them in her heart" (verse 19, NIV).

After a while things settled down. They moved into a house, and the Wise Men visited, bringing their gifts of gold and frankincense and myrrh. Then the word came that they must flee for their lives to Egypt. No mirth there.

For us, Christmas is family and food, bells and music, ribbons and gold and frankincense and mirth. For Mary and Joseph and the little baby Jesus it was anything but.

Lord Jesus, Immanuel, truly God with us, thank You so much for Your incredible gift and for the wonderful example of Mary, Your mother.

ARDIS DICK STENBAKKEN

Change for a Dollar

Dear friends, now we are children of God, and what we will be has not yet been made known. 1 John 3:2, NIV.

WHEN SHE STOOD UP, her voluminous figure commanded attention from her seventh-grade peers. She had listened attentively while several of them described an item most like them. Now it was her turn to talk.

Jo Ed held up a crumpled dollar bill that, like her life, was broken and torn. At 14 she had already had her fill of adult experiences. Boasting several abortions and a bad attitude, she was the pariah of the class. Jo Ed held the dollar bill at arm's length and proceeded to revel in her likeness to it. "I am like this dollar bill because I can go anywhere. People like me. I get handled a lot. I am popular. I get all the attention, just like this buck."

Now it was time for her peers to respond. No one said a word. No one ever said a word to Jo Ed; for if they did, her bad attitude would nail them to the wall. After about two minutes of silence, she spoke up. "Don't anybody have anything to say?"

From somewhere in the room a nervous teen began walking toward Jo Ed, hands in pockets. The room took on an executioner's chill. No matter what he would say or do, he was going to get it. Gazing straight into her eyes like an old sage, his words found their mark: "I am sorry about your description of yourself as being cheap, dirty, and handled a lot—like that dollar bill you are holding." As he spoke he carefully pulled four quarters from his pocket, handed them to her, and pulled the dollar from her hand. He continued: "But like this dollar, you can be changed. You have value. You have worth. It's all in how you look at it."

He turned to greet the applause of the class. Jo Ed cried that day and said absolutely nothing. She was different after that. She got along with the students, and some even invited her to eat lunch with them. The young man's kind words transformed her life.

Christ wants to trade His "change" for our soiled and dirty dollar of a life. He wants to take what we are and change us into what we can become through Him. He yearns to restore worth and value to us. He wants His words "I have loved you with an everlasting love" to find their mark in our hearts. Try Christ for a change.

AMY SMITH MAPP

Love Is a Verb

Freely you have received, freely give. Matt. 10:8, NIV.

"FAITH WITHOUT WORKS is dead." The phrase wandered through my mind as I listened to the speaker talking about our church's participation with the local cold-weather shelter. I'd grown up in a Christian family and heard stuff like this my whole life. But for some reason, lately I'd been struck by it; my faith was a cushy-pew faith. A smile and handshake at church faith. A yes-I-know-about-the-needy-but-I'm-so-busy-and-it-doesn't-really-affect-me faith. An empty faith.

My husband and I discussed the importance of community outreach several times, and we both said we'd like to get involved—if only we knew where to start. God was listening in on the conversation, because He brought the opportunity to us. All we had to do was sign up!

I admit to being nervous, not knowing what to expect, and even went into it a little aloof. After all, I was the Christian, and they were, well, homeless. I was there to do my Christian duty, right?

Opportunities to help at the shelter arose several times over the winter, and I never failed to come away humbled and blessed beyond measure. There's a blessing in serving that can't be had by sitting in a pew. It opened my eyes—every time—to the humanity, the reality, the love of my Jesus. He would be right there handing out hope with the sandwiches.

There we met people who were "better" Christians than most church goers I know, and others who would curse at the mere mention of God. We met men who were too ashamed to look me in the eye, and one who thought he was Woody Woodpecker. I met a woman beaten so badly she could hardly speak, and a rape victim trying to come to grips with the fact that she is probably HIV positive. I met people who were just people without a house—and saw an openness, honesty, and gratitude that is too often veiled in polite society. People. Individuals. Children of my Father God.

Your life is a sermon; it's up to you what gets preached. Talking the talk can do more harm than good if you're not willing to walk the walk. I'm so thankful that I was given the opportunity to take a few steps in my walk and go so far outside my comfort zone. Helping at the shelter doesn't make me better than anyone else. But I'm a better me than I was before. I went to give a blessing, but the one I received was twice as big. God's funny that way.

Vicki Macomber Redden

Ready to Go Home

I can do all things through Christ which strengtheneth me. Phil. 4:13.

THERE ARE DAYS WHEN the hours rush by. Meals to get, beds to change, clothes to wash, gardens to tend, letters to write—endless amounts of work to be done. Sometimes I wonder if my priorities are in the right place. Does it really matter if the house looks neat or if I get the books processed for our church library? Does it really matter if the school board agenda is neatly typed? Does anyone really care? Maybe I can just scribble the agenda or ignore the books and do them later.

Do other people have days like this? Usually I am full of energy, looking forward to my morning devotions. I'm ready to face whatever challenges the day has in store for me. Sometimes it's the head teacher asking for advice, or asking if I can substitute-teach that day if one of our three teachers is ill and no one else is available. As school board chair I try to help wherever I can.

Sometimes it's a church member looking for an address or a phone number. As church clerk I usually have the information they need. Sometimes it's a radio station or one of the local papers asking for clarification on an article I've written, or a radio spot announcement that I've faxed to them. (I am communication leader.) Or it may be one of my Bible class members asking for information on the lesson for that day. And did I also mention that I'm chair of the building committee and that the state fire marshal is mandating that we have a fire hydrant? Sometimes, with all the many hats I wear, I am overwhelmed and say: "Dear Lord, when are You coming to take us home? Is this what retirement is supposed to be? Help, Lord; help me to say no to all those jobs when nominating committee time comes around again."

But then I calm down and remember that my mother-in-law is going on 99. She needs me; my husband and three dogs need me. And, of course, it matters how things are done—I'm working for the Lord. The Lord does things in an orderly fashion, and I must do the same. Tomorrow will be a better day; Jesus will see me through; He will come back to take us home. He promised, and His Word is sure.

You promised to make all things possible, Lord. Now I need help with my priorities in order to know what it is You want me to do today.

LORAINE F. SWEETLAND

God's Healing Power

Is anyone among you suffering? Let him pray. Is anyone cheerful? Let him sing psalms. Is anyone among you sick? Let him call for the elders of the church, and let them pray over him anointing him with oil in the name of the Lord. And the prayer of faith will save the sick. James 5:13-15.

THE NEW YEAR'S PARTY was in full swing. Nearly the whole church was in our head elder's home awaiting midnight to welcome in the new year. I was enjoying myself when I suddenly felt my neck stiffen and an excruciating pain develop in my shoulders. In tears I asked my husband to take me home. Not realizing what pain I was in, he begged me to wait a while. I said I'd lie down in the car and wait. It seemed an eternity before he finally came and drove us home!

It was a sleepless night as I agonized in pain. I really thought I was going to die. I searched my heart and asked God to prepare me to meet Him. The following three days were holidays, so it was the fifth day before I could see our doctor. I underwent an MRI, and the doctor discovered that I had spurs on my shoulders. He said that I had to undergo surgery; meanwhile, I could take some painkillers. Three times he changed the prescription, and three times I went back to him because my stomach couldn't tolerate the medication. Finally he said that I could take Tylenol, although Tylenol was too mild for my pain. I asked, "Doctor, how long should I take Tylenol?"

"For life," he replied.

I went home and said to myself, *I'm not taking any Tylenol; I'm going to ask God to heal me. If He doesn't see fit that I be healed, I'll ask for tolerance for pain.* And that's what I did. I did something else, too. I asked my husband to call the head elder, and I requested anointing.

The elder graciously complied with my request. The three of us—my husband, the head elder, and I—talked about the conditions mentioned about God's hearing our prayers. We knelt in our family room and prayed most earnestly for healing. Then both men anointed me. I trusted God would answer our prayer of faith, and that was just what God, our greatest physician, did. I ruled out surgery and painkillers. I claimed God's promises in James 5:13-15. And God, the heavenly healer, with His saving grace and power showed He was still in control of my life.

OFELIA A. PANGAN

Off With the Old, On With the New!

He has covered me with the robe of righteousness. Isa. 61:10, NRSV.

WHEN I WAS A child I was enamored with my mother's closetful of shoes. I hoped one day to try them on and actually wear them; but alas, when that age arrived, my feet had outgrown my mother's size. Being tall and having feet to match, I've learned several things *not* to do when looking for new shoes. One is never to buy shoes from a catalog. I always ended up returning them because they just didn't fit right.

Finding a shoe store locally that carries my size is a challenge. I've learned the hard way—when I do find something that I like and that feels comfortable, I must buy it then, because it's usually gone long before a sale arrives. I feel really fortunate when I'm able to find shoes I like on sale—and they turn out to be comfortable.

I've discovered that the best place in my area to find shoes is at Nordstrom's. Even if I've tried the shoes on in the store, too often after wearing them for a few hours they don't feel so good anymore. All of which leaves me convinced that women's shoes are designed by men who dislike women! I have many shoes, some of which are marvelously comfortable—and too many that are not.

I wish shoes could be like the wonderful robe that Jesus offers each of us. It's proven to be neat, glorious, and comfortable. Just as shoes protect our feet from rough pavement and rocky terrain, so God's robe protects us as we go through life—up the mountains and down into the valleys of despair. Too often we look in all the wrong places to find this satisfying covering; or we settle for a substitute, which ends up being a waste of time and energy. God's precious designer garment is only offered at one time: when we approach the King of glory. He is the one who provides the best and most complete clothing we can ever hope for. This robe of righteousness is freely given to all who accept Jesus as their Savior.

Dear Lord, come into my heart today. Clear out all the old rubbish in my heart and mind and put Your new robe on me so that I may represent You more clearly each day to come. I praise You for the perfect fit.

PEGGY HARRIS

AUTHOR BIOGRAPHIES

Karen Abdool, whose home is Trinidad and Tobago in the Caribbean, came to the United States to attend Loma Linda University. She is completing the M.D./Ph.D. program at Howard University in Washington, D.C. She did her dissertation research in cancer immunology and plans to become a medical missionary and do cancer research. **Mar. 30, July 25.**

Betty J. Adams is a retired teacher with three grown children, two stepchildren, and seven grandchildren. She is active in community service, prayer ministry, women's ministries, and contributes to her church newsletter; she has been published in *Guide* magazine. Her interests include traveling, gardening, writing, mission trips, and her grandchildren. **Jan. 10, Nov. 2.**

Priscilla Adonis has been married to the same man for 35 years. The women's ministries coordinator at her local church in South Africa, she enjoys sending notes of encouragement; she has also written for the devotional book and sent recipes to various cooking publications. Her daughters live in California; she has one grandson. **Jan. 1, July 1, Sept. 30.**

Sally j. Aken-Linke resides in Norfolk, Nebraska, with her husband, John. Her experiences as a single mother raising two children, and a strong Christian faith, provide a basis for her poetry and short stories. Sally and her husband are active in air medical transport, and are nearly finished building an airplane. She enjoys reading, music, and working with young people. **June 20.**

Linda Alinsod enjoys life in Maryland, but she has also worked in California, Germany, and Zimbabwe. Ten years ago she had a bout with cancer, so praises God for His continued care. Linda is originally from the Philippines; when she has spare time she likes to read. **Feb. 18.**

Maxine Williams Allen resides in Orlando, Florida, with her husband and two small sons. She has her own computer and business consulting company, Tecnocentric; she loves to travel, meet people, and experience different cultures. Her hobbies include writing, reading, and computers. She has special interest in family, children's, and women's ministries. **Feb. 28, Aug. 20.**

Mary M. J. Wagoner Angelin and her husband, Randy, live in Ooltewah, Tennessee. Her hobbies are therapeutic humor, exercising, hiking, writing, and vegan cooking. A stay-at-home mom to two children, she works one day a week as a social worker. She volunteers with the Make-A-Wish Foundation, deaf services, and Regeneration, a Christ-centered 12-step group. **Jan. 14.**

Beryl Aseno is from Nairobi, Kenya, but has worked in Somalia with an international NGO and now is in Togo. Beryl has a master's degree in communications; she enjoys writing, cross-cultural experiences, reading, mission projects, and keeping a daily journal. An accomplished swimmer, she made it to the nationals in her country in 1992. **Sept. 21.**

Audrey Balderstone and her husband operate a garden-landscaping company in England, and both are heavily involved in church and community activities.

Audrey raises thousands of dollars for charity through flower festivals, and is also president of ASI Europe, a business and professionals' association with chapters throughout Europe. **Feb. 15, Nov. 25.**

Jennifer M. Baldwin writes from Australia, where she works in clinical risk management at Sydney Adventist Hospital. She enjoys church involvement, travel and writing, and has contributed to a number of church publications. **Oct. 1, Nov. 11.**

A. Bara (nickname is Molly) is an office secretary in the Northern India Union of her church in New Delhi, where she and her husband, education director of the same union, have served since 1999. They have two daughters: Preeti, studying at Christian Medical College; and Tripti, a student at the boarding school in Roorkee. Her hobbies are listening to music and making friends. **July 12.**

Mary Barrett is paid by the local church to work in pastoral ministry with her husband. She is also a writer and a speaker. She and her husband have two daughters. For relaxation, she loves to be with family and friends. **Feb. 8, Apr. 16, Dec. 11.**

Dawna Beausoleil lives with her hubby, John, in an isolated area of northern Ontario. Besides loving rural life, she enjoys their cats, reading, singing, scrapbooking, and flower gardening. She's been published in many magazines and books. **Dec. 9.**

Annie B. Best is a retired public schoolteacher and mother of two grown children. She enjoys being with her three grandchildren, reading, and listening to music. She has worked as a leader in the cradle roll and kindergarten departments of her church, which she enjoys and finds rewarding. Her husband of 53 years passed away in November of 2001. **May 22, Nov. 21.**

Dinorah Blackman lives in Panama with her husband and her little girl Imani. They own an educational consulting agency. **Feb. 4.**

Sandra Nelson Blackmer is news editor for the *Adventist Review*. She has also worked as editorial assistant for the *Adult Bible Study Guide* and as communication director for the Michigan Conference. Sandra enjoys reading, hiking, and spending time with her husband and grown daughter, as well as their family pets. **June 11.**

Juli Blood, a first-time contributor, has been happily married to Gary since 1994. They were missionaries in Korea for a year. Juli fills her days with reading and writing. She has a cat, Sandy, who didn't enjoy Korea as much as she and her husband did. **Jan. 31, Apr. 5, Oct. 7.**

Evelyn Greenwade Boltwood is a busy wife, mother of two adult children, career woman, student, Pathfinder area coordinator, member of the National Kidney Foundation Board of Upstate New York, and serves on the Kidney Kids Committee. She is a member of Akoma, an African-American community gospel choir. She loves reading and exploring God's world. **Feb. 27.**

Wendy Bradley, as a deaconess, is busy with visiting and keeping in touch with present and past church members. She loves writing for pleasure and keeping in touch with friends. She has recently taken up cross-stitch. She loves going for strolls with her husband; they hope to spend more time together and visit the many beauty spots of England when he retires soon. **Mar. 1.**

Ani Köhler Bravo is a retired secretary who worked at the Brazil Publishing House for 24 years. She returned to college for a bachelor's degree in translating and interpretation. She lives with her husband and son in Eugenheiro, Coelho, Brazil. Her pastimes include reading, cooking, playing the piano, entertaining her friends, writing, and church involvement. **Sept. 16, Nov. 20.**

Carol Bryant is a qualified R.G.N. and midwife, but at present is a stay-at-home mom who is on a four-year open university degree course. She has a 12-year-old son with whom she enjoys cycling and other fun activities. She is a soloist and pianist and enjoys singing and playing songs of praise to our Lord. She also enjoys composing songs, writing poems, and playing piano for the children's department at her church. **Aug. 23.**

Nyarangi M. Bundi is a first-time contributor. She writes from Kendubay, Kenya, Africa. **Dec. 4.**

Darlene Ytredal Burgeson is a retired sales manager. Her hobbies include sending notes and seasonal cards to shut-ins and people living alone. She also enjoys writing, gardening, and photography. **May 15, July 24, Sept. 2.**

Elma Bernhardt de Cardinali is originally from Uruguay, but lives in Argentina. She is a retired primary school director who now teaches Bible classes at the Instituto Adventista Florida in Buenos Aires. She enjoys music, swimming, working on a computer, and attending literary workshops. **Nov. 4.**

Dorothy Wainwright Carey is a happy wife, mother, and grandmother. When she retired from the federal government several years ago, she was privileged to become involved in all levels of church committees. Her interests include church activities, nature, animals, people, and reading. **May 31.**

Beth Carlson is an active wife, mother, and grandmother who is a compulsive keeper of a two-line daily diary "so I know where I've been." **Apr. 27, Aug. 26.**

Antonia (Ann) Castellino was born in the West Indies and moved to London with her parents at an early age. She now lives in the English Midlands with her husband. She is active in her local church, leads Bible studies, and is part of a house group seeking to plant a new church. She is an elementary teacher and aspiring artist. **Apr. 20, Dec. 1, Dec. 25.**

Aucely Corrêa Fernandes Chagas is a nurse with a master's degree in collective health. She works in the hospital in Campo Grande, Brazil. She is coordinator and professor in the graduate nursing course at the Dom Bosco University. She enjoys listening to music, handicrafts, and caring for plants. **Nov. 5.**

Birol Charlotte Christo is a retired teacher. During her active service she also worked as an office secretary and division statistician. She lives with her husband in Hosur, India. The mother of five grown children, Birol enjoys gardening, sewing, and creating craft items to finance her projects for homeless children. **Feb. 21, June 18, July 18.**

Ginger Church, a mother and grandmother, writes from Williamsport, Maryland. She is editor or *Kids' Ministry Ideas* and contract publicist for *Women of Spirit* magazine. She speaks at women's, children's, and other training events and has been published in several magazines. Her latest book is *Ask God for a Miracle.* **June 4.**

Clareen Colclesser, a retired LPN and widow since 1994, has two children, seven grandchildren, and six great-grandchildren. She enjoys family, quiet times with a good book, and her summer retreat near Lake Huron, Michigan. Clareen stays active in her church; enjoys writing letters and short stories, and her collection of interior-decorating magazines. **Feb. 9, Apr. 30, Dec. 3.**

Eva Alice Covey is in her eighth decade of life. She lives alone, has been a teacher, raised a family, and written books. God has given her a young mind and a love for word and as long as they remain she will try to fulfill the purpose for which she is here. **Aug. 6.**

Arul Mary Daniel works in India as an office secretary. She is mother of two blessed children, Elwin and Stalin; and has a wonderful brother, and prayerful mother. Every Friday evening, along with her husband, she goes to a village to share God's love with a group of children. She spends her free time with her children, sewing, and performing household duties. **Feb. 26, July 6, Aug. 11.**

Fauna Rankin Dean, a published freelance writer/photographer, lives near Kansas City with her husband. She is currently working on a book and serves as president of her local Toastmasters Club. They have one adult son, two teenagers, and ten golden retrievers who make every day interesting. **Jan. 19, July 16.**

Tracy Dixon writes from South Wales, United Kingdom. She lives with a congenital disease, spina-bifida, paralyzing her from the waist down and confining her to a wheelchair. She graduated from university with an honors degree in education, taught in two tough inner city schools, and then retrained and now works as a professional psychotherapeutic counselor. **May 8.**

Linda Domeny is a pastor's wife, married for 12 years. Currently she and her husband serve churches in Rawlins and Rock Springs, Wyoming. A physical therapist, she works with children from birth to 5-year-olds. Hobbies include enjoying the outdoors, sewing, sharing recipes, and spending time with friends. **Aug. 25.**

Leonie Donald, with her husband, moved back to New Zealand in 2003 to be near elderly parents. She enjoys reading, exercise, and gardening. Leonie takes an active part in church activities at the retirement village where her parents reside. **Nov. 16.**

Goldie Down died in December 2003, but before that she and her husband, David. did 20 years of evangelistic work in Australia and New Zealand and served as missionaries in India for another 20 years. Goldie was a prolific writer who had 23 books published and numerous articles printed. She was the mother of six children whom she home-schooled. **Jan. 30, Mar. 22, Dec. 20.**

Louise Driver lives in Beltsville, Maryland, with her pastor-husband, Don. They have three grown sons and four grandchildren. At church she is involved with music and women's ministries. She is head of the Children's Department at the Potomac Adventist Book and Health Food Store. Her hobbies are singing/music, skiing, reading, crafts, gardening, and traveling to historical places. **Apr. 21, July 26.**

Donna M. Dunbar is a registered dietitian working for the Department of Juvenile Justice in Arcadia, Florida. She and her husband, Clarence, run the Lighthouse Outreach Center (now a multidenominational soup kitchen). She has two sons, three stepchildren, and four wonderful grandchildren. **May 5.**

Trudy Duncan resides in Woodbridge, Virginia, with her family. She works at the nearby hospital as a medical technologist in the blood bank. She assists in the cradle roll Sabbath school class at her church. Her hobbies include nature activities, traveling, and singing. **Dec. 14.**

Joy Dustow is a retired teacher who enjoys an active part in the social and spiritual activities of the retirement village in Australia where she resides with her husband. They daily receive much spiritual help from these devotional books. It gives them pleasure to know that from the sale of the books many have an opportunity to receive an education in a Christian environment. **May 10.**

Ruthanneke Edwards is a retired elementary teacher. She is an elder and Sabbath school teacher. She enjoys her five sons and 14 grandchildren. Her hobbies are reading, sewing, cooking, writing, and memorizing Scripture in context. **June 25.**

Gloria Stella Felder works as administrative assistant in Queens, New York. She and her pastor-husband are the parents of five adult children; they have five grandchildren. Gloria enjoys singing, listening to music, writing, speaking, and spending time with her family—especially her grandchildren. She is currently working on her second book. **Aug. 17, Oct. 23.**

Leila M. Gomes Ferreira was born in Ipanema, Minas Gerais, Brazil. She likes music and painting. She is married to Pastor Everson; they currently carry out ministry in the state of Para. **June 12.**

Valerie Fidelia, a wife, mother, and grandmother, works as a department director in the Middle East Union, based in Cyprus. She loves her work with women's ministries, and in her local church is involved in small groups and music ministry. **Oct. 30.**

Karen Fisher writes from Hermiston, Oregon. She and her husband have served in Botswana, Africa, and in the Punjab province of Pakistan. They have two grown children and three grandchildren. **July 3.**

Margaret Fisher is retired from 40 years of nursing. She spends time writing poetry and short stories. She and her husband travel in the winter, giving out Christian books and literature. They belong to the Dayton Seventh-day Adventist Church in Dayton, Tennessee, and work with their communication department. **Oct. 21.**

Edith Fitch is a retired teacher living in Lacombe, Alberta, Canada. She volunteers in the archives at Canadian University College and is a member of the Lacombe Historical Society. She enjoys doing research for schools, churches, and individual histories. Her hobbies include writing, traveling, needlework, and cryptograms. **Jan. 24, June 22, Oct. 12.**

Edit Fonseca lives in Curitiba, Parana, Brazil. She is a minister's wife, piano teacher, and director of women's ministries for the South Parana Conference. She has two sons: one a physician, and the other a minister. She enjoys music, writing, and walking. **Apr. 22, July 19.**

Deborah Frans is a graphic artist and writer who shares her Maryland home with two Shetland sheepdogs. She loves to share the gifts of her God-given creativity to bless and encourage others, especially those in the messianic Jewish congregation where she worships and fellowships with other Jews and Gentiles who know and love the King of glory, Jesus the Lord. **Apr. 15.**

Eileen Furlonge grew up in Trinidad. She is a retired nurse who writes from Palm Bay, Florida, where she is Sabbath school secretary and a Sabbath school teacher in her church. She enjoys travel, singing, cooking, baking, reading, and helping others. **May 30.**

Edna Maye Gallington is part of the communication team in the Southeastern California Conference and a graduate of La Sierra University. She is a member of Toastmasters International and the Loma Linda Writing Guild and enjoys freelance writing, music, gourmet cooking, entertaining, hiking, and racquetball. **Apr. 6, Aug. 31, Nov. 23.**

Odessa S. Gentles, born in South Carolina, has lived in the Washington, D.C./ Maryland area for more than 40 years. She is married and the mother of one son. She has worked for the same government agency for 28 years and looks forward to retiring very soon. Hobbies are singing, sewing, cooking, gardening, and making floral arrangements for homes and bouquets for weddings. **Apr. 28, Aug. 14.**

Kristi Geraci, a first-time contributor, writes from Belgrade, Montana. **July 14.**

Evelyn Glass and her husband, Darrell, love having their grandchildren live next door to them in northern Minnesota on the farm where Darrell was born. Evelyn is active in writing for her local church paper and is a member of a local writers group. Since retiring, she has added quilting to her list of hobbies; she continues to speak for various events. **Mar. 15, Apr. 26, Oct. 15.**

Hannelore Gómez, from Panama, currently teaches Spanish in a high school in Virginia. At the same time she is working on her Ph.D. in international studies. Her hobbies are reading and traveling. Knowing the gospel since she was born has been her greatest blessing. **Sept. 17.**

Mary Jane Graves and her husband, Ted, are busy retirees in North Carolina, where they spent their last working years on the staff of a boarding high school. They are involved in delivering meals to shut-ins, church business, gardening, and other activities. **May 16, June 19, Aug. 3.**

Ellie Green, a retired registered nurse, and her husband, Lloyd, live in North Carolina near their adult children. Ellie preaches public evangelistic campaigns in the United States and overseas and is a presenter at women's conferences and retreats. She modestly admits that her two grandchildren are the smartest, most adorable, sweetest, and cutest in the entire world. **Jan. 20, May 2.**

Carol Joy Greene writes from Florida, where she has retired. She is the mother of three adult children and the grandmother of four. She is active in women's ministries in her church. **May 12.**

Glenda-mae Greene is a chronicler of the everyday moments in her life and the author of the recently published devotional, *Green Pasture Moments for Frazzled Urban Dwellers.* She writes from Palm Bay, Florida, where she is actively involved in women's prayer circles and teaching Sabbath school classes at her church. **Jan. 8, Mar. 7, Nov. 9.**

Janet M. Greene is a cardiac rehabilitation nurse, wife, and mother to two girls. Her major objective is that her daughters see Jesus in everything every day. She is active as an associate Pathfinder director, with the expanded goal of having 25 other young people also see Jesus in everything. And yes, she is still a shopoholic. **Sept. 29.**

Gloria Gregory is a director of admissions at Northern Caribbean University in Jamaica. She enjoys encouraging others, writing, and hand crafts. Her two adult daughters and her husband, Milton, are her writing inspirations. She is a frequent contributor to the women's devotional. **Apr. 25.**

Marjorie Hall is personal ministries leader, and investment and ingathering coordinator at her church in Melbourne, Florida. She loves to work with seniors, shut-ins, and those who are ill in the hospital, often bringing them food, flowers, music, and religious pamphlets each Tuesday and Sabbath mornings. **June 7.**

Diantha Hall-Smith writes from Langley Air Force Base, Virginia, and is a first-time contributor. **July 2, Oct. 13.**

Dessa Weisz Hardin and her husband live in Maine. She enjoys traveling, writing, reading, working, or teaching children. An added dimension is grandparenting; she has three adult children. **Jan. 16, July 20, Dec. 21.**

Peggy Harris lives in Maryland with her husband, enjoys two granddaughters, has her own insurance business, writes books, and chairs W.A.S.H. (Women and Men Against Sexual Harassment). **Dec. 31.**

Marian M. Hart, a retired elementary teacher and nursing-home administrator, works with her husband doing property management. As a member of the historic Battle Creek Seventh-day Adventist Tabernacle for 28 years, she has served as a volunteer in many different capacities. Six grandchildren make her a proud grandmother. **Apr. 13, Dec. 22.**

Ursula M. Hedges, a retired teacher/administrator with a master's degree, was born in India. She and her principal-husband have given many years of mission service in the Pacific, Australia, and New Zealand. A church elder and conference women's ministries director in Australia, Ursula has also published books, stories, and articles and is a qualified interior designer. **Apr. 11, Nov. 14.**

Denise Dick Herr teaches English at Canadian University College in Alberta, Canada. She spends many summers in Jordan with her husband on archaeological digs, or camping and canoeing in remote places. **May 4.**

Karen Holford works beside her husband, Bernie, as an associate director of family and children's ministries in southern England. They have three teenage children. Karen has written several books and is training to be a family therapist. In spare moments she likes to make quilts. **May 13, June 30, Nov. 10.**

Jacqueline Hope HoShing-Clarke has served in the field of education as principal and teacher. She is the director of the pre-college department at Northern Caribbean University, Jamaica, and is currently studying for a Ph.D. Jackie is married and has two children, Deidre and Deneil. She enjoys writing, teaching children's Sabbath school, flower gardening, and housekeeping. **Feb. 5, June 24, Oct. 20.**

Lynn Howell is a semiretired teacher who lives on the Sunshine Coast, Queensland, Australia. She's been happily married to Reg for 32 years, and they have two married daughters. Her hobbies include painting, exercising, computing, photography, and reading. She is an ordained elder and enjoys leading out in women's ministries. **Feb. 16.**

Lorraine Hudgins-Hirsch lives in Loma Linda, California. She has worked at Faith for Today, the Voice of Prophecy, and the world headquarters of her church. Her articles and poems appear frequently in various publications. She is the mother of five grown children, and she has 10 grandchildren. **Jan. 13, Dec. 19.**

Bonnie Hunt, retired from 20 years of teaching, coordinates a learning-assistance program for nursing students. She coauthored a book with David Gerstle, *Inspiration PRN: Stories about Nurses—A Collection of Spiritual Lessons.* Hobbies include her children, grandchildren, reading, writing, traveling, and building houses. **June 15.**

Cheryl Hurt is a retired registered nurse and a full-time volunteer working for the Lord. She has been married 30 years to the same smart, funny, gorgeous Christian man the Lord led her to so long ago. **Jan. 12, Mar. 19, Sept. 3.**

Gloria P. Hutchinson is a registered nurse and a single mother to her nephew, whom she "adopted." She works for an elder-care facility and recently completed an Associate of Science degree. In her Palm Bay, Florida, church she serves as Sabbath school secretary and assistant health ministry coordinator. Her hobbies are sewing, reading, and working on the computer. **Aug. 29.**

Grotel Hutchinson was 100 when she wrote this story. She is a great-great-grandmother who lives with her daughter in Palm Bay, Florida. She was, until very recently, active in the sanctuary choir of her church. When she is not traveling or fashioning her own dresses and hats, she is praising her God in the garden. **Oct. 16.**

Shirley C. Iheanacho, originally from Barbados, resides in Huntsville, Alabama, with her husband, Morris, of 34-plus years. She has had the privilege of working in the office of the president of Oakwood College for 20 years, assisting four presidents. She enjoys her two grandsons, playing in the handbell choir, singing in the church choir, and encouraging people. **May 21, Sept. 1.**

Consuelo Roda Jackson is a lover of nature, a conservationist, and environmentalist in practice. She enjoys music, reading, and writing. Consuelo is a volunteer at a community hospital, and holds a weekly singspiration for the skilled nursing facility residents. She holds a doctorate in wholistic nutrition. **July 23.**

Lois E. Johannes is retired from overseas service in southern and eastern Asia, and lives near a daughter in Portland, Oregon. She enjoys knitting, community service work, patio gardening, and her four grandchildren and two great-grandchildren. **Nov. 7.**

Corleen Johnson is women's ministries director in Oregon. She is passionate about evangelism and training women. **Mar. 23.**

Elaine J. Johnson is a mother of four children and has 12 grandchildren. She enjoys working with children and young people and is active in her local church. Elaine enjoys country living with her husband, Peter, of 36 years. Hobbies include electronics, clock collecting, reading, and meeting new people. **May 11, Aug. 18.**

Pauletta Cox Johnson and husband, Mike, live in a small town in southwest Michigan, where she grew up. She's an interior designer and also a freelance writer of mainly children's books; she does gardening, sewing, and crafts. Active in her home church, she has three grown sons, three daughters-in-law, and four young grandsons. **Aug. 16.**

Gladys S. (Guerrero) Kelley came to the United States from the Dominican Republic when she was 17. She has a bachelor's degree in English education and is working on a master's in second-language acquisition. She teaches Spanish as a second language, and loves to write, swim, read, play volleyball, and do extreme sports, such as bungee jumping and skydiving. **June 16.**

Marilyn King is a retired registered nurse with an M.B.A. in business. She and her husband of 50 years live in Oregon beside the beautiful Umpqua River. Family, church, nature, music, and pets add much joy to their lives. **Sept. 12.**

Becki Knobloch is a displaced New Englander living in Lebanon, Oregon. She and her pastor-husband have two girls, Natasha and Karissa. Her profession is health education, but her heart is ministry, so she coordinates the Community Health Improvement Partnership (CHIP). She teaches nutrition and cooking classes to women's groups and enjoys writing. **Apr. 19, June 10.**

Toya Marie Koch is a freelance artist living in Hagerstown, Maryland. She is the director of the Chesapeake Conference worship team, and the junior/earliteen leader at Highland View Academy church. She's married, has no children, but shares her home (and her bed) with two cocker spaniels and two aging cats. She is an amateur musician and photographer. **July 28.**

Linda Mei Lin Koh is the director of children's ministries at the world headquarters of her church. She enjoys working with women by helping them develop income-generating skills so that they can become financially independent. She's married with two grown-up sons. Her hobbies include baking and playing basketball. **Sept. 19.**

Kênia Kopitar lives in Tatui, São Paulo, Brazil. She feels blessed to have been born into such a marvelous Christian family, for having space to care for many abandoned animals, and for having many special friends. **Oct. 3.**

Hepzibah Kore lives in Hosur, India, with her husband. She is presently the shepherdess coordinator and women's ministries director for the Southern Asia Division. She delights in serving the women. Her hobbies are gardening, reading, and listening to music. **Feb. 23.**

Patricia Mulraney Kovalski is a retired teacher, widow, mother, and grandmother. She likes to swim, give English teas, travel, and work for the Lord. **June 6.**

Mabel Kwei is a former university/college lecturer, a mother of three, and a pastor's wife who now lives in New Jersey. She and her husband worked for many years in West Africa. **Feb. 10, Sept. 9, Nov. 13.**

Bienvisa Ladion-Nebres treasures her past two decades of working in Africa and presently enjoys an Asian setting as she teaches in Mission College, Thailand. A mother of three and grandmother of two, she likes music, poetry, church activities, traveling, and writing. **Apr. 23, Sept. 25.**

Nathalie Ladner-Bischoff, a retired nurse, lives with her husband in Walla Walla, Washington. Besides homemaking, gardening, and volunteering at the Walla Walla General Hospital gift shop, she reads, writes, knits, and crochets. She's published several magazine stories and a book, *An Angel's Touch.* **Mar. 29, Oct. 11.**

Mandy LaFave-Vogler is a registered nurse who works part-time at a local health department. Her young children bring her great joy (and challenges). She and her husband live in Manton, Michigan, and at church she helps with cradle roll and kindergarten classes. She enjoys gardening and is a first-time contributor to the devotional book. **Jan. 15.**

Sally Lam-Phoon is the director for education and women's ministries at the Southeast Asia Union Mission in Singapore, as well as the shepherdess coordinator for the seven missions there. Her passion is to help women discover their potential in following God's will. She's married to Chek Yat Phoon, and they have two daughters, Michelle and Rachel. **Apr. 17, Sept. 4.**

Iani Lauer has a bachelor's degree in administration and a master's degree in psychology. She works as a professor at the Northeast Brazil College. She likes to read and talk. Iani is active in the music ministry of her church, rehearsing with groups, and playing the piano during worship services. **July 7, Oct. 17, Nov. 27.**

Gina Lee has had more than 750 articles and poems published, mostly in Christian magazines. She enjoys working at the library and caring for her family of cats. **May 17, Aug. 15, Oct. 8.**

Loida Gulaja Lehmann spent 10 years selling religious literature in the Philippines before she went to Germany and married her husband, Martin. They are active in their church in Hanau, Germany, and are helping to plant churches in the Philippines and supporting lay ministries. Hobbies include traveling, collecting souvenirs, nature walks, and photography. **Mar. 27, June 27.**

Ruth Lennox is the liaison person for women's ministries for her church in Canada. She is a local church elder who likes to write and produce monologues of biblical women, and she enjoys walking. She and her husband have three married children and four granddaughters. **July 10.**

Cordell Liebrandt lives in Cape Town, South Africa. She is a paralegal with an interest in working with people, women's ministries, and evangelism. She is happily married and enjoys the outdoors, walks in nature, and being with family and friends. Her greatest desire is to serve God. **Aug. 24.**

Divonete de Souza Ramos Lima lives in Belem, capital of the state of Para, in the north of Brazil. She is a teacher/leader in the department of ill and impaired individuals in her church. Her greatest pleasure is in reading, experiencing nature, and her two teenage children. **Dec. 15.**

Olga I. Corbin de Lindo, who retired from the United States Air Force, was born in Panama. She and her husband, Richard, have one adult daughter and three grandchildren. She serves her church as a pianist, in women's ministries, and almost every other department for more than 60 years. She still enjoys giving Bible studies, reading, writing, gardening, and playing the piano. **Apr. 4, Nov. 28.**

Bessie Siemens Lobsien, a retired missionary librarian, has been writing short essays, poems, and stories since girlhood. She likes to sew quilts and clothes for her grandchildren and great-grandchildren, as well as for her local Adventist community center. She also collects used eyeglasses to send to Mexico, where she worked as a missionary librarian. **Mar. 14, Oct. 5, Dec. 16.**

Hattie R. Logan, an analyst at Ford Motor Company, has degrees in business administration and human resources administration. Her interests include singing, reading, and visiting sick and shut-in individuals. She has two children, David Paul Logan II and Darnell LaMarr Logan. **Nov. 22.**

Lori L. Mantz, 28, has professional experience in writing, public relations, and marketing for hotels and hospitals. She attends church in Modesto, California. Hobbies include scrapbooking and spending time with her nephews. **Jan. 29, July 9, Sept. 28.**

Amy Smith Mapp, a retired public educator, is a part-time adjunct instructor, aerobics instructor, and reader for McGraw-Hill Publishing Company. Married to C. Bernell Mapp, they have three children and six grandchildren. **Dec. 27.**

Tamara Marquez de Smith writes from Bay Shore, New York, where she lives with her husband, Steven, and their two daughters, Lillian and Cassandra. At her church, Tamara serves where the Lord needs her services. **May 20.**

Kamla Masih is the director of women, family, and children ministries in the North India Section of Jalandhar, Punjab. **July 21.**

Soosanna Mathew has been a teacher for many years and is now an office secretary. Her husband is a minister. They have two grown children, David and Hannah; and one grandchild, Dana. Soosanna enjoys writing and music. **Mar. 10, Sept. 5.**

Debra Matshaya, a teacher at Marian High, Cape Town, South Africa, has had several devotionals published. She enjoys gym and loves gospel music. **July 29.**

Mary Maxson is women's ministries director for the North American Division of her church. She and pastor-husband, Ben, have served in team ministry in Georgia, Carolina, and Missouri, and in mission service in Argentina and Uruguay. Certified in marriage enrichment and as a hospital chaplain associate, Mary has been an editorial secretary and administrative assistant. **Oct. 6.**

Madge S. May practiced nursing in Canada—from Quebec to the Northwest Territories—and Saudi Arabia before moving to Florida, where she now works. She is the director of the Emmanuel Gazelle Adventurers Club at her church in Plant City. **May 29.**

Maria G. McClean lives in Ontario, Canada, with her husband, Wayne, and daughter, Kamila. She attends church in Toronto. **Mar. 9.**

Vidella McClellan is a homemaker and caregiver for seniors in British Columbia, Canada. A mother of three and grandmother of seven, her current hobbies are gardening, crossword puzzles, playing Scrabble, and writing. She belongs to the Toastmasters Club and is active in her church. Her interest in writing began by recording her experiences for casual family reading. **Feb. 24, Apr. 9, Dec. 5.**

Melissa Daughety McClung is a wife and mother of 8-year-old Spencer and lives in Hookerton, North Carolina. She is a juvenile court counselor working on her Master of Science in counselor education. She serves as youth leader, children's ministries coordinator, and church pianist at church. She enjoys RV camping with her family. **Sept. 14.**

Elizabeth McIntosh has been a prayer warrior all her life. This registered nurse, wife, mother of six adult children, and grandmother of nine writes from Palm Bay, Florida, where she is very active in her church, doing whatever God asks. Elizabeth enjoys working in her garden. **May 18, July 31.**

Patsy Murdoch Meeker has enjoyed the company of Tibby, her long-haired calico cat, for a number of years. She has also lived in Virginia for some time, but still misses her home state of California. She likes to read and e-mail friends and, most important, talk to her heavenly Father and Big Brother. **June 2.**

Jônia O. A. Menezes lives in northwest Brazil and works as a women's ministries director for the Sergipe-Alagoas Mission. She enjoys being with people and giving Bible studies. She has a slogan: "There is no limit for a woman who puts her life in God's hands." Her dream is to see every woman with Jesus in heaven. **July 22.**

Annette Walwyn Michael is a high school teacher in New York City. She serves her local church as women's ministries director and is a pastor's wife, mother of three, and grandmother of two. She is author of *Sugar Is All,* a collection of Caribbean short stories and poems set in the federation of St. Kitts and Nevis in the West Indies. **Jan. 7.**

Quilvie G. Mills is a retired community college professor who is actively engaged with her husband, Pastor H. A. Mills, in the operation of their church in Port St. Lucie, Florida. She has a deep interest in young people and finds joy in helping them achieve their goals. Her hobbies include music, reading, traveling, word games, and gardening. **July 5, Oct. 22.**

Susen Mattison Molé was born in India to missionary parents, and spent most of her early life in eastern Asia. She is a full-time mother and teacher to two homeschooled daughters. Occasionally she finds time for her hobbies, which include reading, trekking, and needlepoint. She's married to a naval officer and continues to travel the world. **Jan. 21, June 5, Dec. 6.**

Marcia Mollenkopf, a retired schoolteacher, lives in Klamath Falls, Oregon. She is active in local church programs and has served in both adult and children's divisions. She enjoys reading, crafts, hiking, and bird-watching. **May 27, Aug. 2.**

Esperanza Aquino Mopera is the mother of four adults and a grandmother of five. She is on the staff at Lake Taylor Transitional Care Hospital and is charge nurse. She enjoys gardening. **Aug. 5, Nov. 15.**

Bonnie Moyers lives with her husband and three cats in Staunton, Virginia. She's a musician for a Methodist church, works as a laundry assistant for a nearby bed-and-breakfast, and freelance-writes whenever she can fit it in. She has two adult children and one granddaughter. Her writings have been published in many magazines and books. **May 6, June 14.**

Ethel Doris Msuseni is a single parent, professional nurse and teacher, and pensioner member of her church in Umtata, South Africa. Her hobbies include baking, sewing, gardening, and listening to gospel music. **Mar. 16.**

Lillian Musgrave and her family have made northern California their home for more than 40 years. She enjoys family and grandchildren, and now has a great-grandchild, too. Other interests include music, writing (including poetry and songs), and church responsibilities. **Oct. 27.**

Julie Nagle, a wife and a mother of three, works for the Australian Public Service. She's dedicated to service for God and with God, and is an ordained elder for Christ. Julie is an indigenous Australian who is involved in many ministries, including those to women and the general public. She enjoys public speaking and continual learning. **Feb. 3, Mar. 20, July 13.**

Judy-Ann Neal, a former nurse, is currently a Master of Divinity student at Andrews University, Berrien Springs, Michigan. She is a mother and grandmother who enjoys reading, music, sewing, and camping (when there is a break from all the reading and paper writing that college demands). **Sept. 8.**

Anne Elaine Nelson, a retired teacher, is doing tutoring and testing for schools; and has written the book *Puzzled Parents.* Her four children have blessed her with 11 grandchildren. Widowed in 2001, she lives in Michigan, where she stays active as women's ministries leader in her church. Favorite activities are sewing, music, and photography. **Mar. 4, July 30.**

Desmalee Nevins is a certified health education specialist who lectures in health education and health promotion at the University of the West Indies in Jamaica. She is married with grown children, and is always active in church activities related to youth. **Sept. 18.**

Angèle Rachel Nlo Nlo is a pastor's wife living in Abidjan, Ivory Coast. She's the Sabbath school and trust services director in her local church. Fluent in French and English, she has a master's degree in public law and works in the publishing department of the West-Central Africa Division. Hobbies include reading, travel, Bible study, meeting friends, and cooking. **Dec. 23.**

Maria Sinharinha de Oliveira Nogueira was born in Brazil. She's a retired teacher who is married and has two daughters and four grandchildren. She serves as a deaconess in her church and enjoys reading good books, writing poems, crocheting, crossword puzzles, walks, and physical exercise. **Nov. 6.**

Elizabeth Versteegh Odiyar lives in Kelowna, British Columbia, Canada, where she manages the family chimney sweep business. She has twin sons and a daughter in college. Beth enjoys mission trips and road trips to visit family in the United States. She loves creativity—sewing, cooking vegan, home decorating, organizing—and hopes to be a writer. **Oct. 31, Dec. 17.**

Marly G. Oliveira lives in Rondonia, Brazil, with her husband, Pastor Jose Ari, and their two sons, Fred and Frank. She has a degree in education and likes to preach, teach, and write letters. She enjoys being involved in the women's ministries and children's ministries programs in her church. **Sept. 20.**

Cristine Jeda Orillosa is a student at Pacific Union College in Angwin, California. At the time of this writing she was a student missionary in Chuuk, in the Federated States of Micronesia. She loves Jesus very much and enjoys writing, singing, snorkeling, and swimming. She enjoyed teaching her kindergarten and primary pupils in Chuuk and misses her little angels. **Aug. 21.**

Jemima D. Orillosa works in the secretariat department of the world headquarters of her church. She is active in her local church in Maryland, where she lives with her husband and two daughters. She enjoys gardening and making friends. **May 25.**

Rose Otis spent 23 years in ministry, 10 of those years ministering to women around the world. Currently she and her husband live in Middletown, Maryland, near their two children and four grandchildren. She enjoys mentoring her grandchildren and other women. **Apr. 1.**

Hannele Ottschofski lives in Germany, where she is an elder of her local church. She loves to prepare PowerPoint presentations, and from time to time speaks at women's retreats and evangelistic campaigns in the Ukraine. **Jan. 22, May 28, Oct. 18.**

Claudina Mena de Paco works with her husband, Pastor Noel Paci, in the city of Del Alto La Paz, Bolivia. **Feb. 17.**

Ofelia A. Pangan and her husband are stationed at Mission College in Thailand, where she teaches in the English second language school and her husband is the senior pastor of the college church. She loves her family of three professional adult children, three in-laws, and nine grandchildren. She enjoys reading, walking, gardening, traveling, and playing Scrabble. **Mar. 2, July 17, Dec. 30.**

Revel Papaioannou and her pastor-husband work in Greece. They have four sons and 10 grandchildren. She loves teaching and for years has given Bible studies and taught Sabbath school (all ages), Bible seminars, Pathfinders, vacation Bible school, and English as a foreign language. **Nov. 1.**

Abigail Blake Parchment is wife of Sean, sister of Rachel and Asenath, daughter of Frieda and Albert and the King of kings. She is active in women's ministries in her church in the Cayman Islands. Her ultimate career goal (as yet unrealized) is to be a full-time wife and mother. Until that time she is a family nurse practitioner, working in women's health. **Mar. 31.**

Betty G. Perry lives in Fayetteville, North Carolina, with her retired pastor-husband. They have three adult children and five grandchildren. An anesthetist for 32 years, she is now semiretired. Hobbies include playing the piano and organ, doing arts and crafts, trying new recipes, and, most recently, quilting. **Jan. 5, Aug. 4, Nov. 17.**

Maria Alejandra Lostra de Perucci and her husband have two daughters, ages 16 and 9. She is a housewife, women's ministries director, primary class teacher, teacher of adult literacy classes, and the one who prepares the bulletin for her church in Argentina. She is a fourth-year law student who enjoys reading, drawing, and painting. **Mar. 8.**

Karen Phillips and her husband, John, have four children with whom she has spent the past 15 years as a stay-at-home mom. She has directed Adventurer and Eager Beaver groups, sings in the Omaha Memorial church choir, and is lunch mom at the parochial school. Some of her writings have been published in the Kansas-Nebraska women's ministries newsletter. **Aug. 12.**

Birdie Poddar lives in northeastern India. She and her husband enjoy retirement but keep busy. She gardens, cooks, bakes, sews, reads, writes, and does hand crafts. They have a daughter, a son, and four grandsons. **Apr. 18, July 27, Oct. 19.**

Lanny Lydia Pongilatan, from Jakarta, Indonesia, works as a professional secretary. She was an English instructor for Indonesian Professions in the Indonesian-American Foundation. She enjoys playing the piano, listening to Christian gospel songs, reading religious books, playing tennis, and swimming. **Feb. 19, Sept. 23, Nov. 12.**

Helen Godfrey Pyke is a first-time contributor who writes from Ooltewah, Tennessee. She teaches English at Southern Adventist University. She has three grown children and a husband of 38 years. She enjoys gardening and making pizza and cookies for her students. **May 19.**

Edileuza Nascimento Ramos is a housewife, mother of three, and an avid reader. She is missionary director at her church, as well as an assistant in women's ministries in her district; she also serves as a member of the executive committee of the South Bahia Conference, Brazil. Her greatest pleasure is making friends for Jesus. **Jan. 17.**

Vicki Macomber Redden is the desktop and Web content coordinator for *Insight* magazine at the Review and Herald Publishing Association in Hagerstown, Maryland. She enjoys traveling, photography, scrapbooking, and spending time with those she loves, especially her husband, Ron! **Feb. 13, May 24, Dec. 28.**

Mary Cerovski Reinhold is a retired widow living in Hagerstown, Maryland. She and her late husband, a dentist, served as missionaries in Africa and St. Kitts. She has two married daughters and three grandchildren, with whom she loves spending time. She likes music, travel, swimming, reading, and writing. She's a much-appreciated pianist and organist at her church. **Sept. 27.**

Barbara Horst Reinholtz, semiretired, is the mother of three grown children and grandmother of two. She has served as deaconess and church clerk in her local church. A published author of short stories and children's poetry, she enjoys people, music, crocheting, and crafts. Best of all, she enjoys being wife and best friend to her husband, Laun. **Feb. 14.**

Darlenejoan McKibbin Rhine was born in Nebraska, raised in California, and schooled in Tennessee. She holds a B.A. in journalism, and worked in the plant at the Los Angeles *Times* for 21 years before retiring in 1995. A retired writer, she now lives on an island in Puget Sound, Washington, and attends church in North Cascade. **June 29, Sept. 6.**

Avis Mae Rodney is a justice of the peace for the province of Ontario, Canada, where she resides with her husband, Leon. Wife and mother of two adult children, she has five adorable grandchildren. Avis's hobbies include giving motivational talks, long walks, gardening, and crocheting. **Jan. 11, Sept. 11, Dec. 24.**

Aurísia Silva Brito Rodrigues is the women's ministries director of the Vila Nova Nanuque church in Minas Gerais, Brazil. She is 23, married, and has two daughters: an 8-year-old and a 1-year-old. She likes to read, listen to music, go places, talk, and raise animals. **Mar. 17.**

Teri Deangelia Roulhac, born in Cincinnati, Ohio, moved to La Jolla, California, in 1979, then to Los Angeles in 1982. She has one daughter, age 16, and works as a senior travel consultant contractor in Los Angeles. **Feb. 12.**

Terrie Ruff is director of social services with Alexian Brothers Community Services PACE Program in Chattanooga, Tennessee, and an adjunct professor at Southern Adventist University. Terrie enjoys public speaking, writing, singing, and traveling. Her goal is to be a "beneficial" presence in the lives of all whom she meets. **Mar. 13, Dec. 2.**

Annie Ruiz writes from Negros Oriental, the Philippines. She is a first-time contributor. **June 9.**

Basma Saleem, from Iraq, works with Middle East Arabic language programming for Adventist World Radio. She's an enthusiastic beginners and kindergarten leader in her local church, and is a member of the praise team. Her hobbies include arts and crafts, walking, and music. **Apr. 8.**

Isabela Salles is Brazilian, married, and works in her church's South American Division. She enjoys helping in her church in the area of community service; she likes to read, embroider, and talk with people. **Dec. 8.**

Nicole Salifou, born in the Ivory Coast, came to the United States as a student, graduating from American University. She's married and has three children. She first read the Bible in 1993 and accepted Jesus. Years later she began attending church and is now a deaconess, having been baptized in 2001. She's interested in health issues and in trying vegetable recipes. **Apr. 7.**

Sophia Jasmine Samson is from Chennai, Tamil Nadu, India. Married to a teacher, they are the parents of a 2-year-old daughter, Sheryl Tercia Samson. Sophia works as an office secretary in the Southern Asia Division headquarters in Hosur and enjoys her job and her life, given by God. She enjoys listening to music and cooking. **Mar. 11, June 3.**

Deborah Sanders shares from her personal journal, *Dimensions of Love,* which has become a writing-prayer ministry. She lives in Canada with Ron, her husband of 36 years. They've been blessed with two children, Andrea and Sonny. Sonny is mentally challenged with psychomotor retardation and autism. "Thank you for caring." **Apr. 10, Sept. 10.**

Lilith Rose Scarlett serves as dean of women at Northern Caribbean University in Mandeville, Jamaica. She enjoys early-morning walks, loves helping people, and finds joy in entertaining, listening to good music, and reading. She's still learning to wait on the Lord. **Apr. 2.**

Marie H. Seard and her husband enjoy their ministry of giving women's devotional books as Christmas gifts. She writes a personal message to each woman who receives a book. She and her husband also enjoy traveling and visiting their son and daughter-in-law in California. **Aug. 30.**

Donna Lee Sharp, although retired, enjoys a life that is full with gardening, flower arranging, bird-watching, traveling to visit friends and relatives, volunteering at a migrant farm workers' office, and playing the piano and organ in various churches and community organizations. **Mar. 24, Aug. 8.**

Donna Sherrill lives in Jefferson, Texas, and manages a small country store close to Jefferson Adventist Academy. She's working on an album of songs she's written, and is publicist for a Christian country-recording artist. She enjoys making cards, doing newsletters, and spending time with her grandchildren, who live close by. **Mar. 3, Oct. 4.**

Carrol Johnson Shewmake and her pastor-husband are now retired but still active in prayer ministry. Carrol is the author of seven books and often speaks at camp meetings, prayer conferences, women's retreats, and churches. She is the mother of four adult children and has eight grandchildren and one great-grandson. **June 1.**

Darlene Almeda Showalter, a first-time contributor, writes from Madison, Alabama. **June 28.**

Sherry Shrestha and her husband, Prakash, are family-practice physicians in a small Midwestern ranching community. They have three teenage daughters. Sherry is doing well following chemotherapy for breast cancer. **Dec. 10.**

Rose Neff Sikora and her husband, Norman, live in the mountains of western North Carolina. A registered nurse at Park Ridge Hospital for the past 20 years, her interests include camping in a travel trailer, writing, spending time with her three grandchildren, and helping others. Rose has been published in magazines and books. **Feb. 11, Aug. 13.**

Vera Lúcia Rosembaum Silva attends the Vila das Belezas church in São Paulo, Brazil. **May 14.**

Patricia Fernandes dos Santos da Silva is married and has a 4-year-old daughter. She enjoys reading, singing, presenting the mission report, and telling children's stories. Her hobby is studying and learning more about God. She finds joy in discovering that each day He loves us more and continues to save us. **Mar. 18.**

Sandra Simanton is a licensed independent clinical social worker employed as a therapist in an outpatient psychiatry clinic in Grand Forks, North Dakota. She lives in nearby Buxton with her husband, three children, two dogs, two cats, two gerbils, and a goldfish! **Apr. 12, Nov. 18.**

Heather-Dawn Small is the director for women's ministries at her church's world headquarters. A native of Trinidad and Tobago, she has a college-age daughter and a high school-age son. She says she loves travel, reading, embroidery, and stamp collecting. *Joy* is her favorite word. **Feb. 1, Oct. 14.**

Dolores Smith is a retired nurse and certified midwife. She worked as a nurse practitioner for many years in a large metropolitan hospital. She holds a master's degree in education and received the women's ministries Woman of the Year Award in 1996 for outstanding and dedicated service. She enjoys traveling. **Jan. 27, Sept. 24.**

Candace Sprauve is a retired educator and has three adult sons, a daughter, and three grandchildren. She presently serves as elder in her church and is general Sabbath school superintendent. She volunteers with Literacy Link of America. Her hobbies are reading, gardening, and sewing. **Apr. 24, Dec. 13.**

Feb Stabenow, a psychologist, has a degree in history and education, and a master's degree in education from Brazil Adventist University. She is the mother of a teenager, Rebecca. Feb enjoys reading, writing, and helping people to be in contact with our heavenly Father through nature. **June 21, Dec. 12.**

Ardis Dick Stenbakken recently retired as the director of women's ministries at her church's world headquarters in Silver Spring, Maryland. She and her husband, Dick, a retired Army chaplain, live in Colorado; they have two grown, married children and one granddaughter. Ardis especially enjoys helping women discover their full potential in the Lord. **Mar. 21, Apr. 14, May 1, Aug. 1, Nov. 8, Dec. 26.**

Rita Kay Stevens, a medical technologist living in Albuquerque, New Mexico, is a church administrator's wife. She enjoys traveling and has had the opportunity to live in many different places in the United States and overseas. Her interests include entertaining, walking, reading, and encouraging others. Rita is the mother of two grown sons and one great daughter-in-law. **Apr. 29.**

Risa Storlie, a recent college graduate, enjoys reading, writing, cooking, hiking, and observing and learning lessons from nature. **Feb. 25.**

Iris L. Stovall, a certified personality trainer through CLASS (Christian Leaders Authors and Speakers Services), especially enjoys speaking to women. Iris works in women's ministries at her church's world headquarters. She has three grown children, Greg, J.T., and Jhovonnah; and three granddaughters. **June 23, Oct. 26.**

Grace Streifling, 85, has been diagnosed as a "young 85." She has four grown children. She's a retired nurse who enjoys reading biographies. She served in the mission field, and now enjoys church via the TV most of the time. She still spends pleasant hours making small quilts for small people. **June 8.**

Rubye Sue, a retired secretary and a great-grandmother, works at a small self-supporting school, where she enjoys interaction with the students. Rubye, 83, and her husband, 90, still travel and look forward to visits with their children, grandchildren, and great-grandchildren. **Jan. 26, Aug. 22.**

Carolyn Rathbun Sutton, freelance writer and speaker, lives in Tennessee with her husband, Jim. They enjoy camping, gardening, and sharing Jesus in practical ways. **Jan. 25, Aug. 7, Oct. 28.**

Loraine F. Sweetland is retired in Tennessee with her husband, three dogs, and 98-year-old mother-in-law. She chairs the school board and the Family Life Center Building Committee, as well as volunteering as treasurer for her local food co-op. In her spare time she works on genealogy. **Jan. 23, Aug. 19, Dec. 29.**

Frieda Tanner, a retired nurse, keeps busy by sending Bible-school materials all over the world. She now lives in Eugene, Oregon, to be near her two grandchildren. **Apr. 3.**

Mercedes Almiron de Tapia lives at the Balcarce Adventist Academy in Brazil with her husband and their son, Zuriel. She has worked as an elementary and preschool teacher, and has a degree in social communication. She enjoys handicrafts, children, and working with her church. **Oct. 2.**

Arlene Taylor is director of Infection Control and Risk Manager at St. Helena Hospital in California. As founder-president of her own corporation, she promotes brain-function research. She is a professional member of the National Speaker's Association and has received American Biographical Institute's American Medal of Honor for brain-function education, 2002. **Feb. 2, Aug. 9, Nov. 3.**

Audre B. Taylor, a published writer, was administrative assistant for ADRA International before retiring. She is now a psychotherapist in the Washington Metropolitan area. One of her hobbies is choral conducting, and she won an Angel Award in a national media competition for one of her choral performances. **Jan. 28.**

G. G. (Geneva Gwendolyn) Taylor writes from Florida, where she is church clerk in Palm Bay. A native Floridian, she loves to cast her bread upon the waters, not thinking of the timeliness of its return. **July 15.**

Nola Thom is a first-time contributor writing from Jamestown, North Dakota. **Oct. 25.**

Stella Thomas works as an administrative assistant in the Global Mission office of her church's world headquarters. She enjoys meeting people and sharing the good news of God's love. **Feb. 22.**

Brenda Thornton, a paralegal, resides in Morrow, Georgia. She serves in the youth department at her local church and enjoys shopping, traveling, reading, music, drama, interpretive dance, and art. **May 3.**

Ena Thorpe, a retired nurse, is the women's ministries leader in her church. She's married and has three grown children. She enjoys doing the Lord's work, reading, crocheting, and playing Scrabble. **Sept. 13.**

Margaret Tito works in the Southern Asia Division. She's enjoyed being an educator of children of various ages for almost 28 years. She and A.J., her pastor-husband and communication director of the Southern Asia Division, have three grown children. She is a first-time contributor. **Nov. 26.**

Lynda Mae Vanden Toorn is an administrative assistant for an architectural/engineering firm in Southfield, Michigan. She enjoys reading, writing, singing, computers, hiking, nature, collecting snowmen, and spending time with her husband and their three children. **Jan. 18.**

Nicéia Triandade lives in Niteroi, Brazil. She's married, the mother of three adult children, and grandmother of five (they are her great passion). She enjoys friends, sewing, cooking, and writing poems. Her greatest joy is to travel with her family and to meditate by looking at the sea. At church she is women's and family ministries director and associate Sabbath school leader. **Oct. 9.**

Nancy Neuharth Troyer is a pastor's wife who writes from Georgia. For 25 years she accompanied her husband, Don, around the world while he was a U.S. Army chaplain. Nancy enjoys writing short stories in her weekly church newsletter, making cards with calligraphy, and singing alone in cathedrals. **Mar. 12, Dec. 7.**

Eunice Urbany was raised on a Christian high school campus in eastern Indonesia. She has worked as a nursing instructor and supervisor; taught pediatric nursing and nursing history in western Indonesia; and worked in nursing in Singapore, Hong Kong, and Germany. She has lived in Toronto, Canada; Chile, South America; and California, U.S.A. **June 13.**

Nancy Van Pelt, a certified family life educator, best-selling author of more than 20 books, and internationally known speaker, has traversed the globe for 20 years, teaching families how to love each other. Her hobbies are getting organized, entertaining, having fun, and quilting. Nancy and her husband live in California, and are the parents of three adult children. **Jan. 2, Sept. 15.**

Lovey Davis Verdun, widow and mother of two adult children, lives in Huntsville, Alabama. She is a retired college registrar who serves her church as a local elder and Sabbath school superintendent, and is a substitute teacher in the city schools. Lovey admires beautiful plants and flowers, keeps a neatly manicured lawn, enjoys her friends, and likes playing table games. **July 4, Sept. 7.**

Renee Verrett-Dooley is the women's ministries leader of Valley Crossroads church. Although she works for a major newspaper, she's a homemaker at heart. She loves to sing and longs to sew. She is Wayne's happy wife, and the proud mom of two adult sons, Guy and Gavin Nembhard. **Jan. 3, July 8, Nov. 24.**

Joyce Vickaryous is a wife, mother, and homemaker living in Wilsonville, Oregon. She enjoys reading, writing, walking the Oregon beaches, interior decorating, and anticipating her next new adventure with the Lord. **May 26.**

Donna Meyer Voth is a substitute teacher and volunteer for the American Cancer Society. She enjoys giving Bible studies, watercolor painting, traveling, and camping. She and her husband live in Vicksburg, Michigan. They have a daughter in college. **Jan. 4.**

Nancy Jean Vyhmeister grew up as a missionary kid in Uruguay. She married a Chilean, and served as a teacher, editor, and pastor's wife in Argentina, United States, and the Philippines. She's a mother twice over, and grandmother of three. She finds that retirement barely gives her enough time for all she wants to do. **Sept. 22.**

Lois Wade lives in Michigan with her husband, Mel, 11-year-old son Keith, Intel the dog, and Grumps the cat. Lois is a missionary kid, an elementary school teacher, and a happily married wife of 17 years. Her interests include quilting, painting, crafting of all sorts, hiking, biking, both flower and vegetable gardening, and Bible study. **Aug. 28.**

Cora A. Walker lives in Queens, New York. She's a retired nurse and an active member in her local church. She enjoys reading, writing, sewing, classical music, singing, and traveling. She has one son. **Mar. 26, July 11.**

Nancy Wallack is a parish nurse coordinator and health educator. Parish nursing, a recognized health specialty that combines professional nursing and health ministry, strives to create an environment of compassion and reverence to God through a ministry of physical, mental, and spiritual healing. Nancy has served as a women's ministries director. **May 9.**

Anna May Radke Waters is a retired administrative secretary. She's an ordained elder in the Meadow Glade church, where she serves as a greeter. At the top of her hobby list are her eight grandchildren and her husband, with whom she likes to travel and make memories. She enjoys Internet Bible studies and responding to prayer requests for Bibleinfo.com. **Jan. 6, Mar. 5, Nov. 29.**

Dorothy Eaton Watts is an administrator for her church headquarters in India. Dorothy is a freelance writer, editor, and speaker. A missionary in India for 25 years, she's founded an orphanage, taught elementary school, and written more than 20 books. Her hobbies include gardening, hiking, and birding (with more than 1,400 in her world total). **May 23, Sept. 26.**

Daniela Weichhold is from Germany, but works at the European Commission headquarters in Brussels, Belgium. She likes being with friends, enjoys God's wonderful nature, and traveling. At church she's involved in health ministries. She likes learning foreign languages and discovering cultures. Singing and playing the piano are an important part of her life. **Feb. 7.**

Ruth Gantz Weis, a first-time contributor, writes from Texas. **Mar. 6.**

Lyn Welk works with bereaved children and aids young offenders attending court. She has a full-time pipe organist position at a church in Adelaide, South Australia, and enjoys choir work and Christian fellowship. She loves caravanning and photography in the outdoors. She is the mother of four adult children and has eight grandchildren. **Feb. 6, Aug. 27, Dec. 18.**

Penny Estes Wheeler gives thanks for the value her family put on God's Word. She realizes that she'll never live long enough to read all the books she wants to read or travel to all the lands she wants to see. She and her husband have four adult children and a granddaughter and grandson. Penny is an editor at the Review and Herald Publishing Association in Hagerstown, Maryland. **Oct. 24.**

Vera Wiebe is a women's ministries leader for her conference. She has two adult sons and two grandchildren for whom she enjoys sewing. Her hobbies are sewing, knitting, crocheting, and playing the keyboard. **Nov. 19.**

Lori C. Wiens works for Loma Linda University's Canadian Campus Program as the division secretary. She lives in Lacombe, Alberta, Canada, with her husband, Dave, who inspires her each day to pursue new adventures. **Mar. 25.**

Carol A. Williams lives in Jamaica with her husband and daughter, Shantae. She loves sewing and does so on a full-time basis. She has served her church as women's ministry leader. **Nov. 30.**

Mildred C. Williams is a retired physical therapist who lives in southern California. She enjoys studying and teaching the Bible, writing, gardening, public speaking, sewing, and spending time with her family. **June 17.**

Patrice E. Williams-Gordon lectures in the Natural Science Department at Northern Caribbean University in Jamaica. A minister's wife, she enjoys team ministry with her husband, Danhugh. She delights in her two daughters, Ashli and Rhoni, while trying to keep up her hobbies of reading, speaking engagements, and planning special events. **Jan. 9, June 26, Oct. 10.**

Susan Wooley works as a home health nurse and lives with her husband, Steve, in Florida. They enjoy the beach, their boys, and each other. **May 7, Aug. 10, Oct. 29.**

Velna Wright is a stay-at-home mom of two boys and a girl. Married, she is a deaconess and is active in her church's children's department, Vacation Bible School, children's ministries, and women's ministries. She enjoys home-schooling her children, floral arranging, crafts, sewing, and cooking. **Mar. 28.**

Leni Uŕia de Zamorano has two children and 4-year-old granddaughter she enjoys caring for and reading to. She also works with Community Services in her church and with women's ministries in her area. She likes to walk with her husband, read, and travel. **Feb. 20.**

Prayer Requests

Consecrate yourself to God in the morning;
make this your very first work.
—Ellen G. White, *Steps to Christ*, p. 70.

Prayer Requests

Consecrate yourself to God in the morning;
make this your very first work.
—Ellen G. White, *Steps to Christ,* p. 70.

Prayer Requests

Consecrate yourself to God in the morning;
make this your very first work.
—Ellen G. White, *Steps to Christ,* p. 70.

Prayer Requests

Consecrate yourself to God in the morning;
make this your very first work.
—Ellen G. White, *Steps to Christ,* p. 70.